Jonathan Black is the pen name of] in publishing for over twenty years. School and Oriel College, Oxford, w Theology. His publications include *Essential Writings of Christianity Since the Bible*, co-edited with M. Basil Pennington and Allen Jones. He is the author of the international cult bestseller *The Secret History of the World* and *The Secret History of Dante*.

'Jonathan Black has written a masterpiece. From the moment I began reading this book, I knew Black had accomplished a remarkable feat of repositioning ancient knowledge in such a way that we see truth through yet another lens. I absolutely loved this book'
Caroline Myss, author of *Anatomy of the Spirit* and *Sacred Contracts*

'Jonathan Black is the C.S. Lewis of our time, an inspired seeker after the spiritual reality that underlies and unites so many seemingly disparate traditions. In retelling the age-old stories he holds up a scrying mirror to his readers helping us to see through the veil of materialistic dogmas and detect the operations of the spiritual and the supernatural in our own lives'
Graham Hancock, author of *Fingerprints of the Gods*

'*The Sacred History* is unlike any book I have ever read about spirituality. It challenged my beliefs from the very beginning and has renewed my faith in the fundamentally spiritual nature of reality'
Philip Carr-Gomm, Chief of the Order of Bards, Ovates and Druids

'With *The Secret History* and *The Sacred History*, Black is doing for spirituality what *The God Delusion* and *God is Not Great* have done for materialism'
Sevak Edward Gulbekian, *New Review*

'A completely different way of viewing the universe, via an astounding range of cultural references that takes in art, science, modern cinema, music and literature. This is a book of huge perspectives, dizzying, heady stuff that will change forever the way you view the world'
Good Book Guide

'A new bible for the New Age, weaving mystical traditions from East and West, astrology, alchemy and angels into one amazing, life-enhancing story'
Gyles Brandreth, author of *The 7 Secrets of Happiness*

Frontispiece to John Dee's *The Arte of Navigation*.

THE
SACRED
HISTORY

How Angels, Mystics and Higher
Intelligence Made our World

JONATHAN BLACK

Quercus

Hardback edition first published in Great Britain in 2013 by
Quercus Editions Ltd

This paperback edition published in 2014 by
Quercus Editions Ltd
55 Baker Street
7th Floor, South Block
London
W1U 8EW

PB ISBN 978 1 78087 487 6
EBOOK ISBN 978 1 78087 486 9

11

Printed and bound in Great Britain by Clays Ltd, Elcograf S.p.A.

To Lorna Byrne

Contents

Preface

The stories retold in this book, taken together and told in sequence, represent a sort of folk history of the world.

But more than that, they work on many different levels. They are part of a mystical tradition.

Many describe dramatic events not in the physical world but in the realms of gods, angels and other spiritual beings. Many follow people who entertain gods and angels unawares, or travellers between the worlds who slip through into alternative realities. These stories may show what it feels like when the spiritual realm intrudes on the everyday, when spiritual beings break through, when we suddenly feel a presence, or when we, unwittingly perhaps, step through into a world that is different – upside down and inside out.

Many of these stories have long loomed large in the collective memory but can still quicken the blood today, because they represent great turning points in spiritual evolution – or, to put it in modern terms, turning points in the evolution of consciousness.

According to mystical tradition, this evolution is the unfolding of a divine plan. Great spiritual beings lead us era by era, stage by stage, drawing us out and helping us to evolve. When we fight, when we love, when we are tested to our limits and find a kind of victory in a kind of defeat, we are following in the footsteps of gods and angels, following patterns of meaning and behaviour that they have laid down for us.

But, as with all things mystical, this history is not simply linear. Because time does not operate in the same way in the spiritual worlds, there may be historical events which are in a sense still going on. Events in world history may also be recapitulated in all our individual lives, so that we must each endure an exile in the desert and go on a quest for the Holy Grail. Some events may have been re-enacted as part of religious ceremony. For example, the story that has come down to us as *Cinderella* originated as the sacred drama of Isis, enacted in the temples of ancient Egypt. Some stories, including those of rebirth, may have been part of initiation rituals, where someone was 'born again' into a higher state of being or consciousness. And some of these rituals are still being re-enacted in secret today.

In the form that they have come down to us, these stories are meant to be wise. They are 'teaching stories', meant to work on us at what we today might call a subconscious level, but they are also intended to help us become more conscious of the shapes and mystical patterns of our lives. I will argue that this is one of the reasons why stories are important. Stories, I want to suggest, tend to show the immanence of the divine in human experience.

That is why great events in the unfolding of the spiritual history of the world can be seen in stories which might seem entirely fictional – in fairy stories, tales of the Arabian nights and folk tales of encounters with elemental beings and the spirits of the dead.

No great story is mere fantasy – and neither is fantasy.[1]

*　　　　*　　　　*

These stories are arranged chronologically. In the early chapters I retell the great stories of human beginnings in order to show how epoch after epoch, stage by stage, the fundamentals of the human condition were put together.

Divine intervention and intelligent interaction with spiritual beings, spiritual guidance, spiritual testing – all of this is unquestioned in these early stories and writ large there. The tellers of these mythic tales were not interested in the material world in the way we have become interested in it since the scientific revolution. For them, the great miracle, the great wonder, was not so much the beauty and complexity of the outer world as the beauty and complexity of the *inner* world of subjective experience. They explained how we came to experience life as we do.[2]

So it was because of the passion of Venus for Adonis that desire can sometimes be destructive. It was because Loki, the Norse Lucifer, stole a magic ring forged by the dwarves that even the best of us can become acquisitive and narrowly selfish. Because of Odin and Mercury, we are intellectually curious. Because of the Sun god, we are given the assurance that if we act wholeheartedly and risk everything, we can ultimately defeat the forces of darkness.

Later in the book we will see that because of Moses a passion for justice runs through us like a mighty river. Then because of the Buddha, we are capable of compassion for all living beings, and because of the great mystics of Arabia, we have learned the delights of falling in love.

The story of the medieval founders of Hatha yoga is tied up with the story of Christian Rosencreutz and the introduction of teaching regarding the chakras into the stream of Western mystical thought. We shall see that one of the two great scientists of the spiritual in modern times, Carl Gustav Jung, was advised by a disembodied guide, just as Socrates was guided by his daemon. The other great scientist of the spiritual in modern times, Rudolf Steiner, gave a detailed account of the journey of the spirit after death.

Some themes will recur, and so too will some characters, including the sometimes dangerous and disturbing figure of the Green One, who reappears in different forms and will appear finally to announce the end of the world as we know it.

In the case of some chapters I have unravelled commentaries out of the stories in order to make explicit the turning points in history that they dramatize. In other cases I have been shy of interposing myself.

I take it as axiomatic that, as Ibn Arabi, a Sufi mystic and guiding light in this book, said, 'No single religion can fully express the Reality of God.' Throughout I look at the work and teachings of schools including the Kabbalistic, Sufi, Hermetic, Rosicrucian, Masonic, Theosophical and Anthroposophical, as well as the work of individual mystics such as Plato, Plotinus, Paracelsus, Christian Rosencreutz, Jacob Boehme, Rudolf Steiner and Lorna Byrne, asking if their restatements of the wisdom of ancient times can help us find a language to talk about them in modern terms.

I look, too, at the work of the great storytellers of modern times, writers who ask if there is a mystical dimension to our lives, if the world is shot through with meanings we did not put there, if we really are engaged in interaction with unembodied intelligence. In the age of scientific materialism this is perhaps the greatest philosophical question, and novelists, from Dostoyevsky and George Eliot to David Foster

Wallace, have looked for mysterious patterns, mystic traces and otherworldly influences not in the epic lives of heroes, but in ordinary, everyday lives.

*   *   *

I have written this book partly to ask an outrageous question: *what if the claims of world religions are true?* What would history look like then? Is it possible to give an account of creation which is creationist but cannot be instantly dismissed as absurd by scientists?

What if other large claims are true? What if Joan of Arc really was directed by angels when she defeated the English armies? What if Bernadette of Lourdes *was* visited by the Virgin Mary?

Of course it is not possible to prove these extraordinary events scientifically, but if you weave them together to form a historical narrative, does a coherent account of the world emerge that can be set against the conventional, scientifically correct one? Can a meaningful history be built out of stories of angelic intervention, mystic visions and otherworldly experiences – the rubble discarded by sensible historians?

Is it possible to trace the same patterns in the world today? Do great spiritual beings still intervene in the decisive way that they intervened in the lives of Moses and Joan of Arc? In the last third of the book there are stories of the disturbing experiences of an American president, of miracles witnessed by thousands in Spain, of angels who appeared to Jews persecuted by the Nazis in Hungary and to schoolchildren attacked by a rebel army in the Congo, as well as to people leading apparently ordinary urban lives. *The Sacred History* provides evidence of first-hand experience of the otherworldly across the ages, and I want to suggest that the sheer volume and consistency of this testimony is remarkable. [3]

*   *   *

We live at the intersection between two planes, a mental plane and a physical plane, and we can hop from one to the other. Both planes stretch off into the distance and make us wonder about where we come from and where we are going.

Philosophers have always asked which plane came first and which is more reliable, more knowable. Does one depend on the other for its existence? The philosophical question with the greatest implications for how we face the world is *which is more real – mind or matter?*

Leading on from this, are we here because the universe made us this way, or is the universe the way it is because its *purpose* is to create us? Is mind the primary constituent of the universe? Are value and meaning inherent in the universe? Are fundamental moral laws woven into the fabric of the universe? Or did we invent them?

Did we invent love?

Believing that mind came first and is in some sense more real is the religious or spiritual view of life – and is what nearly everyone believed for most of history.[4] Believing that matter came first is the materialistic and atheist view. It started to become popular with the advent of the scientific revolution and is now the prevailing view, at least among the educated élite. Today the intellectually dominant view asserts that mind or consciousness only came about as a chance fizzing together of certain chemicals.

The philosophical term for the 'mind came first' view is idealism. It's a confusing term, because outside academia it is more often used to mean the pursuit of high ideals, while students of philosophy, at least those studying in the Anglo-American tradition, encounter it as a quaint theory of knowledge which no one really believes anymore and which was last seriously defended in the eighteenth century by Bishop Berkeley.

For most of history, though, idealism was a cosmology and an all-embracing heartfelt philosophy of life. Most people experienced the world in a way that accorded with it – what we might call 'folk idealism'.[5] Most believed that 'in the beginning' there had been a great Cosmic Mind – 'God' in Western traditions. They believed this Cosmic Mind had created matter and meant it to be. They also experienced this Cosmic Mind rearranging the cosmos in response to prayer and their innermost hopes and fears, guiding them, and rewarding or punishing them for their actions. Sometimes they experienced a spiritual presence and sometimes what we might now call collective hallucinations.[6]

Today's intellectual élite, squarely on the side of scientific materialism, tends to mock mystical and spiritual experience, to deride it as woo-woo. Rather than make any serious attempt to engage with the data of spiritual experience, loud and insistent atheists talk as though the question had been settled. But we must not let ourselves be bounced into accepting this. For instance, when it comes to what happened 'in the beginning' there is no decisive evidence – in fact no evidence that is anywhere near decisive. There are only tiny scraps of evidence for the Big Bang and no evidence at all for what went before. When it comes to the beginning of creation, neither believers nor atheists have much to go on. Huge inverted pyramids of speculation are balanced on pinpricks of evidence.[7] In this area, as in many others, certainty is simply an inappropriate response to the nature and amount of evidence we have. In a recent book, the American philosopher Alvin Plantinga argued similarly that we can't rule out that evolution has come about by design – but we can't rule out the contrary either.[8]

*   *   *

If the evidence from science is sparse, are there other sources of knowledge to draw on?

The word 'mystic' comes from *mystae*, from ancient Greece, where certain individuals were chosen for initiation in institutions called Mystery schools, which were attached to the great public temples. Everyone knew of the existence of these schools, but only a few were privileged to discover what was taught in them. In these highly secretive enclosures the *mystae* were educated and put through a series of extreme tests, which might involve long periods of fasting and sensory deprivation, spiritual exercises, sometimes even drugs. The process was designed to induce mystical experiences.

Mystics were enabled to pierce the veil that keeps spiritual beings inaccessible to most people. They were enabled to communicate directly and consciously with the constructive forces of the universe, the forces that according to idealism, control the greater part of ourselves and our environment.

We shall see later that at its core the arcane knowledge that the initiates gained was a practical knowledge of the manipulation of matter by the human mind that started with human physiology. Initiates were taught how to generate psychosomatic effects within the human body and then how to move matter outside the body by the power of mind alone. They were therefore able to work in the world in ways closed to normal, everyday consciousness. They might become prophets or healers or demonstrate other extraordinary gifts. They might originate new ideas in the arts, in philosophy and in science. They knew the spiritual algorithms by which the Cosmic Mind shapes the world around us. Sometimes, as we shall see, they knew this with mathematical precision. Many of the greatest Greeks and Romans, including Socrates, Plato, Aeschylus, Pindar, Ovid, Vergil, Seneca and Cicero, were initiates of these schools.

Then as now, some mystics achieved these altered states and the other ways of knowing that come with them through these techniques of initiation, while other mystics were simply born with the capability. In *The Sacred History* we will learn from the testimony of both types of mystic. The history told here is the human story as related by people with this alternative or higher consciousness, these other ways of knowing. Drawing on the wisdom of mystics down the ages, including Ibn Arabi, Hildegard of Bingen, Rudolf Steiner and the remarkable modern mystic Lorna Byrne, I have tried to make clear what spiritual beings have intended by their interventions in human life.

This book is a visionary history and, as I say, I cannot prove any of it. That would of course be impossible. But it has long struck me that at the level of spiritual and mystical experience, all the great religious traditions merge. The experiences of a yogi in the forests of India, a dervish in the Arabian desert and Lorna Byrne on the outskirts of Dublin seem to be remarkably consistent. Sufi mystics talk about an Otherworld, a place with objective reality but accessed via the imagination. People can enter it through portals in many different parts of the globe, yet convene at the same place and meet the same spiritual beings.

*   *   *

At the end of the book I want to propose what I call 'the argument from direct personal experience': if the universe has been created by a Cosmic Mind, our experience of it should be very different than if it has come about by accident.

How are we to assess our experience, how are we to test it in the light of this? Evidence in favour of a Cosmic Mind will tend to fall in the category of the mystical. But we find it hard to talk about mystical experience in the abstract. Apart from a few little-known mystics, few people have tried to do this, with the result that we have no ready language to describe it. And finding it hard to talk – or think – about mystical experience, we are perhaps more likely to fail to recognize when we are having a mystical experience.

George Eliot wrote about this failure to recognize: 'The golden moments in the course of life rush past us and we see nothing but sand; the angels come to visit us, and we only know them when they are gone.'[9]

So, lacking a conceptual framework, how can we consider such experiences – and the questions of life and destiny? I suggested that stories could be an arena for this . . .

Before the scientific revolution, human consciousness was focused on certain central facts of the human condition: that we have very little say in the great events of our lives, that the events with the greatest bearing on our happiness come at us unbidden, and that there is a controlling intelligence at work which is not our own. Ideas like these are not common currency these days, but the American novelist David Foster Wallace wrote about them in language which is fresh, contemporary and immediate:

Both destiny's kisses and its dope-slaps illustrate an individual person's basic personal powerlessness over the really meaningful events in his life: i.e. almost nothing important that ever happens to you happens because you engineer it. Destiny has no beeper; destiny always leans trenchcoated out of an alley with some sort of Psst that you usually can't even hear because you're in such a rush to or from something important you've tried to engineer.[10]

There is a very great and stark truth underlying all these considerations of meanings of life. Without a pre-existing Cosmic Mind to mean it, the cosmos, life itself, cannot by definition have *any* intrinsic meaning – only the temporary, partial meanings we may choose to project onto it. Without a pre-existing Cosmic Mind, notions of destiny make no sense.

Yet as David Foster Wallace and others have suggested, many of us do sometimes have intimations of higher and absolute meaning. The world is against us, we have a run of bad luck, we duck out of a test and it comes round to meet us in another form, we experience premonitions, meaningful coincidences, dreams that are trying to tell us something, suddenly we understand with total clarity what someone else is thinking, we feel special connections with people we meet, we experience a moment of happiness then realize that everything in our lives has been leading up to it, we fall in love and feel sure it is meant to be . . .

Stories about otherworldly patterns and mystic traces can sensitize us to patterns like these in our own experience. They encourage attentiveness to complex, subtle, inner events which, if idealism provides an accurate picture of the world, are at the same time experiences of the inner workings of the world and evidence for the great forces that weave together to create, maintain and move it. The stories in this book have been chosen to help bring such patterns into focus.

When we read stories, we enter a mysterious place full of paradoxes and enigmas and puzzles, and we may well realize that *life is like that too*. Great fiction opens us up to our own depths and the depths of the world we live in. It can show us a world soaked through with intelligent energy, a world that means to communicate with us . . .

I hope you will enjoy these stories and read them in the spirit they were intended.

The Mystic Vision

'God save us from single vision.'

William Blake

There are people living amongst us who can see the world of angels as clearly as they can see the rocks and stones and trees that the rest of us see. These people have many names, some of them rude, but here we shall call them mystics.[1]

Sometimes they live and work within organized religion, but more often they live apart. They tend to be solitary, perhaps lonely figures.

Organized religion has always found mystics a bit of a worry. If you're a sincere, hard-working priest, who prays for faith but worries in his heart of hearts that he has never really had a mystical experience worthy of the name, it must be hard if a few miles down the road there's a young woman who talks with angels all day long. How can you defend the Church's dogma with confidence when you suspect that others have direct personal experience of realities you only know about in theory?

It goes without saying that atheists are hostile to mystics too. For them, visions of angels are simply delusions. I'm only too aware that if certain psychiatrists of an authoritarian bent got hold of some of my friends, they'd try to have them certified as schizophrenic.[2]

In the face of such hostility, one common misunderstanding needs to be cleared up: the mystical vision is not necessarily inconsistent with the scientific view. Mystics aren't calling into question the evidence of our eyes. They're not even saying that life isn't happening in the ordered way that science describes. What they are saying is that events are happening *because angels and other spiritual beings are planning them*. Because they're working behind the scenes to make them happen.

How do they know this? Sometimes mystics see only what we see – the physical world. Sometimes they enter a visionary state in which the physical world fades from view and they see only the spiritual world.[3] At other times they see the two worlds interweaving. A mystic may see an event with their two physical eyes – such as a mother deciding to double-check the seatbelt that holds her baby's car seat in place – while at the same time seeing the same event with a third, more spiritual eye. From this perspective the mother's guardian angel is at her shoulder prompting her to turn and look again, because the clip isn't safely clicked into place. As she does so, the baby's guardian angel smiles with gratitude and is illuminated with the brilliant clear blue light of understanding.

What the third or spiritual eye sees may lie outside the physical world, but that isn't to say that it is *inconsistent* with what the two other eyes see. Rather, it opens up a new dimension that weaves in and out of the physical world.[4]

It's important to bear this double vision in mind as we come to consider the creation. Here, mystics and scientists are, I believe, looking at the same series of events. *They are merely looking at them from very different points of view.*

If you turn to Chapter 1 of Genesis in the Authorized Version of the Bible, the sequence of events is as follows:

> And God said Let there be light . . . Let there be a firmament
> . . . Let it divide the waters from the waters . . . Let the dry land

God creating the world with mathematical precision. (Illustration to Brunetto Latini's *Li Livres dou Trésor*).

> appear . . . Let the earth bring forth grass . . . Let the waters
> bring forth abundantly the moving creature that hath life . . .
> Let the earth bring forth . . . the beasts of the earth . . . Let us
> make man . . .

If you strip out the poetic language, what is this describing? It is a sequence in which subatomic particles ('light') are followed by gas ('firmament'), followed by liquids ('the waters'), solids ('dry land'), primitive vegetable life ('grass'), primitive marine life ('the waters bring forth abundantly the moving creature that hath life'), land animals ('the beasts of the earth') and finally anatomically modern humans ('let us make man'). Looked at this way, Genesis is consistent with the modern scientific view.

Atheists who want to discredit the biblical account of creation always point to the idea that it took place in only seven days. But the Bible clearly never meant to say that the world was created in seven days in the modern sense of the word 'day', because a day is the measurement of the revolution of the Earth in relation to the sun, and in the beginning neither Earth nor sun existed. In Genesis the word 'day' must mean some

The Archangel Raphael sent to Adam and Eve.
(Illustration to Milton's *Paradise Lost* by Gustave Doré)

vast unit of time like an aeon. Genesis is giving an account of events before time as we know it was measurable, perhaps before it even existed.

So, what's the problem? Why the bad blood? Because Genesis says that *God planned this sequence of events. He meant creation to happen and made it happen.* He said, 'Let it happen,' and saw that it was good.

*　　　*　　　*

What is even more provoking is that the Bible also says that angels helped carry out his intentions and rejoiced at them.[5]

The Bible is the source of many stories of angels, but there are other sources, too, some just as ancient. The myths and legends of the Jews, the Talmud and the mystical traditions of the Kabbalah, which we will examine later, expand on the descriptions of angels in the Bible.[6] Mystics have always claimed to have insights into the role of the angels that may not be explicit in scripture but are perhaps alluded to and encoded within it. In Jewish and Christian mystical

St Michael helping to mould the human form. (Italian miniature of the thirteenth century).

tradition, the Archangel Michael had a special role in the creation of human form, for instance, and the deeds and personalities of Michael and other angels lie hidden between the letters and words of Genesis. As we shall see, there are also sacred and mystical traditions from other religions that seem to be telling the same stories about the same beings.

Let us now gaze into the great vistas opened up by these mystics and visionaries, the panoramas of armies of angels, dynasties of angels, angelic leaders, angelic heroes and, yes, bad angels. In what follows we will see galaxies expanding and collapsing and angelic civilizations rising and falling.

Are the battles of angels the product of human fantasy, as the atheists insist?

Or are our lives and loves echoes of the lives and loves of angels?

Softly Falls the Dew . . .

In the beginning there was no time, no space, no matter – only darkness.

Scientists have almost nothing to say about this time – and neither do mystics. Whichever way you look at it, it's almost impossible to discover anything at all about this darkness or even to find any words to begin to describe it.

But whilst scientists claim it was nothing more than nothingness, believers claim it was nothing less than the teeming mind of God.

It is from this point of disagreement, on an issue about which both sides should admit that they know almost nothing at all, that great epoch-making arguments have flowed – the inquisitions, the persecutions, the imprisoning, the torture, the executions, the wars that continue into modern times.[1]

One thing we all know for certain, whichever side we are on, is that in order to get to where we stand today, there must have been a transition from a state of no matter to a state in which matter began. Scientists have offered theories to explain this very mysterious transition, such as the 'steady state' theory that says that matter is coming into existence all the time, that it is steadily precipitated out of the darkness. Then, of course, there is the Big Bang theory. This says that matter and space and time all sprang into being at once, bursting out of a single dimensionless, timeless point called 'the singularity'. But whether it happened steadily or in one quick splurge, that is to say whatever the *speed* of the process, if you had been there with two physical eyes and been able to look at these events through the most powerful microscope, you would have seen very fine, at first almost abstract subatomic particles evolve and take shape as atoms. The cosmos was becoming suffused with *stuff* in the form of a very thin mist.

You might have been reminded of the wonder you felt as a child when you woke at dawn and went out into the garden to find that dew had precipitated out of thin air. Even though it looked as if it hadn't rained overnight, the early rays of the sun revealed a lawn sparkling with drops of water. In Jewish mystical tradition the mystic dew of creation is sometimes thought of as softly falling from God's great shaggy mane.[2]

Or you might have been reminded of the wonder you felt in the chemistry lab when amongst the Bunsen burners and racks of test tubes you first saw beautifully shaped crystals forming in a solution, as if ideas from another dimension were squeezing into our material dimension. And if you are a believer, that is exactly what did happen – and that other dimension, the one that lends shape and form to our material dimension, is nothing less than the mind of God.

In the visions of the mystics, the process of creation began when God began to think – when thoughts began to emanate from the mind of God, wave after wave of them. And in the same way that wave after wave dashing upon the shore smoothes the pebbles on the beach, so wave after wave coming out of the mind of God fashioned the first matter.

Look at this mystic version of events more closely, look with imagination, and you can see that these waves of thoughts are actually made up of millions of angels. The first wave is made up of gigantic angels who fill the whole cosmos. Next comes a wave of lesser angels which the greatest angels have helped to create, and together these generate a third wave of smaller angels. This sequence flows down until we finally reach minute spiritual beings. They work to weave together what we recognize as the material world around us, the rocks and stones and trees.[3]

Equating the thoughts of God with angels may seem odd. These days we tend to have a lowly conception of our own thoughts, seeing them as abstract things which hardly *exist* at all. But there is an older, perhaps more illuminating way of looking at thoughts that comes from the great religions. This sees thoughts as *living beings*, with a level of

God brooding. Creation myths describe how matter came to be and how the fundamental laws of the universe were put in place. Because time is a measure of the movement of objects in space, what they describe can be said to take place before time as we know it started to tick over. According to the Big Bang theory, matter and the fundamental laws of the universe came into being after a very short interval of time – sometimes said to be a fraction of a second or a few seconds – after the initial explosion. But in a sense, if time had not yet started, any measurement of this interval is arbitrary. It could equally be thought of as long enough for the battles of angels, the loves of the gods and the rise and fall of civilizations that mythology describes. For an animated representation of this, see: http://www.youtube.com/watch?v=PeasdIUJ86M

independent existence and a life of their own as we send them off into the world to do our bidding.

We will return to this way of looking at thoughts later, but suffice to say here that everyone who prays believes something similar. People who pray are engaging in an activity that is an echo of God's creation of the cosmos.

*　　　　*　　　　*

The question is, when you pray, when you wish upon a star, if you want something strongly enough and in the right way, does the cosmos respond? Or does the influence only go one way – from matter to mind? This question – of whether or not there is an interaction between mind and matter – lies right at the heart of today's cutting-edge intellectual debate.

Any sincere attempt to answer this important question involves considering your innermost feelings, your deepest, most private fears and highest hopes. It also calls on your subtlest powers of discernment and most subjective interpretations of your experiences. Only you know what you pray for in your heart of hearts. Only you are capable of assessing how your prayer has been answered. You are the best judge of what any particular moment means to you. We are talking about

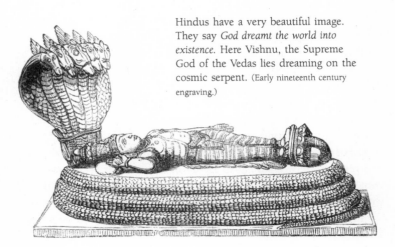

Hindus have a very beautiful image. They say *God dreamt the world into existence*. Here Vishnu, the Supreme God of the Vedas lies dreaming on the cosmic serpent. (Early nineteenth century engraving.)

the subtlest shifts and shades of the interior life here – not issues that are accessible to measurement or scientific testing.

Sometimes scientists try to argue that the only questions worth asking are the ones that admit of scientific testing. But this point of view is *only scientific* and does not take account of areas of experience where science has nothing useful to contribute. The militant atheists among scientists tend to be highly suspicious of these areas and to suggest that we don't really have these experiences. In his essay *On Life* Tolstoy wrote about this encroachment, this attempt to trick us into believing we are not experiencing what we are in fact experiencing: 'The false science of our day assumes we cannot know the one thing we really do know: what our reasonable consciousness tells us.'

For an atheist, physical objects are the measure of what is real. According to idealism, on the other hand, mind is *more real* than matter. The cosmos is imbued with mind, charged with it. Matter is alive with it and pulsates with it and responds to it. Mind is rearranging matter all around us all the time.[4] And we too can have a say in that. We may change the course of history just by sitting alone in a room, being quiet for a while and thinking about it . . .

Belief in the power of mind to move matter is what distinguishes religious and spiritual thinking, and this moving is the quintessential supernatural event.

And yet we who call ourselves religious or spiritual often behave as if there were no such thing as the supernatural. We often go along with the atheistic view. Perhaps it's that we tend to compartmentalize our spiritual beliefs? For example, we tend to accept an account of history in which God and the supernatural play no part.

*　　　　　*　　　　　*

Mystics assert that as well as working together to create the material world, angels have guided humanity to great turning points in history.

I have been fortunate in the writing of this book to have the help of a remarkable woman called Lorna Byrne. She has seen and talked with angels all her life. She has always had a very special relationship with one of the higher angels, an angel who has played a vital part in the human story and who has a particular mission in our own age – the Archangel Michael.

Shortly after I heard about Lorna, a friend told me that the head of a religious order in Rome had been to see her, and a senior theologian at a Dublin college consulted her if he wanted to know if what he was writing about the different orders of angels was right. Since then Lorna and I have become firm friends. Sometimes I have been able to read her some of the stories preserved in mystical tradition and ask if the angels agree, and on occasion she has helped stories and traditions about angels come alive for me.

*   *   *

Does the mystic dew still fall?

From birth we are creatures that are part coming into being and part dying. As we age, we become fixed in our ways and the dying part begins to predominate. The skull pushes its way outwards, against the skin. But even in old age we still receive vivifying influences, especially when we are asleep. Then the mystic dew is precipitated again, sparkling in the deep dark depths of our minds. We wake up refreshed, with renewed life and purpose.

This may be seen as the work of angels standing at our bedside, protecting and teaching us and preparing us for morning. They commune with our spirit while we are sleeping. They embrace us and comfort us, and so we wake up knowing somewhere deep inside us what we need to do.

Mother Earth and Father Time

'What's this war in the heart of nature? Why does nature vie with itself, the land contend with the sea?'

Opening lines from *The Thin Red Line*,
directed by Terrence Malick[1]

If human eyes had existed in the beginning, they would have seen vast waves of mist, finer and more subtle even than light. This soft and nurturing mist, carrying the potential for all life, was Mother Earth.

Then, says the Bible, 'Darkness was upon the face of the Earth.'

By drawing on the legends of the Jews and the creation myths of neighbouring cultures, we can see some of what lies behind the biblical account. Myths all around the world tell this story:

Mother Earth was blasted by a searing dry wind. To human eyes it would have looked as if the mist was being churned up by a typhoon, but mystic vision detects something like a human form hidden in the storm – a long-boned giant, hooded, with scaly white skin and red eyes. The darkness was the spirit of Saturn. He was armed with a scythe, and he swooped down, pressing himself on top of Mother Earth with black delight.

'Don't be afraid. Let me just . . . lie on you.'

Did he want to make love to her? Or was his only desire to squeeze the life out of her? There was an ambiguity to his deeds that would leave a scar, a chasm in the deep structure of the cosmos.

You might have thought that Mother Earth would be terrified as she felt the giant's cold breath, his exhausting, leaden presence weighing more and more heavily on her. You might have thought that she would fight him off, try to push him away. But she knew this *had to be*, that it all had to happen according to plan. So, as he tried to cover her, she spread out and embraced him. She held him so he could not rise up and fly away again.

'You're a man!' she coaxed him.

Ah yes, he thought – but he then found he couldn't look up. He could only manage another thin metallic hiss.

She wanted him to draw her in closer, as close as it is possible for one being to be to another. She wanted him to work his way down into her and she up into him.[2]

To Saturn it seemed as if her reserves were limitless, as if she were absorbing all his strength, draining him. But the irony was that for her part she began to fear she couldn't hang on much longer either. It felt to her as if she had nothing left, that he was the stronger. He was succeeding in suffocating all the life out of her, and if he did, she knew the consequences: there would never be life anywhere in the universe. It would forever be a place of the sifting of dead matter . . .

'Let there be light.'

Just when all seemed lost, there came a sound like a trumpet, and suddenly, out of nowhere, light arrived in the form of a beautiful youth with a golden mane on a golden chariot pulled by golden horses. Seven golden rays radiated from his shining brow and he rode fearlessly straight into the middle of the storm, scattering the darkness.

That this rescue had come in the nick of time set a pattern deep in the structure of the cosmos. Forever after, rescuers would come at the eleventh hour – Robin Hood rolling under the portcullis before it clanged shut to rescue Maid Marian, the US cavalry arriving to save the wagon train.

The young Sun god fought Saturn and vanquished him. Saturn is one of the names of Satan, the spirit of opposition, and creation myths all over the world would preserve a memory of these events in the stories of Saturn oppressing Mother Earth and the Sun god then vanquishing the monster.

Saturn was banished to the outer limits, where he lay coiled around the cosmos like a great serpent with his tail in his mouth. He was evil, but a *necessary* evil. Because of him the mists of proto-matter were no longer formless. As atoms formed, individual objects started to exist.

This grisly old tyrant would be remembered for eating his own children. What this myth points to is that *what comes into existence can also go out of existence*. This is the thing about being a thing – you are limited. If you can begin to *be*, it follows that you can also cease to be.[3]

In his hour of triumph the Sun god warmed Mother Earth back to life. As he did so, he sang her a beautiful song, at first soft and gentle, but rising to shake the whole cosmos. It was a song of victory and love. The song of the Sun god caused all the matter in the universe to vibrate. There's a beautiful phrase preserved by Christian mystics to describe this agitation of primal matter: 'the dance of the substances'. As a result of this dance, the substances began to coagulate and form myriad patterns. If you scatter powder, such as talcum powder, on a smooth surface such as a pane of glass and draw the bow of a violin across the edge, the powder will form pattern after pattern as the music and its vibrations change. The patterns formed on the glass will be like the patterns that formed then – the shapes of primitive fernlike plants.

The Greeks had a name for the Sun god who formed the world in this patterned way: they called him 'the Word'. The Word was with God and the Word was God's greatest, most important thought. The Word sang life into existence. When St John talked about the Word in the opening verses of his gospel, he expected his readers to understand what he meant by 'the Word that shines in the darkness'.[4]

In the last chapter we saw the mysterious transition from no matter to matter. Now, with the arrival of the Sun god, we are seeing the equally mysterious transition from no life to life – the creation of the first vegetable forms.

Single germs joined together and formed vast floating nets of interweaving luminous threads that dissolved and came together again in ever more complex patterns. At the centre of these patterns there formed a trunk with its branches stretching everywhere. This vast vegetable being at the heart of the cosmos, whose soft and luminous limbs stretched to all corners of it, was Adam.

Plants don't reproduce in the sexual manner characteristic of animals. Typically a seed breaks away to form a new plant. Scientists call this plant-like method of reproduction parthenogenesis, and in creation stories it was in this way that Adam's limbs broke off to form Eve. Adam and Eve were the vegetable seeds of what would eventually become humanity, and this is what the Bible means to tell us when it says Eve was created out of Adam's 'spare rib'.

By parthenogenesis, then, Adam and Eve populated the whole cosmos. Their children and their children's children evolved into complex vegetable life forms, including plants' sense organs shaped like flowers. In time the universe was as full of these gently palpitating flowers as the night sky is full of stars.

This vegetable stage of development is remembered in the Bible as the Garden of Eden. Because there was as yet no animal life in the cosmos, Adam was without desire and so without care or dissatisfaction. He lived in a world of endless dreamy bliss. Nature yielded a never-ending supply of food in the form of a milky sap, similar to the sap in dandelions today. Angels tended this garden and humanity lived in uninterrupted communion with them and could see beyond them and gaze on the kind face of God Himself.[5]

Throughout history a rumour has persisted that it is possible for individuals to regain this blissful state. Later, we will follow this rumour to its source and ask if it is true.[6]

The Angel Michael
and the Serpent

There is something horrible in life. We don't know what it is, but it is coming towards us whether fast or slow, from in front or behind, from inside or out, or in a strange knight's move through a dimension we do not know.

And in those first moments, amid the green shoots and the flowers, something was stirring. A whiff of sulphur was followed by a flash of lightning and a clap of thunder. The peace of the sun-drenched garden was rent by a livid red-horned snake, sparkling all over as if covered with diamonds, sapphires and onyx, and with an emerald on its forehead. Coil upon coil quickly unravelled. This snake was so bright that foliage in the garden cast shadows by its light. It shot with dazzling speed up to the trunk in the middle of the garden and wrapped itself around Adam.[1]

Adam began to thrash around, feeling something never felt before. Never had *pain* been felt anywhere in the world before, because up till then the only living things had been plants.

In the mystic vision of the snake and the tree we see the clearest possible image of the development of the spine, and the spine is of course the defining anatomical feature of animal life. This is creation's third mysterious transition – from vegetable to animal life – and again the mythical and biblical account is not inconsistent with the scientific account, merely expressed in a different, more visionary way.

Adam saw a winged figure swooping down, armour flashing. Archangel Michael, champion of the Sun god, had arrived to save him before he became completely maddened by pain.

Fire flashed from the serpent's eyes as it turned away from Adam to confront Michael. Its body puffed up with poison.

As Michael made a dive for the monster's neck, it unleashed its coils and shot high into the air to drive him off. Michael saw his chance and plunged his spear down into the belly that now lay exposed before him. There it became stuck in the tough hide. A disgusting stench spread from the wound. Michael recoiled, but as the snake swooped low to dislodge the spear, Michael was quick and strong enough to pull it free and thrust it upwards, this time right through the neck of the snake. He pinned it to the top of the trunk of the tree.

For a few moments the great serpent writhed there and Michael glimpsed the green jewel fall from its forehead.[2]

The serpent was now deflating before Michael's eyes, but all the time it held his gaze, challenging him. The serpent was looking at him as if it had somehow got the better of him, as if Michael were stupid!

Still leaning on his spear, Michael reached down and pulled his sword from its sheath with his other hand, intending to decapitate the snake with one blow.

For an instant it seemed to Michael as if the snake was made of glass and that his sword had shattered it. Then he saw to his horror that that wasn't precisely what had happened. The snake had dissolved into millions of smaller snakes that were even now escaping, shooting off in every direction and burying themselves in the life of the forest.

Michael had won the day, but it was a victory that mixed bitter with sweet. In defeat Lucifer did indeed bring forth a sweet and wonderful thing. Because of Lucifer the light of animal consciousness was introduced into the world, and what the story of Adam and Eve tells us is that with animal life came desire.

But with desire came suffering.

And after desire came death. Because a plant reproduces by shedding a part of itself, the new plant is in a sense a continuation of the old one, and therefore in this sense a plant does not die. But an animal's body dies completely and irrevocably.[3]

The spine and nervous system that are characteristic of an animal's body bring animal consciousness and also the possibility of knowledge.

Desire brings death (fifteenth-century engraving by Sebald Beham).

Of course, with knowledge comes the possibility of error. Because of Lucifer we are animated, both in the sense that as animals we can move across the surface of the planet and in the sense that we are propelled by desire. And because of him we are in permanent danger of taking the wrong path and losing control.[4]

So, like Satan before him, Lucifer is necessary – but an evil nonetheless.

I say Lucifer is 'like' Satan because, really, in the Bible and in the world's great creation myths there are two great primordial stories about the battle of the Sun god with a serpent monster. Of course these stories are similar and tend to become entwined in our minds, but it is worth disentangling them because they tell us related but different things about the human condition. They both tell us why life is hard – but 'hard' in two different senses. Life is hard in the sense that it brings us discomfort and pain and pushes us to our limits. It is also hard to understand.

The stories of the two snakes reflect this. The Saturn snake – Satan – attacks from outside, while the Venus snake – Lucifer – insinuates itself inside us. Because of Satan, the spirit of opposition, life is often hard to bear. Because of Satan, we are attacked. Because of Satan, we – like Mother Earth – are tested to our very limits, to the point where we want to give up.[5]

Lucifer attacks us in different ways. Lucifer makes us liable to make mistakes. He endowed matter with a glamour that would dazzle people and blind them to higher truths. He injected a paradoxical, tricky quality into the heart of the universe and at the same time injected a perverse quality into our hearts that responds to the tricky quality 'out there'. It is because of Lucifer that, as St Paul puts it, 'the good that I would do, I do not, but the evil which I would not, that I do'.

This is right at the heart of what it means to be human. There is no easy way out and no easy answer. The road is always fraught with the danger of death, but if we do not take that road we will die in our beds without ever having lived. We must put at risk what we value most or we will lose it anyway. Beyond a certain point there is no return. That point must be reached.

*   *   *

We have been retelling stories involving planetary gods – Saturn, Mother Earth, Venus and the Sun god. How is it possible to square these with the biblical account?

The answer lies in the series of emanations of angels from the mind of God. There is a little-known but deep and widespread tradition that one of the orders of angels is especially closely related to the planets: *the gods of the planets are a type of angel*.

The Bible is full of stories of different types of angels – including archangels, the Cherubim and the Seraphim – and St Paul refers, too, to different orders of angels: 'In Him all things were created, in heaven and on earth, whether Thrones or Dominions or Principalities or Powers . . .' (Col. 1.16). St Paul doesn't bother to explain his lists of the different orders. Like St John when he is writing about the Word, he expects his readers to know.[6]

The beings called gods by the Greeks and Romans were the order of angels called Powers by St Paul.

Of course people from different parts of the world have always encountered disembodied beings they have called gods, angels or spirits. How people see them is coloured by the culture they have been brought up in. Spiritual beings also adapt themselves and take different forms suitable for different cultures. A sacred Tamil dedication addresses the deity as 'Thou that takest the form imagined by Thy worshippers'.[7]

The scientifically correct view of these accounts would of course be that they are all nothing more than delusions. But if they are something more, if they are encounters with something real, if there really is a spiritual dimension, then we would expect to find beings there that are recognizably the same, albeit in different cultural clothing.

Lorna Byrne has direct, daily experience of the spiritual realm in a way that matches the accounts of great mystics of the past. Because she is badly dyslexic, and has, besides, many distractions of an angelic nature, she has never read a book in her life. She knew nothing of this mystical tradition before she met me, but has always experienced St Michael as the Archangel of the Sun and Gabriel as the Archangel of the Moon.

I remember when we first discussed this. We were walking beside a river in the countryside near Dublin – and I was surprised because

Unembodied intelligence was commonly depicted as winged beings in ancient cultures. These three beautiful images from *The Dictionary of Greek and Roman Antiquities*, illustrated by numerous engravings on wood, edited by William Smith, 1848, show a winged genius – from the base of the column of Antoninus Pius – a goddess inscribing a shield and the conjuring of a spirit from a bowl.

Lorna had just offered to teach me how to fish! She laughed out loud, openly delighted, when I told her that Michael as the Archangel of the Sun and Gabriel as the Archangel of the Moon was a tradition not only in Christianity and Judaism but in Islam as well.

So, there may be conflict between religions at the level of doctrine and dogma – contradiction even – but, as we shall see, the stories and the experiences seem much the same. In what follows I try to weave the stories of gods and angels and great men and women guided by gods and angels into one story.

The Spider Woman Weaves
her Spell

*'By recollecting the myths, by re-enacting them, we are
able to repeat what the God, the Heroes, the ancestors
did* ab origine. *To know the myths is to learn the
secrets of the origins of things.'*

Mircea Eliade, *Myth and Reality*

Changing Woman lived in the canyon of the Navahos. Hers was a
beautiful land, but its people were terrorized by giants and monsters
who picked off travellers and ate them.

There was one great giant with a furrowed brow who could see
Changing Woman was on her own. He was always hanging round.
He wanted her, but she could see that his heart was black and full of
hatred.

One day he noticed her twin sons' footprints in the sand and jealously
asked who had made them. Changing Woman said she'd made the
tracks herself with her hands. But she wasn't sure the giant was
convinced, and on days when she feared he might be returning she'd
hide her sons in a hole in the middle of her hut which she would then
cover up with a slab of sandstone.

The boys survived to grow tall and strong and when it was time for
them to learn how to hunt, she helped them to make bows and arrows.
But this provoked a strong yearning in the boys. They said they wanted
to hunt with their father. It was only natural.

'Who is our father?' they asked.

'You have no father,' she said. But they persisted and eventually she admitted that their father was the Sun god who lived far away, far beyond the Grand Canyon on an island in the middle of the great ocean. She told them that it would be impossible for them to find him, that they would never survive the journey – the traps, the difficult terrain, the ravening monsters . . .

But then, when she saw how determined they were, she let them go, with great sadness in her heart but also her blessing. She warned them about the Raven, the Vulture and the Magpie. She said they were spies for the monsters that wished to devour them.

So, when the two boys set off before dawn, they were aware as they passed between the trees that they were being spied on every step of the way.

In the early morning light, as they were approaching a sacred mountain that loomed above the trees, they saw a trail of smoke rising from a hole in the ground. Curious, they peered down into the gloom and saw an ugly wizened old woman dressed in black tending a fire. It was the Spider Woman.

'Who are you and what are you doing here?' she rasped.

'We don't know who we are,' they admitted. 'And we don't know where we are going.'

They explained that they were the sons of Changing Woman and that they were on a quest.

'Are you trying to find your father?'

When they nodded, the Spider Woman beckoned with a grey scaly hand. 'Come down into my lodge.'

They squeezed down to find that the underground walls were covered with webs as thick as cloth and clogged with bones.

'Don't be afraid,' she said. 'I will tell you how to find the House of the Sun god.'

She explained that the journey ahead of them was long and dangerous and that their father lived on the far horizon on the other side of the ocean. To reach him they would have to pass deadly obstacles – through rocks that would clash together to try to crush them, through a forest of reeds that would slash them to ribbons and across dunes of boiling sand that would burn the flesh off their bones.

'No man can survive these tests without the talisman I am about to give you,' she said. She handed them a hoop made of three feathers torn from live eagles and instructed them to hold it in front of them. She told them to look their enemy in the eye and say:

> Put your feet down with pollen.
> Put your hands down with pollen.
> Put your mind down with pollen.
> Then your feet are pollen.
> Your body is pollen.
> Your mind is pollen.
> Your voice is pollen.
> You are beautiful.
> You are still . . .'

They set off again armed with the artefacts and wisdom of the Spider Woman. The rocks of the Grand Canyon parted to let them through, the reeds softened and the dunes quietened and lay down. Then on the shore a rainbow suddenly appeared in front of them and they crossed over the ocean by walking on it and at last reached the House of Sun.

Their father would not at first believe they were his sons. He made them wrestle him and then made them endure a sweat lodge that would have killed any ordinary man. When they survived these tests, he finally recognized them and gave them helmets made of flint and arrows of lightning and deadly sunbeams. He said, 'My sons, these are the weapons you will need to destroy the monsters that are ravaging your mother's kingdom – but I am the man who must strike the first blow. Because it is I who must kill the great giant with the furrowed brow.'

And so it was that the three men set off to make the return journey arm in arm . . .

Many years later, when the fighting had ceased, the battle had been won and the monsters eradicated, when it was again safe for children to go out alone, a little girl was playing in the woods. She saw a trail of smoke emerging from a hole in the ground. She peered down into the gloom and all of a sudden a gnarled old face thrust up in front of hers.

'Come down, my dear. Come down and sit with me.'

The little girl climbed down a rickety old black ladder and took a seat next to the Spider Woman.

The wise woman

'What's that called?' she asked.

'That's a loom, my dear, and what I am doing is called weaving,' said the Spider Woman.

And for the next three days and nights she taught the little girl how to weave. The little girl watched open-mouthed as the Spider Woman's hand flitted rhythmically backwards and forwards across the loom. The Spider Woman hummed as she worked in complex patterns of light and colour, going round and round like the stars and the planets, as if she were bringing the very world into existence with form and colour and harmony and secret meaning. The girl perhaps had an inkling, even if she couldn't have said so, that a cosmic web was being woven into existence in which every part was related to every other part, and all centring on a hole in the middle of the cloth.

'Always leave a hole in the middle of the blanket, my dear, won't you?' warned the Spider Woman. 'Like spiders always do. Otherwise you may get caught in your own web!'[2]

'I am all that has been and is, and shall be, and my veil no mortal has hitherto raised.' The Graeco-Roman historian saw this inscription on a shrine in Sais in Egypt. It was dedicated to Athena, but Plutarch believed that it had originally been dedicated to Isis. The little Navaho girl encountered a creator goddess known by many different names in different parts of the globe.

In the course of this book we will meet this mysterious Initiatrix in many different forms, some of them very familiar. She is the medium through which the divine enters our lives. She is frightening because she employs the supernatural to combat dark forces, but we will see in the next story how her intervention foiled a Saturnine plot to deprive us of the divine altogether.

*   *   *

From the point of view of materialism, myths like these represent elements of the subconscious – in the Freudian account they are memories of our infancy, the gods being our parents in fancy dress. From the point of view of idealism, on the other hand, they represent a historical account of how human experience was put together, the laying down of successive silts that would become the aggregates of the human psyche.

I first came across the Spider Woman in Joseph Campbell's *The Hero with a Thousand Faces*, which contains a shortened version of her story. Campbell's great achievement was to see the essential unity that lies behind myths and legends from all over the world and to show how the same stories are told in different cultural guises. Perhaps partly because of the influence of Jung, he tended to understand myths as embodying great psychological truths rather than historical truths.

The Angel of the Night
(from *L'Art Byzantine*).

The journey of the hero through his sequence of trials is the journey of everyman and everywoman through their own life. The myths reveal the great patterns of the unconscious.

I think that is a great truth and an important aspect of reality that we all intuitively respond to and believe to be true, but I also think it is not the whole story. Something which is nowhere laid out explicitly and systematically in the writings of the great Austrian mystic Rudolf Steiner but is everywhere implicit in it is that myths and legends originate from different stages of human development. Looked at in this way, prompted and guided by Steiner, as I have been in these chapters, you can see that on one level myths are collective memories of great turning points in human evolution and that they may be put in a proper chronological order.

Isis and the Mystery
of the Perfect Fit

Once upon a time there was girl who worked tending the fire in the kitchen of a great palace. It was a hard life and because she was permanently blackened by soot from the fireplace, everyone called her Cinders.

Although she was at the bottom of the heap, much put upon by the family and other servants, she dreamt that one day her prince would come . . .

The story of Cinderella is a version of a drama acted out in the temples of ancient Egypt. In the original, Cinderella was blackened with soot because she was in mourning, because the prince she was dreaming of was missing, presumed dead. She had been roaming the world, searching for his remains, and her quest had reached its climax – in pantomime terms its 'transformation scene' – while she was working in disguise as a servant in the kitchens of the palace of the king of Syria.

In this original version, she was called Isis and her prince was called Osiris:

Osiris was a popular king, a mighty hunter who rid the land of many monsters that were ravaging it. One day he returned from one of these hunting expeditions to find that his giant of a brother, Seth, was organizing a gala dinner for him.

After dinner there were games and Seth announced he had made a beautiful wooden chest, inlaid with gold and silver and precious stones. He said that whoever fitted the chest perfectly could keep it.[1]

One guest after another tried the chest, but they were all too fat for it, too thin, too short or too tall. Eventually Osiris tried. 'Look,' he cried, 'it fits! It fits me like the skin I was born in!'

Everyone looked on, amazed, but they were even more amazed when Seth and his henchmen leapt forwards and slammed down the lid. They hammered in nails and filled all the holes with lead. The chest was now a coffin.

Seth and his men carried the chest down to the banks of the Nile and launched it onto the waves. There it floated for many days and many nights until it washed ashore.

A tamarisk tree gradually grew around it, wrapping it in its branches until it became entirely enclosed in the tree. In time this tree was chopped down and used as a pillar in the new palace of the Syrian king.

In her grief Osiris's young wife, Isis, had cut her hair short and covered herself in ashes. She roamed the world looking for her man.

Eventually she pitched up at the court of the Syrian king. She no longer had any of the trappings of royalty and could only find work as a skivvy in the kitchens.

But one night she had an extraordinary vision: she saw Osiris imprisoned in the old tree that held up the central hall of the palace.

The next morning she fought her way into the throne room and managed to convince the king of her true identity. He allowed her to cut through the bark of the tree and prise open the coffin. She was also allowed to carry the body of Osiris away from the palace to a small island, where she began to use oil and magic arts to revive him.

But Seth had magic powers too. He and his cohorts were hunting by moonlight when they saw Isis cradling Osiris on the banks of the island. Swooping down on them, they snatched the body and gleefully hacked Osiris to pieces. Seth wanted to make sure this time, so he had the pieces of the corpse buried in remote parts of the land.

Isis had to set out again on her travels, accompanied this time by her darker-skinned sister Nepthys. She transformed herself into a dog,

Osiris and Bastet. Different civilizations from different eras remembered the gods at different stages of their evolution. On the way to helping humans to evolve the anatomy we know today, and before all animal forms had been absorbed into the human form as the crown of creation, the gods adopted the anthropomorphic forms remembered by the Egyptians.

the better to seek out and dig up the parts of the corpse.

Eventually they assembled them all and took them to the island of Abydos. There Isis bound the parts together with a strip of white linen and brought just enough life back to her husband so that he was able to impregnate her.

Isis, the mother goddess, was now carrying Horus, the future Sun god.

Today Horus is known to many children as Jack, because, like the story of Cinderella, the story of Horus's battle with the giant Seth would also come down to us as a fairytale. Because he would return to overthrow his gigantic uncle and rule as king of the gods, we know Horus as Jack the Giant Killer.

The story of Isis, Osiris and Horus is a very strange one, isn't it? How can we make sense of it? Can we consider it as being in any way real or historical? I think they may begin to understand by retelling another famous fairy tale, *Sleeping Beauty* . . .

Once upon a time in a land far away, in a very happy, blessed kingdom, a beautiful baby girl was born to the king and queen. They rejoiced and organized a ball to celebrate. They invited the good and great of the land, including six of the seven fairies who lived there.

In turn each of these six fairies waved a wand and gave the girl a present in the form of a blessing that would help make her life a full and happy one.

But the seventh, a wicked fairy, was enraged at not being invited. With a flash and a bang she appeared in the middle of the ball and cursed the child. She cursed her unto death: 'She will prick her finger and die!'

One of the good fairies stepped forward and countered the wicked fairy's black magic with her own white magic. The sentence was commuted from death to a deep dreamless sleep that would last at least a hundred years and could only be broken by the kiss of a prince.

The king and queen had every sharp metal object removed from the palace – every pin, needle and pair of scissors, every knife and fork. The baby grew into a beautiful young girl with long dark hair and eyes that flashed when she spoke. She was loved by everyone in the palace, courtiers and servants alike.

One day she was a bit bored and happened to be wandering around the palace when she came to a part she couldn't remember ever visiting before. She found an entrance to a tower and climbed the stairs to the top. There, in the little chamber underneath the roof, she came upon a little old woman with a gentle face and kind eyes, working on a spindle.

The princess sat and watched for a while and chatted with the old woman, and after a while asked if she could have a go on the spindle.

'Of course, my dear.'

'Ouch!'

And so it was that the princess dropped to the floor in a dead faint, blood ballooning out of the tip of her finger.

Seven is a sacred number in all religions and the seven fairies in this story should alert us to the fact that it has a secret mystical meaning.

Mystical teachings from around the world say that when the spirit leaves the body after death it spirals up through the seven spheres of the planets. These spheres are sometimes also called 'heavens'. For example St Paul wrote about being taken up into the third heaven, and the phrase 'in seventh heaven' comes from this tradition too.

Having ascended to the seventh heaven, the spirit is reabsorbed into the great embrace of God. It then spirals down again. As it passes through each and every sphere, it receives a gift from the angel of the planet of that sphere. This is a unique and special gift it will need in its next incarnation if it is to have a happy and fulfilled life. So, for example, from the angel of Venus the human spirit receives loving qualities, from the angel of Mars the qualities of boldness, and so on.[2]

But the angel of the sphere of Saturn is satanic – the evil fairy. Her aim is to deaden the spirit forever by trapping it in the material world.

If we bear in mind the fact that in the fairy tale the handing out of the six blessings and the curse takes place *at the ball*, it becomes easy to appreciate the very strange topsy-turvy nature of this tale. Because we can now see that everything that happens when Sleeping Beauty is apparently awake and alive really happens when she is dead, and only when she is in her deep death-like sleep, which is to say dead to the spiritual world, is she alive on Earth![3]

The similarities between *Sleeping Beauty* and the story of Isis and Osiris are too obvious to need drawing out. When Osiris is dead and nailed in his coffin he is really alive on Earth. These stories, like the other stories we have been retelling, *are not really about what happens in this world at all*.

In fact all the stories we've looked at so far – the overthrow of Saturn by the Sun god, the snake in the garden, the Spider Woman, Isis and Osiris – are accounts of events that took place in the spiritual dimension, and that's for a very good reason: because the world of physical objects that we are familiar with today hardly existed then. The material world was like a mist, a vague, unformed, ephemeral anomaly floating in the midst of a bright and brilliant, fully formed spiritual world. The bodies of nymphs, monsters, animals, even humans were closer to phantoms than to the sort of creatures encased in solid bodies we are today.[4]

So, in a way you might look again at everything we've seen so far and say, as many storytellers say . . .

After all, it was only a dream . . .

*   *   *

I have suggested we remember ancient stories because they preserve turning points in human history, great events that prepared the way for life as we experience it. The great turning point in the history of humanity that Christianity calls the Fall was actually the fall into matter. Human spirits had been phantoms like the gods, the angels and the giants. As their bodies became harder and fleshier, they began to experience new joys – and new dangers too.

The story of Isis and Osiris is about how we came to be born and live in the material world for a certain limited time – and what it felt like.

Osiris was the Egyptian god of regeneration. He would die in winter and be reborn in spring. Osiris dolls, representing his corpse, would be planted with seeds that would then sprout in spring.

Because of the Osiris angel, the human spirit would become deeply immersed in the material world for the interval of a life on Earth. Because of Osiris, the tasks the human spirit faced would run deeper and be more exacting, more individual, than they could be for any free-floating spirit . . .[5]

Godly Lovers and Angelic Wives

'Angels are the powers hidden in the faculties
and organs of man.'

Ibn Arabi

Jupiter looked down from his throne on Mount Olympus and stroked his beard. He was looking at the flanks of a nymph clambering over rocks beneath a sacred waterfall. Io had come on since he last looked. Her skin was white and soft and with his godly telescope-like vision he could see it flecked with spray. He licked his lips.

Gods flew through the air as fast as thought itself.

As Jupiter appeared beside her, the nymph turned to slip among the trees and hide. But she heard a great booming laugh immediately behind her.

As he pinned her to the sacred grass, the muscles on his neck stood out.

Jupiter's wife, Juno, could always see what he was thinking. In fact she could see what he was seeing, and when he closed his eyes with pleasure, she took her revenge. She who was called 'the cow-eyed' because her eyes were large and lovely, transformed the nymph into a white cow.

Jupiter opened his eyes and looked at Io in amazement. Even as a cow, she was lovely.

In the jovial age when Jupiter ruled the world, he and his fellow Olympians flew across the clear blue sky, and every tree, every rock, every river, every stream had its god and its spirit. Things were constantly morphing into other things. It was a magical time when creation was not yet fixed. It was a time of clear vision clouded never by doubt, never by hesitation, only by desire.

From an engraving taken from *Jupiter and Europa* (by the initiate painter Paolo Veronese). The bull looks out of the picture and asks, 'Wouldn't you?'

If Io had been placid and gentle, Daphne was more of a tomboy. *This* young nymph liked to play in the woods, to gather berries and make bows and arrows. She had no thoughts of a man, but she was too beautiful to escape.

Apollo wanted her as soon as he saw her. He imagined rearranging the hair that was at that moment falling about her neck and back.

Alighting on the ground next to her, he wanted to tell her he loved her. But, perhaps knowing better than he did what he was after, she turned to run.

He called after her, 'Don't run away! I won't hurt you!'

Now she was scrambling up a hill.

'Be careful!' he called. He worried she might scratch herself on brambles.

Just then a gust of wind blew her dress aside and the sight of her straining thighs made him move faster.

She could feel his breath on her neck. She cried out to her father, a river god, to protect her, and as Apollo grasped her hair he felt only leaves. As he put his hand round her waist to turn her and pull her towards him, her stomach became enclosed in bark and her feet took root in the earth. She had been transformed into a laurel tree.

The Afro-Roman poet Ovid, who preserved this story, told us that even now Apollo still loved Daphne. He looked at the tree he was clasping and saw that it was good.

Being very beautiful is like being the only sober one at a party: your beauty makes everyone else delirious.

And they don't care if you feel left out. They just want to bend you to their will.

Adonis had two older women after him, Venus and Persephone. He had been put in Persephone's care when he was orphaned as a young child, and then, when he had grown into a beautiful youth, her attentions had begun to make him feel very uncomfortable. He was starting to loathe her coming anywhere near him, and when she touched him it was as if everything faded to grey.

But now, as beautiful slim-hipped Venus came towards him, smiling, her arms outstretched, a blur around her like the flapping of evanescent wings, he felt as if he were being dragged under. She was talking to him and he wasn't listening to what she was saying,

From an engraving taken from *Venus and Adonis* (by the initiate painter Titian).

but he knew she was offering him a thousand honeyed secrets.

It was hot, midday in a clearing in the woods. There were primroses on the ground and he could hear a droning like a million bees. It was true what they said – Venus was very, very beautiful. She was as beautiful as he was.

She seized his sweating palm and tried to smother him with kisses and Adonis could feel the sap rising in his veins too – so why not?

Because he was being overwhelmed, and he turned and ran from her.

'Flint-hearted boy!' she called after him. 'Thou art not a man!'

The last thing he heard was her screaming as he speared himself on

the horns of a wild boar that was at that moment charging out of the undergrowth.

As he lay outstretched, blood flowed from his side onto the ground, and where the ground was soaked, anemones began to grow.

Venus knelt to smell the flowers and caught a trace of the boy's sweet breath.[1]

*   *   *

If Jupiter and Apollo and the other gods of the planets *were* angels, isn't it odd that they behaved in such an immoral way? We expect higher moral standards from our angels.

There is a key passage in the Bible that may well be glossed over at Sunday school – and you may not hear many sermons on it either. Genesis, Chapter 6, reads: 'The sons of God saw the daughters of men that they were fair: and they took wives which they chose . . . when the sons of God came in unto the daughters of men, and they bare children to them, the same became the mighty men of which were of old.' The phrase 'the sons of God' is used elsewhere in the Old Testament to mean the angels. The Bible is here alluding to the stories of the loves of the gods.

Another thing to bear in mind is that these stories, whichever part of the world they come from, describe things that happened long before humanity devised any notions of morality. They describe what have come to be known as *natural* forces – and this is a clue to the historical events that lie behind these particular myths.

ΣΑΛΠΙΩΝ
ΑΘΗΝΑΙΟΣ
ΕΠΟΙΗΣΕ

Engraving taken from the vase of Salpion. It is easy to underestimate the intellectual sophistication of the Greeks when it came to the gods. According to Macrobius, the Orphic initiates saw Dionysus as being the principle of Mind which was divided up into individual minds. The intellectual élite considered Apollo and Dionysus to be different aspects of one divine principle. Their view was by no means crudely anthropomorphic. The Greek gods of the planets are agents of the perfect fit between humanity and the cosmos. We have seen this expressed in storytelling but it was also expressed by them in numerical terms. The ancient Greeks attributed numerical values to the letters of their alphabet. Adding up the numbers attributed to letters in a word or name could yield a significant number, and it is astonishing but demonstrably true that the names of Apollo, Zeus and Mercury yield mathematical constants according to which the natural forms of the world are constructed. The numerical values of these names are the numbers that describe the shapes of equilateral triangles, squares, cubes, pyramids, octahedrons and tetrahedrons. Musical harmony is in proportion to these numbers too. (For a fuller explanation and a demonstration of the maths, see *Jesus Christ, Sun of God* by the brilliant David Fideler.) In modern times we make a distinction between quality and quantity, with mathematics being a description of quantity that is indifferent to human concerns. This is very far from the ancient way of thinking based on idealism. The ancients lived in a cosmos concerned for humanity, and higher mathematics was one way of describing that concern. Some people are hostile to mysticism because they see it as a lapse into lazy or infantile thinking. That is not the case here. The thinking is extraordinarily complex and insightful – but it is not empirical thinking. It is the thinking of idealism working itself out in the world and discovering the way the world works by means of this way of thinking.

We've seen how the Bible and various myths may be seen to be not inconsistent with the scientific history of creation, but as giving an account of the same series of events from a different perspective. Io is transformed into a cow, Daphne into a laurel tree, the beautiful youths Adonis and Hyacinth into flowers, Arachne into a spider, Callisto into a bear . . . What these stories are telling us about is the proliferation of biological forms. They describe the coming into being of the many different species we know today – the plants, the flowers, the trees, the animals, the burgeoning of the world's bio-diversity.[2] Because matter was not fixed and bodies were soft and phantom-like, we see the proliferation of biological forms taking place with dizzying rapidity and magical ease.[3]

*   *   *

The Greek stories may be the most familiar versions, but essentially the same stories have been told all over the world. The Celtic tradition, influential on Tolkien and much modern fantasy, includes a Welsh story about a boy called Gwion:

Gwion was employed by a witch to stir a cauldron. She was brewing a transformative elixir for her ugly stupid son.

One day, as Gwion was stirring this brew, it suddenly bubbled up. Three drops spat out of the pot and landed on his hand, scalding it. Without thinking, he put his hand to his mouth.

The witch saw this and came rushing towards him. 'That's not for *you!*' she screamed in a rage.

Gwion shapeshifted into a rabbit to flee, but she instantly changed into a greyhound and soon gained on him. Reaching a river, he turned himself into a salmon, but she leapt in after him in the form of an otter. Suddenly he soared out of the water as a bird, but she transformed herself into a hawk, snapping at his tail.

In a panic he looked far down below and spotted a pile of wheat. He threw himself downwards and landed in it, transforming himself into a grain of wheat. *It will be like looking for a needle in a haystack,* he thought.

But the witch turned herself into a hen and pecked and pecked at the pile until she had eaten every last grain.

After a while the witch found she was pregnant, even though she

Gwion

had found no one willing to impregnate her. It seemed the grain had grown inside her, and when Gwion was reborn it was as a baby with all the beauty and wisdom that the witch had wished for her son.

Someone cried out, '*Tal iesin!*' which means 'How radiant his brow is!'

And that is how a great spirit was incarnated as Taliesin, the famous Welsh bard.

We love stories that involve flying, don't we? On a recent weekend with some old friends, including the one who had introduced me to the Welsh myths and legends, we were sitting around discussing scenes in films that make you cry. Of course there's the death of Bambi's mother. Someone suggested the moment when Baloo the Bear turns out not to be dead in *The Jungle Book*.

Someone else said, 'When ET turns out not be dead.'

I thought of the end of that film, where the boy is cycling along with ET in the basket on the handlebars and they suddenly lift off and fly through the sky. It's like in pantomime when Peter Pan suddenly takes off and flies over the audience – that makes us want to cry too. I think there is something deeply moving about human flight, perhaps because we all carry within us memories of the time before our material bodies were fully formed, the time when we *could* fly, when we were spirits living freely among spirits in a world bathed in the ineffable light of a spiritual sun. We are, I believe, deeply nostalgic about that time, and we long, too, for a time when we will be purely spiritual beings again.

That is the arc of human history as it is told in all the world's religions. We are dipped briefly into matter and one day we will rise again and fly free of it.

The time is coming when we will soar once more.[4]

Odin and the Angelic Theory of Evolution

'First you were clay, then from being mineral you became vegetable, from vegetable animal and from animal man . . . and you have to go through a hundred new worlds yet . . .'

Rumi

Different angels and spirits come to prominence in different times and different places and different traditions. If the Greeks and Romans remembered the deeds of the angel of Jupiter particularly vividly, in northern Europe it was the deeds of the angel of Mercury that fired the imagination. The Norse people remembered this angel as Wodin or Odin.[1]

The stories of the Norse planetary gods, like the stories of the Olympian gods, show them and their rule threatened by giants but also undermined from within.

Odin knew he had to suffer to prepare himself for his world-saving mission.

Engraving of the image of
Norse deity on a gold-foil coin
called a *braceate*, found
in Denmark.

He was wounded by a spear and hung himself on the gnarled and windswept World Tree for nine days and nine nights, while the leaves whispered to him the secrets of the runes.

Then he travelled down through dense mists to dark caves, the realm of the Black Dwarves. He intended to learn from them the secrets of forging the elements.

Finally he travelled along the roots of the World Tree to find the Fountain of Wisdom. This fountain was the source of all memories, and the elderly giant who guarded it was called Memir (or Memor, 'Memory'). He refused to let Odin drink from it unless he sacrificed his most precious possession. Odin plucked out one of his eyes. It sank in the waters of the fountain and lay in the depths, glimmering.

In the spiritual vision of the peoples of northern Europe, the World Tree stood at the centre of the cosmos. The world of humans was called Midgard or Middle Earth and the World Tree sprouted out of the middle of it, towering high into the heavens.

Near the top of the World Tree was a golden throne. Odin sat there with a raven perching on either shoulder, and every day the ravens flew all around the world, returning in the evening to tell him what they had seen.

The World Tree also held Asgard, the great city of the gods, in its branches – twelve golden castles, each decorated with the sign of one of the constellations. The only way into this golden kingdom was via Bifrost. This bridge, made of air, water and fire, appeared to the people down below in Midgard as the rainbow. Heimdell, the watchman of the gods, stood by the bridge. It was said that his senses were so keen that he could hear the grass grow in the ground or the wool grow on a sheep's back anywhere in a hundred-mile radius.

Led by Odin on his eight-legged horse, the gods would ride out over Bifrost to battle against the giants and the trolls. The Kingdom of Midgard was bounded by mountains and beyond these mountains lived the Ice Giants, the Fire Giants, the Sea Giants, Hill Giants and the Rime Giants.

The dwarves and trolls were allies of the giants. Green-eyed and dark-skinned, the dwarves bred like maggots in the body of the Earth. Trolls lived in small villages made of mounds, surrounded by human heads on poles. Inside these mounds they hoarded treasure, but they also enjoyed living in squalor, their dirt floors crawling with worms and snakes.

The giants and their allies were held in check by the gods, above all by Thor, the great god of thunder, who rejoiced in his title 'Bane of the Giants'. As a baby he'd astonished the older gods by lifting ten huge bales of bearskins with one hand. Challenged to a fishing contest, he'd snapped the head off a passing ox and used it as bait.

Thor rode in a chariot pulled by two fierce butting goats. Thor's hammer would fly through the stormclouds to shatter the head of a giant then return to his hands. He liked to say if it hadn't been for him, the land of the gods would have been overrun by giants.

The iron in our blood hammers round our bodies, powered by Thor, the god of war.

*   *   *

The Norse myths, like the Greek, Roman and Hebrew, are an account of an evolving world in which great spiritual beings called angels in some traditions and gods and spirits in others are the agents of creation.[2] Again, they are not *necessarily* inconsistent with the data collected by science. Alfred Russel Wallace conceived of the theory of evolution of the species according to natural selection at the same time as Charles Darwin and independently of him; as a mark of this, they co-presented it to the intellectual élite of the day in the form of the Linnaean Society in 1858. Whilst their joint theory gradually compromised and eroded Darwin's religious faith, Wallace believed that natural selection was guided by creative intelligences, which he identified with angels.

Today such creative intelligences have been reframed by the biologist Rupert Sheldrake in his theory of morphic resonance.[3] In a recent book, *The Science Delusion*, he pointed up the lack of philosophical sophistication of the leading militant materialists, showing that the version of science that they used to beat spirituality was a broken old stick. Mary Midgley, one of the UK's senior philosophers, reviewed it in the *Guardian*:

> The unlucky fact that our current mechanistic materialism rests on muddled, outdated notions of matter isn't often mentioned today. We can't approach important mind-body topics such as consciousness or the origins of life while we still treat matter in 17th century style as if it were dead, inert stuff . . . We need a new mind-body paradigm.[4]

In myths the gods and angels of the planets have a special role in the forming of the human condition. They work to give it its fundamental structure – to make an arena in which we can grow and endure, struggle, love and develop a faculty for free will and free thinking. Myths belong to idealism, to a world-view where matter is only there in order to help us have experiences. That is what it is for. Myths are an account of the human condition *subjectively experienced*, and they may be as precise as it is possible to be.

*   *   *

I have written elsewhere about the origins of the idea of evolution in religious thought. Evolution means evolving into something *better*, and religious and spiritual thought and experience always yearn for this.

But religious thought, as expressed in these myths, is also always highly conscious of how precarious this process of evolution is . . .

By drinking of the Fountain of Wisdom Odin had learned of the transience of all things, and he knew too that the giants would not be held in check forever. In the halls of the gods the feasting on roast boar, the necking of mead, the boisterous sporting contests and the knockabout practical jokes helped keep anxiety at bay, but it was all shot through with a strain of melancholy.

No one caused more merriment or made Odin laugh harder than Loki – and Odin loved him for it. Loki is the angel called Lucifer in Christian tradition. He lived with the other gods in Asgard and was always accepted by them – but he was mischievous, and his mischief turned slowly into evil.

Loki disappeared for a while and then it emerged that he had taken as a lover one of the enemies of the gods, a giantess. Worse, it turned out that this giantess had given birth to three monstrous children. Loki had kept these children secret as long as he could, but they had grown too large to hide any longer, and now Odin ordered him to bring them to Asgard.

The other gods shrank back in horror when they were dragged into the hall, but Odin was afraid of no living creature. He stepped forward and seized the first of the monsters, a great snake. He hurled it into the ocean and pulled it tight around the Earth so that it was imprisoned there, its tail fixed in its mouth.

The daughter of Loki and the giantess was called Hela. She was hideous, half alive and half a blue rotting corpse. Odin threw her out of Asgard and she fell for nine days until she reached a dark and dank kingdom in the bowels of the Earth. Odin ruled that she could never leave this kingdom until the end of the world. Named after its queen, this hell could only be approached by paying a toll, then crossing a freezing underground river and by evading a blood-drenched hell hound chained by its gates.

Odin was less sure what to do with the third monster, Fenris. The Fountain of Wisdom had shown him this giant wolf in a prophetic vision. He knew it was a deadly threat to him. By the laws of Asgard it was forbidden to kill a guest, even a wolf, but day by day it grew larger and stronger, howling in the courtyard of Asgard and shrugging off the strongest chains the gods could forge as easily as if they were cobwebs.

Then, remembering the secrets of forging metals he had been shown in the realm of the Black Dwarves, Odin sent a messenger to them. But this messenger returned with a tiny chain as delicate and soft as a ribbon.

'That will never hold Fenris!' cried Odin.

The messenger protested that the dwarves had sworn it would hold the wolf until the day of the Last Battle. It was a *magical* chain, he explained, made from the pad of a cat's footsteps, the beard of a woman, the roots of a standing stone, the nerves of a bear, the love-call of a fish and the saliva of a bird.

The wolf had now grown big enough and strong enough to resist any attempt to put a chain round his neck. He was confident in his strength, afraid of no chain except a magic chain. The gods promised no magic had been used in the manufacture of this new chain and Fenris agreed to have this new chain put around him provided that one of the gods placed his hand in his mouth as a token of this promise.

When the others hesitated, the war god Tyr stepped forward and placed his hand in the slavering jaw. Then Thor draped the chain around the neck of Fenris and fastened it to a rock in the centre of the Earth.

The moment it was fastened, the chain tightened, digging into the neck of the wolf. Fenris roared and howled with rage, and strained and shook his head so violently it was all a blur. After a while he was still again and everyone saw that he was indeed held fast – with the severed hand of Tyr clamped between his jaws.

So Fenris was enchained – for now. But Odin knew well enough that good could not come from evil and that ultimately evil would result from evil. There would be a price to pay for tricking the wolf, even if they had done it for the best of reasons.

The human condition is very precarious. It is threatened on all sides. And it could – and can – easily be destroyed by something as seemingly slight and evanescent as a hidden intention.

*   *   *

How come we are here then? How come all the extraordinarily unlikely coincidences, the delicate series of checks and balances needed for the creation of intelligent life have come together to create us and give us a chance to evolve? Scientists agree that the odds against this happening by chance are almost infinite.[5]

According to the ancient answer, the perfect fit is not an unlikely accident. It has come about – and we are as we are – because every *thing* is directed and informed by the intelligence of angels. In the mind-before-matter account, every thing is charged with intelligence, every thing is full of mind.[6] The material world was made to cradle the vegetable world, which was formed to cradle animal life and that was created to cradle human consciousness in turn.[7]

We are not routinely conscious of this intelligence and the way it informs every part of the material world. We may see evidence of intelligence at work all around us, but fail to recognize it. Yet even the most inert-looking object, such as a mountain or an escarpment, is full of intelligence and intent. It just moves very, very slowly.[8]

In pre-scientific times, all the sharpest minds were idealists. They had more of a sense of this intelligence both in the world 'out there' and inside us. They had an acute sense of the role of the planets in particular in forming both our physical and our mental make-up, of the cycles of the moon influencing the forces of generation and of the cycles of Venus influencing the kidneys to produce desire in the form of testosterone. They knew that Mercury worked through our limbs, enabling us to move through space and think spatially, and that the sun had called the eye into being and caused it to grow as a sunflower grows up to meet it.[9]

Our conscious self is like an infant emperor carried aloft by a bustling train of nursemaids, ministers, bodyguards and generals – and these helpers are the great forces of intelligence in the universe.

These forces are much greater than our own conscious intelligence, and they are at work below the threshold of our consciousness. They know how to perform complex chemical operations, for instance breaking down food to isolate and convey substances to different parts of the body, absorbing oxygen into the blood, converting inorganic substances into vital fluids, converting vibrations in the ear into the sounds we hear. A vast number of intelligent operations that you or I may barely begin to understand take place below the threshold of our consciousness.

In the ancient world the agents of these complex processes in different parts of the body were seen as spiritual – as gods or angels. Today we have a complex and sophisticated sense of the human body as made up of parts with a degree of independence working together with other elements inside and outside the body – a sense of the body as a living machine. The ancients had a similar sense of an individual's spiritual make-up. They saw a human being as a spiritual machine made up of many different living parts working in co-operation and at the behest of spiritual beings. Basiledes, a pupil of St Peter's, called the human being 'an encampment of different spirits'. Ibn Arabi, a spiritual master among the Sufis, said, 'Angels are the powers hidden in the organs and faculties of Man.'

The retinue that carries the infant emperor aloft is therefore made up of St Michael, Odin and Mars, of the great gods and angels of the planets and stars, and the lesser angels and spirits at their command. The common academic criticism of belief in gods and angels is that they are an example of the fallacy called anthropomorphism. This is a matter of looking at natural phenomena, such as thunder or volcanoes erupting, and projecting human characteristics onto them in a primitive or childlike way. A thunderclap shows the gods are angry.

The trouble here is that scientific materialism is so entrenched in our society that it may sometimes be difficult to even begin to understand the ancient spiritual wisdom that informs the stories of the gods and angels. The aim here is to try to see what is good and wise in the ancient way of thinking about these things. The ancients liked to dwell on an important truth and to draw out its implications. One of these important truths is this: the human being is a continuation of its environment. We have evolved as a reflection of and in reaction to qualities in the cosmos. Therefore there are qualities 'out there' in the universe that make us human.

Ancient peoples called these qualities gods and angels. On this view, what we like to think of as our intrinsically human qualities have been lent to us by angels.[10] They have projected their qualities onto us, not the other way round.

The Story of the Precious Ring

'We wants it, we needs it. Must have the precious.'

Gollum, *The Lord of the Rings*

One day Odin, Loki and Honir, Odin's brother, were walking the Earth together disguised as men. They were passing a green and silver waterfall when Loki saw an otter sunning itself. He picked up a smooth pebble and threw it at the otter, killing it instantly.

The others applauded Loki's skill and they all carried on until they came to a great hall. There they were greeted by a dark-skinned man wearing magnificent bejewelled robes. He introduced himself as Hreidmarr the magician, but he seemed friendly enough.

Loki said they were poor travellers and had no great gifts to bring to such a great lord, but, he said, pulling it out of his bag, they could offer him this freshly killed otter for dinner . . .

Hreidmarr's welcoming smile vanished and in an instant the three gods found themselves pinned to the floor by two more dark-skinned men. Hreidmarr was standing over them with a double-headed axe, roaring that they were about to die.

'Why would you want to kill us?' spluttered Loki.

'My youngest son, when he went fishing, liked to turn himself into an otter!'

'We didn't know!' said Honir. 'How could we? What will you take to set us free?'

Hreidmarr went in to a huddle with the other dark-skinned men, who were his two elder sons. At last he returned: 'As the price of your freedom we will accept enough gold to fill the skin of the otter . . .

until not a single hair remains to be seen. Two of you will remain here in chains while the third is released to fetch the gold.'

Loki was retracing their steps beside the waterfall, wondering what to do, when he thought he saw a glint in the pool below. Peering into the depths, he saw a pike hiding in the entrance to an underwater cave.

Loki wasn't fooled by the disguise. He recognized that the pike was really the dwarf Alberich, the famous guardian of a store of treasure. The glint in the water provoked an answering glint in Loki's eye and he went off to fetch a net to dredge the pool and land the pike.

Alberich disguised as a pike

A few minutes later he grabbed hold of the flapping, suffocating fish and cried: 'You don't fool me! I know who you are.'

He told Alberich he would kill him unless he handed over all his treasure. Then he watched while the dwarf repeatedly emerged from the water with armfuls of treasure, until a great teetering pile stood on the flat stone where Loki had first seen the otter. The dwarf told Loki that this was his whole store of treasure. Loki told him he could go, but as the dwarf turned to dive back into the pool again, Loki espied a glint on his finger. It was a golden ring. Loki was drawn to it and demanded the dwarf hand it over.

'Let me keep just this ring,' begged the dwarf. 'It's a magic ring. I can use it to replenish my store of gold and this magic won't work for anyone but a dwarf.'

'No, give it to me!' said Loki, wrenching the ring from him.

'Then I curse you and I curse whoever wears this ring,' said Alberich, as he slipped back into the pool in the form of a pike.

Loki returned to Hreidmarr's great hall carrying the huge pile of gold and wearing the precious ring. Odin noticed it and demanded Loki hand it over at once.

Then, under the watchful and vengeful eye of the magician, the three gods began to fill the otter's skin with gold. Because it was a magic skin, it kept expanding, but finally it seemed completely covered with gold and they asked to be set free.

Hreidmarr was on the point of agreeing, but then he said, 'No, there is a hair on the snout that is uncovered with gold.' But he wasn't looking at the hair, he was looking at the ring on Odin's finger. He ordered him to give it up.

And so it was that a fateful curse entered the stream of history.

Later, when Hreidmarr refused to share the gold with his two remaining sons, they murdered him. Then they fell out with each other, until one turned himself into a dragon in order to keep the ring and all the treasure for himself.

The other brother was called Reginn. He wasn't brave enough or strong enough to fight the dragon himself, so he needed to trick someone braver and stronger to do it for him.

He noticed a young man, Siegfried, arrive at court, and heard a rumour that his sword was forged from fragments of a sword that Odin had given his father. So, he befriended him and told him about the dragon that was guarding a store of treasure.

Together they followed the track across the heath that led to the dragon's cave.

Reginn said that the dragon left the cave every day to go down to the river to drink and advised his new friend to dig a trench along its route, then hide in it. When the dragon slithered over it Siegfried would be able to plunge his sword into its heart.

But just as Reginn slipped off to hide behind some rocks in order to watch Siegfried's progress from a safe distance, an old man appeared by Siegfried's side. He was wearing a long blue cloak and a low-slung wide-brimmed hat that hid his eyes. He warned Siegfried that if he was underneath the dragon when he struck it with his sword, he would be drenched in its deadly venom and die.

The old man disappeared, but Siegfried took his advice and dug a side trench. And as the dragon slithered overhead, he managed to slip into it to avoid the torrent of dragon's blood.

Siegfried slays the dragon (in a nineteenth-century illustration).

Reginn emerged from behind the rocks, exultant at the death of the dragon, his brother. He asked Siegfried to cut out its heart and roast it.

But as Siegfried was roasting the heart, he was splattered by boiling blood. A drop singed his finger and he put it into his mouth to soothe it – and instantly found he could understand the language of the birds. The woodpeckers were warning him that he was being tricked and that if Reginn were allowed to eat the dragon's heart, he would become the cleverest man in the world and no one would be able to stand against him. He would rule the entire world.[1]

Then the increasingly urgent chatter of the woodpeckers warned Siegfried that Reginn was creeping up behind him.

Siegfried span round and did to Reginn what Reginn had intended to do to him, slicing off his head with one swipe of his sword.

Now the birds began to sing a new song, a song of a beautiful young woman bound by the briars of sleep.

In the morning, as Siegfried saddled his horse, he saw a great light on the horizon. He rode through trackless regions towards it and saw a great wall of flame at the top of a mountain.

Spurring his horse forward and up the mountain, he leapt over this wall of flame to discover, lying there as if dead, a knight in golden armour. He dismounted and removed the knight's helmet, to find a sleeping beauty with long golden hair and dazzling white skin.

As he leant down to kiss her, he saw the thorn of a hawthorn stuck in her side. When he pulled it out, she awoke. She said she was Brunhilde, and that Odin had put her to sleep, telling her she could only be woken by the man called Siegfried the Dragon-slayer.

As they looked deep into each other's eyes, knowing they were destined to be together, Siegfried placed the golden ring that he had taken from the dragon's hoard on Brunhilde's finger.

Instantly, she changed. She told him that before they could live together, he must prove himself worthy: he must go and conquer a kingdom for her to rule as queen.

In this way the evil influence of the dwarf's ring continued to ripple outwards.

*   *   *

In mythology one of the main markers of chronology is the successive generations of the gods. In Greek mythology, for example, there is the generation of the parents of Zeus, the generation of Zeus and his brothers and sisters, the generation of the children of the gods who were themselves gods – Aphrodite, Ares, Athene – and then the generation of demi-gods and heroes, who were the children of the union between god and human. This last generation had superhuman qualities. They were usually stronger than other men, who could not usually stand in their way, but they weren't as powerful as gods. For example, being only half divine, they weren't able to fly of their own accord. They were, however, often able to rely on the help of the gods and communicate with them. In Norse mythology Siegfried is a demi-god or hero and therefore belongs to the same generation – and era – as the Greek heroes.

These different generations show different stages in creation. As the material world grew denser, the age of the great gods came to an end. The gods of the planets had played their part in creating a world for humankind, and myths of the later generations show that these gods were seen increasingly rarely.

But the evil influence of the ring was spreading not only outwards but also downwards. Life on Earth would often be hard and full of struggle.

The Mighty Men, the Men of Renown

'. . . the sons of God came in unto the daughters of men, and they bare children to them, the same became mighty men which were of old, men of renown.'

Genesis 6.4[1]

A king called Acrisius imprisoned his daughter, Danae, in a tower plated with brass. This tower had only one small window high up in the wall of his daughter's cell. He committed this terrible crime because a soothsayer had told him that Danae would give birth to a boy who would one day kill him.

But Danae was beautiful and one day Jupiter looked down from the clouds and spotted her. She gladdened his eye and one night he visited her stealthily, coming through the small window in the form of a shower of golden rain.

She gave birth to a boy called Perseus. The king dared not risk killing a son of Jupiter, so he set Danae and the baby adrift on the sea locked in a wooden chest.

Danae loved the boy. She cooed to him in the dark and was glad when he was rocked to sleep by the gentle motion of the waves.

Eventually the chest was washed ashore, to be found by a passing fisherman. He took an axe to it and broke it open. This fisherman was a good man. He took Danae and Perseus in and looked after them, and in time the boy grew big and strong.

Although the fisherman had chosen a simple life far away from the court, he was in fact the brother of the local king, Polydectes. One day Polydectes saw Danae walking by the shore. He wanted her immediately, but she would have nothing to do with him. Perhaps when you've made love to a god, no mortal, even a king, is particularly appealing?

The king came up with a plan to get Danae's protector, Perseus, out of the way. He announced he was holding a banquet. All the young men of his kingdom were commanded to attend and each was to bring the king a horse as a gift. They all did, except for Perseus – the stepson of a simple fisherman having no horse to give. The king rubbed it in and all the other young men laughed in a grovelling and lickspittle way. Red with shame, Perseus rashly tried to save face by saying he could bring the king whatever gift he cared to name. He had fallen right into the trap.

'Bring me the head of the Gorgon Medusa!' demanded the king, beaming.

The Gorgon Medusa was one of three monstrous sisters. She was so ugly that anyone who looked at her was instantly turned into stone, and many would-be heroes had died in an attempt to destroy her.

Perseus didn't know what to do. He was sitting by the seashore praying for help when two tall, luminous figures appeared shimmering beside him. He somehow knew they were Athene, the goddess of wisdom, and Mercury, the messenger of the gods. They comforted him and assured him they would protect his mother while he was away. Mercury gave him a flint sickle, sharp enough to decapitate the Gorgon Medusa, and Athene said she would lend him her shield, shiny like a mirror. She advised him to use its reflection to guide the sickle down onto the monster's neck, so he wouldn't have to look at her directly.

They told Perseus that he must first go on a long journey to find the Grey Sisters. They would set him on the right path and tell him how to gather the other magical artefacts he would need.

Perseus journeyed north until he found the Grey Sisters in a bleak cave at the foot of a mountain. They looked as if they had been born ancient. They had only one tooth and one eye between them. They were forced to pass these between one another and use them in turn. Perseus crept up on them and snatched the eye as it was being passed between one sister and the next. They were powerless to catch him and he made them swear to give him good advice if he gave them back their eye.

So the Grey Sisters advised Perseus how to find his way to a mysterious country that lay at the back of the North Wind. He followed their instructions and found there wraithlike creatures who could fetch for him the other magical things he would need to complete his mission – the winged Shoes of Swiftness, sandals that would enable him to fly through the sky like Mercury, a magic pouch that could contain the Medusa's head without being dissolved by its poisons, and the Helmet of Invisibility.

Finally Perseus flew off in search of the Gorgons. Alighting on the ground, he soon found himself walking through a forest of standing stones. After a while he realized that these stones were the petrified forms of people and that the Gorgon Medusa must therefore be nearby.

Then he heard a hissing sound and saw the three monstrous sisters stretched out, asleep and sunning themselves on an expanse of rock. They had green-gold wings the shape of bats' wings, yellowing tusks, and instead of hair they had a writhing mass of snakes.

Donning the Helmet of Invisibility and using Athene's shield to guide himself, Perseus crept up on them. Careful not to turn away from the reflection, he sliced the head of the Medusa with one sweep of his flint sickle.

But the snakes on her head did not die with her and their frenzied hissing awoke the other sisters, who came for him. Wearing the Shoes of Swiftness, Perseus leapt into the air and shot off towards the horizon. Drops of blood fell from the pouch, and wherever they fell the land became infested with venomous snakes.

Perseus was longing to see his mother again, but as he neared the island he thought of as home, he changed course. He had seen a beautiful girl with long red hair, chained to the rock by the seashore, naked except for a necklace of emeralds and streams of tears. Now he stopped in mid-flight to hover around her.

Graeco-Italian gemstone carving
of the Gorgon.

She said her name was Andromeda. She was being sacrificed to
a giant sea monster, because her mother had boasted about her
beauty . . .

Just then the surface of the sea began to bubble and foam and
suddenly a great serpent reared up towards Andromeda.

Perseus shot high in the sky then swooped down to hack at the great
neck of the monster again and again until it collapsed into the sea. As
the commotion in the water subsided, he cut Andromeda free.[2]

Perseus and Andromeda arrived at the court of Polydectes. Encircled
by the rich young men who had jeered at Perseus, the king still felt
brave enough to mock him, refusing to believe that he really had
succeeded in his mission. But then Perseus reached down into his
pouch and brandished the head of the Gorgon Medusa. As the king
and his court drew breath in horror, they were turned instantly into
rocks.

The king's brother gave up fishing to take the throne and married
Danae.

Perseus and Andromeda set sail to found a new kingdom, but on
the way they chanced upon some games and stopped off for a while.
Perseus wanted to take part. Here was a chance to enjoy his prowess.
He excelled at all the disciplines, but especially the discus. In fact he
threw the discus with such force that it flew out of the performance
area of the stadium and into the crowd. When the spectators parted,
Perseus saw that the discus was embedded in the head of an old man.

Gemstone carving of young Hercules wearing a lion headdress (from *Antique Gems* by Rev. C. W. King). Though lions are scarce and hunting them is banned, warriors of the Maasai tribes are occasionally cornered and forced to kill a lion in self-defence. Then they will wear its pelt as a headdress in the same way. It's the mark of a great warrior and attracts a lot of women.

Perseus, the head of Medusa and Andromeda traced among the constellations (from a fourteenth-century Spanish manuscript).

This old man was Acrisius, who had set his daughter Danae and her child afloat in a chest in order to overturn the prophecy that his daughter's son would one day kill him . . .

*   *   *

On his travels the king of Athens fell in love for the first time and fathered a son. He was a restless man, an adventurer. He didn't stay for the birth, but left a pair of sandals and a sword hidden under a great boulder. He told his young lover that when their son was strong enough to lift it and retrieve these possessions, he should seek him out.

So it was that at the age of eighteen Theseus set off for Athens. He arrived to find his father now old and worn out by an unhappy marriage.

His father didn't recognize him, but as soon as Theseus strode into court, the queen saw in the firm line of his jaw the handsomeness that her husband now retained only in traces. Fearing that Theseus might interfere with her control of the king, she demanded that this young stranger be sent out to bring back the great Cretan bull that was then ravaging the countryside.

Many had died in the attempt, but of course Theseus led the bull back to Athens by the nose. The king decreed it should be sacrificed at a great feast. The queen planned to take the opportunity to poison Theseus, but as the young hero brandished his sword to carve the meat on the bone, the king recognized the sword he had left under a boulder all those years before. Father and son were reunited with much rejoicing. The queen slunk away.

The morning after the night before Theseus was surprised to wake to weeping and wailing in the courtyards of the palace. When he asked what was going on, he was told that this was the day of the year when the Athenians were bound to send a tribute to Minos, king of Crete. Every year seven youths and seven virgins were sacrificed to the Minotaur, a terrifying bull–man hybrid.

Straightaway, Theseus volunteered to be one of the seven. His father pleaded with him not to go. When Theseus insisted, his father made him promise that if he survived the Minotaur he would, before he set sail for home, change the black sails on his ship to white, as a sign to his loving father that he was still alive.

When Theseus arrived on the island of Crete, Ariadne, the king's daughter, fell in love with the young adventurer. She came to him in the night and told him the secrets of how to defeat the Minotaur, which was kept in a labyrinth. All the previous victims had become lost and disoriented before they were attacked. Ariadne brought Theseus a ball of thread and told him to tie one end to the entrance. Then he should unravel it as he progressed through the passageways, leaving a trail behind him so that he could retrace his steps.

She also told him the secret of how to find your way round a labyrinth, which is to choose the path that seems to take you away from where you want to go.

Theseus followed the path this way and that until at last he penetrated the chamber at the centre of the labyrinth. There the Minotaur leapt on him with a great roar. Theseus found the beast's hide too thick to penetrate with the sword Ariadne had given him. Throwing it aside, he wrestled with the monster until eventually he was able to grab hold of its horns. Then he pulled its great head back and back – until he heard an almighty snap.

Slipping out of the palace before dawn, Theseus and Ariadne ran hand in hand down to the harbour and set sail before her father awoke.

On the voyage back to Athens, they stopped at the island of Naxos.

There the god Dionysus was hidden, watching the beautiful young woman from among the trees that abutted the beach. He waited until she wandered off on her own, then he came to her.

Dionysus was a beautiful, soft-bellied and slightly feminine young man, and he had a sinister air. He offered Ariadne wine, wooed her with it until she forgot all about Theseus, forgot where she was going and why.

When the time came to leave, Theseus could not find Ariadne. He called for her, but she would not come. So it was that Ariadne abandoned Theseus, as his father had abandoned his mother.

The handsome prince was so distraught he forgot to change his black sails for white ones. His father saw the ship come over the horizon with black sails and, assuming his son had been killed by the monster, threw himself off the cliffs into the sea.

*   *   *

The stories of Perseus and Theseus both end with the death of the father. In the older story it's the fulfilment of a prophecy, in the later a cruel accident which is the result of thoughtlessness.

The earlier story is packed with fantastical supernatural elements. As well as prophecy, magical talismans and transformations and the attendance of otherworldly beings, Perseus uses the power of the supernatural to overcome every challenge he faces.

In the story of Theseus, there is only one overtly supernatural element – the existence of the beast itself – and the suggestion is that this monster is kept in its elaborate cage because it is a rarity.

When the demi-gods slew monsters, they were also slaying the bestial part of themselves and of humanity – because in the mystical view of the world we all share in a spiritual dimension and are connected there, even if we appear separated into different bodies in the physical world. Humanity had been given animal consciousness, but that gift carried with it a danger for every human being – the danger of turning bestial and monstrous.

A darker, colder age was dawning. The lives of all Earth-dwellers were becoming harder. If bodies had once been densified imaginations, more like phantoms than flesh and blood, gravity was now weighing them down as bones were thickened and became more rigid. Humans dragged themselves more slowly over the surface of the Earth. They lived in a bloody death-drenched world, a world gone wrong.

And in an ironic twist of fate they discovered that as they were less and less able to depend on the gods, the gods in some strange way turned out to depend on them . . .

The Gods Turn to Humans for Help

The Titans, the progeny of Saturn, had been held in check, but every so often they came storming over the horizon and threatened to end the rule of the gods – and therefore the evolution of humankind.

The most fearsome monster the world had yet seen was called the Typhon. When this Titan first emerged out of the sea a shout of fear echoed around Mount Olympus. With terrifying speed he headed straight for Olympus, spitting fire from his mouth and blocking out the sun with bat-like wings. He had the head of a gigantic goat, and when he shook himself free of the waves to mount the shore, the gods saw with horror that below the waist he was a writhing mass of snakes.

Jupiter tried to slow him down by hurling thunderbolts at him, but they merely bounced off the Typhon and clattered to the ground. As the monster was almost upon him he just managed to grab an ancient flint scythe – the one Perseus had used to behead the Gorgon Medusa. But before he had time to swing at the Typhon, the snakes were crawling all over him, wrapping themselves around his limbs.

When the god was held fast, another serpent snatched the scythe from his hand and set about filleting him of all his sinews. A god like Jupiter could not be killed outright, but he could be rendered completely helpless.

The Typhon gathered up the sinews and took them away with him to a cave, where he planned to rest and recuperate from his wounds.

Apollo and the goat-god Pan had been watching and they devised a plan. They tracked down Cadmus, a dragon-slaying hero who had been forlornly wandering the Earth looking for his long-lost sister, and promised him that if he did what they asked, they would help him complete his quest. Pan gave him his pipes and, disguised as a shepherd, Cadmus set off to search for the monster.

Reclining in his cave, the Typhon was wondering what that wonderful sound was. He had never heard music before, but he could feel it soothe and heal him. He crawled from the cave to see.

Startled by his hideous and bloody appearance, Cadmus stopped playing.

'Don't stop!' the Typhon roared. 'What is that? Make that noise again!'

'Oh, this is nothing,' said Cadmus. 'The music I can make with my lyre is much more beautiful. The music I make with my lyre would make you whole again.'

'Why don't you play your lyre, then?'

'Sadly, the sinews I use for strings are broken and I don't know where I can find new ones.'

The Typhon went back into the cave to fetch Jupiter's sinews and handed them to Cadmus.[1]

Cadmus said he had to go back to his hut to restring his lyre, but of course he went back to Jupiter.

Restrung, Jupiter was able to ambush the Typhon, and this time he overpowered the monster and buried him under a mountain.

Many aeons later, in the time of the ancient Greeks, the Typhon's rage would occasionally erupt from the top of that mountain and come streaming down the sides as molten lava.

We have just seen something new, something unprecedented in the world, which marks a tectonic shift in power: the gods have been forced to call on Cadmus for help.

As well as being called on by the gods to rescue Jupiter, Cadmus was remembered by the Greeks as the inventor of writing. But despite his deeds and achievements, he remains a mysterious figure.

*   *   *

There is a mysterious figure in Hebrew tradition who is also said to have invented writing and been called on by angels to save them.

Enoch was a cobbler, large-boned and broad-chested. Somewhat solitary and forbidding, with black glancing eyes and a heavy beard, he shrank from the wickedness he saw infecting humankind.

One day he was walking alone in the desert, in a stony and desolate place, when he heard a voice calling him from the sky: 'Enoch! Enoch!'

'Here I am.'

'Arise, leave the desert and go and walk among the people to teach them the ways of the Creator.'

Then he saw a great vision spread across the sky. A radiant cloud was engulfed by a swirling darkness. Then there came a Holy Word, a Voice of Light that caused everything within the vision to glow and vibrate.

The Enochian literature is rich and extensive.[2] In one strand of it Enoch understood that another of the names of this Holy Word was 'Master Builder'. He saw this Master Builder build seven Spirits of the Planets, Seven Governors. Each was to give humankind a part of its nature.

Great turning points in history are new beginnings, but also endings. What is ending here is the period when humans living on Earth could gaze upon the gods and see them as clearly as we now see physical objects. This capability would henceforth decline and they would enjoy it less and less frequently and then only under special conditions. So they were losing something precious, but they were gaining something too – the ability to *understand* how the world works, to frame it in language.

Enoch's visions were given to him so that he could preserve the vision of God and angels that had been the common experience of earlier humans – and the medium by which it was preserved was language. This is why Enoch, like Cadmus, has been remembered as the inventor of language and writing.

In some traditions Enoch inscribed this new wisdom on two monumental pillars, one of granite and one of bronze. These were built to help measure the movements of the heavenly spirits that people could no longer see as living beings. They were massive, sturdy structures, because Enoch intended them to survive a great catastrophe that would soon overtake the world. Other traditions speak of a lost book or library.[3]

It was said to be Enoch's vision of the stars and planets that inspired him to invent language. He saw an alphabet in the heavenly bodies spread across the sky. The consonants were images of the twelve signs of the zodiac and the vowels were images of the planets, and the patterns of language in a sentence reflected their patterns in the sky.

When Enoch returned from the desert with the gift of language, people came to him from all over the world, including kings and princes. His message was compelling and people adored him for it. Crowds pressed round him, wanting to hear him, to touch him. Sometimes he felt hemmed in and needed to escape. Sometimes he travelled into the wilderness to live in solitude and commune with great spirits. More and more he needed to be alone.

At first he absented himself for three days at a time, returning on the fourth to be with the people. Then after a few years he only appeared once a week. His appearances always caused great excitement. After a year's waiting, the crowds were desperate for his return, but when he reappeared his face shone so brightly many had to avert their eyes.

Some of the stories of Enoch remind us of the ministry of Jesus Christ, who also attracted vast crowds but then wanted to withdraw and spend time in solitude. One of Enoch's titles was 'Sun of Righteousness', a title also given to Jesus.[4]

What had he been doing on his retreats into the wilderness? He had certainly been experiencing more visions: 'And my eyes saw the secrets of lightning and thunder, the secrets of clouds and of the dew . . . I saw the chambers out of which come the Sun and the Moon and where they go.' *The Third Book of Enoch* is one of the great repositories of angelic lore and knowledge of the different orders of angels.[5]

The stories about Jupiter and the other Greek and Roman gods mating with humankind are full of light, beauty, joy and good humour. They are charged with astonishment at being alive in the world. The account in the Enochian literature shows a darker side. Here the angels who take human wives are Fallen Angels, otherwise known as the Watchers. Their offspring, called the Nephilim, are evil and destructive giants who caused wars, ate human flesh and drank human blood. The whole of creation would become corrupt as a result of these unnatural unions.[6]

The Fall of the Angels (in a nineteenth-century engraving).

God told Enoch to go to the Fallen Angels and warn them that they would find no pardon and their children would only suffer violence and ruin, and that they would find no peace.

But when Enoch went to the Fallen Angels, they trembled with fear and asked him to intercede with God on their behalf. They were too ashamed to talk to God or even raise their eyes heavenwards.

Some of Enoch's followers reported seeing a vision of a gigantic horse in the sky. When they told Enoch, he said, 'This means that the time is coming when I will have to leave you.'

Enoch retreated into the mountains, where the ground was inhospitable and the weather stormy.

Thousands tried to follow and gave up, but a few persisted. He turned on them and told them to return to their tents: 'It's dangerous to follow me. You will die.'

On the sixth day of his journey he again addressed a last ragged band of followers who had been trying to keep up with him. But again they refused to turn back, saying that only death could separate them from him. He did not speak to them again.

On the seventh day a strange object appeared flying through the clouds. It was a chariot pulled by horses of fire. Enoch mounted the chariot and rode off.

Later others went looking for him and for his band of followers. At the point where the trail ended they cut through snow and ice and found the dead bodies of the followers, but there was no trace of Enoch.

Enoch had not died. God had taken him to a place where they walked together. God had more work for him to do.

In the stories of Cadmus and Enoch we have seen a shift in the spiritual economy of the cosmos. Where once humanity seemed to depend entirely on angels and gods, now spiritual beings are looking to humans for help.

In the spiritual history of the cosmos what takes place is the unfolding of a plan. In this chapter we have begun to touch on the mysteries of this plan.

The next stage of the plan called for another hero – but a new type of hero . . .

Orpheus, the Sphinx and the Timelock

God decided to teach humankind to think. And the method he chose to do this was music.

Orpheus lived with his mother and her sisters. He had no father to look up to, no men to be role-models. Then one day a friend of his mother's arrived. There was great excitement. A rumour had reached them that this great lord was interested in marrying one of the sisters.

Everyone told Orpheus this was a very important person.

The visitor drove a high royal chariot pulled by magnificent white horses. He emerged out of the sun so that Orpheus could not see him properly at first, but he could tell immediately that this lord was a good two or three feet taller, a man on a different scale from everyone else.

Orpheus held back as his mother and aunts rushed forward to surround the golden-haired visitor. He felt shy, perhaps shrinking from a meeting that on some level he knew would be momentous.

Apollo looked beyond the women encircling him: 'Who's this?'

'This is my son, Orpheus,' his mother proudly said.

Orpheus could now see how brightly the man's eyes shone, how intently, and how hard it would be to say 'no' to him.

Apollo came over, put his arm round the boy's neck and spent a lot of time talking to him. As the day progressed it seemed he was more interested in Orpheus than in any of the aunts. And before he left he gave him a present. Orpheus hadn't seen anything like it before. It looked a bit like a sieve, except that it had only seven strings and it was made of gold. Apollo showed him how to stroke the strings to make an extraordinary sound quite unlike anything he had ever heard before . . .

An extraordinary melody can induce a change in consciousness, like an awakening. Imagine you lived in a time before music had been invented and then suddenly you heard a swelling melody, beautiful harmonies, a hypnotic rhythm. *What on Earth is this?* you would think. Music would seem like an enchantment, as if the air was suddenly different in quality, full of significance, gelling with meaning.[1] Listening to this strange new sound, it might seem as if your mind were expanding. You might feel faint and suddenly aware of yourself, as if you could hear the river of your blood thundering round your veins like the Milky Way.

Orpheus grew into a young man who sang and played the lyre so compellingly that birds and wild beasts gathered around him, as did trees, even rocks.[2] He could heal with his music, restoring the natural harmonies of body, soul and spirit.

He met up with other heroes and together they joined Jason on his quest for the Golden Fleece. Orpheus sailed on the *Argo*, in some traditions the first sailing ship, with Hercules, Theseus and the others, and Jason would not have been able to complete his quest without him. They had to sail past the Sirens, bird-like seductive demonesses perched on jagged rocks. Their eerily beautiful singing filled men with a sweet lethargy that made them want to throw themselves overboard to swim over to the Sirens, where they would be torn apart by the rocks. The music of Orpheus wove beautiful new harmonies around the song of the Sirens, transforming a song of sexual desire into something higher. And the men continued on their quest.

When Orpheus returned home he fell in love with a nymph called Eurydice. At their wedding she was wandering off by herself by the banks of a river when a satyr lunged at her. She ran away as fast as she could, failing to notice a snake in the long grass. Its fangs sunk into her ankle. Her eyes swam with tears and her life ebbed quickly away.

Her sisters set up a cry that echoed around the mountain tops and lonely Orpheus walked along the shore, singing a song of love and loss.

Then he approached the entrance to the Underworld, and the whole world held its breath. As he descended the dark path that led to the marshes beside the river Styx, shades of the dead swirled around him like flocks of starlings. But as Orpheus sang, the dead dispersed.

Then he sang to Acheron the ferryman, who agreed to row him over, and he sang to the Furies, their hair plaited with snakes. The beauty of his music made them weep, and made Cerberus, the three-headed dog, keep his jaws clamped obediently shut.

The pathway spiralled downwards and eventually Orpheus reached the great chamber where the king and queen of the Underworld sat.

He sang for his loved one, pleading to be able to take her back to life. The king and queen agreed, on one condition: that while Eurydice followed him towards the daylight, he must not look back at her.

So Orpheus began the long, steep climb, and Hermes was tasked to bring Eurydice up behind him.

After the pathway had spiralled nine times, Orpheus and Eurydice were nearly free. But just as daylight became visible on the rocky walls ahead, Orpheus became anxious. What if the gods of the Underworld had been toying with him? What if he'd been tricked? With only a few steps to go he paused.

'He's turned round!' cried Hermes and from down below there were three great crashing sounds like a monumental building being torn asunder.

Orpheus saw Eurydice reaching out to him, straining to catch hold of him – but only for a moment. 'I'm being called back!' she cried. He tried to grab her, but it was like trying to get hold of a wisp of smoke, and a moment later he found himself standing alone outside the gates of hell.

For seven months he wandered aimlessly, crossing the snowy wastes of the north, then charming tigers and the beasts of the jungle. The whole world echoed to the name of Eurydice. Everything was charmed by his music except Orpheus himself.

One day he climbed a hill to find a flat, grassy plain. Trees moved up the hill with him in order to listen to his music. Oaks leant forward to hear better. Ash, cypress and elm, wrapped around with ivy, and sweet-smelling wild strawberry plants climbed the hill too.

But suddenly another sound filled the air. A band of barbaric women, followers of Dionysus, wine-soaked and wearing only animal skins, were on the rampage, mad with lust, howling, beating their breasts and yelling drunkenly. They danced with their throats upturned to the sky and their hair thrashing wildly, banging drums with sticks and clashing cymbals.

They could see but not hear the beautiful young man. They called out to him to join them, but he was sunk too deep in grief to notice. Angry now, they began to throw stones and clods of earth at him and to tear branches from the trees and throw them too. When he still wouldn't respond to them, they threw themselves on top of him in a frenzy. Their eyes sliding to the side as they bit into him, they tore him limb from limb. So Orpheus died in great pain and after a life of great pain.[3]

Later his head and his lyre were seen floating downstream towards the shore, his lips still murmuring, 'Eurydice, Eurydice!'

A sea wind began to play his lyre as they floated out to sea and came to rest in a cave on the island of Lesbos.

Eventually a shrine was built.

The two main sources of the story of Orpheus are Ovid and Horace, both of whom were initiates of the Mystery schools. Their poems are saturated in mystical history, and I have added elements, too, from Rainer Maria Rilke.

Horace's version of the Orpheus story comes in the *Georgics*, a series of poems with anecdotes of farm life. The story is embedded in a long poem on bees. After telling the story, Horace describes a religious ceremony in honour of Orpheus. Funereal poppies and cattle are led to the grove for sacrifice, and then, as the flanks of one of them is cut open, out swarms a buzzing cloud of bees.

According to mystical philosophy, individual animals don't have spirits like humans, but each animal species has a spirit. So animals don't each have a private, individual mental space, but animals of the same species share a mental space. A group of animals can therefore move with one mind. We have all seen, for example, a flock of birds wheeling together in the sky with perfect understanding. Rudolf Steiner talked about the group spirits of animal species moving across the surface of the Earth like trade winds.

But perhaps nowhere in the animal kingdom is the mystery of shared mind more intriguing than in the case of bees. Bees in a hive behave in very complicated ways, communicating telepathically and highly intelligently. For example, they can keep an appointment. A single bee may find food and return to the hive to tell the others when and where they need to be, communicating the information by a sort of dance, sometimes called the tail-wagging dance. The encoded information includes – as experiments in the 1940s showed – the angle of the Earth's rotation! So, whilst a single bee may be thought of as having very limited intelligence, a hive of bees is intelligent in some ways which are above and beyond human intelligence. Today biologists talk of them having a 'hive mind'. For Steiner, a beehive is wise because it is guided by the higher spirits of Venus. The bees work together out of love – a love of community rather than sexual pleasure.[4]

Another way of looking at it is to see a human head as like a beehive. We tend to be proud of our private mental space. We like to take credit for the good ideas that flit into it. But the truth is that angels and spirits perpetually weave through our mental space, helping to create the texture of our mental lives.

Music may enhance our sense of the unity that exists between our mind and the mental life of the cosmos. Great music sometimes instils in us a sense of the creative goodness of the cosmos. The music of Orpheus helped awaken in humankind a sense of cosmic order. Later it would help give rise to mathematics.

But there are discordant notes in music, too, and chords waiting to be resolved.

*　　　　　*　　　　　*

It started with an ordinary traffic dispute, about right of way . . .

And it was all so pointless. Oedipus was only travelling down that road because of a misunderstanding.

Oedipus loved his father. He had always been good and kind to him. But one day a strange old woman had taken him aside and warned him that he would murder his father and marry his mother. Oedipus was afraid of his own temper. He decided to leave home at once and set off on a long journey in search of a new home.

Eventually he arrived at a crossroads where a stupid old man in a chariot blocked his way. There was an argument and the old man tried to barge his way past. Oedipus was walking, and when he refused to give way the old man tried to run him over and the chariot's wheel trundled over his foot. In agony and a blind rage, Oedipus dragged him from his chariot as easily as if he were a doll and killed him.

Oedipus continued on his way. He was travelling over a mountain pass. The air was thick with flies and the stench of carrion. Then, through the miasma, Oedipus saw a strange monster with the face of a woman, the body of a lion, the wings of an eagle and the tail of a serpent.

Her mouth was red with blood.

The Sphinx sat on a ledge by the side of the pass and asked any traveller attempting to pass a riddle: 'What creature has four feet, two feet, then three feet?'

When travellers failed to answer, as they always did, she leapt at them, savaged them and spat their remains into the chasm below.

But inspiration struck and the answer came to Oedipus: 'A man crawls on all fours as a baby, grows to walk on two feet, then in old age needs a walking-stick.'

With a howl of rage the Sphinx flung herself into the chasm.

In the city that lay the other side of the pass, Oedipus was acclaimed a hero. It turned out that the old man on the chariot had been the tyrannical king of this city. Oedipus married Jocasta, his beautiful widow, and was himself crowned king amidst much rejoicing.

But he felt uneasy. His lust for Jocasta was for some reason tinged with disgust and at times the marriage bed felt like a wasteland. He couldn't sleep and walked wearily in a labyrinth of thought. He began to see death lurking everywhere – in the fields, in the earth, in the air, in wombs of the women he saw in the city.

He summoned a famous seer, Tiresias, who was blind. Tiresias was so old he was like an insect, his skin shiny like a carapace. He was so old he was sexless, but it was rumoured he knew the secrets of both men and women.

The Sphinx
(in a nineteenth-century
engraving from a marble
statue found on the
island of Delos).

Standing before the throne, Tiresias seemed nervous and reluctant to tell Oedipus what he demanded to know – what shame writhed beneath the city's surface? What was the cause of his suffering?

'To be wise is to suffer,' he nodded.

'Don't give me platitudes!' Oedipus told him to stop prevaricating and reveal the source of the evil afflicting himself and the city.

'It is *you* who poison this city,' said Tiresias finally.

'No – on the contrary, it was I who *saved* this city, because I was able to answer the riddle "wise" men like you couldn't answer. How dare you accuse me?'

Oedipus was losing his temper, but this seemed to give Tiresias the courage to speak more plainly: 'I don't care what you do to me,' he said, and went on to tell Oedipus and the assembled court that the city was under a curse because of the murder of the old king.

Jocasta tried to calm Oedipus, but then he was distracted, because a messenger arrived with the news that his father was dead . . .

Oedipus had loved his father, but a weight lifted from him because he now knew that the prophecy that he would kill him could never come true.

The messenger explained that he had come to take Oedipus back to attend the funeral. Oedipus declined to go, though, explaining that to go back home would be tempting fate. He had in mind the second half of the prophecy, that he would marry his mother.

The messenger tried to reassure him, telling him he had nothing to fear.

'What do you mean? How can you say that?'

'My lord, you are not a blood relative of the king and queen you know as your father and mother.'

The messenger explained that he had come across Oedipus as a baby being carried along by a herdsman with his feet nailed together on a plank of wood. The messenger had taken the baby from the herdsman, removed the nail from his feet and carried him to court, where a royal couple had adopted him and brought him up, loving him as their own son . . .

Oedipus was astounded and demanded that the herdsman be found and brought to him to confirm this story.

Meanwhile Jocasta had gone white. She begged Oedipus to let it lie. What good could come of all this delving into the past? 'We are who we are. We are happy together. What difference can it make?'

'No, I must unlock the secret of my birth,' said Oedipus.

Later, he realized he hadn't seen Jocasta for a while. He found her hanged and the truth of his birth and the cruel twists of his fate came home to him.

Taking a brooch from her hanging body, he blinded himself. 'What do I need with eyes,' he said, 'when the whole world is hideous?'

In the age of the demi-gods the net of matter had been tightening, and now people felt another net: the web of destiny.

*   *   *

How do I come to be here, now, experiencing this? I have consciously chosen only a small part of it. The greater part in terms of time and space, such as the era in which I was born, the country, whether I was

The frieze from the Theseum in Athens, Theseus and the Minotaur far right. On one level the labyrinth is an image of the spirit in matter. The spirit works its way to the middle, completes its divinely appointed task, then works its way out again. Living in matter, we have a certain amount of free will, but it is limited. Every so often we can choose to go this way or that. We cannot see the overall pattern and are in that sense largely working in the dark. According to idealism matter prevents us from seeing the overall pattern so that we are free to make our own choices. More particularly, the labyrinth is a model of the brain. According to idealism, the brain is a very special species of matter. It filters out spirit, like all matter, but it is also designed to let certain spiritual elements through.

born in peacetime or war, rich or poor, the personality of my parents, whether they loved me or not, whether they raised me well, was not chosen by me – not in this lifetime, anyway. And my capacity to change these things is at best limited.

We live in two different worlds, regulated by two different sets of laws. The laws that govern these parallel universes are similar, but in some respects different. There are the laws of physics and then there are human values. The human condition is constructed so that all humans crave happiness, goodness, meaning. We want to do the right thing, but we are anxious about failure. We are the animals that look at the world in fear, because we know all the ways things can go wrong.

So we lead two parallel lives. There is the life of facts, of data, numbers – the life that can be measured. Then there is the life that matters to us. This is the life in which our chances of happiness turn sometimes on great events, but more often than not on immeasurably small

and subtle things – the smile that fades, the too-quick look away. The important events in this other life, this other universe, may not be intimately tied to the world of facts, of weights and measures, of war or peace, rich or poor. I'm talking about the events that determine whether or not we are happy and fulfilled. Will I meet a stranger who turns out to be the love of my life? When that happens, will I find the right thing to say? Will I be struck down by sudden illness? Will I have children? When will my parents die?

The most extraordinary aspect of the human condition has to do with these questions of quality. And it is the great miracle of human consciousness that all these questions – about our happiness or unhappiness, our safety and survival, our fulfilment or lack of it, our goodness or badness, our salvation or damnation, our understanding or lack of it, our goodness or evil, love or hate – all of these lie in a permanent state of balance.

Life continually presents us with tests, mysteries and dilemmas. The story of Oedipus shows a man experiencing life engaging with him, dealing with him in terms of human values. Stories like this give an account of a cosmic intelligence that is immanent in our lives. The cosmos has plans for us and tries to engage us in an intelligent exchange of ideas – a dialogue almost – concerning our own well-being.[5]

Today we have no language to talk about life being shaped, about fate or destiny, apart perhaps from astrology, which the intellectual élite is never going to take seriously.

That is one of the reasons why these stories are important: they may help us to bring into consciousness qualities in our own lives – mystic traces – that we may otherwise find hard to put into words.[6]

We saw that Orpheus invented music and laid the ground for mathematics. He was a transitional figure because he had the power to move animals, trees, even rocks, by the power of his music, but by inventing numbers he also laid the foundation for science.

Daedalus was a contemporary of Theseus, Orpheus and the other demi-gods who joined Jason on the quest for the Golden Fleece, sailing the *Argo*.

But Daedalus looked forward to a new stage of human development. He had engineered the labyrinth that housed the Minotaur and he tried to make wings for himself and his son Icarus, using bird feathers and wax. Credited with the invention of the saw, the potter's wheel and both the ship's sail and its prow, Daedalus did not deal in the power of the supernatural.

Daedalus sat on the stony shore repairing his boat. He hit a nail with his hammer and in the answering echo he heard the death cry of the gods.

Noah and the Waters of Forgetfulness

Noah (in a painting from the catacomb of Callixtus).

One stormy night, when the whole world was roaring like a bull, I heard a voice whispering to me through the reeds of my hut. It said, 'Pull down these reeds, pull down this hut to build yourself a boat. Give up material things and seek life. Take the seed of all living things and stow them in your boat, which must be built according to the dimensions I give you.'

I replied as we were taught, 'My Lord, it is my honour to obey.'

In the morning everyone set to work. The reed-binder began to take my house apart, the carpenter fetched his axe and even the little children were set to work carrying the pitch and bitumen needed to fuse and seal the wood and the reeds together and make the boat watertight.

By the fifth day we had built the basic structure. It was massive. It took up a whole acre and was six decks high, but I was only doing what I'd been told.

I was killing sheep every day and supplying wine – red and white – to keep the workers strong and happy in their work, and then on the seventh day I hammered in the water-plugs and the boat was finished. We took poles aboard to help steer her and food supplies were carried on board in baskets.

We then tried launching the boat on the water. It proved hard – we had to take out some planks and reposition them – so we decided to wait until it was in the water before loading on what we had of gold and silver.

Finally my family boarded and we took in all the animals too – domestic animals like cattle, but wild beasts as well. Then I told the craftsmen to go aboard, closed the gate and sealed it with bitumen, and I battened down the windows.

It must be time, I thought. The winds were gathering.

We passed the night peacefully, but at dawn I saw a huge black thundercloud on the horizon. Shafts of lightning were soon causing forest fires over on the hills, and the next time I looked, the vast cloud was overhead, filling the whole sky. The entire world had gone black. The rains began and soon I heard sounds loud enough to make the gods themselves quiver: it was as if the whole world was being lifted up and smashed like a clay pot. I heard a woman's voice wail: 'Oh Lord, let daylight return!'

We were tossed about the inside of that boat for six days, then suddenly on the seventh day all was suddenly still. I broke open a hatch and poked my head out. I was glad to feel the light on my face, but what I saw next made me sit and weep: the sea was clogged up with people, their bodies floating in patches like spawn.

Our boat had come to rest. It was stuck fast on the top of a mountain, and sea stretched in every direction as far as the eye could see. I thought to myself, *Humanity is being returned to clay*.

I released a dove, but it came back, because it had found no place to settle.

The next day I released a swallow, which circled around and came back too.

On the third day I released a raven, and eventually it came back with clay on its claws. Then I released many birds that did not return and I gave thanks to my Lord.

*   *   *

This is a version of the story that most people know as the story of Noah. It's taken from Sumerian, Mesopotamian and Babylonian sources, but the same basic story is told all over the world, from China to South America. In the version in the *Book of Jubilees* the purpose of the Flood is to destroy the monstrous progeny fathered by the Fallen Angels. In the myths of the Hopi it is the Spider Woman who saves humankind. She cuts down giant reeds and hollows them out so that they float like canoes to carry the survivors.[1]

The biblical account that has Noah lead the animals in two by two is saying something about humankind as the crown of creation. In mystical philosophy the human form has all the other forms of nature in some sense absorbed and perfected within it. There is a legend, too, that only one animal was left off the ark and therefore did not survive the Flood – the unicorn. This, too, says something about human form, because in mystical history, while humans were still largely spiritual creatures and not fully materialized, they had a spiritual eye with which they perceived gods, angels and other spiritual creatures. We have seen this as the eye of Odin.[2]

But by the time of the Flood, though, human form has been fixed in the form we now know.

We said that gods helped create the human condition. Often they would lead humans into some aspect of this by first assuming it themselves. For example, the ancient Egyptians remembered gods like Osiris, Isis and Horus as anthropomorphic creatures. These cosmic memories recalled far distant times when the gods were leading humanity towards the human form.

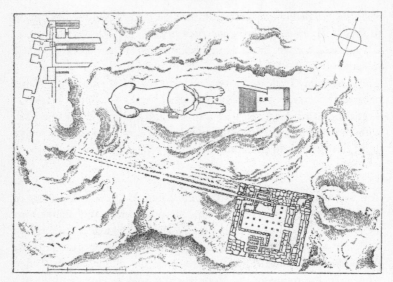

Nineteenth-century aerial plan of the Gizeh plateau.

The Sphinx was carved on the Gizeh plateau to mark the completion of this process. It is made up of four creatures – the lion, the man, the bull and the scorpion – which in the Judaeo-Christian tradition are called the Cherubim. There are twelve Cherubim altogether. These are the angels of the twelve constellations, but the four Cherubim at the cardinal points of the zodiac – Taurus, Scorpio, Leo and Aquarius – together mark a cross on the cosmos and together they are also the four elements that, according to traditional metaphysics, make up the matter of the cosmos: earth, air, fire and water.[3] The Sphinx therefore marks not only the fixing of the anatomy of the human being but also the fixing of matter, which finally became solid and much as we know it today. It's because of these Cherubim that objects are, as it were, four-sided.

The history in the twelve preceding chapters has seemed phantasmagorical partly because matter was not until this point fully fixed, but with the carving of the Sphinx out of the sandstone of Egypt, the age of metamorphosis was finally over.

The fixing of matter makes it possible to fix dates too. The Belgian author and engineer Robert Bauval has made a convincing argument to suggest that the Sphinx was carved on the Giza plateau in 11,451 BC. The Flood is recorded in all cultures as taking place at the end of the Ice Age, covering over what was remembered as a world of hybrid creatures, giants and dwarves, when gods had flown through the air and humans had rubbed shoulders with demi-gods and heroes.[4]

There is a strange epilogue at the end of the Sumerian story of the Flood. Xisuthros builds a fire out of cedar wood, myrtle and reeds to celebrate the Flood's abating and make a sacrifice (probably of sheep, but we cannot tell because the text is mutilated). The gods smell the sweet scent and then swarm all over it like flies. It's a disconcerting simile, but what we are being told is that the gods have been starved of human company.

Rama and Sita – the Lovers in the Forest

Rama (from *The Gods of Greece, Italy and India*, Sir William Jones, 1784).

Fleeing floods and the destruction of the old antediluvian way of life, migrating peoples were drawn westwards, partly by rumours of a magic mountain. In the *Mahabharata*, the great Hindu epic that has its roots in the Neolithic age, this mountain is said to be to be unapproachable by the sinful. It was rumoured to lie in a remote and inaccessible region at the back of the Himalayas. There heavenly dew settled on its peak and formed rivulets. These combined, flowed and divided to form four great rivers that spread out over the plains, and it was here that the first of the great post-Flood civilizations was founded.[1]

If you had been alive then and looked at the landscape using modern frames of reference, you would perhaps have seen little evidence of the stories we are about to retell. The surviving scraps of archaeological evidence would suggest only a few fairly unimpressive dwellings and a few primitive stone and bone tools. What will give us a better understanding of what it felt to be alive then? What will tell us more about the reality of being human in this period – scraps of evidence and scientific theories as to their significance, or the great sacred stories that live on in the human psyche?

*   *   *

The hero of the archaic Indian civilization was called Rama, and his story was written down by a robber called Valmiki.

Rebuked by wandering holy men for stealing food, Valmiki sat alone in the forest and meditated so deeply and for so long that eventually he was entirely covered over by an anthill.

Some time later the holy men were walking along the same path and, wanting to see if he had progressed at all and being unable to see him, they called out his name. Valmiki burst from the anthill in a shower of dry mud and, now a reformed man, he wrote down the epic story called the *Ramayana* . . .

On the great plain where the Ganges ran down from the mountains the king was feeling his age. He was missing his youngest son too. Everyone loved handsome, broad-shouldered, strong-armed Rama. It was hard not to. People were drawn to him as rivers were drawn to the sea. There was something good and true about him.

Rama was in fact on his way back to see his father, having just won the hand of Sita, the princess of a neighbouring kingdom. Her father had set a task that suitors had to complete in order to win her hand. Many had failed. But Rama had picked up with one hand the bow that none of the others had been able to lift at all. Then he had strung it with such ease that it had snapped with a loud crack! Rama was potent like a bull, and Sita's father was glad to give him her hand in marriage. Sita herself placed a garland round his handsome bullish neck.

When he saw the happy couple, the old king decided to abdicate and appoint Rama as his successor. His three other sons were as delighted as he had expected them to be. *Who wouldn't be?* he thought.

But still he had a vague feeling of disquiet. He remembered an incident from his youth. He'd been down by the river when a gurgling sound had caused him to jump to the conclusion that a wild animal was about to spring on him. He had spun round and shot through with an arrow a boy who was there filling a pot. The boy's parents had put a curse on him – that he would lose his own son.

What the old king didn't know was that a hunchbacked old servant, a maid to the one of his wives, was now whispering in her mistress's ear, telling her that her own son should be crowned king, not Rama.

'If Rama becomes king,' said the wicked old servant, 'you and your son will be banished. Rama thinks that you and your sons are beneath him. You know how proud he is.'

The king had once been completely besotted by this wife and rashly promised her two boons. Now she went to him and asked him to keep his promise. She demanded that her son be crowned king and Rama be banished for fourteen years.

The king begged her to release him from his promise, but she insisted. Bewildered, he turned to Rama, hoping he would see a way out of this dilemma, but his son was determined to do the right thing. So Rama, his favourite brother, Laxman, and his new wife, Sita, cast off their silks and jewels, put on bark-tree clothing and slipped away unnoticed.

When they reached the Ganges, they built a raft and pushed off to the far bank, then plunged into the forest. Walking single file down the narrow pathways, pushing through the lush vegetation and the low-hanging creepers, they wondered at the strange, strongly perfumed flowers, the exotic birds and the monkeys high in the trees. In the evening they stopped to build themselves a wooden hut.

Suddenly there was a commotion – movement in the forest, a cloud of dust, the cracking sounds of animals fleeing through the undergrowth. Laxman climbed a tree and reported that their brother Bharata was heading their way at the head of a column of soldiers. 'They're coming to kill us!'

Rama refused to hide, and stayed to greet Bharata.

Bharata arrived with the news that their father had died. He did not himself want to be the new king and asked Rama to come back and take the throne. Now their father was dead, he said, there was no need for anyone to be bound by his promise.

But Rama refused. He had agreed to live in exile for fourteen years.

Bharata went down on his knees and asked Rama for his wooden peg sandals, saying if he really wouldn't go back with him, his sandals would remain on the throne until the day of his return.[2]

Rama, Sita and Laxman journeyed deeper into the forests, happy with their humble way of life, eating fruit and roots, hunting deer and drinking water from streams. For many years they enjoyed exploring the land and experiencing the passing of the seasons. Rama said he was as content with this life as he would have been with the life of the court.

But even hidden in the depths of the forest, Rama's perfection was an affront to the evil powers in the world. They would not let him alone. Living in the forest was only *like* living in Paradise.

One day a beautiful scent like an expensive perfume filled the clearing in front of Rama, Laxman and Sita's hut. Then a beautiful white-skinned woman stepped into the clearing and smiled at Rama with shining eyes. He noticed her long fingernails, greyish purple in colour and curved like claws.

'I've had my eye on you for a long time,' she said, 'and I've loved you from the first moment I saw you. Why do you live like this – dirty, with matted hair, in that disgusting little hut? You are wasting your life with this plain woman. Marry me instead and we will rule the world and make it a beautiful place.'

Rama exchanged a sly glance with Laxman. 'My brother here is unmarried. Why don't you marry him?'

'But I'm only a servant to my brother. That would make you a servant too,' Laxman smiled. 'It's him you want to marry.'

Realizing she was being teased, the demoness resumed her normal shape with a huge distended belly, coppery curls and bulging eyes. She rushed at Sita. But Laxman quickly stepped between them. Drawing his knife, he sliced off her nose and ears, and the demoness ran off into the jungle screaming.

Life returned to normal until one day when Sita was sitting in front of the hut and saw a golden deer run through the clearing. She called on Rama and Laxman to catch it for her and they dashed off after it. Every time they got anywhere near the deer, though, it slipped away again out of sight, and they were drawn further and further from home.

After a while Sita heard some soft, muttered chanting. An old hermit appeared, begging for food. 'What a beautiful girl you are,' he said. 'I think you may be the goddess of love with your perfect white teeth and shapely round hips.'

Sita thought this language a little strange from a holy man. She fetched some food nonetheless.

As she handed it over, however, a hand shot out and grabbed her arm. She tried to pull away, but the old hermit pounced on her like a tiger, revealing himself in his true form – a ten-headed demon with eyebrows like writhing snakes. 'Yes, my duty to avenge my sister is going to be a real pleasure!'

This was Ravana, king of demons. After Laxman had maimed his sister, she'd gone to him and demanded he take revenge. He had sent her back in the form of a deer to lure Sita's protectors away. Now he snatched Sita, dragging her into his magic chariot pulled by donkeys. They flew away over the trees.

Returning from the hunt, Rama and Laxman were dismayed to find Sita missing. They called out and searched for signs of a struggle, or for a trail she might have left.

Rama then found in the bushes something he at first thought was a horribly deformed demon. In reality it was the bleeding, mutilated form of a giant bird, its wings and legs sliced off and barely alive. With his dying breath, the king of the vultures explained that he'd seen Ravana abducting Sita in his chariot and had tried to come to her rescue, but Ravana had got the better of him. He told them Ravana was taking Sita to his palace on the island of Ceylon.

Rama and Laxman solemnly burned the remains of the king of the vultures, then set off in pursuit.

They trudged through the forest over many days. The sky grew darker, the clouds massing like armies of demons. As they approached the sea, Rama and Laxman travelled through parts of the forest where only the stumps of burnt trees remained, where the earth was blackened. They came across the burnt remains of ashrams and villages.

As they breasted the last vegetation and reached the open shore, they looked across the sea, aghast. Ceylon was so far away. How could they possibly reach the island?

Rama knelt on the shore to pray. He was loved as much by the animal kingdom as by humankind, and now all the creatures of the forest came to help. They were led by Hanaman, king of the monkeys. Monkeys and bears carried logs and rocks. Insects and spiders helped to weave together a gigantic floating bridge.

Rama crossed at the head of a great army of thousands of monkeys, to be faced by an army of demons. The battle between monkeys and demons raged for seven days.

Rama's monkey army

Rama hacked his way through the demonic hoards until he cornered Ravana. Every time he cut off one of his ten heads, another grew in its place. Then he drew his great bow and shot an arrow through Ravana's heart. The demon king fell from his chariot, blood spurting from his ten mouths. He had been called 'Brave in Three Worlds' and now three worlds were finally free of him.

Rama went in search of Sita, pounding down the corridors of the palace. He found her in Ravana's secret, secluded garden. When he saw her, he was shocked. He did not rush to embrace her. She was thin and her flesh was greying and unhealthy.

Her voice breaking with pain, she told Rama that Ravana had threatened to cut her into little pieces, to make mincemeat of her, to kill her if she wouldn't sleep with him – but she swore that she never had.

Just to be sure, Rama made her undergo an ordeal by fire. She emerged from the conflagration untouched, because she was pure.

It was now fourteen years since they had gone into exile, so Rama and Sita mounted Ravana's chariot, newly bedecked with flowers, and flew back across the sea and over the forest canopy, to be greeted with garlands and great celebrations by Bharata and all the people. There was dancing and chanting and processions with golden flags and soldiers in golden armour. The Monkey King attended the celebrations swirling a white umbrella.

This was the story told by Valmiki who had burst from the anthill.

The reign of Rama was a golden age that Mahatma Gandhi often said he hoped would return. But sitting on golden thrones Rama and Sita never quite recovered the happiness of their life wandering in the forest. Also, going about the streets of the city in disguise, Rama caught wind of rumours that Sita had given in to Ravana. There was a famine and some said that this had been caused by Rama taking her back after she had lived with another man.

One night Laxman came to Sita and sat beside her.

'Why are you crying?' she asked.

He explained that Rama had told him to take her back into the forest, into exile.

Laxman escorted Sita to the other side of the river. As she stood on the riverbank, watching the lights of Laxman's boat recede, she thought she was losing her mind. How could this make sense? She couldn't bear to live without her Lord Rama.

'Don't do it.' She heard a voice behind her. 'Don't drown yourself.'

She turned and saw a very old man, a hermit. 'Who are you?'

'I am Valmiki. The forest is my home.'

When Valmiki took Sita in, she was pregnant. She gave birth to two sons and Valmiki became their tutor.

Many years later, when the boys were grown men, he took them into the city and encouraged them to sing a song he had composed, called the *Ramayana*. When Rama heard it, he was overjoyed to recognize them as his own sons. He sent for Sita, commanding her to return to him – but also saying that she would have to undergo another trial by fire to prove her purity.

Sita was reluctant, but she did her duty.

Rama felt a surge of joy when he saw her, very frail but dressed in robes of red and gold.

She asked, 'Do I have your permission to prove my purity and innocence to you?'

Yes, she did, he said, and so it was that Sita proved herself by dying on the spot. Rama saw her soul ascend to heaven.

There are many different versions of the *Ramayana* and it also poses awkward questions. Why is Sita treated so harshly? Doesn't the way she is dealt with by Rama seem horribly unfair? It is drenched with nostalgia, too. Rama and Sita want to get back to Paradise, to the garden, to a time before life became hard and full of responsibility.

This then is a story about spiritual evolution – but also about the pain it brings. Rama and Sita defeat demons who are unambiguously evil, but they are themselves defeated by moral ambiguities. Rama's wife does not deserve to be suspected of infidelity, but she *is* suspected by the mean-minded in the kingdom, and Rama's wife must be above suspicion. She has to suffer for the sake of the community, so that others can be purged of their dark thoughts.

Although we are separated on the physical plane by being confined in individual bodies of flesh, on the spiritual plane we are all connected to the great Cosmic Mind, which is the hub of the cosmos, like Mount Meru.

Why doesn't Rama take the throne when everyone wants him to? Because his father has accidentally killed a boy by acting too hastily, too rashly. Rents caused in the fabric of the cosmos must be repaired by all of us.[3]

Krishna, Snow White and the Seven Maids

At the beginning of the fifth millennium BC a great spiritual leader was born in a region west of India.

The land we call Iran was dangerous then, a place of looting, raiding, warring tribes. We must picture a bleak, rocky landscape. Small farming communities and their cattle were menaced by rival tribes and outlaws – bandits and witches – and by wolves. Disease was rife. Cleanliness and purity were always under threat. Blood within the body was sacred, but once spilled it became unholy. The dead were not buried but staked out in the open, so that their bones would be picked clean by vultures. To these communities, the darkness outside the enclosure seemed clawing, snarling, slashing, hurtling. Huddling in their huts, they told stories of Satan rushing on creation like a gigantic fly.

As soon as Zarathustra[1] was born, he laughed – the only time in history this had happened. He grew up to be fearless of evil, determined to fight fire with fire, but he was also puzzled by it. Some of his thoughts have come down to us, ancient hymns called the *Gathas*. 'Why was I created? Who made me? I am bound by maleficent bloodlust, by anger and violence . . . One is not to know the Truth . . .'

At the age of thirty he met seven tall shining beings who showed him a vision of the spiritual history and reality of the cosmos.[2]

He went to the court and preached what the shining beings had told him. He told the king to turn away from evil to good, and preached woe to evil-doers and that the destiny of the world was in the control of angels. He was the first of a line of prophets, telling kings what they did not want to hear.

The king's counsellors were priests of Saturn, and they persuaded the king to throw Zarathustra in prison. He escaped and retreated to remote mountainous regions. There, in caves, he initiated his followers as the shining beings had initiated him. Through these terrifying ordeals, which killed them and brought them back to life, his followers learned not to be afraid of death. When they were initiated, they became confident they had confronted and faced down the worst that life and death had to offer. Afterwards Zarathustra sent them out into the world to do battle with demons. These warriors for good were called magi, from an old word, *magu*, meaning 'priest'.

At the age of seventy-seven Zarathustra was tending the sacred flame in one of his mountain hideaways when an assassin crept up behind him and stabbed him to death.

The demons had won the battle. The war moved to a new phase.[3]

*   *   *

A council of gods gathered in a parallel dimension, on the shore of the Milk Ocean. They implored the Sun god to incarnate. They said it was the only way they would be able to defeat the dark forces that were winning the war for the world.

One of the leaders of these evil forces was a king called Kamsa. He had been an evil child. As a young prince, he had murdered other children, the children of the poor. Later he had imprisoned his own father and usurped the throne. He held court amid luxury and extravagance, and local children continued to disappear, but no one dared question the king.

When his sister, Devaki, married, he gave an extravagant dowry that included elephants, horses and hundreds of servants. He was riding his chariot back from the wedding, pleased with his generosity, when he heard a voice cry out from the crowd, calling him an idiot and predicting that Devaki would have a son who would kill him.

Even Kamsa hesitated to murder his own sister. Instead he had her and her new husband thrown into the deepest dungeons of his great stone prison. But in her dark cell Devaki was sustained by strange and luminous dreams. She heard beautiful music, as if harps and flutes were playing in the cell next to her, and she saw great beings of light.

In time Krishna was born. On that momentous day on the stroke of midnight the gaolers fell into a deep sleep and the manacles and gates that held the prisoners magically sprang apart. They fled, Krishna's father carrying the baby wrapped in blankets.

They came to a great wide river on the edges of the city. Uproar in the streets behind told them that the king's soldiers were almost upon them. They seemed to be trapped, but then the waters of the river miraculously parted and they were able to wade through the mud to the far bank before the waters closed.

Kamsa had sent his soldiers out into the streets and houses. He had given orders that all the newborns in his kingdom were to be slaughtered.

But after the massacre, when he consulted an attendant demon, he discovered to his rage that his deadly rival, his nephew, was still alive.

That night he had a dream. He was looking at himself in a mirror and he was headless . . .

Meanwhile Krishna was carried to safety. The fugitives walked through the deep green corridors of the forest until they saw Mount Meru up above the treetops. They settled in a remote cedar-scented village of cattle farmers.

Krishna grew into a beautiful boy with big eyes and a wide smile. He was full of sweetness. Everyone who saw him instantly fell in love with him. The milkmaids who worked on the farm would forgive him when he was naughty. He would steal butter from them while they slept and feed it to the monkeys. Sometimes he let the cows roam free shortly before milking time, and sometimes as the milkmaids carried pots of milk back from milking, he would deliberately knock them from their heads, then run away laughing and make them chase him.

If Rama's life story turns on strictly observed principles, Krishna's repeatedly and joyfully breaks the rules. If Zarathustra's life seems a terrifying initiation test, Krishna's life is a vision of a cosmos with divine playfulness as its ruling principle.

Sometimes Krishna's mother found him playing with deer. Once she found him wrestling with young panthers. On another occasion she heard he had been eating mud. He shook his head and denied it. She ordered him to open his mouth. Peering inside, she saw for moment the whole cosmos opening out and new dimensions unfolding.

Meanwhile Kamsa redoubled his attempts to kill Krishna. One day when Krishna was all alone he saw a woman approach the farm. Telling him she was a nurse, she scooped him up and put him to her breast. In reality she was a demon witch called Putana, sent by Kamsa, and her nipples were smeared with poison. Krishna fastened on to her breast and sucked and sucked until she crumpled, all the life sucked out of her. As she died, she resumed her monstrous form and fell like a great black tree, crushing huts and out-houses.

In his teens Krishna loved to flirt with the milkmaids. Once he stole their clothes while they were bathing in the river and hid in a tree to watch them emerge. Seven milkmaids loved him because of his sweetness and because he had grown into a great beauty. They liked to hear him play the flute, and sometimes on autumn evenings they danced around him in the moonlight. It always seemed to each milkmaid that Krishna was facing her and holding her with both arms.

Krishna with a milkmaid
(from an image in an
eighteenth-century Indian
wall hanging).

Kamsa decided to lure his nephew out of hiding. He sent out messengers advertising a festival. There was to be feasting and dancing and a wrestling tournament with great prizes for the winners. So it came about that as they were entering adulthood Krishna and his brother decided to make their way to the city.

As they arrived, dressed as poor country folk, they met a poor young girl, horribly deformed by leprosy, selling perfumes to try to scratch a living and feed herself with scraps. Krishna stopped and asked her to give him some perfume for free. When she handed it over without hesitation, he kissed her and she was cured and made beautiful.

Rumours of this miracle spread rapidly. By the time Krishna and his brother had reached the main square, a crowd had gathered around them, showering them with petals.

When Kamsa saw this procession, he seethed with rage. It seemed to him that the people were acclaiming Krishna as their new king. He had planned for an elephant to be driven towards them and trample them to death. But now Krishna's brother stepped forward and knocked the elephant out with one punch.

There are different versions of what happened at the end of the fair. Some say Krishna hauled Kamsa into the wrestling arena and killed him then and there. In others Krishna and his brother escaped back to the woods.

*   *   *

In some respects the story of Krishna reminds us of that of Snow White, but with the genders reversed. Both Krishna and Snow White live in the woods. Krishna's Satanic uncle and Snow White's aunt repeatedly try to kill them, attacking them in the guise of kindly strangers. Uncle and aunt both check the progress of their plans in otherworldly mirrors. Krishna is surrounded by seven maidens, as Snow White is surrounded by seven dwarves. The number seven tells us that both these sets of seven are the planets revolving around the sun.

Let us unravel the mysterious connection between these two stories. Psychologists tell us Snow White represents the self and that her story is the archetypal story of all our childhoods. In oriental philosophy, the great Cosmic Mind is called the Self, and all our individual selves are reflections of this Self.[4] Though we may remain unaware of it for the greater part of our lives (believing that we contain the ground of our own being), the relationship between Self and self is in this view about as intimate as it could be. As the German mystic Meister Eckhart put it, 'The eye through which I see God and the eye through which God sees me is the same eye.'

Krishna is the Self. He has been called the Indian Christ and, to put it in Western terms, he is a manifestation on Earth of the Word, the Sun god whose vital intervention stopped Saturn from squeezing all the life out of Mother Earth, as we saw in Chapter 2.

As we shall see now, Indian scriptures contain a description of Krishna, revealing himself as the Self.

*   *   *

Two ruling families were about to go to war. Time had passed and Krishna had survived his uncle's attempts to kill him in order to play a decisive part in a great battle.

The dispute between the two families had arisen out of a game of dice in which one family had lost everything to the other. Now this dispute would be resolved by Krishna. 'I am the cleverness in the dice,' he said.

On the morning of the Great Battle (the *Mahabharata*), Krishna became the charioteer of Arjuna, a warrior leader.

Arjuna was about to sound the conch horn that signalled the start of battle and lead one of the two armies forward. But as he surveyed the enemy and recognized many friends and relatives in their ranks, and as he thought about the unprecedented slaughter that this battle would bring, the great warrior hesitated. He stepped down from his chariot and his bow slipped from his hand and fell to the ground.

Then Krishna dismounted too, and came and stood in front of him. He told Arjuna that the battle he was about to fight was a battle that would open the very gates of heaven. He told him that he could not kill anyone, and neither could he himself die, because what was eternal in humankind moved between the worlds.

Then he allowed Arjuna to see him in his divine form, saying, 'Through me all creation comes to be, through me all creation rolls around. All things have their life in me. I am their beginning and their end. I am the power in the powerful and I am desire in the pure of heart. I am the beauty in all beautiful things and the good in all that is good. I am the Way. I say to those who love me, you are in me.'

Arjuna looked and saw, where a man had been standing, the light of a thousand suns, countless forms, endless universes unfolding, infinite space and infinite time. He saw Krishna with the sun and the moon for his eyes. He saw him being adored by all the gods and spirits he had ever heard of and many more. (This incident in the *Bhagavad Gita* may bring home to us a strong sense of what it would be like to meet the incarnated Christ.[5])

Then he heard Krishna say, 'Arise, Arjuna, with your spirit ready to fight!'

So Arjuna stepped back up onto his chariot and blew the conch horn. For eighteen days the great plain shook with war cries, the

The Caves at Elephanta (from a nineteenth-century engraving). According to a legend, these caves were first carved by Pandava, a hero of the *Mahabharata*.

neighing of horses, the roaring of elephants, trumpets, the whistling of arrows, the crashing of golden maces and the cries of dying men, until finally Krishna's advice in the ear of Arjuna enabled him to triumph over superior forces.[6]

There are different versions of Krishna's death. In one version he was tied to a tree and martyred by archers. In others he lived in a terrible time of disaster and disease. Everything seemed to go wrong for him. He retreated to the forest and was meditating under a tree when a hunter accidentally mistook his foot protruding from behind a tree trunk for the ears of a deer and shot him with a bow and arrow. What the stories agree on is that the date of his death is determined by astronomical cycles – and that it marks the end of one great cycle and the beginning of another, the Kali Yuga, the Dark Age.[7]

The beginning of the Kali Yuga was also the beginning of the age of the founding of the first great cities and the first great civilizations. Rama and Sita, Zarathustra and Krishna lived in the wild. The heroes of the next age would be the first to confront the loneliness, the alienation and feelings of futility that come with life in the city.

Gilgamesh and the Elixir of Immortality

'People lived in a lawless manner like the beasts of the field. Then one day a beast emerged from out of the sea which borders Babylonia. The beast was called Oannes. The body of Oannes was that of a fish, but under his fish's head he had another head, like a man's head, and his feet were like a man's too, joined to a fishy tail. He was able to speak like a man, and he talked to the people living by the sea, teaching them how to distinguish the different seeds of the earth and which fruit to pick. He taught them writing and mathematics. He showed them how to use geometry to build cities and to found temples, and also gave them a body of law – everything they would need for city life.

Every evening Oannes would stop talking and return to the sea, because he was amphibious.'

This fragment, from the ancient Near East, is an account of the founding of the first city, Uruk, in about 3000 BC in what is today southern Iraq, an area between Basra and Baghdad. It clearly means to say that the transition from tribal society to cities was brought about by super-human intelligence.[1]

The later story of Gilgamesh, the fourth king of Uruk, is in part about what people felt as they adapted to city living. This strange and wonderful story was lost for thousands of years until 1872, when George Smith, a scholar at the British Museum, announced he had deciphered tablets excavated in the library of the last Assyrian king. Inscribed on lapis lazuli, it had been locked up in the temple of Venus inside a copper box . . .

Sumerian hunter-hero (engraving from a cylinder seal).

Gilgamesh was a young buck. He was taller and stronger than everyone else, lion-chested and very handsome, with beautiful curly hair. His restless energy, his voracious appetite for life, drove him to charge around hunting, clearing mountain passes, digging wells, building up the city walls – and seducing young women. And still he was restless. He wanted to compete, to wrestle, to test his strength, but there was no one to stand up to him, and this made him lonely.

Then a trapper who worked in the nearby forests noticed that something or someone was disabling his traps, filling in all his pits and helping the game to escape.

One day at a watering hole used by gazelles, this trapper saw a strange, wild, hairy man and he watched as this ape-like creature drank then ambled off in the company of the gazelles.

Meanwhile Gilgamesh had been having dreams of a friend who would be coming his way with the impact of a meteor, and when the trapper told him what he had seen, he thought, *This must be the one – this must be the friend I've been waiting for!* and a plan was devised to lure the wild man to the city.

The trapper returned to the watering hole with one of the temple prostitutes. They lay in wait for a while, seeing only small creatures drinking at the watering hole, but on the third day the gazelles returned and the trapper saw that the wild man was still with them. He said to the girl, 'Go to meet him and bare your breasts. You can tame the savage man.'

So the wild man saw what he had never seen before – a naked woman. She spread her cloak on the ground and they made love for seven days and seven nights. Then the wild man, who was called Enkidu, tried to leave and run with the animals again. But he found that he could no longer run fast enough and, besides, they had become afraid of him.

The woman said, 'Enkidu, why do you run with the wild beasts? You are beautiful, like a god. Come with me to the city.'

She took him first to a cottage, where she washed and clothed him and taught him to eat bread and other cooked food and he drank seven jugs of beer, which made him sing with joy!²

She told him more about life in the city – the crowds, the fine clothes, the great buildings, the festivals and the music. She told him more about the tall, handsome young king, Gilgamesh, but when she told him about his ruthlessness with women, about how he took the women of the city as if by right, Enkidu resolved to challenge him and stop him.

The long-awaited clash between Gilgamesh and Enkidu happened in the market square. Gilgamesh was taller than Enkidu, but Enkidu was thicker-set. Enkidu blocked Gilgamesh's way, and the walls and timber of the buildings shook as they wrestled for four days. They were nearly evenly matched, but in the end Gilgamesh was able to throw Enkidu onto his back and pin him to the ground.

Then they felt a brotherly love for each other. They hugged, and from then on they were seldom out of each other's company.

But after a while Enkidu began to miss life in the wild. He complained of feeling listless and lazy. He said his arms were losing their strength. Gilgamesh proposed they go on an adventure together. They would slay a monster called Humbaba, who preyed on travellers passing through the cedar forests of Lebanon. It was said that his hideous face, a labyrinth of wrinkles and ridges, was as ugly as a plate of guts.

Gilgamesh and Enkidu crossed the mountains, tracked him down in the forests and sliced off his head.

Scarcely had they arrived back in Uruk, however, than a giant bull began ravaging the countryside. Soon it had killed 300 men. Some people said that the very gates of hell were being shaken down, and that the dead would emerge and start eating the living.

As Gilgamesh and Enkidu went out to meet the bull, a great chasm opened up in front of them. Enkidu was tipped in, but managed to hang on to the edge. Then he jumped up and grabbed the bull by the horns. He yelled to Gilgamesh to insert his sword between the nape of the neck and the horns – the place that matadors use today. They cut off the horns to hang on the wall back home.

But when they returned again to Uruk, they found the city had been struck by plague. People said that the bull had been sacred to Enlil, the king of the gods, and that now he was angry.[3]

Enkidu fell ill. Gilgamesh wept and prayed over him. Enkidu cursed the trapper who had found him and the temple prostitute who had tamed him and trained him to enjoy civilized life. His eyes began to dim. He had a dream in which he was led along a road of no return to a House of Dust, where people only ever ate dust and drank dust. He could not see Gilgamesh and believed his old comrade had deserted him. In his dream he cried out in agony.

A worm slipped out of his nose and Gilgamesh let out a shriek. He pulled a sheet over his friend's face. Enkidu, who had been as swift as the panther, would move no more.

Pacing backwards and forwards, Gilgamesh tore off his fine clothes and cut off his beautiful curly hair. 'He was my axe, always in my hand,' he cried out. 'He was the dagger in my belt.'

He ordered a statue to be made of Enkidu, then he left the city and began roaming the wilderness, grieving for his friend. Then a terrible new thought struck him: *If Enkidu could die, then so too could he.*

As men sank deeper into their bodily, animal natures, as their experience and memory of the spiritual realms grew fainter and dimmer, so their dread of death grew greater.

Gilgamesh remembered stories he had been told of his ancestor who had survived the Flood by building an ark. It was rumoured that this ancestor had never really died and that he lived on a sacred mountain to the east. Gilgamesh determined to go and find him to discover the secrets of life and death.

He crossed the wilderness. He killed lions and took their skins for his clothes. He entered gates guarding a narrow pass to a mountainous realm. The light on the mountain pass grew darker, until he came to a brilliantly lit plain, where the trees were made of gold and their fruits were rubies, emeralds and other precious stones. From among the trees his ancestor came to greet him.

Gilgamesh said, 'I was expecting you to look strange, but you look like a man, just like me! I was going to *make* you tell me your secrets, but now I've met you, I find I can't even raise my arm against you.'

The old man smiled and began to tell Gilgamesh his own story.

'One stormy night,' he said, 'when the whole world was roaring like a bull, I heard a voice whispering to me through the reeds of my hut. It said, "Pull down these reeds, pull down this hut to build yourself a boat. Give up material things and seek life. Take the seed of all living things and stow them in your boat . . ."'

The old man ended his story by explaining how after the Flood the king of the gods had boarded the boat and he and his wife had bowed down before Him. God had touched them on the forehead and blessed them, saying that now they would live for ever.

Then the old man said he was going to give Gilgamesh that same gift. In order to receive it, though, he must neither lie down nor sleep for six days and seven nights.

But Gilgamesh was exhausted by his journey over the mountain pass and he was overcome by sleep the moment he sat down.

When he awoke he knew he had failed the test. 'What am I to do?' he pleaded with the old man. 'Death is all around me, in my every footstep, my every breath, my clothes, my sheets. It is clutching at my flesh.'

The old man dismissed him angrily, gesturing to him to return the way he had come, but then his wife intervened. She said, 'Gilgamesh had been travelling for a long time and was exhausted when he arrived. Give him some hope, something to take back with him.'

So the old man relented and told Gilgamesh where to find a very special plant. 'It grows,' he said, 'on the bottom of the ocean. This plant is prickly like a bramble, like a rose, but if you can dive down far enough and find it and bring it up to the surface, you need never grow old.'

Gilgamesh went to sea, to the place his ancestor had told him about, and attached stones to his feet to pull him down to the ocean's floor.

Down, down, down, he sank through the different levels of the sea. At last he found the plant and although it pricked him and tore the flesh of his hand, he was able to pull it free from the seabed. Then he cut himself loose from the stones and swam to the surface with all speed.

While he was lying on the shore gasping for breath, a snake smelled the wonderful scent of the plant. It slithered over and carried the plant away. That is why the snake can slough off its skin and regenerate itself.

And that is why from that day forward Gilgamesh was doomed. He had failed in his quest to find relief from what had been afflicting humankind. He had found nothing to ease his pain or disperse the gathering darkness.

Gilgamesh, king of Uruk, had the wrong idea. He looked in the wrong place. It was another inhabitant of that city, a very different type of man, who set humankind on the right path . . .

Abraham, the Father of Thinking in the Head

There is a story in the Talmud about a boy named Abram reaching a certain age and asking his father where he could find the God who had created heaven and Earth.

'My son, the creator of all things is here with us in this house.'

'Then please show him to me, father,' said Abram.

His father led him to a secret inner room, where he pointed out twelve large idols surrounded by many smaller ones, with traces of food and other burnt offerings scattered in front of them.

'Here they are, my son – the gods who created everything.'

Abram seized an iron rod and smashed all the images except one, furious with his father: 'You bring guilt upon your soul, the same guilt for which your ancestors were punished by the Flood. Cease, father, to serve such gods, lest evil fall upon your soul and the souls of all your family.'

In this story we hear the questioning that would become one of the great gifts to the world of the Jewish people. Abraham, as he later became, was famous throughout the ancient world because he brought this new quality into it.

Abraham's family came from Uruk, the great city ruled by Gilgamesh. Gilgamesh may have still been alive when Abraham was born. According to Hebrew legend, Abraham's father worked for Nimrod, the mighty

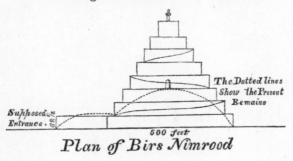

The Tower of Babel (illustration from *Evidence of the Truth of Christian Religion* by the Rev. Alexander Keith, 1833).

hunter referred to in Genesis, who may have been Gilgamesh's successor as king. Some have even identified Gilgamesh with Nimrod.

But as we move from the story of Gilgamesh to that of Abraham, it is immediately obvious we are encountering a very different mindset.

There is a tradition that Abraham was expelled from Uruk for refusing to work on the construction of the Tower of Babel. This tower was the tallest of the great ziggurats or step pyramids that loomed over the city. Why was it being built?

It was becoming increasingly difficult for great spiritual beings to sink down through the heavens to Earth. We have come a long way in this history from the time when God walked with Adam and Eve in the garden and from the sense of direct knowledge, even direct experience, of the deeds of the gods we find in Greek myths. Stories of life before the Flood present us with a bright parade of heavenly activity, but this begins to tail off in the time of the demi-gods. Post-Flood heroes such as Rama and Krishna find themselves battling with demons – in the stories of Zarathustra the sky is even darkened by demons – but the higher-order angels, the gods, are by no means a constant presence for them.

According to Rudolf Steiner, the priests of Egypt and Sumeria believed that the nearest point to the Earth that many powerful higher-level beings could approach of their own volition was the moon. The moon, therefore, became a kind of staging post, and the great pyramid of Egypt and the ziggurats of Sumeria were designed to draw these high-level beings down from it.

The pyramids of the ancient world can be seen as a great cry of spiritual pain, monuments to a gigantic sense of loss – loss of the great cosmic vision and of the great unifying cosmic purpose. This is what lies behind the story of the Tower of Babel. When the Bible says that as punishment for trying to storm the ramparts of heaven, different peoples began to speak different languages, what is meant is that different peoples no longer shared one cosmic vision. Instead they saw only a short way into the spiritual realms – shadowy visions that left them at odds with one another and unable to see the purpose they shared.

Abraham felt this sense of loss, but he wouldn't make use of the ziggurats to try to fulfil this spiritual yearning. He would develop new methods – for himself and for humanity.

It was about 2000 BC when Abraham left Uruk and the skyscrapers of the ancient world in order to wander the desert. He was trying to find a meaning, a pattern, a unity in what was happening in the world, and he would succeed by means of a series of mysterious encounters and finally a famous test, the true meaning of which is revealed, as we shall see, in a secret, mystical tradition.

God said to Abraham, 'Get thee out of thy country and from thy father's house, unto a land that I will shew thee.'

This was the first mention of the Promised Land.

Abraham was seventy years old when he and his wife, Sarah, and his nephew, Lot, travelled south into Canaan. Years of famine forced them to abandon the nomadic way of life to spend a while in Egypt. Then later, as the numbers of their followers and cattle grew, Abram and Lot parted company.

Later still, Lot was captured and taken prisoner by a local king, and Abraham armed and trained 318 followers to rescue him.

He was celebrating Lot's release at a place called Salem – later called Jerusalem – when he had a strange visitor:

And Melchizedek, king of Salem, brought forth bread and wine: and he was the priest of the most high God. And he blessed him, and said, Blessed be Abram of the most high God, possessor of heaven and earth: And blessed be the most high God, which hath delivered thine enemies into thine hand . . . (Genesis 14: 18–20)

The face of Melchizedek
(drawing from a statue on
Chartres cathedral).

The name 'Melchizedek' means 'king of righteousness'. There is another reference to Melchizedek in the Old Testament in Psalms 110.4: 'You are now a priest forever according to the order of Melchizedek.'

These two short passages contain all the Old Testament has to say about the mysterious figure of Melchizedek. But in the Letter to the Hebrews, (7:17) Jesus Christ is referred to as *a priest forever in the order of Melchizedek* – alluding to Psalm 110. Jesus is therefore said to be in some sense following in the footsteps of Melchizedek. Paul also says of Melchizedek (Hebrews, 7:3) that he is 'without father, without mother, without origin, without beginning or end but made in the likeness of the Son of God'. Melchizedek is evidently a quite extraordinary figure. As time passed, artists and architects would understand this. He would also become a hugely important figure in Church iconography.

What is his secret?

There is a clue in an early Christian text, the *Pistis Sophia*, where he is called 'the great receiver of Eternal Light'. This is one of the titles of Manu, the Son of the Sun and survivor of the Flood in Hindu tradition – the individual we know as Noah. There is also a Talmudic tradition that as a boy Abraham had gone off alone to learn at the feet of his ancestor Noah.

Melchizedek, then, is Noah in disguise, the keeper and teacher of ancient pre-Flood wisdom. He had not died in the normal way. He had been the ancestor Gilgamesh had sought out. Gilgamesh had failed the test, hadn't asked the right questions. His aspirations had been limited and materialistic. Now Noah/Melchizedek presented the true teaching on eternal life to Abraham, symbolized in the ceremony of the bread and wine.

God then made Abraham a promise: 'Look now toward heaven and see the stars. Thy seed shall be like them.' (Genesis 15:5)

As with the Melchizedek passage, there is a secret meaning to this promise. God doesn't just mean that Abraham's descendants will be *as numerous as* the stars, but also that they will be *ordered* like the stars. They will be ordered into twelve tribes, as the stars are ordered in the twelve constellations of the zodiac, and their destiny will be mapped out according to the movements of the angels of the stars and the planets – according to a unified plan and pattern.

But would God's promise come true? On the face of it, this looked extremely unlikely. Abraham and Sarah were childless and already extremely old.

Sarah offered her servant Hagar to Abraham as a second wife, and at the age of eighty-six Abraham became a father. Hagar, an Egyptian girl guided on her path by an angel, bore him a son called Ishmael, from whose lineage would rise Islam when the world needed it. (Hagar and the angel. Illustration from *The Chronicle of the World* by Rudolf von Ems, early thirteenth century.)

When Abraham was ninety-nine years old, he had more mysterious visitors. One day he was sitting in his tent, sheltering from the noonday sun, when he looked up into the sun and saw three men approaching. He rushed out to greet them, bowed low before them and offered water to wash their feet. Then he asked them to rest under a tree and asked Sarah to bake cakes and fetched butter, milk and meat to feed them.

He was, 'entertaining angels unawares', and one of them told him that Sarah would shortly bear him a child. Sitting in a nearby tent, Sarah overheard this and laughed. Not only was Abraham ninety-nine, she had reached ninety.

Another of the angels warned Abraham of the destruction of Sodom and Gomorrah, where his nephew was living.

Lot was sitting at the gate of Sodom when he saw some visitors approaching. Like Abraham, he bowed down before them. He invited them into his house, offering them water to wash their feet and feeding them. But when it was time to go to sleep, he heard people surrounding the house, demanding to know who the strangers were.

The Departure of Lot and his Family from Sodom (by the initiate artist Peter Paul Rubens).

What had made the people of Sodom suspicious? Were they feeling guilty? Did they feel someone had come to spy on them and judge them? They demanded that Lot bring the visitors out, and when he refused, they tried to batter the door down.

The mysterious visitors somehow exercised a supernatural power that struck the attackers blind, and the assault on the house subsided.

Then the angels explained to Lot that the Lord was going to destroy the city and that he should leave before first light with his wife and two daughters.

When the time came, the family hesitated. The angels told them to hurry. They took them all by the hand and led them out of the city to the safety of a mountain.

When the sun rose, 'the Lord rained upon Sodom and upon Gomorrah brimstone and fire from the Lord out of heaven'. (Genesis 19:24)

Abraham was a hundred years old when Sarah bore him a son. She said, 'God hath caused me to laugh, so that all who hear will laugh with me.'

They named their son Isaac, meaning 'Laughter.'

The boy grew fit and strong, and was of a naturally sunny disposition. Some years later, when he was about fourteen, Abraham said to Sarah, 'I am going to take Isaac with me tomorrow.'

She loved her son very much and didn't like to let him out of her sight. 'Please don't take him too far – or for too long.'

She managed a smile, but that night she couldn't sleep. As she lay awake she had a premonition, and in the morning she hugged Isaac to her and wept: 'My only boy, my only child, my hope.' Then she turned to Abraham and said, 'Watch out for the boy. He's only young. Don't make him walk in the heat. You know he tires easily.'

As they went along, Isaac noted that his father was collecting the wood needed to make a sacrifice. 'Father, where is the sacrificial lamb?' he asked.

'Our God has chosen you, a creature without blemish,' said Abraham, 'as an acceptable burnt offering in place of the lamb.' He took him by the shoulder and looked him in the eye: 'Are you without blemish? Is there any secret evil in your heart? If there is, now is the time to tell me.'

'I feel . . . no regret,' said Isaac.

After walking for three days they reached the holy mountain that God had chosen, and Abraham built an altar and laid wood across it. His son helped. Then Abraham tied him to the wood.

'Bind me tightly so that I don't struggle,' said Isaac. 'Tell my mother I died bravely.'

Abraham turned away so Isaac couldn't see the tears in his eyes.

'Now quickly, father, do the will of God.'

Was Abraham being asked to sacrifice the beloved son for whom he and Sarah had waited for so many years?

The angel of the Lord called unto him out of heaven and said, 'Abraham, Abraham.'

'Here I am.'

'Lay not thine hand upon the lad, neither do thou anything unto him.'

And Abraham lifted up his eyes and looked and saw a ram caught in a thicket by its horns. He went and took the ram and offered him up for a burnt offering instead of his son.

Here the deep and mysterious stream of secret meaning that lies just beneath the surface of the whole story of Abraham rises again. The horns of the ram caught in the thicket represent what in Hindu mysticism is called the crown chakra, the two-petalled organ of spiritual vision that, when open, enables people to see into the spiritual world and commune with gods, angels and spirits. Abraham is here sacrificing this ability. He is eschewing the ecstatic, atavistic forms of religion practised on the ziggurats, the deranging of the senses that led to chaotic visions. The people of the pyramids yearned for the dreamy form of consciousness of earlier times, and if they could not encounter the higher spiritual beings, they wanted to encounter the lower ones, even demons. On some level Abraham understood that humankind would have to reject this atavistic way of seeing. If spiritual reality were less immediate, less invasive, humankind would be able to develop a faculty to reach out to it.

The story of Abraham is the beginning of the quest for the Promised Land, and on an important level it is the story of the nurturing of a new form of consciousness. In sacred history, human consciousness is never static but continues to evolve, and in Genesis and Exodus the

Jews are shown evolving new faculties on behalf of the whole of humankind.

Abraham is sometimes called the father of monotheism. He stands at the head of Judaism, Christianity and Islam. But it is important not to indulge in any anachronism here. The people of the Old and New Testaments, and indeed the people of the Koran, were not monotheists in the sense that we often use that word today – the sense of believing in a totally undifferentiated divine being, or that there are no other distinguishable spiritual beings apart from God. Their world remained crowded with gods, angels, demons and other spirits. St Paul admits the existence of other gods in 1 Corinthians 8.5: 'Even though there be so called gods whether in heaven or on earth – and indeed there are such gods – yet for us there is one God.'

Abraham was the founder of monotheism because he intuited a great Cosmic Mind behind everything, planning everything. Monotheism did not mean that there were no other gods or spiritual beings but that there was a unified plan in the world and – crucially – that humankind would have to develop the faculty of intelligence in order to discover that plan. Because of monotheism humankind would be enabled to make sense of the whole of life and the cosmos, and in order to be able to do that, would develop the faculty for sustained abstract intellectual thought.

*   *   *

On their journeys the Israelites moved through barren and hostile lands. Famine drove them back into Egypt, where they became enslaved. The nomadic way of life was replaced by a life among the gigantic stone monuments, obelisks, pyramids and temples.

The land of Isis and Osiris preserved ceremonial lore going back to the beginning of time. Gods and the spirits of the ancestors might appear in the smoke and incense at the climax of ceremonies. Egyptian civilization was death-obsessed and the cityscape resembled a vast necropolis.

The most famous of the Israelites became an Egyptian prince. He and his brother Aaron would compete with Egyptian magicians in the performance of spectacular magical feats.

The forces of materialism had murdered the world teachers Zarathustra and Krishna. The light of the messengers of the Sun god

Jacob's Ladder (from the Lübeck Bible). 'When he reached a certain place he stopped for the night because the sun had set. Taking one of the stones there he put it under his head and lay down to sleep. He had a dream in which he saw a stairway resting on the earth with its top reaching to heaven, and the angels of God were ascending and descending it . . . I am with you and will watch over you wherever you go. Early the next morning Jacob took the stone he had placed under his head and set it up as a pillar and poured oil on top of it.' (Genesis 28:11–12)

It is interesting that Jacob is not swept up by the angels and given a tour of the heavens like Enoch or, later, Mohammed. He views the orders of angels as it were from a distance, and this distance gives him the space to *think* about them. He has a later, more intimate, encounter:

'So Jacob was left alone, and a man wrestled with him till daybreak. When the man saw he could not overpower him he touched the socket of Jacob's hip so that his hip was wrenched as he wrestled with the man. Then the man said, 'Let me go, for it is daybreak.' But Jacob replied, 'I will not let you go unless you bless me.' Then the man asked him, 'What is your name?' 'Jacob,' he answered. Then the man said, 'Your name will no longer be Jacob but Israel, because you have struggled with God and with men and have overcome.' Jacob said, 'Please tell me your name.' But he replied, 'Why do you ask my name?' Then he blessed him there.' (Genesis 32:24–29)

Note that Jacob's wrestling with the angel is not a trial of strength, but a test of cleverness. It is chess-like.

was dimmed and there spread from China a new form of wisdom, cut off from the spiritual realms. It taught people to be prudent and look after their own material interests.

God and the angels had always intended that human spirits would fall into matter, but they were falling too fast and too far. Not only were they progressively being shut off from the spiritual realms and spiritual influences, but they were also progressively being cut off from one another. New forms of cruelty arose.

For the first time in history we hear of tyranny, slavery, exploitation, mass slaughter. There are famous carvings of atrocities, glorying in them, on the walls of temples at Karnak in Egypt. Because people no longer had the vision of the higher orders of angels ascending to the great Cosmic Mind, they came to see lower orders of the spiritual beings as the highest gods. They claimed one or other of these beings as the god of their own tribe or city – and in a strange and terrible reversal, the God of Abraham became a war god too.

Moses and the Gods of War

*'On the plane of illusion the divine fire
is the divine wrath.'*

Rudolf Steiner

*'Man is under the illusion that thoughts are enclosed
in his skull, but they are only reflected there.'*

Rudolf Steiner

The life of Moses sees a series of supernatural interventions on a scale and decisiveness that has few parallels. The supernatural attends Moses at every turn. Angels help him to put his shoulder to the great cosmic wheel and to push open the great cosmic door.

To begin with, an angel appeared to Moses in the burning bush and he became a wonder-worker. Later, when he was told to stretch out his hand, and with it his rod, Yahweh stretched out His hand and smote Egypt repeatedly with the plagues, culminating in the killing of the firstborn.[1] The Red Sea was parted by supernatural means to allow the Israelites through. God sent a pillar of smoke to guide the Israelites by day and a pillar of fire by night. When they were in need, He sent quail and manna from heaven, and he told Moses to strike the rock of Horeb with his hand, causing water to pour from it. Yahweh covered Mount Sinai with smoke and fire and talked to Moses there. Moses, Aaron and seventy elders saw a vision of Yahweh over a pavement of sapphire stone. Yahweh gave Moses sapphire tablets on which the command-ments were written 'with the finger of God'.[2]

Moses and epic demonstrations of divine power, (engraving from an illustration in
The Christian's New and Complete Family Bible, 1790)

Engraving from John Martin's *Seventh Plague of Egypt*, 1872.

When Moses came down the mountain a second time his face shone brightly, in a way that may remind us of the story of Enoch. The Tabernacle was built, a model of the whole cosmos, and the 'glory of the Lord' appeared in it before all the children of Israel.

But one day God informed Moses that he wasn't the wisest man on Earth. Moses was intrigued. God also told him where to find this wise man – at the 'confluence of the two seas'.[3]

We can identify this place as Bahrain, which means 'two seas' or 'twin waters'. Divers off the coast of Bahrain can still descend through sea water today to swim in streams of fresh water.[4] This mysterious phenomenon – caused by vents on the seabed which emit fresh water from vast underground lakes – is called 'the divine springs from which flow the paradoxes of life' in the commentaries on the Koran. In Islamic mysticism, the pure water is a manifestation of the spirit that 'in the beginning' gave rise to the opposite of spirit, which is to say matter.

The salt water, on the other hand, is a manifestation of this matter, and this coming together of opposites accounts for the mysterious and paradoxical quality of life.

We will return to this paradoxical quality, but here we may take it simply as a sign that the story we are about to hear is a strange one.

Moses set out with his servant to find the wise man. They travelled a long way along the seashore and by midday Moses was growing weary. He told his servant to prepare their meal. At this point the servant had to confess that when they'd stopped to rest earlier, he'd left the fish for their supper behind on a rock.

'What! You forgot it? We must go back and fetch it.'

'No, the strange thing is that the fish – which was well and truly dead, I was certain of it – was just lying there when a large wave crashed against the rock and a drop of water landed on it. Suddenly it came alive again and leapt from the rock into the sea!'

Moses recognized this was a vital clue. The seemingly miraculous rebirth of the fish meant that they had been close to the confluence of the two seas.

They retraced their steps and Moses was surprised to find sitting on the rock a wild-looking old man, bearded and dressed all in green. He looked forbidding, angry, perhaps even a little mad. He made no gesture of welcome or recognition.

'May I walk with you,' said Moses, 'so that you can teach me your superior wisdom?'

'You won't be able to keep up with me,' said the old man, 'and besides, you will understand nothing of what I do or say – nothing!'

'I'll ask God to help me understand,' said Moses. 'And I will obey you in all things.'

'If you must follow me around,' said the man, 'I have one condition: you must not question anything I do.'

Moses followed the old man as he set off along the shore with surprising speed. After a while they came to a harbour. The old man found a boat moored there. He sprang into it and stamped furiously on the bottom of it until water glugged in. As he stood back to admire his handiwork, the boat started sinking.

'What on Earth have you done?' said Moses. 'Do you want the owners of this boat to drown?'

'You have already forgotten your oath?' asked the old man.

Moses apologized.

They set off at the double and after a short while Moses saw a young man coming towards them from the other direction. He was astonished when, without warning, the old man drew a sword from somewhere within his cloak and ran him through, killing him.

As they stood over the bleeding corpse, Moses was breathless. 'Are you mad?' he said. 'You've killed an innocent man!'

The old man raised a reproving finger. 'What did I tell you? You can't bear God's wisdom, can you? You can't cope with it.'

Moses said that if he ever questioned the old man again, he'd accept that they would have to go their separate ways.

The old man moved off with great speed again.

In the evening they came to a small, isolated village. It appeared poverty-stricken. No one came out to greet them. The old man bustled over to a ruined wall and began to build it up again with prodigious energy. Moses dared not question him. When the wall was finished, he merely commented that the old man could have charged for all that work.

The old man said, 'This is where you and I go our separate ways, but before we part I will explain to you what I have done today. The boat belongs to a poor family. Local landowners are requisitioning all the boats in the area to fight a war. They won't bother with a boat that needs repairing. The boy I killed was full of evil intent. He was planning to convert his family to demon worship. Now a new, loving child will be born to his parents, who will be a joy to them all their lives. That wall belongs to young orphan boys. Their father had hidden some treasure under it and died before he had the chance to tell them. If the wall hadn't been repaired, the treasure would have come to light while the boys were still too young to defend themselves. Now they will find it at the right time.'

Moses kept his head bowed while he listened, wanting to concentrate and make sure he took it all in. When he looked up, the old man had disappeared.

Who is this strange figure to whom the mighty Moses defers? He reappears in different guises in the course of sacred history and we shall meet him again shortly.

*   *   *

The Old Testament has different names for different aspects of God, including the Elohim in the act of creation, and Adonai, or 'the Lord'. Yahweh represents a particular aspect of God to do with helping humanity to develop a capacity for reflection, for thinking. We saw in Chapter 8 that in earlier times the whole body was experienced as an organ of consciousness and of perception. As well as head consciousness people had a heart consciousness, a kidney consciousness (expressive of desire), and so on. This sense of different centres of consciousness within the human body was suppressed in the time of Yahweh, as humanity began to forge a 'mono-consciousness' envisaged as having its seat in the head.

Mount Sinai, where Yahweh made his revelation to Moses, is literally 'the mountain of the moon'. In esoteric terms, Yahweh is seen as reflecting the sun's light by means of the moon, a cosmic arrangement that makes human reflection possible.[5]

Modern science has come to appreciate how necessary the moon has been for the development of life on Earth. It is responsible for the tilt of the Earth that keeps our climate within the narrow band suitable for organic life. Science has also begun to measure something that folk wisdom has always appreciated – the effect of the phases of the moon on human psychology. A statistical survey on lunar cycles and human aggression carried out in Florida by the *Journal of Clinical Psychiatry* and published in 1978 showed that violent assault and murders peaked around the full moon.[6] But esoteric and mystical philosophy also proposes something altogether more fundamental: *that it is only because of the positions and cycles of the sun and moon in relation to each other and to the Earth that we are able to think.* The moon reflects down to us the light but also spiritual life of the sun, and because reflected light is weaker than direct light, we can as a result consider spiritual influences that would otherwise dazzle and overwhelm us. Because of the moon we have the capacity for free thought and free will that the angels – who see God directly – do not.[7]

The second of the ten commandments brought down from the mountain of the moon, not to 'make any graven image or any likeness of anything that is heaven above' is a commandment to stop thinking in pictures and start thinking conceptually and in abstract terms. It is interesting that scripts said to have been dictated by angels are usually pictorial in content, not conceptual. Again, it may be that we are capable of conceptual thinking in a way that angels are not – and that this is part of what they need from us.[8]

*   *   *

It was in about 2500 BC, at the beginning of the period that historians call the Late Bronze Age, that Moses travelled towards the Promised Land, carrying with him this newly developing mental faculty. He caused great havoc and destruction among the tribes that stood in his way.

The king of the Moabites, afraid for himself and his people, sent messengers to a seer called Balaam. When Balaam eventually reached the king, he told him the last thing he wanted to hear: that Israel would succeed in battle.

This turned out to be true. God sent an angel out before the Israelites to drive out the Moabites, the Canaanites and other indigenous peoples. Some parts of the biblical narrative giving an account of the Israelites' progress towards the Promised Land make uncomfortable reading. In one grisly episode thousands of Israelites were slaughtered on God's instructions. God sent plagues and deadly, fiery serpents. Chapter 31 of the Book of Numbers makes outstandingly hard reading. Inspired by God and commanded by Moses, the Israelites killed all the local kings, took women and children as prisoners and burned the cities. Some commanders were reprimanded for allowing the indigenous womenfolk to live and told to kill all male children. Thirty-two thousand virgins were kept as slaves.

Rainer Maria Rilke, the great poet of angels in modern times, was asked whether, if he cried out to the hierarchies of angels and an angel responded and suddenly held him to his heart, he would be utterly destroyed by it. 'Beauty,' he said at the beginning of the *Duino Elegies*, 'is nothing but the beginning of a terror we are scarcely able to bear.' In Rilke's poetry, angels are the agents of the care the cosmos has for us – but we are ill-equipped to understand them or their work. The fire of divine love may appear as a terrifying and destructive force.

The prophet Balaam was riding his donkey to see the king of the Moabites, but the donkey refused to cross a bridge. The prophet beat him with his staff until something extraordinary happened: the donkey turned his head, looked back to where Balaam was sitting on top of him and said: 'What have I ever done to you to make you hit me like that?'

'You won't obey me and you've deliberately hurt me.'

'You've known me all your life. Have I ever disobeyed you or hurt you before?'

Then a veil was lifted from Balaam's eyes and suddenly he saw what the donkey was seeing: an angel was standing in the pathway with a sword poised to strike Balaam.

Balaam threw himself on the ground before the angel, who now spoke to him. 'Why did you strike your donkey three times? Your donkey saw me and turned aside three times. If he hadn't, I would have killed you.' (from Numbers 22:21–38)

So, when reading accounts of atrocities in the Old Testament it may be hard to refrain from judging Yahweh in modern, human terms – hard, indeed, not to make the same sort of moral judgements Moses made when he encountered the wise old man – but, as a medieval Arabic saying points out, ascribing human morality to God can be as crudely anthropomorphic as imagining that He has a beard or smokes a pipe.

The Yahweh of the Old Testament *is* warlike, full of wrath. Perhaps it is that He is fiercely protective of the first tentative, delicately flickering flames of the human intellect? These flames were always in danger of being snuffed out, as the people he has chosen to be its crucible made their perilous journey.

As the Israelites neared the Promised Land, Moses's apprentice, Joshua, encountered a stranger and challenged him: 'Are you for us or against us?'

'I am captain of the Host of the Lord,' replied the stranger, identifying himself as the Archangel Michael.

Joshua prostrated himself.

'Take off your shoes,' Michael told him, 'for the place you are standing on is Holy ground.'

Guided by an angel, Joshua took the city of Jericho and its inhabitants were slaughtered too.[9]

If great spiritual beings no longer manifest themselves on the material plane as frequently as they once had, it seems that in the Late Bronze Age they still appeared at great turning points in history. In the historical books of the Old Testament angels not only take part in spiritual warfare, they also take part in battles where flesh is cut and blood is spilled: 'That night the angel of the Lord went out and put to death a hundred and eighty five thousand men in the Assyrian camp.' (2 Kings 19.35) But although the Old Testament alludes to angels intervening in battle, it doesn't give us much of a sense of what it was like to be there.

*　　　　*　　　　*

We can perhaps find more of this sense in the epics of Homer, writing about the siege of Troy, which took place perhaps some two hundred years after the siege of Jericho.[10]

There are some nights, Homer writes, when the air is still and cloudless and the stars stand out in all their glory – and this helps us to think great thoughts. In the *Iliad* Homer looks down on the plains and sees how the gods of the stars and planets shape events below. You can feel him exulting in his power as a storyteller as he describes the gods exulting in their own powers:

Athene and Apollo turned themselves into vultures, perched high on a massive oak, enjoying the sight of the soldiers on the plain ranged against each other, rank after rank like wave after wave, rippling and sparkling with nodding helmets of horsehair plumes, glittering swords, shields and spears of ash, beams of bronze flashing out everywhere into the infinite depths of the sky. The earth was shaken by the feet of marching men with murder in their hearts . . .

Homer takes us, too, down into the midst of the battle to see the gods fighting at close quarters. His descriptions take us into the heart of the action and we see what happens when – to use the famous phrase quoted by Shakespeare – the gods 'let slip the dogs of war':

Struck by a crushing blow on the thigh, Prince Aeneas fell to his knees, steadying himself with one hand, as darkness began to fall within him like nightfall. Then Aphrodite swept down and gathered up her son in her white arms and threw her shimmering robe around him, so that flying spears clattered harmlessly to the ground around him . . . Ares was striding like a giant amongst the soldiers, striking out with his great death-dealing hands, when the spear of the hero Diomedes thrust up into the lower part of his abdomen. The war god let out a terrible cry of pain as loud as nine or ten thousand men, so that the soldiers on both sides of the battlefield quaked with fear. Then the god swirled back up into the sky like a tornado of smoke . . . Zeus donned his golden armour and seized his golden whip, and mounting his blazing chariot flicked this whip at his two great white horses with golden manes, and he came careering out of the sky, steering a course between the ground and the stars, and he hurled a thunder bolt down amongst the Greeks, scattering them and causing the colour to drain from the cheeks of every soldier, turning their hearts to water.[11]

The way that consciousness evolves through history was discussed by German philosophers, beginning in the early nineteenth century. (Later we will look at Hegel's extraordinary account of the evolution of consciousness in relation to Napoleon.) This way of thinking about the evolution of consciousness received support from an unexpected source in 1976, when Julian Jaynes of Princeton University in the States published *The Origins of Consciousness in the Breakdown of the Bi-Cameral Mind*. This book attracted a lot of attention and continues to be controversial. Jaynes points out how easy it is to read modern consciousness into ancient literature like the *Iliad*. He argues that if you read the text carefully you can see that there is in it little or no notion of introspection. In Homer's text, he argues, there is no language to describe mental states. The men and women do not think about what they are going to do and then decide. What we experience as impulses of the interior mind, they experienced as exterior – as coming to them from the outside. Achilles does not decide not to strike Agamemnon – Athene pulls him back by the hair.

What is more curious, perhaps, is that the men and women of that time seem to have no sense of a private mental space as we do today, but only of a communal mental space. Therefore it is not just lone individuals who see the gods of war and wisdom striding through the ranks of the enemy and pushing them back, it is everyone present on the battlefield. These are evidently what we might – and Jaynes does – classify as 'collective hallucinations'. The siege of Troy and the complex civilizations of the Bronze Age were directed by these collective hallucinations.[12]

A collective hallucination is an event which cannot happen in the universe of scientific materialism – except as an extremely unlikely coincidence of individual hallucinations or as a mass hysteria that deludes people into believing they are hallucinating the same thing. In the universe of idealism on the other hand, the appearance of a god or an angel to a multitude of people may be a manifestation of a higher reality. In idealism we can share a mental space even if it is partially and temporarily interrupted by matter. According to the contemporary

Greek gods in battle (engraving taken from the Pergamon Altar, Berlin Museum).

accounts, these 'collective hallucinations' were directing battles and ordering highly complex societies.

When we read accounts of human experience written in earlier times we often find that they assume the world is an arena for supernatural events and that people regularly experience visions, collective hallucinations and other manifestations of the supernatural. In fact the literature of the ancient world is forthright and unquestioning on the subject of the appearance of gods and angels, either to individuals or to groups. Their appearance before large groups of people is wonderful and magnificent, but to these writers and their contemporaries it is not unexpected. The writers of these accounts are not trying to pull the wool over our eyes. They haven't even begun to suspect that the world might be other than they describe it. If the appearance of gods and angels was a delusion, it was a mass delusion shared by the whole of humanity. That was their reality.[13]

Solomon, Sex and Beauty

'Who is she that looketh forth as the morning, fair
as the Moon, clear as the Sun, and terrible as an
army with banners?'

Song of Solomon 6.10

We have seen Homer describe in glorious language that ripples on the page how the gods intervened in battle.

He describes the gods intervening in other ways too. In the *Iliad* he has a wonderful description of Paris, whose elopement with Helen had brought about the ten-year siege:

Paris quickly put on his shining, bronze armour and ran down from his house high in the walls. He ran through the town like a stallion that has broken away and gallops across the fields in triumph towards his favourite bathing place. He tosses his head so that his mane flows back over his shoulders, and off he goes, running so fast his hooves barely touch the ground. And Paris arrived like this, awesome in his armour, shining like the sun and laughing, and he knew that he was beautiful.

Paris and Helen belonged together because they were beautiful. He had visited the court of her husband, Menelaus. He had looked into her eyes and seen his destiny there.

In this era, at the beginning of what historians call the Iron Age, the Venus serpent inside the human body began to thrash with unredeemed sexual energy. We saw in Chapter 3 how the cosmos was put together so we would crave happiness. The story of Moses is the description of how we came to have another great desire running through us in an unstoppable torrent – the craving for justice, for fairness.

In the stories of Helen, David and Solomon, we see these two great cravings clash.

Worldly beauty is not a tranquil thing, even though a beautiful person may look tranquil and composed. 'Beauty is not only a mysterious thing,' said Dostoyevsky, 'it is a terrible, frightening thing.' Beauty is where all the contradictions clash, 'where God and the devil contend – and the field of battle is the human heart'. Great beauty attracts demonic powers.

We live in a paradoxical world, a world of opposites yoked together so that they can be hard to distinguish. Beauty can make us happy. Somewhere deep inside us, it stirs a vision of creation as it could, perhaps should, be. It can charge us with a sense of purpose and meaning. It can lead us to a feeling of being at home in the world. The ecstasy in physical love that beauty can inspire can be very like a mystical experience.

But if we are deceived by it, beauty can bring about the fall of empires.

Good people, even very great people, can behave badly.

*   *   *

Like his contemporary Odysseus, David slew a one-eyed giant. He grew up to become the first king to unite the settled tribes of Israel in one kingdom. He was a great king, but a flawed one – loving Bathsheba he sent her husband away to fight in a war so he could have her to himself.

David and his son Solomon both reigned for forty years. Solomon would build the temple his father had promised to build.

One night Solomon had a dream in which God asked what He should give him. Solomon considered the question before giving his reply. *If I ask for gold, silver, jewels and so on,* he thought, *God will give them to me and that will be that. But if I ask for wisdom, I will be able to earn riches myself and much more besides . . .*

So he said, 'Lord, give to your servant an understanding heart.'

When he awoke, he wandered in the fields. He heard the chatter of the birds, the crowing of the rooster, the braying of the ass, and he found he could understand what they were saying.

Solomon is traditionally said to be the author of what theologians call the 'wisdom books' of the Bible: Proverbs and Ecclesiastes. This 'wisdom literature' is not primarily concerned with spiritual matters. Proverbs give practical rules for a happy and successful life. This is what proverbs from any tradition are doing when they advise you to look before you leap or make a stitch in time. In his dream Solomon acted prudentially, and when he awoke he continued in this vein. The Talmud says that he had the power of understanding nature, the properties of trees and plants, and that he taught 'concerning the beasts, the fowls and concerning the creeping things, and concerning fishes' (I Kings 4.33). In the Koran he was able to bend the world to his will in many ways, including controlling the *jinn*.[1]

Solomon's reign brought his people unprecedented wealth and prosperity. Trade opened up new channels for wealth to flow in and also new ideas. Solomon built his palace and then four years into his reign he began to build his Temple. A thousand labourers cut down cedar and juniper trees. They hauled logs down from the Lebanese mountains and over to Jerusalem. Thousands more workers quarried the local limestone and carved rough ashlars into perfectly cut stones.

Solomon's Temple was not as massive as you might expect of a building that looms so large in the collective imagination. According to the measurements recorded in the Bible, it was only the size of a small country church. But what awed people about it was that in its Holy of Holies, in its thick darkness, lived God Himself.

The Temple was made to be God's body. Like the temples of Egypt and the Christian cathedrals of Europe, it was built according to ideal human proportions – not just the shape and proportions of the physical body but also the qualities of the higher, spiritual bodies. The four, seven and eightfold shapes found in temples and cathedrals work on our soul and spirit and through them our physiology. It is possible to feel this when walking into even a small country church. Craftsmen of earlier generations had absorbed this working, spiritual knowledge.

Martin Luther wrote about the threefold structure of the Temple that revealed itself as you moved from the vestibule through the long hall to the Holy of Holies. This, he said, reflected the threefold nature of the human being – physical body, soul and spirit. Then the light of God was revealed in the seven-candled candelabra that stood in front

Interior and pillar from Rosslyn chapel
(nineteenth-century engraving).

of it, so that the rays of the seven Thoughts of God were working as one.

The twin pillars were fashioned by Hiram Abiff, master craftsman and worker in bronze, the architect Solomon had employed to design the Temple and supervise its construction. Called Jachin and Boaz, these pillars stood outside Solomon's Temple, marking the furthest point of the sun's rising at the equinoxes. But they also represented smaller human-scale rhythms which interlock with the cosmic rhythms like cogs in a clock – the rhythms of human evolution, life and death, night and day, and breathing in and out.

The red column, Jachin, represented the absorbing of the oxygen in red blood – and also the absorbing of spiritual influence, of Self by self. This had happened freely before humans developed material bodies. Now it happens in between incarnations when the spirit rises up into the spiritual worlds in order to be refreshed, and it happens, too, in a smaller way at night when the spirit emerges from the physical body.

The red column was the Tree of Life, representing the animal life that red blood makes possible. The blue column was the Tree of Knowledge. It represented carbonated blood and what we as individuals contribute to cosmic and human evolution by our thoughts and deeds during our lifetime, during the day and moment by moment, by what we decide to think and do. It is what we take with us into life after death, and what we contribute to the mysterious alchemical process which is the gradual evolution of humankind.

The Temple of Solomon was not indestructible, but it looked forward to a temple that would be indestructible. It was a prophecy in stone. In the future, after the world and humanity had passed through many stages of evolution, and when the human body had been spiritualized, according to the process alluded to in the pillars, and when humanity had rediscovered its ideal nature, then it would be indestructible. This is the Masonic wisdom built into the Temple: as the craftsman carved the stone, divided it with his compasses and penetrated it with his chisel, so will the human being be mastered and made perfect.

Solomon's wisdom, his wealth and his amazing buildings with strange wonder-working properties, attracted people from afar.

: FORTVNA : FENESTRALIS

The king is surprised as good fortune comes in by the window.
(Emblem by Jean Cousin, 1568.)

The Queen of Sheba was famous for her beauty. She arrived with gifts of gold, frankincense and myrrh. Solomon waited for her in a room made of mirrors – the walls, the ceiling and the floor – and when she first saw him she thought he was standing on water.

Sheba was shy of walking on this glass. She had a secret that a mirrored floor would reveal – that her feet were webbed like the feet of geese.

The king beckoned her forward. She now saw she had to cross a stream to reach him, but as she was about to step on a wooden bridge, something made her hesitate. She stood still for a while. She was having a premonition, and she wanted to wait until she was sure she understood it. A moment later she realized what it was that she was being told: that one day a god would be crucified on this piece of wood.

So she stepped sideways, avoiding stepping on the bridge and choosing to wade through the stream instead. When she emerged on the other side, she was overjoyed to see that her feet had been healed.

Solomon came forward to meet her.

Solomon and Sheba were attracted to each other. 'I am black,' she said. 'My beloved is mine, and I am his: he feedeth me amongst lilies.'

She teased him with riddles. She gave him an emerald with a curved hole in the middle and challenged him to push a thread through it. Solomon sent a silkworm to crawl through the hole drawing with it a silken thread.

There is another twist to the story of Solomon and the Queen of Sheba. We are excavating the deeper layers of the human psyche here, aggregates of spiritual turmoil.

Sheba met someone else, another kindred spirit: Hiram Abiff. As queen of the Sabeans, Sheba would have worshipped Venus under the name of Astarte. As a Phoenician, Hiram would have worshipped Astarte too, constructing the Temple so that at certain times the light of Venus rising would shine in through a dormer window into the Holy of Holies. Masonic temples are still built with the same orientation today and as a candidate for initiation is born into the brotherhood his attention is drawn to the rising of the five-pointed star of Venus.

The Temple was nearing completion and, visiting it, Sheba asked Solomon if she could meet the man who had designed this marvel. Solomon was reluctant, but she insisted.

When Hiram was summoned, he gave the queen a glance that melted her inside. Solomon noted this glance, and he also saw the queen look away with downcast eyes, keeping her thoughts to herself.

She then asked Solomon if she could meet the builders too.

'Impossible,' said Solomon. He explained that they were scattered all over the place and, besides, far too busy. But Hiram jumped up on a stone, holding up the sign of the tau cross, and immediately hundreds of men swarmed in front of them.

Solomon knew that Hiram was planning the unveiling of his greatest architectural and alchemical marvel: the molten sea. Knowing, too, that the queen was to be present at its unveiling, Solomon appointed three apprentices to work on this project. He had good reason to believe these three were incompetent, and he hoped they would spoil Hiram's demonstration.

On the day the molten sea was to be cast, when molten metal and water were to be poured into the mould, Solomon, the Queen of Sheba and many nobles gathered to watch. But because the apprentices poured the molten metal and water in the wrong proportions, the casting went disastrously wrong and a scalding cloud of steam enveloped the crowd of spectators.

Hiram felt humiliated. His reputation was destroyed. But that night he had a vision of an angel who presented him with a hammer and golden triangle. When he awoke he found these artefacts lying next to him and he understood that he was to wear the triangle around his neck. It had a word written on it, and he understood that this was the secret name of God. If pronounced perfectly, it would return humanity to the state of perfection it had enjoyed before the Fall.

His optimism restored, Hiram Abiff set to work again. He would make another attempt to manufacture the molten sea, this time using the hammer that had been given him in his dream.

One day, when this work was well on the way to completion, he met the Queen of Sheba in a courtyard of the palace. They confessed their love for each other and made secret plans to leave the kingdom. They planned to meet up again somewhere they could be safe.

Solomon did not directly ask the three apprentices to kill Hiram. He merely wondered out loud who would rid him of this turbulent man.

That evening they attacked Hiram, demanding to know the secrets of a Master Mason.

'Your life or the secrets!' they cried.

'My life you can take, my integrity, never,' he replied, before one of the ruffians felled him with a single blow to the head.

Just before he died Hiram was able to toss the golden triangle down a well. And that is how the Word came to be lost.

As we shall see, the quest for the lost Word is, like the quest for the Holy Grail, intimately tied up with the mysteries of human physiology.[2]

The significance of Venus to the writers of the Old Testament is perhaps not obvious. But Psalm 19's description of the sun coming out of his chamber like a bridegroom is based on an earlier Canaanite passage describing the sacred marriage of the sun and Venus. Perhaps more interesting and more important, as author Robert Lomas has pointed out, is the frequent recurrence of the number forty – the number of years in the Venus cycle – in the Old Testament account of history. For example, Israel wandered in the desert for forty years, Saul reigned for forty years, David reigned for forty years, Solomon reigned for forty years. According to 1 Kings 6.1, the Jerusalem Temple was built 480 years (12 Venus cycles) after the Exodus from Egypt. The historian Josephus recorded the tradition by which Solomon began to build the Temple 144 years (36 Venus cycles) after the Flood. Clearly this recurrence is meaningful. Either the writers were aware of a tradition that the movements of Venus exerted a controlling influence on the pattern of history and therefore fudged the dates to fit. *Or Venus does indeed have such an influence and the authors of the Bible recorded it accurately.*[3]

Elijah in between the Worlds

Three apostles accompany Jesus up a mountain. Suddenly they see him in the sky. He is shining – 'transfigured'.

Moses and Elijah are up in the sky beside him, and he is talking to them, though the apostles cannot hear what is being said.

This transfiguring is the spiritualizing of the body talked about in the mystical teachings of all the world's religions. The Transfiguration looks forward to a time when all human bodies will have been spiritualized in the same way. Moses and Elijah are beside Jesus because of the important part they play in this process.

Moses was an almost godlike figure, a thunderer who attended some of the most spectacular supernatural interventions in history. Elijah was also a thunderer. Fired by righteous anger, he too called down fire from heaven to kill the enemies of Israel. He seemed to live in storms and Slavic tribes in eastern Europe believed him to be the same figure their ancestors had worshipped as Perun, the god of thunder and lightning.

And, like a god, Elijah was not a constant presence. He came and went in an unpredictable and mysterious way.[1]

Elijah first appeared in the reign of Ahab, king of Israel. Ahab was a successful king who had built up the wealth and the army of the nation. He had defeated a neighbouring king in battle and made a strategic marriage to Jezebel, daughter of the king of Tyre. She was a follower of Baal, the great spirit of Saturn. In Judaeo-Christian terms, he is Satan of course. She persuaded Ahab to build a temple to Baal, and her followers began to persecute the people who remained faithful to the God of Moses.

It was then that Elijah appeared at court in order to rebuke the king. Elijah had long, unkempt hair. He wore a black hairy coat and a leather belt. Ahab mocked the disconcerting tramp-like figure. In return Elijah cursed the land: 'There shall be neither dew nor rain these years, unless I say so . . . '

Abraham and Moses had been the political leaders of their people as well as their spiritual leaders. By the time of Elijah, the people were settled in the Promised Land and there had been a transition. The king was a politician by nature. He had – and was – compromised. Elijah came to his court as one of the first Hebrew prophets expressing their anger at leaders who fall away from spiritual ideals. These prophets were severe. Like Zarathustra, they said what people in authority did not want to hear.

Elijah disappeared as suddenly as he had appeared. He knew he had to hide if he wanted to survive. In a land blighted by drought because of his curse, he was a solitary, even lonely figure. He seemed to live in a visionary state, a sort of world between the worlds.

One day as he was wandering through the parched wasteland he came to a brook, and ravens brought him bread and meat.[2]

Elijah wearily moved on. He called out to an old woman he saw gathering sticks, asking her to bring him a cup of water. Then, as she turned to fetch it, he called out again, asking her to bring him something to eat. She explained that she only had a handful of meal in a barrel and a little bowl of oil, and that she needed this because she and her son were starving. Elijah told her that if she made some cake out of the meal and gave him a morsel of it, she and her son would want for nothing. She did as he asked, and the barrel then seemed to have an endless supply of meal and the bowl magically replenished itself too.

But the boy still grew weaker and after a while he died. The woman said to Elijah, 'Did you come to slay my son?'

Elijah took the boy's corpse to the loft where he lived sometimes and laid him in his bed. They stayed in the loft for three days and three nights. Somewhere deep inside the boy there was a spark of life . . .

He felt he was being shaken awake. He was lying in the bottom of a ship that was being tossed about on the ocean. He was being shaken awake by the crew members, who were wild-eyed and scared to death. They were speaking an unfamiliar language but he gathered they thought he would be able to explain to them what had caused the storm – and what they could do to cause it to abate. They asked angrily if they were being punished for his sake? Had he committed some great crime that was bringing about this misfortune?

The boy told the sailors to throw him overboard. He felt the waves close over him, the darkness of the deep surround him and weeds wrap themselves around his head.

Suddenly a great whale loomed up and swallowed him and he remained in the belly of the whale for three days and nights, until his soul was fainting in him and he cried out to God . . .

And he awoke in an attic to find an old man with long hair and a hairy coat staring down at him.

Jonah and the whale

What did the boy think when he was brought back to life, to sunlight and the world above ground? Elijah is a fierce, unpredictable figure, but children seem to intuit that underneath he is benevolent. In Jewish households at the start of Passover a fifth cup is reserved for Elijah at a ceremonial meal called the Seder. The door to the street is opened,

Elijah is invited in and children may look for a ripple on the surface of the wine in this cup as a sign of his presence.[3]

The boy in Elijah's loft would grow up to become a prophet. Mystical tradition reveals his secret identity: he was Jonah, famous for his story about the whale and how it was that he came back from the dead.

Meanwhile the drought in the land of Israel was biting harder. Cattle and horses were dying and the people were suffering badly. After two years King Ahab sent out a search party to try to find the strange man who had predicted the drought. Eventually, after a long search, Elijah was found and persuaded to go to the court.

'Is it you who brings this trouble on Israel?' the king demanded to know.

Elijah told him that trouble had come about because he, the king, had followed Baal. Then he challenged the priests of Baal to a contest on the top of Mount Carmel to show the difference between their god and the God of Israel.

From dawn to dusk 450 priests of Baal called on their god, invoking him and asking him to set light to wood they had laid under a sacrificial bullock. They chanted and flayed themselves to feed the sacrifice with their blood – to no avail.

Then Elijah also made an altar and prayed, and straightaway fire came down from heaven and set up a blaze beneath his sacrifice. The sky blackened, there was crack of thunder and blessed rain began to fall on the parched earth.

'Get up,' he said to Ahab. 'Eat and drink, because there is an abundance of rain.'

There was much rejoicing in the capital, but for a second time Elijah knew he had to run and hide. Jezebel, the priestess of Baal, would certainly try to kill him now.

On the run in the wilderness Elijah eventually sat down heavily in the shade of a juniper tree. He told God that he had enough, that he wanted to die. Totally exhausted, he fell asleep.

An angel touched him and told him to get up and eat. He awoke and by his head he found a cake baking on coals and a jug of water. He ate and drank and lay down to sleep again, and an angel touched him a second time and told him to arise and eat, because he had a terrible journey ahead of him.

Elijah went into the wilderness for forty days and forty nights. He travelled to the mountain where Moses had heard God speak to him from a burning bush. Would God speak to him with the same clarity he had spoken to Moses?

Elijah was sheltering in a cave on the side of the mountain when a great wind began to tear the land apart. Great boulders began to bound down the mountainside past the entrance to the cave.

But Elijah knew that God was not in the wind.

Then the whole mountain was shaken by an earthquake, but Elijah knew that this was not what he had hoped for. God was not in the earthquake.

Then a sheet of fire lit up the entrance to the cave, but Elijah knew that God was not in the lightning.

The bushes in front of the cave were now on fire, but God was not in those burning bushes as He had been for Moses.

Elijah's face fell and he wrapped it in his mantle. And as he did so, he heard a still small voice inside him, saying, 'What are you doing here, Elijah?'

This voice, which he recognized was truly the voice of God, told him to continue his mission and to appoint his successor.

Later he walked past a man ploughing the fields with oxen. The man stopped what he was doing and followed him. This was his successor, Elisha.

The story of the 'still small voice' is an account of one of the most profound turning points in human history. We saw in earlier chapters how in the religious account of history, the account seen through the lens of idealism, the formation of the physical world went hand in hand with the equally gradual formation of a distinctively human consciousness. We saw how in Homer's descriptions of the siege of Troy and in the biblical account of the parting of Dead Sea the divine operated 'out there'. Now, with Elijah, the sphere of divine operation has shifted inwardly.

The fire that had set light to that bush was, Elijah now saw, also a spark inside him, lit within the cave of his skull.

Elijah was the herald of an inner dawn.

Like Noah and Enoch, Elijah did not die in the ordinary way. Like Enoch, he retreated further into the mountains and was carried up to heaven in a fiery chariot drawn by fiery horses. This was watched only by Elisha, whom he had chosen as his successor and onto whom, as a mark of this, he let slip his mantle.[4]

The Bible tells us that a few years after Elijah's death the king received a letter from Elijah rebuking him and prophesying plague. This is not a misprint, as some have speculated, but confirmation that the fact of Elijah's physical death did not diminish – and does not diminish – his ability to work in the world. It is said that with four beats of his wings he can cross the surface of the world – because he is an angel. The Torah says that sometimes he looks like an ordinary man, sometimes he takes on the appearance of an Arab, sometimes of a horseman, now a court official, now a prostitute.

In Jewish tradition he appeared to teach many great teachers, and some people say that in Arab traditions he appears as the disconcerting old man, Khdir, the Green One, who took Moses on a hair-raising journey.[5]

This is not the last time we shall meet him.

*   *   *

Assyrian armies often seemed to be on the point of overrunning Israel but were repeatedly frustrated. It seemed to the Assyrian king that his enemies always knew in advance where he was going to deploy his forces. It was as if they could overhear what he was saying in the privacy of his bedchamber. Suspecting some kind of super-natural intervention at work, he sent a spy to discover the whereabouts of the famous prophet Elisha. Then he sent a large army to the hilltop town where Elisha was staying.

So it came about one morning that Elisha and his young servant awoke and looked down to find the town and the hill completely surrounded by an Assyrian army.

The servant was terrified. 'Master, what on Earth are we going to do?'

'Fear not,' said Elisha. 'We have more up here on our side than they have down there.' Then he prayed, saying, 'Lord, I pray thee, open his eyes that he may see.'

The young man looked again and saw that vast armies of angels in chariots of fire were ranged around them to protect them.

The eyes of the soldiers at the foot of the hill were blinded that morning so that Elisha and his servant could walk through them unharmed.

Soon, however, Israel was surrounded on all sides. As long as Elisha remained alive, his mere presence was enough to keep the enemy armies at bay, but on the day of his burial, Israel was invaded.

*   *   *

The history told in the Old Testament shows angels intervening in the affairs of men and women, both in great public events like the Exodus and later in the period of the settlement and periods of exile.

Engraving from *Tobias and the Angel* by Antonio del Pollaiolo. During the Assyrian captivity in about 700 BC an old man called Tobit was blinded. According to the Book of Tobit he sent his son Tobias on a journey to fetch some money that he had left in the care of a friend. Tobias took with him as a companion a man called Azarius, who was the Archangel Raphael in disguise. On their return to Tobit and his anxiously waiting wife Anna, Raphael enabled Tobias to cure his father's blindness. Angels are an expression of the cosmos's care for us; in ancient Jewish lore it was Raphael who taught Noah the art and science of healing herbs.

Angels are shown intervening in the lives the good and the great, like Elijah, Jonah, Elisha and Daniel, but also in the lives of the humble, such as Tobit, Anna and Tobias.

We will see later evidence that both these things are equally true today.

Fiery two-winged wheels. Thrones. (From *Christian Iconography* by Adolphe Napoleon, 1843.)

The prophet Isaiah (engraving taken from Michelangelo's frescoes in the Sistine Chapel). The Seraphim are traditionally depicted as angels with six wings, as they appear in Isaiah 6, 1–7: I saw also the Lord sitting upon a throne, high and lifted up, and his train filled the temple. Above it stood the Seraphim: each one had six wings; with two he covered his face, and with two he covered his feet, and with two he did fly. Then flew one of the Seraphim unto me, having a live coal in his hand, which he had taken with the tongs from off the altar: And he laid it upon my mouth, and said, Lo, this hath touched thy lips; and thine iniquity is taken away, and thy sin purged.

Ezekiel's vision of the Cherubim. 'And I looked, and, behold, a whirlwind came out of the north, a great cloud, and a fire enfolding itself . . . out of the midst thereof came the likeness of four living creatures . . . As for the likeness of their faces, they four had the face of a man, and the face of a lion, on the right side: and they four had the face of an ox on the left side; they four also had the face of an eagle.' (Ezekiel 1.4–10) The four Cherubim are the angels of the constellations at the four cardinal points – Aquarius, Leo, Taurus and Scorpio – which work together to fix matter and also mark the four great turning points in the year. (Engraving from Matthew Merian's Bible of 1630.)

When Jews were again being held in captivity, this time in Babylon, 597–538 BC, the prophet Daniel was thrown into a den of lions and the cave was blocked shut for the night. In the morning Daniel was unharmed, because, he said, an angel had stopped the lions' mouths. (Engraving from a nineteenth-century Bible.)

The Buddha's Story

Jorge Luis Borges, the Argentinian short story writer, essayist and poet, liked this story told by the Buddha:

> A man was wounded in battle. He was lying on the field in agony, an arrow embedded in his side. His friends and supporters were tending him. They all knew the arrow had to be pulled out or he would die, but it was a risky procedure and the wounded man was anxious. He was in increasing pain and fearful and he wanted it to be done right, or more precisely he wanted to *be sure* it was done right. So he asked where the arrow had come from. 'What's it made of?' he asked. Then 'How long is it? Who was the archer?' and '*What caste is he*?'
>
> But while he was asking these questions and his friends were trying to answer them, he slipped away and died.
>
> The Buddha told this story to his pupils. 'I will teach you how to pull out the arrow,' he said.
>
> 'But what is the arrow?' they asked.
>
> 'The arrow is the universe.'

This is a story, like *Sleeping Beauty*, that pulls the world inside out. We think the world holds and sustains us, but according to the Buddha really it is killing us. We can get caught up in it and think it is everything there is. We ask the wrong questions and get lost in a labyrinth of deadening thoughts.

But in the context of the wider and greater spiritual reality, this physical world is a small thing. When the arrow is pulled out of us, the world will be pulled inside out and we will be able to see the greater spiritual reality.

The Buddha's own life story is another version of the story of the man shot by the arrow.

The queen of a small kingdom in northern India had a dream that she was carried on the wind on a long journey to a lake in the Himalayas. There a white elephant, wise and powerful and with six tusks, entered her left side. She was being 'overshadowed'.[1]

Later the pregnant queen set off to stay with her parents, feeling that her time was near. Her mother would look after her, she thought. On the night of the full moon in May she was passing through gardens and orchards. She went over to look at some flowering trees. It was time. A fig tree leaned towards her so she could grasp it and steady herself. She looked down to see that her son had already been born and was standing on his feet.

Siddhartha took four steps to the north, south, east and west and announced his arrival with the roar of a lion: 'I am the greatest, I am the first, I have been born for all that lives!'

That night all the creatures in the woods and orchards were silent and at peace.

The baby was born the size of a six-month-old child and grew with astonishing speed. He quickly became a handsome athlete, a bowman and wrestler like Rama and as lovable as Krishna. His smile was dazzling, his eyes holding all other eyes. The scholars in the temple were astounded by his wisdom when he was still a boy. At sixteen he married a beautiful princess and they had a son.

All the while his father sought to protect him from the world. He wanted to shelter his son from life's harsher realities, to wrap him up in cotton wool. Siddhartha was dressed in the finest, softest silk and wherever he went servants held parasols over him to protect him from the sun. He would recall: 'I was delicate – so delicate!' If he ever felt like venturing out of the palace, the roads before him and his gilded chariot were made clean and beautiful, bedecked with flowers, banners and flags. Beautiful, shiny, happy people pushed forward to meet him.

Every sign of life's sadness and ugliness was cleared away. Yet as he matured, something in him rebelled against all this pampering, and one day he spied something horrible through the slats of a wall.

What he saw filled him with fear – was it a demon? It looked semi-human, but scarred and twisted, red-eyed, moving with ugly, jerky insect-like steps. Siddhartha demanded to know what it was. His charioteer didn't want to disobey the king's orders, but eventually he had to admit: 'This is a human being. He was a baby once, then a young man like you, but now all his strength and beauty have gone and it's painful for him just to move.'

'How is it possible?' said Siddhartha. 'How can the world be made in this way – to create such suffering?'

From then on Siddhartha was more observant and soon he noticed a woman covered in leprous sores lying in a ditch. Again he was appalled that such things could happen in the world and the charioteer had to explain that anyone could fall ill at any time. Siddhartha wondered how people in the neighbourhood could be laughing and singing and carrying on as normal when one of their kind was suffering in this way just around the corner.

Then he saw a man with waxy white skin being carried by other men. The charioteer had to explain that the man was dead and was being carried to the funeral pyre.

'*Dead*?' said Siddhartha, thoroughly alarmed. 'Is he the only one? Are there any other people in the world who are "dead" like this?'

The charioteer had to explain that everyone died.

Siddhartha saw that the world his father had constructed for him was unreal, and it seemed wrong to him that some people should live in the way they did in the face of such terrible, universal suffering. He wanted to understand it – and more than that, he wanted to put a stop to it.

Later Siddhartha and his charioteer met a travelling monk, wearing a simple robe and carrying a begging bowl. His eyes were shining, full of a deep peace.

'Who is that man?' said Siddhartha. 'Why does he look so peaceful?'

'That is a holy man,' said the charioteer. 'He has given up everything: family, company, wealth, position, ambition – everything. He eats by begging. He lives alone, seeking enlightenment.'

At that moment Siddhartha became less troubled, because he could begin to see what he had to do.

That evening the prince went to the king and told him he wanted to leave the kingdom to search for an answer to the problems of suffering and death. The king offered him his kingdom to stay. Siddhartha refused. So the king agreed to let him go – but secretly ordered that all the gates should be locked and the guards doubled.

After dark, Siddhartha went to see his wife and son. He found them sound asleep, his wife's hand resting on their son's head. He wanted to hold them and say goodbye, but knew that if he woke them up it would only delay his departure. So he kissed his wife lightly on the foot and left.

He raced in his chariot towards the city gates. They were locked, but the guards had fallen into an enchanted sleep, and miraculously the horses pulling the chariot rose up and flew over the wall.

They raced on until they reached the forest. There Siddhartha dismounted, stripped himself of his fine clothes and told the charioteer to cut off his long hair with a sword. When a hermit appeared from between the trees, Siddhartha exchanged his fine robes for the holy man's simple, coarse one.

Siddhartha disappeared from sight between the trees when he was twenty-nine years old.

For six years he lived among the hermits, the matted-hair ascetics and the communities of priests hidden in the depths of the forest. He practised their meditations, took part in their rites and tried to find enlightenment through self-denial. Eating no more than one grain of rice per day, he found his body wasting away. His skin lost its colour and became like that of a deep-sea creature. His tendons, nerves and veins protruded. His drying blood moved through his veins like sludge. The gleam in his eyes receded until it was like the gleam of water seen at the bottom of a deep well.

But he still hadn't found what he was looking for. He managed to drag himself to the edge of a river and lay there exhausted for a while. Then he noticed the branch of a tree leaning down towards him and managed to pull himself up and set off down the path.

The daughter of a local farmer found him resting under an apple tree. She brought him milk rice, made with milk from sacred cows in a golden bowl and covered by a snow-white cloth.

As he ate, Siddhartha's strength returned. He knew he was about to find perfect understanding, a solution to the problems that had troubled him since he'd first seen the elderly, the sick and the dead.

He came across a farmer mowing a field and begged an armful of grass from him. Then he spread it out in front of a sacred fig tree, sat and waited to see what would happen. In his mind's eye the tree at his back swelled up and became a great world tree, connecting him to the whole world on all its many levels and in all its different dimensions.[2]

A handsome young prince was waking up in his harem. He looked at his wives, all of them smiling in their sleep. He thought, No wonder they call me the Lord of Desire.

Even in the dark recesses of the palace where he lay, the sharp morning air reached him and pinched his nose. It was time to be up and doing. He decided to check on his domains, to see if any fences or iron gates needed repairing. He yelled at the top of his voice to alert his servants that he was on his way. He intended to set their hearts pumping like hammers, ready and able to do his will, and to set his packs of hunting dogs barking and slavering.

However, he had only gone a few steps from the bedchamber when he sensed that something was wrong. The strings on the instruments of the court musicians that had been played so beautifully the night before were now broken. He stepped out into the courtyard. The fountains had been switched off. Who had given permission for that? He began to burn with anger. He went to the well that supplied the palace. It was almost dry. He could only catch a very faint gleam in its depths.

It was an ill wind. Somebody somewhere had come to challenge him, to try to end his dominion. The handsome young prince, who was called Mara, called for his armoured iron-clad elephant, mounted it and let out a full-blooded roar that was heard all over the world. At his summons, a mighty army began to emerge from the forests that surrounded the palace. There were tigers, lions, monstrous insects, snakes and other reptiles that had been hiding in the depths of the forest since before the Flood. And demons too.

But as they mounted their attack on Siddhartha, still sitting beneath the tree, their arrows turned into flowers before they reached him, and Siddhartha refused to give way to fear, despite the rocks, the mountains that Mara hurled at him. All floated down around him like straw. Thunderbolts turned into gentle perfumed breezes. Then, as evening came, under a blood-red moon Mara sent his three beautiful daughters to try to tempt Siddhartha. He only laughed at them.

Finally, Mara himself approached the seated prince. He looked down from his elephant and asked by what right he sat there. Siddhartha replied that he had lived many times and had worked his way towards this moment over many millennia. Mara said that he had done the same and that his armies ranged behind him would vouch for it. Who would vouch for Siddhartha?

Siddhartha reached down and touched Mother Earth. She vouched for him and at that moment he was transfigured: his physical body shone and he became the Buddha.

Mara and his army melted into the night. The sky rained petals and the moon now shone with a clear white light.

The Buddha continued to sit under the tree for forty-nine days. Then he set out and preached for forty years. With only a few possessions, including a yellow robe, his begging bowl, a water strainer, a razor and a needle, he walked freely and easily, sometimes twenty miles a day, staying in monasteries or temporary shelters. He would rise early and after ritual purifications spend a while in solitary meditation. In the late morning he would walk to beg for food, then spend the rest of the day meditating, teaching or walking again.

Like Krishna, the Buddha preferred to spend his time with humble people who herded sheep or cattle, or with craftsmen such as blacksmiths.[3]

The Buddha's teaching was suffused with a marvellous clarity of intellect. It was abstract and conceptual rather than visionary. It was as bare of imagery as a small country church with whitewashed walls.[4]

It is the fruit of an adolescent being royally entertained in his father's palace, yet knowing there must be more to life. As a young man, the Buddha had wanted to understand the meaning of life, and now he did.

This is the human condition, he said. We are unhappy because we can't always be with those we love, because we often have to be with those we don't love. Because we can't have what we desire every moment of our lives, we are unhappy. This is what we all experience. But there is a way out of this.

> Self is an error, an illusion, a dream. Open your eyes and awake. He who is awake will no longer live in fear. He will see that what he thought was a snake is really a piece of old rope, and he will cease to tremble.[5]
>
> Cleaving to things, desire for things, sensuality, all this is inherited from former lives, from the old life of our ancestors. It is the cause of all suffering.
>
> He who has discovered there is no self will let go of all selfish desires, all egotism.
>
> Stop grasping and you can achieve calm and peace of mind.
>
> By giving away our food, we gain more strength; by giving away our clothes, we gain more beauty; by giving away our wealth we gain more treasure.
>
> Give with reverence.
>
> Only by compassion for all living things, by continuous acts of kindness and giving can we reach the immortal path.
>
> See the eternal quality and the holiness in every living thing.

The Buddha put great emphasis on having the right intention. So, the inwardness we saw in Elijah evolved further here. Because all things, including our innermost thoughts, are connected, the same action performed twice but with two different intentions will have very different results. A gift given as a formality and a gift given graciously will change the cosmos in completely different ways, even if physically the gift and the act of giving are exactly the same. It is the thought that counts. In idealism the thought is more real than the object, and the physical world is contingent on the world of thought. A good intention ripples out and has wide effects in the world of thoughts – our own and everyone else's. As the Buddha says in the *Dhammapada*:

Clinging to yourself is a continuous dying.

Hatred can only be overcome by non-hatred.

If a man does me wrong, I will offer him in return my full love.

The Buddha had rejected the extreme methods of the ascetics. He knew that it is possible to achieve great spiritual and supernatural gifts by their methods. But, he explained, they are highly dangerous – to the individuals concerned, to others, to the world – if they are developed without developing a feeling for morality at the same time.[6]

Late in life he rebuked a disciple for being too eager to take over from him, and the man tried to kill him by driving a mad bull-elephant towards him. But just as many years later a giant wolf that was terrorizing the countryside would lie down in front of St Francis and obey him like a pet dog, the elephant knelt gently in front of the Buddha. He lifted his right hand and gently patted the animal on the forehead.

Finally, at the age of eighty, he felt the end drawing near. The rainy season came and he fell ill. He lay down between two blossoming trees with his head towards the Himalayas. He was silent and a great silence rippled out over the land. He spoke to his disciples for the last time, saying that all created things must strive to be free, then he sank deeper and deeper inside himself and achieved Nirvana.

The Buddha began to lead the way out of natural cycles, out of the animal, vegetable and mineral world into which humanity had fallen. He carried with him the promise of the spiritualization of the world – the promise that we can all escape as he did.

Socrates and his Daemon

The Emperor asked a sage to be brought to court. 'What is the highest truth?' he wanted to know.

'Total emptiness . . . with no trace of holiness,' said the sage.

'If there is no holiness, then who, where or what are you?'

'I don't know,' the sage replied.

Question everything. Test it with reason. Look at the assumptions behind it, take those assumptions apart and question your questions too. Awareness of ignorance is the beginning of wisdom.

In the West, this way of thinking started with Socrates. It is because of him that we place such a high value on knowing. Socrates is the father of Western academic philosophy – and also, as we shall see, intellectual integrity.[1] Yet he had his own personal daemon, an uncanny adviser who had supernatural knowledge of the world, who often knew better than him and who repeatedly whispered in his ear, telling him what he should do. 'It began in my early childhood,' he said, 'a sort of voice which comes to me.'

Socrates was born around 470–469, in the golden age of Athens, the time of its great flowering in the arts and sciences. He was the son of a poor sculptor and a midwife.

There is a story that one day the young Socrates was trying to carve a statue of Apollo's daughters, the Three Graces. Frustrated, he threw down his chisel, saying he would rather carve his own soul.

He was spotted by a wealthy man, who paid for his education.

In his twenties, while the finishing touches were being applied to the Parthenon, Socrates was talking with the great thinkers of the day. As a soldier, he also fought for Athens with great courage, and he was a hero, too, at drinking strong drink. He was physically strong, but ugly with a flat nose. His face looked like the face on statues of the centaur Chiron, people said.

But what really distinguished him were the voices – the voice of his own private daemon and his own voice, questioning everything.

As he reached middle age, he was still poor. He went around barefoot in a dirty old cloak. He could have been earning a living as a teacher, but he had always refused to take money for his teaching. It was also said that at the market he didn't concern himself with how much things cost or how he was going to find the money to pay for them, but with listing all the things he didn't need or want. 'I contend that to need nothing is divine,' he said, 'and that the less a man needs, the nearer he approaches divinity.'

Be that as it may, as his wife might have said, he wasn't a good provider for his family. His wife used to nag him. On one occasion her anger and frustration exploded and she emptied a chamber pot over his head.

The Athenians seemed to regard him as what we today might call 'a bit of a character'.

His daemonic voice was internal. No one else could hear it. It would come to him unbidden.

Early one morning while on a military campaign Socrates fell deep into thought in the middle of the camp. He just stood there. People were astonished to see him still standing in the same place at midday and then that night soldiers pulled their beds out of their tents so they could watch him. Only in the morning of the next day did he come to, appear to say a prayer to Apollo and walk away. Then, it seemed, his voice warned him not to attempt to cross a particular river until he had performed a rite of atonement.

His daemon evidently foresaw the future. On another occasion he was walking with friends through the city streets, when he suddenly stopped because his daemon told him not to take a particular route. His friends, who would not be advised by him, did take that route – and found themselves run over by a herd of pigs.

His daemon also advised about bigger things. During the battle of

Silenus and a panther, from an antique gem, probably Roman (from *Antique Gems* by the Rev. C. W. King, 1866). There is a tradition that Socrates was a reincarnation of the satyr Silenus, which is reflected in the statues of them, which have the same face. It's hard not to see the influence of the daemon of Socrates on the account of daemons in Philip Pullman's *His Dark Materials* trilogy.

Delium it advised Socrates to take a particular route that enabled him to rescue Alcibiades and two other famous Athenians. The comrades who declined to follow this advice were overtaken by the enemy and killed.

During the Peloponnesian War Socrates was also told that Athens should not send out a particular expedition. Yet again his advice wasn't heeded and the expedition duly turned out to be disastrous.

Why was Socrates privileged in this way? Why did this voice come to him? According to his pupil Plato, we are all given a daemon at birth to guide us through our earthly lives. According to the historian Plutarch, we are all able in principle to hear its divine promptings, but Socrates could hear them more clearly than most people because he was not as distracted as most of us are by the passions that enflame bodily nature and cloud the mind.

Someone went to consult the oracle at Delphi, asking if there was anyone alive wiser than Socrates.

The priestess simply said, 'No.'

When he found out about it, Socrates questioned what the oracle had said. He wanted to know the exact words.

'How can I be the wisest man in the world?' he said. 'I know nothing!'

He knew that the pronouncements of the gods – in this case Apollo – were never straightforward, often enigmatic, ambiguous and open to misinterpretation. In his view these pronouncements demanded thinking and questioning.

Later Socrates decided that Apollo had given him a divine mission to question *everything*. He thought it was *good to know*. He believed that if anyone faced with a choice knew which was the better course of action, knew all the implications and knew all the good that would result from choosing it, then that person would naturally feel unable to choose the worse course of action. For Socrates, then, knowledge was virtue.

He wanted to try to work out how we should live. Happiness, he argued, did not come from wealth or power or other external things, but from knowing what was good for you, for your soul. The oracle at Delphi advised, 'Know thyself,' and Socrates tried to work out in reasonable, logical terms what that meant.

In the person of Socrates the human intellect was beginning to find out what it might be capable of – to flex its muscles. Socrates would rush about the city talking to everyone, not just the statesmen, generals and philosophers, but the tradespeople, shopkeepers and courtesans. Just as Gilgamesh had rushed around trying to find someone strong enough to give him a good fight, so Socrates looked for someone who could match his intellectual strength.

And so he tested everyone. He would draw people's opinions out of them, unravel the assumptions behind these opinions, then look for contradictions and try to reduce them to absurdity. He could be charming, funny and fascinating, but sometimes he was also teasing and sarcastic. Perhaps he didn't know his own strength? Where he found ignorance, he mocked it, and he sometimes teased people in a way that made bystanders laugh.

'Philosophy,' he said, 'is the greatest kind of music.' His philosophy – his powers of reasoning – often had a strange effect on people. It charmed them – but not always in a pleasurable way. Sometimes people engaged in conversation with Socrates found they no longer knew what they knew or believed, sometimes so much so that they went into shock – as someone said, as if they'd been stung by a stingray. Of course they weren't used to being tied up by logical argument.

A friend told Socrates that he was wise not to travel, saying that if he behaved abroad as he did in Athens, he'd be arrested as a wizard. Of course, being a wizard, the friend reminded him, was often punishable by death.

The comment was prophetic. Socrates *was* making enemies. Not everyone found him amusing. A group of young men had gathered around him and some of the Athenian élite found this sinister. Was he subverting them? Also, if Socrates said that he knew nothing, what did that say about the great and powerful men he so easily trounced in public debate? Not everyone appreciated being made to look stupid.

We saw that by the time of the prophets, the political leaders of the Jews were no longer their great spiritual leaders. Socrates and his young follower Plato believed that political leaders should still be 'the ones who know' or, as Plato would put it, 'philosopher kings'. Socrates mocked Athenian ideas of democracy, calling it an amusing entertainment, and he also mocked politicians for partying with chorus girls.

Athens had been losing some of its self-confidence. It had suffered defeats in the Peloponnesian War and behaved in an unjust and cruel way to some of its enemies. Some people felt uneasy, and perhaps thought that all Athenians should pull together. It wasn't a good time to be 'off message'.

Socrates was summoned before two officials who told him of a new law by which he would be forbidden to use his questioning, reasoning methods to influence the youth of the city.

'Can I ask you a question – just to make sure I understand your orders?' he said.

'You may.'

'Of course I want to obey the law – but are you telling me that I am forbidden from teaching the young in a reasonable way? Is the implication that . . .'

'Because you are a fool, Socrates,' said the official, angrily, 'I will put it in plain language that even you can understand: you are forbidden to talk to the youth of Athens in any way whatever.'

Socrates had two particular enemies who became his leading accusers: a poet he had humiliated in a public debate and a rich merchant who did not like the influence Socrates had on his son. He was brought to trial before 500 judges and accused of corrupting the youth of Athens and not believing in the gods of Athens – believing instead in his own private daemon.

Asked why he taught the young and did not take part in debates in the great public assemblies, Socrates said – in what must have seemed to the assembled leaders and officials to be a calculated insult – that his daemon had advised him not to take part in politics because it would stain his soul and make him less able to see the truth. 'Surely you don't want to punish me for telling the truth?' he said.

According to Socrates, a philosopher should not dwell on the petty, transient affairs of men, but fix his attention instead on the eternal realities to be seen in the patterns that the stars and planets make in the sky. He was here referring to the work of the great spirits of the stars and planets in forming the world and directing it.

Socrates was questioned on the report that the oracle of Delphi had said he was the wisest man on Earth. He suggested that Apollo might have been joking, and the assembly roared its disapproval.

It did likewise when Socrates was questioned about his daemon. He said it was important to note that the daemon never *made* him do anything. A daemon seeks to take you over and use you, but Socrates' daemon left it up to him to decide what to do.[2]

As his trial continued, Socrates referred to many instances when his daemon had accurately predicted the future. But everything he said seemed to speak to his judges of his arrogance.

When asked if he had prepared a defence, he said he laid his whole life before the judges. He said that he had always spoken for truth and justice – and that that should be his defence.

Later he was asked why he had not used his usual eloquence to sway the judges, and he said that his daemon had told him not to. He continued: 'I have been told that if I am caught questioning the young and philosophizing, I shall die. I should say to you, men of Athens, that I reverence you and love you, but as long as I breathe and am able, I shall not cease to philosophize. I am about to say something at which

The prison where Socrates was held (engraving by a nineteenth-century traveller).

perhaps you will cry out, but I pray you not to do so. For you know well that if you should kill me, you would not hurt me as much as you would hurt yourselves.'

He was found guilty.

When asked if he would like to suggest a sentence, he proposed that either they gave him the highest honour that they could bestow or fine him the smallest coin there was. He seemed not to take his accusers seriously, even under threat of death.

A second vote was taken and he was condemned to die.

He said calmly, 'There has befallen me that which men may think and most men do account to be the greatest of evils.' And yet, he went on, his daemon had given him that morning no sign, either at home or here in the court, that by being condemned to death he had been overtaken by any evil.

'What has happened to me seems to me to be a good thing, and if we think death to be an evil, we are making an error, so be of good hope, my judges. Know too that I am in no way angry with those who have accused or condemned me, though they have condemned and accused me with no good will but rather with the intention of hurting me. Life after death will surely be a place where they don't condemn a man to death just for asking questions.'

He was condemned to drink hemlock, and the sentence was to be carried out in a month's time.

Friends urged him to escape, but he refused to do so.

On the appointed day he said, 'Soon I must drink the poison, and I think I'd better take a bath first, so the women won't have the trouble of washing my body after I am dead.'

He briefly saw his wife and three sons. His wife was crying, but he sent them all briskly away.

When the time arrived, his executioner, too, burst into tears. Socrates told him: 'I return your good wishes and will do as you bid.'

As he raised the cup to his lips and drank, quite cheerfully, his followers were weeping. He rebuked them, saying that he had been told that a man should die in peace.

His legs began to fail and he lay down. 'When the poison reaches my heart, that will be the end.'

He covered his face up. Then after a while a movement was heard and they uncovered his face to find that his eyes were set.

Socrates had finished carving his soul. He had tried to teach how to live; now he tried to teach how to die.

Because our age is so soused in materialism, we may find it hard not to wonder if Socrates really did want to die. It occurs to us to doubt his sincerity. But the fact of the matter was that at that time almost everyone believed in a spiritual reality. For Socrates the body was 'the tomb of the spirit'. The spirit had fallen into matter, which had gradually hardened around it, but in between earthly lives the spirit was free to ascend to higher, spiritual realities.

It has been suggested that Socrates was executed for introducing a new god or gods in the shape of his own daemon. But Athens was a thriving marketplace for new ideas, new beliefs, new gods. It prided itself on open discussion of these matters and tolerance of a huge range of different gods. No, what offended the Athenians, what was unacceptable, was that this new god – Socrates' daemon – was private to himself and internal. Only a few hundred years earlier the gods of Homer and the God and angels of Moses had acted, as we have seen, in huge public events witnessed by thousands. They were awesome powers active in the world. In the story of Socrates, as with Elijah and the Buddha, we see that a new arena for divine intervention was opening up.[3]

Socrates was a martyr. He died for the inner life.

*   *   *

Plato was twenty-five when Socrates died.

The works of Plato give us the first systematic account of idealism. Idealism, as we have seen, is the belief that mind came before matter, that matter comes from mind and is dependent on it, and that mind is in some way more real than matter. It had never been written down as a philosophical system before Plato, but up until that point pretty much everyone in history had believed in it without question.

Because we are most likely today to encounter idealism as dry academic theory, usually as a theory of knowledge, it is easy for us to forget that for most of history it has been a philosophy of life. People experienced the world in a way that accorded with it. They experienced the physical world responding to their mental acts, in prayers for example. They had religious, spiritual, mystical experiences, and saw

The omphalos (from *Architecture, Mysticism and Myth* by W. R. Lethaby, 1891). In Greek thought Apollo was the Logos or Word, the source of the world's harmony, weaving in eternal song all that is and will be. The most sacred thing at Delphi was the omphalos stone that marked the sacred centre of the world and the place where all worlds met. This stone was covered by a net, mathematically generated by the numbers of the gods' names. This net depicted the world's soul. It caught the thoughts or ideas of the great Cosmic Mind and pulled them into the material world. We each have a sacred centre like this in our body.

Nineteenth-century illustration of the cave of Plato. The material world is made up of shadows cast by the spiritual world.

the world working according to patterns that just wouldn't be there if the world were only a place of atoms knocking against atoms.

Plato wrote down his philosophy of idealism just at the time when its opposite, materialism, the view that matter came before mind, that mind is dependent on matter and that matter is more real than mind, was first conceived. Plato argued for idealism just at the point when it was no longer what everyone automatically believed.[4]

Plato's greatest pupil was Aristotle, whose categorical style of thinking prepared the way for modern science. Aristotle became tutor to Alexander the Great. In the last and most expansive flourishing of ancient Greek civilization, which historians call the Hellenistic, Alexander founded a mighty empire stretching as far as India.

Just as later the Roman Empire would become a vehicle for the spread of Christianity, so the spreading empire of Alexander the Great carried with it the philosophy of Socrates, Plato and Aristotle. It was a great time for the exchange of ideas and philosophies, a time when, for example, a Buddhist, a Jew and a follower of Plato might find to their surprise that they had much in common.[4]

It was in the midst of this great maelstrom of ideas that a great being would be born who would bring them all together in spirit.

Jesus Turns the World Inside Out

Portrait of Christ (from the cemetery of St Callixtus, Rome).

'Are you the one we've been waiting for? Or do we need to seek another?'

Matthew 11.3

One day at the beginning of the first century in the town of Tyana in modern Turkey, a child was about to be born. His mother lay down in a field and swans came up from the river and formed a protective shield around her, singing and flapping their wings.

and emperors. He was politically influential, courageously criticizing Nero and Domitian. He was an original thinker, accepted as an authority in schools that had been founded by Pythagoras, Socrates and Plato. He preached a universal religion that was progressive in its day, and because of this he was credited with helping to reform the thinking of late Roman emperors in ways that would later help Christianity to survive. Emperor Hadrian collected his works and he was looked up to by the great philosopher-emperor Marcus Aurelius. His brand of Pythagorean philosophy was influential on Neoplatonism, which was in turn highly influential on the mystical stream of Christian theology. 'How is it,' complained the Church father Justin Martyr, 'that the talismans of Apollonius have the power to prevent the fury of the waves, the violence of the winds and the attacks of wild beasts, and that whilst our Lord's miracles are preserved by tradition alone, those of Apollonius are most numerous and actually manifested in present facts?'

Yet Jesus Christ changed the world and Apollonius didn't.

Elijah, the Buddha, Socrates and Apollonius brought spiritual aware-ness and understanding to the world – the knowledge that we are all interconnected, that we should show compassion to every living thing, that we must play our part in the world's evolving. They all knew on some level what was happening and what had to happen, but it was Jesus Christ who brought the power that made it happen. He had the power to turn history on its hinges. Elijah, Buddha, Pythagoras brought faith and hope, but Jesus Christ brought love.

When Jesus was tempted by Satan in the wilderness, he was by his refusal repudiating magic, because magic meant working with the lower spirits. Jesus worked with angels.

As we have seen, angels appeared at key moments in history as told in the Old Testament, but in the time of Jesus they came out of the shadows. The New Testament throngs with angels: announcing to Zechariah that his wife will have a son, the annunciation to Mary, telling Joseph to marry Mary, announcing the birth of Jesus to the shepherds, telling Joseph to take his wife and son and flee to Egypt, ministering to Jesus after his temptation in the wilderness, communing with Jesus in the Garden of Gethsemane, strengthening Jesus on the cross, rolling away the stone from the tomb of Jesus and appearing to

Paintings of the crucifixion often show an angel holding a bowl to catch the blood of Jesus as it flows from the wound in his side made by the Spear of Longinus. (Miniature from the Syrian Gospel of Zagba.)

Mary Magdalene and the disciples to tell them about the resurrection. Later angels direct Philip to go south to Ethiopia and direct the centurion Cornelius to fetch Peter. An angel appears to Paul by night, asking him to take the gospel to Europe.

The early chapters of this book told a story of the cosmos common to all religions. Matter was precipitated from the great Cosmic Mind, then vegetable life arose out of that, then vegetable life formed a cradle for animal life and animal consciousness.

The image of the snake on the tree is, as we saw, the clearest possible image of the origins of the animal consciousness that prepared the way for distinctively human consciousness. Then, as the story continued, matter became denser and hardened around human consciousness. Humans became more and more cut off from and less aware of the Cosmic Mind. Spiritual leaders like Zarathustra, Krishna, Moses, Socrates and the Buddha helped lead humanity through this lessening of spiritual awareness.

But by the time of the Roman Empire humans had become almost completely cut off – not only from the spiritual dimension, but from one another too. The legal system which was to be the Romans' greatest contribution to civilization barely managed to keep in check a terrible, bloodthirsty culture of cruelty. The spiritual vision was dimmed to such a degree that it became possible to doubt its reality, giving rise to the atomism and atheism of Democritus and Lucretius.[2]

Now, as the Fall reached its deepest, darkest point, the crucifixion and resurrection of Jesus Christ marked the beginning of the ascent.[3] Just as animal consciousness was pinned to the tree in the Garden of Eden, now divine consciousness was pinned to the cross of matter. Like animal consciousness being absorbed into vegetable life and enclosed in matter in order to create human beings, divine consciousness would be absorbed into matter too.[4]

Divine consciousness would begin the process of dissolving matter, spiritualizing it.[5]

*　　　　*　　　　*

Jesus and the four elements (from an illustration to *Le Propriétaire des Choses* by Bartholomaeus Anglicus, 1490).

We can see indications that the whole structure of the cosmos was changing in the story of Mary Magdalene.

She first appears by name in the Bible as one of a group of women who help look after Jesus. She may have been wealthy. She is often portrayed in a yellow robe with long hair, which is often reddish. She seems to glow with an inner mystic light. There is something tender and a little sad about her.

She is often portrayed with an alabaster jar. This is because in Catholic tradition she is identified with Mary, sister of Martha whose story is in Luke's gospel.

The sisters were entertaining Jesus in their home. Martha became irritated because while she was rushing round organizing everything and doing what had to be done, her sister was sitting at their guest's feet, listening to him talk and sharing a moment of intimacy.[6]

When Mary later took expensive scented oil from an alabaster jar and anointed the feet of Jesus, one of the disciples suggested that this was a waste of money. He said the money should be spent on the poor instead, but Jesus replied: 'Leave her alone. She was always meant to use this oil on me, and to save some for my burial.'

The story looks forward, then, to the death of Jesus, when Mary Magdalene will come to the fore.[7]

We don't know for certain that Mary Magdalene and Martha's sister Mary are the same person, but both shared a care for the person of Jesus, and both had a relationship with him that seems intensely personal. When Jesus said Mary was right to anoint him with the expensive oil, he was not being selfish, he was saying something about the cosmos as Christianity understands it: that the God of Christianity is a personal God and we live in a personal cosmos. The cosmos has been created to give us the qualities that make us human, and beyond that it has been created to give each and every one of us our own personal experience of it, with tests, dilemmas, mysteries, conflicts and blessings tailored to our own individual strengths and weaknesses. Our individual personalities, with all their weaknesses, are the crown of creation and we should cherish them.

Mary Magdalene was one of the three women who stood at the base of the cross and witnessed the crucifixion there. She witnessed, too, Joseph of Arimathea's burial of the body and she was the first person to see the risen Christ.

In John's Gospel Mary went to visit the tomb early in the morning when it was still dark. She saw that the stone blocking the entrance had been rolled away, so she ran and told Peter and John. The three returned and found the linen in which the body had been wrapped lying there – but no sign of the body. It seemed that it had been stolen.

Peter and John left. Mary was standing, weeping, outside the tomb, when through her tears she looked back inside and saw two angels in white, one standing where the head of Jesus had lain, the other where the feet had been.

'Woman, why are you crying?'

'Because they have taken away my lord, I know not where.'

Then in the garden outside the tomb she saw a figure that she assumed must be the gardener. He spoke to her: 'Woman, why are you weeping?'

She replied that if he had taken the body away, would he show her where? But then when she heard him say 'Mary' she recognized him by the quickening of love in her heart.

She rushed to embrace him, but he stopped her: 'Touch me not, because I am not yet ascended.' He asked her to go and tell the disciples what she had seen.

The 'resurrection body' of Jesus, the transformed body that is the first of the transformed bodies that will spiritualize the entire material dimension of the cosmos, looked different from his former, fleshly body. We are given to understand the same thing in the story of the stranger who accompanied two of the disciples on the road to Emmaus. They too will fail to recognize the risen Christ.

When Jesus told Mary not to touch him, it was because this resurrection body was in some mysterious process of transition that would be complete by the time Thomas was invited to touch the wounds in it.

How did the disciples respond to being told by Mary that their master had risen from the dead? A suspicion that some of them might have been jealous of Magdalene, resentful of her intimacy with Jesus, occurs in Christian texts written at around the same time as the four canonical gospels.

In the Gospel of Thomas, Peter asks Jesus to tell Mary to leave, as 'women are not worthy', but Jesus refuses and says: 'I will make Mary a living spirit.'[8]

In the Gospel of Philip it is said that Jesus 'loved her more than the all the disciples and used to kiss her often on her mouth'.[9] The disciples complain that he loves her more than all of them, and he does not deny it. This passage has led people to speculate that Jesus and Mary were married, but, as we will see later, what is being referred to here is an experience of intense mystical bliss, a 'mystical marriage'.

The fragments of the Gospel of Mary Magdalene that have come down to us describe events after the resurrection – perhaps shortly after Jesus has told Mary to go and tell Peter and the others that she has just seen his resurrected form. Peter asks Mary to reveal to them the teachings that Jesus had taught her. Mary then describes the successive stages by which the spirit has to free itself from attachment to the Earth before it can re-ascend to God. She talks about a vision that Jesus allowed her to see in which the spirit ascends through seven realms and is tested in each. She describes how the spirit is tested in turn by seven powers – by the powers of darkness, by desire, ignorance, death-wish, enslavement to the flesh, worldly wisdom and anger. She is presenting a world-view in which the human spirit is locked into matter. She is saying that the human spirit needs the supernatural power that Jesus can bring in order to unlock itself and escape.

Isis loved the Sun god, Osiris. She helped usher him through into another world where he would be king. Now the wisdom of Isis was working through Mary Magdalene.

There is a tradition still alive today that Mary Magdalene travelled by boat to the south of France with her brother Lazarus and lived out the rest of her life there. It is significant, too, that this region is closely associated with the Holy Grail. We will examine later the real meaning of the Holy Grail.

As Mary herself says in her gospel, 'Where the mind is, there is the treasure.'

Jesus Christ carried the cross towards Golgotha. On the other side of the world a great and powerful man was dragged out of his sanctuary.

The entrance to his cave was carved and painted to form the mouth of a snake. People had been afraid to go there, but now soldiers emerged with the god-king as their prisoner.

Because of him the corn had grown to such a size that a single ear was almost too heavy for a single man to carry. It was said that he talked to plants and that immediately they grew and bore fruit. Because of him, hunger was no more. Domestic animals would breed and multiply with astonishing rapidity, and wild animals would become docile in his presence and do his bidding. Vast numbers of wonderful sweet-singing birds – some of them species never seen before – gathered in the cities and serenaded the people.

Did the king really have power over the forces of growth and reproduction? The beautiful women of the kingdom bore him many beautiful golden babies, a new race perhaps – and there was some disquiet about this among the people. What would become of their own children?

Then storms came and washed the crops away. The flocks of birds began to grow bold and steal food, even attack children. There were rumours of mutants emerging from the cave and scampering into the forests at night. One day a prophet arrived and told the people that their king had been working black magic. He pointed to the dance of Venus and Mercury, close to the sun, now hidden, now revealed. The prophet had a compelling quality like the king – and they believed him when he said they must crucify the king.

So the king was dragged, his long snake-like body covered in green feathers, through the sacred groves, where the roots of the trees were carved to look like snakes. They took him to the Hill of Skulls, and there he was nailed to a cross between two criminals. Hanging on either side of him, these criminals abused and insulted him.

In those days people were killed by being hung on a cross and shot with arrows. The king's body was painted all over with suns in mockery of his claim to be the sun's emissary.

A small group of women stood on the hill strewn with skulls and bones and watched the execution. One of them was the Spider Woman, and she rejoiced because now her own children would be saved and the great rent in the cosmos would be repaired.[10]

Engraving of serpent-bird from the relief in the Temple of the Foliated Cross, Palenque, now in the British Museum.

*   *   *

With the life of Jesus, history enters a hall of mirrors. The life of Jesus is like the life of Apollonius yet also its opposite – and so is the crucifixion in America. The world we live in is a paradoxical place, but the appearance of Jesus caused paradoxes to proliferate beyond all measure.

In the spirit world, natural laws don't apply or are reversed, so paradoxes arise when the spirit world breaks through into the material world. Paradox was Jesus Christ's characteristic mode of utterance. Paradox was what gave his sayings their rhetorical force:

Whoever seeks to save his life shall lose it.

The meek shall inherit the Earth.

He who is near me is near the fire.[11]

The world, then, is a place of mutating paradoxes. Just when we feel certain, we are met by the opposite of what we expected. The Chinese sage Lieh Tzu, who lived shortly after Jesus Christ, said:

When the eye can make out the pointed tip of a single hair, it is about to go blind. When an ear can make out the beating wings of a gnat, it is about to go deaf. When the tongue can distinguish between the taste of the water from one river and the water of another, it is about to lose the sense of taste. When the nose can tell the difference between the smell of burning silk and that of burning linen, it is about to lose the ability to smell. When the body takes special pleasure in sprinting, its limbs are about to stiffen. When the mind distinguishes very acutely between right and wrong, it is about to make a mistake.

If there were no humans to observe it, the universe would not be beautiful or rich or strange. It would not be a shame when the universe collapsed, when its vast extent, its mutating patterns, its complexities were no more, because these are expressions of value and without mind all is valueless and meaningless.

The life of Jesus Christ illustrates a vast convergence of spiritual beings and forces. His life was so mysterious, so momentous, that we still struggle to understand it in all its cosmic dimensions, but one aspect is this: there is a special law which operates like the law of thermodynamics. If we try to do something purely good, then because of the Saturnine influence in the world, a force of evil which is equal and opposite to it will rise up to meet us. But there is another law, a law of a higher order: if we try to do something purely loving, the power of love inside us will grow.

The Sun at Midnight

'I have seen the sun at midnight.'

Apuleins, *The Golden Ass*

'We have seen the Sun wandering on the Earth.'

St John Chrysostom

The crowd left their cloaks with Saul so they could throw with more enthusiasm. As Philip was stoned, Saul looked on with approval. He was an authority figure, a Pharisee, and he had sanctioned the stoning of this follower of Jesus.

In those days the Pharisees were the keepers of Jewish mystical wisdom, which may have helped prepare Saul so that when the time came he would be able to understand the subtle and complex change that was taking place in the cosmos. Saul was conversant with the ideas of Plato as well as the thoughts of cutting-edge Jewish philosopher Philo and the ideas of a personal conscience that were being developed by the Stoics. He felt passionately about such things. Reading the epistles of Paul, you may recognize someone who cared more than most people about being right. There was nothing in his nature before or after his conversion that said 'Let it slide . . .'

Now Stephen sank to his knees, cried out, 'Lord, do not hold this sin against them!' then he slumped to the ground dead.

Soon Saul was powering up the road to Damascus, determined to eradicate the subversive ideas of the Christians with all possible zeal wherever he found them. He conducted house to house searches, dragging men and women out and into prison, condemning some to death.

He was approaching Damascus when a bright light shone down from the sky onto him and his followers and he heard a voice. The others seem to have seen the light and heard something but not understood it, but what he heard was: 'Saul, Saul, why do you persecute me?'

He fell to the ground. 'Who are you, Lord?'

'I am Jesus, whom you persecute. But rise, enter the city and you will be told what you must do.'

When Saul stood up he found he was blind. His followers took him by the hand and led him into the city. He would be blind for three days.

Meanwhile a local resident, a follower of Jesus called Ananias, also had a divine revelation. He was told to go to find Saul in a house on the Street Called Straight. He was reluctant at first, knowing of Saul's reputation, but in the end he obeyed. When he laid hands on Saul he was cured of his blindness – and he had been converted.

What had he seen in his blindness to convert him from Saul to Paul?

The Second Letter to the Corinthians talks about the extraordinary experiences of 'a person he knew', but most commentators believe Paul is really talking about himself. He says this friend was 'caught up to the third heaven – whether in the body or out of the body I do not know – and [he was] caught up into Paradise and told things that are not to be told, that no mortal is permitted to repeat'. (2 Corinthians 12:2–4)

The idea that Paul was told things he wasn't permitted to repeat may remind us of the initiation ceremonies of the ancient world, where candidates were kept in a trance state for three days. The mention of the third heaven may also remind us of Enoch, taken to the Third Heaven, where Paradise is and where God walks.

Later in Athens Paul met a man called Dionysius and converted him on the Mount of Mars, the Areopagus, the place where Socrates had defended himself in vain.[2] Dionysius the Areopagite, as he became known, wrote about the heavens and we can understand something of what Paul meant by the 'third heaven' through his writings.

When Paul refers in passing to different orders of angels, he clearly expects his readers to know what he is alluding to, but in *The Celestial Hierarchies* Dionysius expands on Paul's comments, giving a systematic account of the nine orders of angels. The lowest is the Angels and above them come the Archangels, including Michael, Gabriel and Raphael.

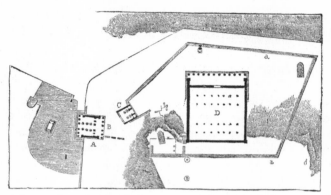

Plan of the temple enclosure of Eleusis. As with Freemasonic lodges today, everyone knew that the Mystery schools were there, but no-one knew what went on inside.[1]

The third order in the hierarchy is called the Principalities by Paul. These have a care for nations. The next order is called the Powers. These are the angels of the planets, who have a special role in the shaping of biological forms and also human consciousness. They are the spiritual beings referred to in Genesis as the Elohim. The angels above the Powers are the Virtues, the Denominations, the Thrones – the 'Timelords' – and the Cherubim, the twelve angels of the constellations. The highest order is made up of the Seraphim, the six-winged angels seen in a vision by Isaiah and, as we will see later, by St Francis. The Seraphim are the highest thoughts of God.

These nine orders are divided into three groups, each sometimes thought of as occupying a 'heaven'. So when in Corinthians Paul describes being taken to 'the third heaven', he means to the heaven occupied by Thrones, Cherubim and Seraphim, the orders of angels who are perpetually in the presence of God.

Paul's experience of the heavens made him aware that some very great and very mysterious event was taking place there. Something tremendous was happening. 'Behold I tell you a mystery. We shall indeed rise again . . . in a moment, in the twinkling of an eye . . . then shall come to pass the saying that is written, Death is swallowed up in victory. O death, where is thy victory? O death, where is thy sting?'[3]

Paul was saying, then, that the cosmos was undergoing a transformation, some fundamental shift. But on the surface nothing seemed to have changed. Everyone continued to age, become sick and die. There wasn't even a political revolution.

So what *had* Paul seen in his conversion experience, his three days of blindness?

Insofar as we can piece together what happened from texts like *The Golden Ass* by African-Roman writer Apuleius, it seems that in the initiating procedures that lasted three days in the Mystery schools of the ancient world, candidates were sometimes shown a vision of the Underworld before finally being guided upwards to a glorious vision of the heavens. Did Paul experience something similar?

There are some scattered allusions to a great event in hell in scripture. Acts says that 'Hell could not hold him' and Peter wrote of Jesus making a proclamation to 'the spirits in prison'. In the apocryphal Gospel of Peter, Jesus is asked 'Hast thou preached to them that slept?' In the Christian Creed believers still assert as one of their central tenets that Jesus Christ 'descended into Hell'.[4]

To find a detailed account of what happened we must turn to an early Christian literature ascribed to Nicodemus.

Like Saul, Nicodemus was a Pharisee. He was also an initiate of the Mysteries who had visited Jesus one night to listen to his teaching and later helped Joseph of Arimathea prepare the body of Jesus for burial.[5] The gospel that bears his name preserves a description of the Harrowing of Hell. It is given in the words of two men who have risen from the realm of the dead and are therefore able to give an eyewitness account of the arrival there of Jesus Christ:

When we were placed with our fathers in the depth of hell in the blackness of darkness, on a sudden there appeared the colour of the sun like gold, and a purple-coloured light lit up the place.

The mighty Lord appeared in the form of a man and enlightened those places that had ever been in darkness and he broke asunder the fetters which before could not be broken and with his invincible power he visited those who sat in the deep darkness by iniquity and the shadow of death by sin. Trampling upon death, the Lord seized the Prince of Hell.

Then Jesus stretched forth his hand and said, 'Come to me, all you who were created in my image, who were condemned by the tree of forbidden fruit and by the devil and by death.'

Presently all the saints were joined together and taking hold of Adam by his right hand, the Lord ascended from hell and all the saints of God followed him. Then the Lord delivered Adam to Michael the archangel and he led them all to Paradise, filled with mercy and glory.

And two very ancient men met them and were asked by the saints, 'Who are you, who have not been with us in Hell, and have your bodies placed in Paradise?'

One of them said, 'I am Enoch, who was translated by the word of God and this man who is with me is Elijah the Tishbite, who was translated in a fiery chariot.'[6]

Jesus was leading the dead out of the jaws of hell and up to heaven and it was perhaps this that caused Paul to announce the end of death.[7]

I said at the beginning of this history that I was going to tell it as much as possible from the point of view of spiritual beings. Here we see that in the time of Paul while it might be true that the physical world had not changed much, the spiritual worlds had been completely transformed.

Like Moses, Jesus was leading his people out of captivity. Like Joshua, he was leading them into a land of milk and honey, up and into the light.[8] He had a mission to the dead as well as to the living, and in the light of this the living and the dead were seen as belonging to the same community.

Although humankind had in previous ages enjoyed free interaction with the spirit worlds, so that people felt assured of continuing to live in the spirit worlds after death, over time this vision had become dimmed. About 1,200 years before the time of Jesus, Odysseus had travelled underground to meet the grey ghost of Heracles and the dead had appeared to him then as lifeless shades, flitting, criss-crossing like bats. Likewise, Achilles had said, 'I would rather be a slave in a poor man's house than a lord in the land of the shades.' The Psalms of David had talked of death in terms as going down to the Pit, a dull, shadowy and dreary place of half-existence. By the time of the Roman Empire a few people had even begun to wonder whether there was life after death at all.

It was into this darkness that the resurrected Jesus Christ suddenly

came, shining with such brightness and lighting up the spiritual worlds so brilliantly that Paul was knocked over. Then, blind to the material world, Paul was shown extraordinary visions, culminating in death, descent into hell and the resurrection of Christ making possible the resurrection of all.[9] And, as we know from his epistles, he spent the rest of his life applying the best intellectual equipment and philosophical frameworks of his day to making sense of what he had seen.

To understand the grandeur of these cosmic events, it is important to remind ourselves of the essential shape of history according to idealism. What is being described is not merely psychological. In fact it isn't to do solely with individuals, or even humanity as whole: it is concerned with nothing less than the transformation of all matter. At this point, which was also the darkest point, the midnight of world history, Jesus Christ had penetrated to the centre of the Earth and planted in it the seed of his Sun-nature. After many ages of preparation, the Sun-seed was finally planted at midnight. This seed would grow so that the Earth might become a sun.

This is Christianity's great cosmic vision – one that is not often clearly laid out in these materialistic times. In the beginning matter was precipitated from the great Cosmic Mind. It grew denser, colder and harder until human souls were trapped in it, isolated and blinded and cut off from the great Cosmic Mind. But in the middle of history the Cosmic Mind sent an emissary containing its creative essence which would begin to loosen matter so that eventually human bodies, all bodies, the whole

(*opposite page*) Angel rescuing St Peter from prison (engraving from an eighteenth-century Bible). Herod Agrippa was persecuting the Christians. He had James, the brother of Jesus, killed and he arrested Peter and had him put in prison. The night before Peter was to be brought to judgement, he started to pray. He was chained to two soldiers and others were guarding the gates. Suddenly he felt himself prodded in the side and realized he had been sleeping. He heard a voice say, 'Arise up quickly,' and his chains just seemed to fall from his wrists. The guards were sleeping, he noticed, and the Archangel Michael was saying, 'Do up your belt and your sandals,' like a father tenderly hurrying a child off to school. 'Put on your cloak and follow me.' Peter left the prison, went past the sleeping guards and out into the dark and empty street. When he reached some iron gates he saw that Michael had disappeared. He hurried to a house where Christians lived. (from Acts 12:3–19) of material cosmos would dissolve and be spiritualized.

Though the Mystery schools of the ancient world may not have known the name of Jesus of Nazareth, they shared the same vision of world history and the role of the Word – the Sun god – in that history.

The Gospel of Matthew records that that night the dead were seen walking the streets of Jerusalem. Great events in the spiritual worlds are always followed by great events in the physical world, and now events in the spirit worlds caused an explosion of supernatural events to erupt on the surface of the Earth. Fifty days after the resurrection of Jesus Christ the apostles were sitting together in the upper room of a house when suddenly they heard a sound like a great rushing wind. It seemed to fill the whole house. Then they saw tongues of fire hovering over themselves like crowns and began speaking fluently in languages they had never known. For Peter, this was the fulfilment of a prophecy by Joel: 'I will pour out my spirit upon all flesh and your sons and daughters shall prophesy and your young men shall see visions and your old men shall see dreams.' The disciples found they could perform miracles, heal, predict the future, see spiritual beings and understand the minds of others.

At that point of midnight, when Jesus lit up the interior of the Earth, he also lit up the interior of the human skull. With Jesus came the idea that we all take for granted now that we each have inside us a mental 'space' that is as infinite, rich and various as the material cosmos. 'The Kingdom of God is within you,' he said – a whole kingdom! And when people were prompted to look for an inner kingdom and duly found it, they became Christians.

Humanity was experiencing a great and sudden change. Men and women were having extraordinary inspirations and insights. It was a complete revolution in consciousness.

*　　　　　*　　　　　*

In Persia, in 216, Mani, 'put on an earthly body' as he himself would phrase it. His family belonged to a Jewish-Christian sect. As a child he had visions of angels. As a young man he performed healing miracles. He seemed to his friends to be able to appear suddenly whenever and wherever he was needed, and he also could hear the voices of plants. He had a vision of Jesus as suffering in all of humankind and all of nature – plants as well as animals. He understood that matter was a coat that it was painful for the spirit to wear, and because he had been born a cripple, this may have been literally true for him.

Mani had tremendous visions of cosmic history. Born in the land of Zarathustra, he tried to understand the dynamic relationship between light and dark, spirit and matter. He said that the struggle between light and darkness would end when the sparks of light had worked to transform matter.

Like Pythagoras and Apollonius, Mani travelled to India to learn. He understood the parts that Krishna and Pythagoras had played in the evolution of humankind – that they had been sent to prepare the way for Jesus Christ. 'Wisdom and goodness have been brought down to each age in succession by the prophets according to a perfect plan,' he said. 'They were brought to India by the prophet Buddha, to Persia by the prophet Zarathustra and later in the West by Jesus . . . I am the true prophet of Babylonia and the present age.'

His writings also show that he was versed in Egyptian mysticism. At the age of twenty-five, after years of thinking, meditation and spiritual striving, Mani had a vision of his heavenly Twin.

The Twin said, 'Greetings to you, Mani, from myself and the Lord, who has sent me to you and chosen you for his mission. You will go to the people and announce the joyful news of the Truth.'

Mani would later say of his heavenly Twin, 'I recognized him and understood that he was my Self from whom I had been separated.'

His Twin told him to leave the community where he had been brought up and to found his own community.

Mani taught his followers to be pure in all things, forgoing meat, drink and sex. He preached a gospel of non-violent resistance to evil. He also taught his followers to respect the light contained in all living things, including plants. They should not plant or grow crops, only eat what they found. Mani wanted to return to ways of Paradise before the Fall. 'Every part of the vegetable world is singing a song,' he said, 'and breaking forth a secret of the divine mystery.'

His Twin also deepened his understanding of the war between light and darkness. Evil could only be fought with good, but humans would only be strong enough for this fight if they were able to give birth to their Higher Self. Mani worked on his inner self as on a statue, straightening out what was crooked and purifying himself so that the divine light would shine out of his centre.

Mani's uncompromising nature, and his refusal to heed warnings to stay away from the court of the Persian king, led to his crucifixion.

After his death, Manichaeism, as his way of thinking became known, grew quickly to become a religion in its own right. St Augustine, the greatest theologian of the early Church after St Paul, was a Manichaean for nine years.

Something very like Mani's notion of a heavenly Twin or guardian angel was taught in early mainstream Christianity. *The Shepherd of Hermas,* one of the earliest Christian texts, contains instructions on how to distinguish the good angel that attends every individual from the bad angel that also hovers near:

> The angel of righteousness is gentle and modest, meek and peaceful. When he ascends into your heart, he talks to you of righteousness, purity, love, contentment. But the angel of iniquity is angry and bitter. When he ascends into your heart, know him by his works. When anger comes upon you or harshness, know that he is in you, or when you are attacked after a longing for things improper, by overreaching and pride and blustering. Now that you know his works, depart from him. Be a man or woman ever so bad, yet if the works of the angel of righteousness ascend into his or her heart, he or she must do something good.

The Church father Origen, and St Gregory of Nyssa also wrote about the guardian angel and the bad angel that attend every human being.

There are degrees of certitude in Church teaching. The existence of angels is *defined doctrine*, the highest level of certitude. That the good angels are sent by God to act as guardians of men is *De Fide ex Jugi Magisterio*. It is *theologically certain* that all believers have guardian angels. That everyone has a bad angel is not certain in the same way.[10] The seventeenth-century mystic Jacob Boehme has an explanation for the relative weakness of these bad angels: 'Devils see only the darkness of the wrath of God.' The theologian and exorcist Martin Israel agrees with this, explaining that the dark angel has restricted vision and little understanding of 'his place in the cosmos' or of cosmic history. Dark angels are virtually blind and also of limited intelligence. It is only

The Guardian Angel (by Jacopo de' Barbari, fifteenth century).

because of these limitations that they are able to exert an evil influence. If they saw clearly all the implications of the evil they were proposing, they would not be able to do it.

Angels of light, on the other hand, have a clear understanding of the direction of the cosmos and their part in it, which makes them more powerful.

*　　　　　*　　　　　*

For the early Christians the cosmos was a battlefield where the forces of good were ranged against the forces of evil, and everyone had both a good and a bad angel trying to win them over. The battle between the forces of good and evil, therefore, was fought in many different dimensions – in the heavens, on Earth, in the realms of the dead, and in the kingdoms inside each human being.

Here we may begin to understand more closely what the point of the material cosmos is. In the beginning human beings were naturally overwhelmed by the presence of God and could not do other than what He asked them to do.

Matter was created partly so that they would have the ability to evolve free will. As matter formed and hardened and encased human spirits in material bodies, it formed a barrier so that they were no longer overwhelmed by God. From the point of view of idealism, that is what matter is *for*.

Through the course of the history of the cosmos a complex, finely tuned metaphysical engine containing delicate checks and balances was set up that would enable people to discern just enough spiritual reality to enable them to make up their own mind without the evidence being overwhelming.

And that arrangement is reflected in the universal human experience today. It is often hard to work out what is the right thing to do. The right thing and the wrong thing may look very similar. Life can be misleading. It often tempts us to do the wrong thing and to delude ourselves into thinking that what is wrong is right, but, as the mystical mathematician Blaise Pascal said, 'There is just enough light for those who want to believe, and just enough shadow for those who do not want to believe.' The history of the world according to idealism gives an account of how the human condition comes to have this extraordinary quality.

24

The Age of Miracles

The centuries after the death of Christ seem the great age of miracles. Many stories have come down to us about miraculous appearances, healings and transformations of the type famously collected in *The Golden Legend* of Jacob de Voragine and depicted in paintings.

We naturally tend to think of these phenomena in Christian terms, but there are records of pagan gods appearing both to crowds and to notable individuals extending surprisingly late into antiquity. In his *Life of Marcellus*, Plutarch reported that the temple of Enguinum in Sicily was revered because of the apparitions of the mother goddess that took place there. Philostratus reported frequent manifestations of Aesculapius, the god of healing, at a temple at Tarsus. Pliny reported apparitions of the gods above a consecrated stone seat in the temple of Hercules at Tyre. In his thesis *On the Nature of the Gods*, Cicero, that most reasonable of Romans, reported frequent apparitions of the gods in his own time: the divine twins Castor and Pollux were seen coming to the aid of troops in battle, fauns were frequently heard in the forest and gods had appeared in many forms.

A contemporary of St Paul's, a famous doctor from Rome called Thessalus of Tralles, left an account of travelling up the Nile to the great temples of Egypt. When he reached Thebes, an old priest promised to secure him an interview with either a god or a ghost. After three days of fasting, the priest shut Thessalus in a specially prepared cell containing a seat for the god. The god was an apparition of indescribable beauty, who answered the doctor's questions on medicinal herbs.

There are many reports of miracle cures too. One of the more intriguing healing miracles in late antiquity happened to man called Phormion, who lived in the town of Kroton. He was wounded in battle, and when the wound did not heal he was told by an oracle to travel to Sparta to visit a shrine to Castor and Pollux. Following these instructions, he took hold of the door handle and suddenly found himself holding the door handle of his own house in Kroton. He was at home and he was healed. Later we will see other stories of miraculous translocation involving personal transformation.

The Epidaurian temple, like the shrine of the divine twins, was a place of healing snakes. Its record of apparitions and miracle cures includes the story of a man who fell asleep one day outside the temple. Passers-by saw one of the temple's tame snakes come and lick his sore toe. He awoke cured and said he had had a dream in which a handsome young man had put a dressing on his toe.

Image from a coin from the temple of Epidaurus.

Both of these stories point to another realm or dimension we may enter in order to be healed. We will return to this theme later.

A miracle is not then an exclusively Christian phenomenon, but the idea does seem to have become more current in late antiquity. As we have seen, as Christianity spread, an ancient myth, like the story of Perseus, does not present the extraordinary events it describes as miraculous, because it is understood that they took place in a world where the laws of nature were not yet fixed. By the time of Christ, people were becoming more curious about the material world. They were collecting information – geographical, biological and historical – and categorizing it in the Aristotelian style, discerning patterns in it and beginning to take note of natural laws, or what some Arab philosophers called 'customs'.[1] A miracle was then an event which apparently contravened these natural laws. (We will return to this area of thought when we come to the Enlightenment and the Scottish philosopher Hume's famous attack on miracles.)

But although the concept of miracles arose when materialism was being formulated, idealism was still vibrant, still the dominant philosophy. Idealism explained the precipitation of matter from mind in terms of a descending scale of emanations from the Cosmic Mind. The many different religions and philosophies of this time show a unified view of this scale or hierarchy, though modified by the culture in which they appear – for example the Greek-flavoured idealism of Neoplatonism, the Jewish-flavoured idealism of the Kabbalah and the Egyptian-flavoured idealism later called Hermeticism. Some scholars have also detected the influence of Persian and Indian-flavoured idealism on the Neoplatonism of Plotinus, and by this time Buddhist monks had travelled as far as Greece.

Whatever the particular flavour of the idealism they adopted, people experienced the world in a way which matched their belief. Plotinus wrote about working with what he called the World Soul in the act of creating the physical world: 'I am vision-loving, and I create by the vision-seeing faculty within me. I create the objects of contemplation, as mathematicians imagine and draw their figures. I gaze within and the figures of the material world take being as they fall from my brooding.'

Experiencing the world as responding to your innermost thoughts and prayers, as the Apostles did, and working in the act of creation with the Cosmic Mind, as Plotinus described it, are the quintessential experiences of idealism and the basis of all religious and spiritual philosophy.

Look at the world through the lens of idealism and miracles are not impossible or even improbable. In fact they are what you might expect.

A history of the world according to idealism ought to be able to suggest outlines of a plan unfolding behind these apparent manifestations of the divine, scattered though they are through diverse cultures. If there is an Otherworld intruding into the mundane world and influencing it, we ought to be able to find some hints at least of co-ordination, of a unified plan.

*　　　　*　　　　*

In the fourth century two factions were fighting for control of the Roman Empire. Both were pushed into battle by dreams. Maxentius had a dream telling him that if he took his army to fight outside the walls of the city, Rome's greatest enemy would be defeated. His army was well dug in and protected inside Rome, but prompted by the dream, he led his army out to meet Constantine – not realizing that he was himself Rome's greatest enemy.

The bridge over the Tiber had been made impassable in order to block Constantine's advance. So, on 28th October 312, a pontoon bridge was hastily constructed in order to carry Maxentius and his army across. It collapsed, and thousands of men, including Maxentius himself, were drowned.

Meanwhile Constantine had been wrestling with theological uncertainties. Many different religions and philosophies were being put forward. Constantine wanted to know who the real god was, the greatest god, and he prayed for this god to reveal himself and stretch out his hand to help him in his hour of need.

That day, as the sun began to sink, he had a vision. He saw a shining, radiant cross just above the sun and there also in the sky was written the words: 'Conquer by this.'

Constantine was awed by the vision, but he didn't know what to make of it. Then that night he had a dream in which Jesus Christ appeared to him, carrying the same cross he had seen in the sky. Jesus told him to make a copy of that cross and to carry it into battle, that this would bring victory.

In the morning Constantine called his most highly skilled workers together, described to them in detail the cross he had seen and told them to make a replica of it.

With this cross carried before him, Constantine was able to defeat his enemy and unite the Roman Empire. He had been victorious with the help of the God of the Christians, so he issued an edict ending the persecution of Christians and began a process of Christianizing the empire.

Once Christianity had been a local, exclusive sect; now it became the official religion of Rome.

Our dreams are for the most part jumbled perceptions of the spirit worlds that are hard to understand. But sometimes when spiritual beings have something important to communicate, dreams are their vehicle. They are then much clearer. In the story of Maxentius and Constantine we see spiritual impulses working in concert through the dreams of different individuals to bring about a great turning point in history.

Some historians doubt Constantine's sincerity, though it is surely much in his favour that he chaired the Council of Nicea, which decided Church doctrine, and that he even guided the discussions. He had later visions of St Michael, built the Church of the Holy Sepulchre and the Church of the Holy Nativity in the Holy Land and the Basilica of St Peter in Rome, and he laid the foundations of Hagia Sophia in Constantinople. His mother, Helena, who shared his enthusiasms, journeyed to the Holy Land and unearthed the Spear of Longinus, which had pierced the side of Jesus Christ on the cross.

There is no doubt of Constantine's burning desire to understand spiritual reality at the most profound levels. He did not promote a narrow and dogmatic Christianity that denied the spiritual reality of other religious traditions. He said that reading of the birth of a solar saviour and the dawn of a new golden age in Vergil's fourth *Eclogue* had helped convert him to Christianity. Before he died he moved the capital of the empire to Byzantium – renamed Constantinople after himself – because of a Sibylline prophecy of the fall of Rome. As a mark of this, he had a holy relic, the Palladium, a small wooden statue carved by Athene, buried under a column in the middle of the new capital. In the ancient world it was believed that a city containing the Palladium would have special, divine protection.

*   *   *

A fifteen-year-old girl was tending a flock of sheep belonging to her stepmother. Her natural parents had made her leave her home in Antioch because they wouldn't tolerate her Christianity. But she was making a new life for herself in the countryside and she was happy.

Then one day the governor of Antioch was walking through the fields and spotted her sitting by a well. He saw how beautiful she was and he was consumed with desire for her. He said to himself, 'I'll take her for my mistress.'

He waited until he was back in town and surrounded by the accoutrements of power, then he told his servants to bring her before

The initiation of a Roman poet (by the French initiate painter Nicolas Poussin).

him. But she refused. They reported back: 'She says she doesn't give a hawthorn berry for all your power!'

He told them to bring her before him, by force if necessary. 'I'll change her mind for her soon enough.'

When she was dragged into his chambers, he demanded to know who she was. She said that she was called Margaret, that she was of noble lineage and that she was a Christian.

The governor vowed to himself that he would make her love him. He offered her gold and asked to marry her. But it was he who was falling in love . . .

When he could see she really would have none of it, he became enraged and told his men to bind her hand and foot. Then she was hung up on the wall and beaten until blood ran from her body like water from a spring.

'Maid Margaret,' said the governor, 'is this pain good?'

Still she would not relent and in the end the governor had to cover his face with his cloak, because he could not bear to see so much blood. He told his soldiers to take her down and throw her into prison.

That night, as she lay feverishly on the blood-soaked straw, she saw a great horned snake as green as the grass in summer glide towards her, opening its loathsome mouth as if to swallow her whole.

'Get away from me, you evil spirit!'

She struck out at it, flung it away from her. Then she struggled to her feet and planted one foot on it, pinning it to the floor.

She said, 'Lie still under the feet of a woman.'

The next morning she was found with her foot on the unconscious form of one of her jailers. The governor knew then that his love for her was hopeless and he condemned her to death.

*   *   *

In 380 a Spanish mystic called Priscillian was excommunicated, accused of conducting the Mass in the nude and of impregnating a young woman who was part of his flock. In 386 he was tortured and executed, the first Christian to be martyred by other Christians. The Church fathers looked on with approval.[2]

*   *   *

204 | THE SACRED HISTORY

Genevieve was born in 419. A simple young shepherd girl, she moved to Paris to join a convent. She was prone to fits and visions. She talked of the different orders of angels described by Dionysius, and warned of dark angels – which is why she is often depicted with a demon on her shoulder.

She made people nervous. Some wondered if she was possessed and they plotted to throw her in the Seine.

One night she was walking through the city with a group of nuns, their way home lit only by a solitary candle. It was a still night without a breath of wind, but suddenly the candle was snuffed out. The others were afraid, saying that a demon had done it, that it was a sign that Paris would fall to Attila the Hun. Genevieve took hold of the candle herself and immediately it flared up again.

Attila *was* approaching. As his armies came over the horizon, people started to panic. Many began leaving, yielding the city to the invader. But Genevieve had a vision. She went about the streets crying, 'I see it! I know it! They will not come! Let the men flee if they want to. We women will pray so hard that God will surely hear our prayers.'

She calmed the people and persuaded them not to abandon the city.

Her vision proved accurate: Attila promptly turned south.

St Dionysius – St Denis – and Genevieve would become the patron saints of Paris.

*   *   *

In 438 Constantinople was destroyed by an earthquake. The population huddled in the nearby fields, praying for the tremors to cease.

Suddenly, from the middle of the crowd, a child was swept up into the air by an invisible force, ascending until people could see him no longer.

After a while he floated back down and he told the assembled crowd and the emperor himself that he had been present at a great concert given by angels in the sky, praising the Lord.

The bishop of Constantinople later wrote that the entire population of the city had witnessed this event.

*   *   *

In the rest of this book, as we move into modern times, we will see if it is still possible to experience the world as Socrates, St Paul, Plotinus and Mani experienced it, interacting with disembodied intelligence, and we will ask if the same supernatural patterns can be seen weaving around us.

Do people today wield the same supernatural powers as the Apostles?

Gregory the Great sending missionaries to convert the English (miniature from the tenth century attributed to St Dunstan). Gregory saw angels on many occasions, as well as collecting the accounts of others who had done the same. He was curious about the mental states in which spiritual perceptions were achieved, distinguishing between the 'shadow mixed with light', when the power of the imagination was mixed with reason, and the great visions which could only be achieved through the highest forms of contemplation. (Carol Zaleski, *Otherworld Journeys*, Oxford University Press, 1987, 89–90)

The Temptation of St Antony (from a wall painting in S. Sepolcro, Barletta). 'The golden haloes around the heads of pagan gods and Christian saints refer both to their being bathed in the glory of the sun and also to the fact that a spiritual sun within their own natures is radiating its *glow-ray* and surrounding them with celestial splendour. Whenever the nimbus is composed of straight radiant lines, it is solar in significance; whenever curved lines are used for beams, it partakes lunar nature; whenever they are united, it symbolizes a harmonious blending of both principles.' W. and G. Audsley, *Handbook of Christian Symbolism*, 1865.

The Mountain Comes to Mohammed

'All men are asleep. They only wake up when they die.'

Traditional wisdom quoted by Mohammed

This is a history of the world that includes the parts that conventional historians have discarded – stories that have nevertheless loomed in our collective imagination.

The phrase 'believe in magic' can be used in two ways. It can either mean that you believe you are justified in using it or that you believe that it works. If you haven't given in to the materialistic view that mind is just a by-product of matter, you may well use it in the latter sense.

Mohammed certainly believed in magic in this way. He said, 'The influence of the evil eye is a fact.' A large part of his mission was to stamp it out.[1]

We saw earlier how the Harrowing of Hell caused a surge in demonic activity and appearances of the spirits of the dead. The barrier between the physical and spiritual worlds seemed very thin then, and the proliferation of religions, philosophies and sects continued. Mystery centres in places like Luxor, Karnak, Delphi, Corinth and Eleusis, where entry into the spiritual worlds was managed under controlled conditions, were closed down. Priests, magi who knew how to practise these techniques, were driven underground. Many fled south to Arabia, which is perhaps one of the reasons why that region looms large in the human imagination as a land of enchantment.

We have been tracing the development of the unique human faculty of free will. Individuals were now able to exercise this faculty to try to compel spiritual beings to do their bidding.[2]

A follower of Apollonius called Alexander of Abonoteichos kept a very large tame snake he named Glycon. He put the mask of a human face on it, made out of linen, and people came to visit, looking for miraculous healings and fortune telling.

There were reports of brass bottles sealed with lead stoppers that were being caught in fishermen's nets and washed up on shores of Africa. It was said that if you broke the stopper a blue-ish smoke would emerge and fleetingly take a human form – and that these were bottles in which Solomon had imprisoned *jinn*.

Simon Magus was the pupil of an Arabian magician. He travelled widely, accompanied by a beautiful woman called Helena. He claimed she was a reincarnation of Helen of Troy. It was said that his power as a magus came in part from the sex magic he performed with her.

His many well-attested feats of magic included healing the sick and raising the dead, making statues come alive and speak, flying and making himself invisible. It was said that he could command legions of demons.

He taught that each human being had in their innermost depths the root of the universe, a source of endless power.

Late in life, when his own powers and fame seemed to be fading, he allowed himself to be buried alive for three days, promising he would rise from the dead. But when people gathered to witness this, his cries were heard echoing up from hell. Pope Paul I had a church built over his grave just to be on the safe side.

*　　　　　*　　　　　*

Mohammed was born in 570. He was raised in a land where people had once believed in a supreme creator, but now set their sights lower and worshipped idols carved out of wood, granite or agate.

Their greatest shrine was the Ka'bah at Mecca, which had hundreds of idols of wood and stone around and inside it, many of them bedecked with jewels. Some were in the form of animals – for instance Nasr, the vulture god. Others were deities of the stars and planets, including three moon goddesses. There were statues of Moses and Jesus Christ and a painting of the Virgin Mary. Sacrifices were made there, sometimes of hundreds of camels at a time. Mecca was also a great commercial centre, with great caravans arriving to sell camels, slaves and women. Doctors and magicians rubbed shoulders with thieves, gamblers and prostitutes.

When he was six, Mohammed's mother died and he was sent to live with his grandfather. He worked as a shepherd, as a cameleer for merchants and then, when he was twenty-five, he began to manage the estates of a rich widow called Khadijah.

Mohammed liked to wander alone around the countryside, sometimes pitching his tent on Mount Hirah with its magnificent views of the city and the plains. Something was troubling him – a thirst for the infinite. The cults of the Ka'bah would not do. He didn't speak to anyone for several months. He became unkempt and wild-eyed. He was hearing voices he knew weren't human.

One day he heard a new voice in the wind: 'You are the chosen one. Proclaim the name of the Lord.'

He fled up Mount Hirah to a cave. But he saw the outline of a giant figure standing near him. Was it a *jinn*? He felt this being's eyes upon him and heard it say with a voice that was as clear and distinct as any voice he had ever heard: 'Recite!'

'I can't recite . . .' He had never been able to recite, because he had not been taught to read.

'Recite!'

Some lines of text appeared in the air in front of him in blazing letters of fire. They were what would become the first lines of the Koran, and now he found that he *could* read.

Mohammed left the cave and climbed to the top of the mountain. The voice spoke to him, closer now, in his ear: 'Thou art the messenger of God, and I am Gabriel, His Archangel.'

Gabriel continued to come to Mohammed. As he moved about the streets he often felt the archangel's eyes on him. Sometimes Gabriel came to him in his house, often during the night, sometimes as a voice, sometimes in human form, and gradually he taught Mohammed the truths of the Koran. So it was that a simple illiterate man, not particularly articulate, created the greatest, most complex, most beautifully phrased, most sublime, supreme work in the Arabic tongue.

Eventually Gabriel said, 'Step forth and preach the new faith to the world.'

Mohammed's wife was the first to accept his message, then soon a small group of followers gathered around him.

'Pray to God, be good to the captive and the poor and the orphan, and give alms . . . feed the hungry, be compassionate and helpful . . . be steadfast in justice, witnessing before God though it be against yourselves, or your parents or your kindred, be it rich or poor.'

Mohammed also taught that whenever a group of people gathered to remember God, they would be surrounded by angels.

He began preaching in public. The crowd called on him to perform miracles, but he refused. He pointed out that Jesus had performed miracles and despite this he had not been widely believed. 'I am but a man like the others,' he said.

Later he went to Ka'bah and stood beside the statues of the moon goddesses. 'They are nothing, only what your fathers created!'

There were angry shouts.

'There is no god but Allah, and Mohammed is his prophet.'

Men in the crowd said he was a dangerous madman.

In the days that followed, children and slaves began to throw stones at Mohammed in the street. Once he had to plead to be let back in through the city and when he returned home his face was covered in blood.

He was lying on his bed, nearly despairing, when he saw a figure enter the room. He started, knocking over a cup of water.

It was Gabriel, wearing golden robes and leading a creature with the body of a horse but the head of a human. This was Buraq, the heavenly steed.

'Ride with me,' said Gabriel. 'I will show you great things.'

They flew over the deserts to Jerusalem, where they saw the ladder that Jacob had seen. They climbed it and when they knocked on the silver doors of the first heaven, they were admitted by Adam.

From there they travelled through the seven heavens, meeting Moses and Abraham. They saw an angel with a body made of fire and ice and another with 70,000 heads. Each head had 70,000 mouths and each mouth had 70,000 tongues, and each tongue spoke 70,000 languages – and they were all praising God.

In the seventh heaven was a house of prayer. Gabriel told Mohammed that 70,000 angels visited it every day. Now Mohammed joined the angels encircling the house of prayer seven times.

God was sitting on his throne above the seventh heaven, seventy veils covering his face. He laid his hands on Mohammed and taught him the deeper meaning of prayer. He then commanded that Mohammed be shown the inhabitants of hell, and afterwards Buraq carried him back to Mecca and to his bed.

The cup of water he had knocked over had not yet hit the ground.

Like Enoch and Paul, Mohammed had been taken on a heavenly journey that would change history. But when he first tried to tell the inhabitants of Mecca about it, their hostility towards him increased.

The reality was that Mohammed's message of justice for all threatened the privileges of the ruling élite and his attacks on the cults that surrounded the Ka'bah threatened their commercial interests too. Mohammed was driven out into the desert.

There, among the Bedouin tribes, he began to find mass support. The modern world was coming into being in the desert, not only in this message of freedom and equality but in Mohammed's continuing refusal to countenance miracles. For Mohammed, the material world, the world of the senses, was miraculous enough. For the rest he persuaded people to follow him because his universal truths were reasonable. The emphasis on logic and on what was clearly or demonstrably true, would make Islam the starting point for modern science.

Mohammed helped build a simple house of prayer out of mud bricks, dried in the sun. In front of it was a courtyard to shelter the homeless.

He told a fable:

When God created the Earth, its form was not fixed and it shivered, so God took mountains and put them in place to keep the Earth still. The angels said to Him, 'Allah, is there anything in creation stronger than mountains?'

'Iron can break mountains.'

'Is iron the strongest thing in creation?'

'Fire melts iron.'

'Is there anything mightier than fire?'

'Water puts out fire.'

'Is there anything mightier than water?'

'Wind can overpower water.'

'O merciful God, what is the mightiest thing on Earth?'

And Allah replied: 'The most beautiful thing in creation is a compassionate person who gives alms. If he gives with his right hand without his left hand knowing, he is stronger and more powerful than all things.'

Mohammed was fifty-two. It seemed to him that he had a message the whole world needed to hear, but that people were corrupt, idolatrous and living in misery. Solomon had spoken very wisely and Jesus had been mild and performed miracles, but Mohammed saw that neither had been able to turn all the peoples of the world into believers in the One God.

So Mohammed sent out a proclamation that anyone who wished to serve Allah and his messenger should assemble at a well near Medina. Three hundred men arrived. They had between them just two horses and seventy camels.

Mohammed's enemies, on the other hand, had mustered an army of two thousand. The two armies faced each other. Mohammed raised the black flag of war, picked up a handful of sand and threw it in the direction of his enemies, saying, 'May confusion cover their faces.' The wind carried the sand and brought angels over the horizon, casting terror into the unbelievers' hearts.

A strange sword was found in the sand, too, and Mohammed took it up. It was seven yards long and had two blades. The enemy fell away before Mohammed and his men. Afterwards, he said, 'The angels of God brought our victory today.'³

When Mohammed rode into Mecca in triumph, he headed through the deserted streets straight for the Ka'bah and circled it seven times. Then he took his staff and smashed the idols till they lay in pieces in the dust, even the statue of Abraham.

When the people realized that Mohammed didn't mean to harm them, they began to come out of hiding. They stood gazing at the mounds of broken idols. Then they all heard a sound and looked up.

'Arise for prayer. Prayer is better than sleep.'

It was a black man, a former slave to whom Mohammed had given the honour of making the first *muezzin*.

Mohammed died in 632. After his funeral there were reports of a strange old man with a white beard. He was first seen standing at the back of the crowd, but then he seemed to move spring-heeled through the people until he stood by the side of the body. There he paid his condolences to Mohammed's closest companions.

Afterwards, when he had disappeared, these companions explained that they had been talking to Khdir.

We have met this old man before. He is a green thread running through this book.

Charlemagne and the Paladins of Pain

Islam spread north into Europe until the tide was stopped and turned back by Charlemagne, the Holy Roman Emperor. The greatest military hero in Christian history, he fought to defend what Constantine had established.

Charlemagne was over seven feet tall and had piercing blue eyes. He had twelve paladins (noble lords), and one of them was a traitor.

Eventually, after seven years of fighting, Charlemagne drove the Muslims out of Spain and was master of all except for a small enclave near Saragossa.

Forced to sue for peace, the Muslim king sent emissaries to Charlemagne. They found him seated on a golden throne in an orchard, white-bearded yet still handsome and proud of his manly bearing. They delivered this message to him: 'If you cease this unhappy war and return to France, our king will give you 400 mules loaded with gold and fifty cartloads of silver, along with bears, lions, 700 camels and 1,000 falcons. He will also go to Aix to be baptized.'

Charlemagne consulted his paladins and decided to accept.

But the Saracen king also had been holding secret talks with Ganelon, the Judas among the paladins.

'What do you think of Charlemagne?' the Muslim king had asked. 'Through how many lands has he carried that old carcass of his? It's very strange how he never seems to tire of fighting.'

Ganelon replied that Charlemagne would never give up war while he had by his side his favourite knight – his nephew and right-hand man. 'It's Roland,' he said, 'who gives the old man the taste for war.'

So they devised a plan. Ganelon advised Charlemagne to put Roland in command of a rearguard which would be detailed to stay near the entrance to the Pyrenees at a place called the Valley of Thorns. They would be told to stay there to protect the rear of the French army while it wended its way through the narrow mountain passes back to France.

So it came about that Roland stood on a high rock and waved as he watched the French army recede. It was about to disappear. Charlemagne waved back, then faced forward, and his army resumed its march. The ground shook with the heavy tramp of the mailed horses and the emperor wept silently. The previous night he had dreamt about hunting in the forests of the Ardennes and being attacked by a boar and a leopard, and now he worried about his nephew's safety.

After thirty miles the French soldiers knew they were reaching the far side of the Pyrenees and a shout of joy went up when they saw the sunny fields of France ahead.

Meanwhile Roland had come down from the high rock to rejoin his troops. The valleys were gloomy, but the sky was blue and the shields of Roland's soldiers flashed in the sun.

Suddenly they heard the sound of hundreds of trumpets. Roland's brother knight Oliver climbed a pine tree and looked into the valley behind them. There were thousands upon thousands of Saracen soldiers approaching. They had walked into a trap.

'Brother Roland, I pray thee, blow your horn. Charlemagne will hear and come to our aid.'

'I need no aid except my sword, Durandal,' said Roland.

Durandal was the wonderful sword that had belonged to Hector.

'Watch it flashing in the thickest part of the fighting,' said Roland, 'and it will soon be dyed in Saracen blood.'

'But I've seen the size of their army,' said Oliver. 'We've never fought against such overwhelming odds. Please, brother, blow your ivory horn.'

'Don't say another word,' said Roland. 'The emperor himself entrusted us with this mission.'

'Roland, for the love of God, blow your horn!'

But Roland pointed Durandal towards heaven and cried, 'The day shall be ours!'

Then thousands of swords leapt from their sheaths, as the Saracens swarmed over the rocks and joined the French in battle. They hemmed the French in on every side and soon only sixty Frenchmen were left alive.

At last Roland placed the horn to his lips and blew a mighty blast that echoed through the narrow gorges until it was heard thirty miles away.

'Roland's horn!' said Charlemagne. 'He's in trouble!'

'You're growing white-haired and flowery,' said Ganelon, riding next to him. 'You're too indulgent. Roland is fond of blowing his horn. He does it all day long.'

The horn again.

'Don't fret,' said Ganelon. 'He's only hunting.'

Roland blew his horn a third time. He blew it so hard that blood vessels burst in his temples and blood poured from his mouth and ears.

Charlemagne heard him falter and knew he had been tricked. He gave orders that Ganelon should be thrown in chains – he would deal with him later – and turned his great army round to go to the aid of his favourite nephew.

After a while he saw in the distance that only two Frenchmen were left standing, and they were surrounded. He ordered his trumpeters to blow, and when the Saracens heard it and saw what was coming, they made a last frantic effort to kill Roland. They knew that if he survived, the war between Muslim and Christian would last forever.

Roland lay dying, but he was proud that Charlemagne would find forty dead Saracens for every dead Frenchman. He stretched his right glove heavenwards and an unseen hand came down and took him.

Arriving in the valley, Charlemagne found only piles of corpses. Then he saw a cloud of dust in the distance and ordered his men to set off in pursuit.

The chase ended after the Saracens had been reinforced by a fleet and by the leadership of the emir. Two great armies met on a plain by the sea.

Roland in the Valley of Thorns (drawing from a window in Chartres cathedral).

Now there were giants among the Saracens who had great bristles along their spines like wild boar, and men with hides so thick they had no need of armour.

The battle raged all day and then in the evening, amidst the crumpled shields, entwined chainmail and creaking hauberks, Charlemagne shouted, '*Mountjoie!*' and the emir shouted the Muslim battle-cry, '*Precieuse!*' and they recognized each other's voices high and clear above the tumult. They rushed towards each other to finish it.

Their spears shattered against each other's shields and both slid from their horses. They were quickly on their feet, drawing their swords. The emir struck the emperor on his helmet with such a blow that it was split in two. The sword cut through his hair and took the skin off his scalp to a hand's width. Charlemagne was staggering back, wanting to fall, but then he heard Gabriel talking to him, saying, 'Great king, what does thou?'

The vision of Charlemagne (from a miniature in the *Chroniques de Saint-Denis*, thirteenth century).

And, finding himself called into question, he also found the strength to lift his sword, *Joyeuse*, one last time and bring it down on the emir's blazing jewel-encrusted helmet. He cut his head in two all the way down to his beard, so that his brains were caught up in his sword.

The battle was won.

Back home, lying in his bed, Charlemagne received another visit from the archangel: 'Charlemagne, you shall summon up your empire's army again and rescue another Christian king . . .'

'God, what a life of toil is mine!' said Charlemagne, and he wept until his beard was soaked with tears.[1]

*   *   *

We noted earlier that Solomon's Temple was much more modest in scale than we tend to imagine it. The battles around the siege of Troy were no doubt on a much smaller scale than Hollywood imagines them, and history tells us that in reality the battle in the Valley of Thorns was little more than a skirmish. The magnificent visions that have come down to us are much greater and more meaningful than they would perhaps have seemed if we had been there and observed events with the physical eye, because they describe the spiritual worlds breaking into the material world, the boundary between the two dissolving and gods and angels intervening in human affairs.

We have seen that the growing tip of the spiritual evolution of humankind has passed from one civilization to another, from Tibet and India to Persia, to Sumeria and Egypt, to the Jews and the Greeks, to Rome, Jerusalem and Arabia. If the siege of Troy marked the beginning of the ascendancy of Greek civilization, this battle in the Valley of Thorns marked the beginning of the ascent of European civilization, as the advance of Islam was finally checked.

And yet paradoxically the great flowering of European culture came from Islamic seeds. Charlemagne famously exchanged gifts with Haroun al Raschid, the caliph of the *Tales of the Arabian Nights*, who sent him some remarkable mechanical toys quite unlike anything that had ever been seen in Europe. Much has been written about the way that Arab intellectuals preserved and developed scientific ideas and techniques that later became key to the scientific revolution in Europe.[2] The Arab influence on the spiritual growth of Europe, on art, literature, philosophy and indeed on the whole of human nature as it was then evolving, was more evanescent but, as we shall also see, no less illuminating and transformative.

*   *   *

Mohammed listed the seven signs by which you could tell a 'friend of God'. They are similar to the gifts of the Holy Spirit. Friends of God have the power of truth, so that no one can oppose them. They have the gifts of clairvoyance and inspiration. Anyone who hurts them receives swift retribution. Everyone praises them – except the envious. Their prayers are always answered. Wonderful things happen around them. They are sometimes seen suddenly disappearing into the ground, walking on water – or speaking with Khdir.

Khdir is a wonder-worker in big but also intimate things, an inspiration to poets who also helps people to confront their greatest fears. We have already met him at the confluence of the two waters, when Moses met the mysterious and irascible old man.

A Sufi mystic, Ibrahim ibn Adham, wrote about his life in the desert.[3] Hungry and thirsty, he was at first glad to come across another human being. But then he quickly realized that this very old, impoverished hermit had nothing to give him.

Nevertheless they stayed together and in the evening the old man performed the evening prayer and said things Ibrahim could not follow. Then Ibrahim looked and saw food in his bowl and water in his bottle.

The old man stayed with him for several days, during which time he taught Ibrahim the Supreme Name of God. Soon afterwards, he left.

Sometime later, hungry and thirsty again, angry with the world and his place in it, Ibrahim called out for help, using the Supreme Name. Immediately he felt someone clutching his waist and heard an urgent whisper: 'Ask and it will be given!'

He trembled with fear. Then he recognized the old man's voice.

'Do not fear,' the old man said. 'I mean you no harm. I am your brother Khdir. But never use the Supreme Name in anger again, because it will cause great destruction in this world and the next . . .'

And with that the old man disappeared again.

Khdir, sometimes identified with Elijah, is the unseen teacher of Sufism. Sufism is a mystical dimension of Islam, though its roots are older and have been absorbed into Islam from earlier spiritual traditions. Sufis in the Caucasus mountains in Turkey trace their traditions back to Melchezedek's meeting with Abraham.

Stories about Khdir generally involve the supernatural. He changes himself into a log and floats downstream. He enables a schoolboy to remember the whole of the Koran instantly. He asks a man to eat an apple, and looking at the apple the man sees an ocean running from the throne of God to the Earth and shining like the sun. A wicked king keeps trying to execute him, but he keeps reappearing – and this extraordinary magical figure will keep reappearing in this book too.[4]

Dean Stanley, a Victorian theologian famous in his day, found a

Muslim chapel dedicated to Khdir on the seashore near Sarafand, north of Tyre. Fascinated, he ventured inside to discover an empty tomb. When he asked some local peasants why it was empty, they said that Khdir wasn't dead yet, but flew around the word, appearing wherever he was needed.

*   *   *

Green is the colour of regeneration. The Green Knight who arrived at the court of King Arthur was beheaded but 'sprang up again and so amazed them all'. In alchemy green is the colour of the life forces that work in the subtle borderland between mind and matter. It is the colour of imagination that sees into the inner life of things, and by doing so, changes them.

'Wisdom awakens to wetness and greenness and to flowing waters. Wisdom says I am the rain coming from the dew that causes the grasses to laugh with the joy of life.' Here, in the writings of Hildegard of Bingen, a Christian nun of the twelfth century, we come very close to the spirit of Khdir.[5]

It is a sign of what is to come.

Perceval Makes a Fool of Himself

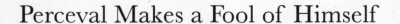

'It is only with the heart that one can see rightly;
what is essential is invisible to the eye.'

Antoine de Saint-Exupéry

Following the Muslim threat which had arisen in the seventh century, and which led eventually to the crusades, the profession of knighthood was Christianized in the form of chivalry. Early on knights were made when, at the climax of the ceremony, a squire was tapped on the head with a sword – an echo of the initiation ceremonies of the ancient world.

Perceval's mother decided that she would never tell him he was the son of one of Charlemagne's paladins.[1] Her husband had fought and died with Roland, and so she tried to shield her son from the glamour of knighthood and the obligations of life at court.

Mother and son were a world unto themselves. They lived deep in the woods where no one could find them. The mother dressed her little boy in a coat made out of rabbit skins with a pointed hood like a fool's cap. They washed in the stream and lived on fruit, berries and roots and the milk of the goats until the boy was old enough to hunt for birds' eggs and make himself a bow, so that he could kill small deer. His mother noticed that he was growing strong and handsome. He was a fast runner too.

One spring day he was alone in a clearing in the woods when he heard a strange clanking sound. Three knights in armour rode into the clearing. Perceval had never even seen a man before and when he saw these knights in shining silver and gold armour, quite dazzling in the shafts of sunlight coming through the trees, he thought he must be seeing the angels that his mother had told him about.

The knights laughed at him, but in a kind way, and Perceval knew he wanted to be like them.

His mother was heartbroken when he eventually told her he wanted to leave and find his place in the world, but she knew she had to let him go. She told him to honour and serve all women, to be courteous to all men, to avoid untrodden ways and to enter every church he saw.

As Perceval left their home in the forest, his loving mother kissed him goodbye and smiled, knowing she had nothing left.

On his wanderings the boy came upon the cave of a hermit, who told him it wasn't manly to mention his mother quite so much. Then he fitted Perceval up with a horse and a lance. 'Life is a proving time,' he told him.

Perceval wanted to be a man, to be a knight, but he was rubbish at it. He was laughed at, especially by women. A knight in red armour laughed at him behind his back, calling him a rustic youth in a fool's cap. He tried to joust with a dwarf knight who looked like a monkey on a greyhound, but the dwarf unseated the would-be hero. One night a beautiful young woman slipped into his bed, but he didn't know what to do.

He was restless. He decided to go back and visit his mother, not knowing she had died of heartbreak. But he got lost and couldn't find his way back to the woods of his childhood.

One evening he was riding by a grey and misty lake when he came across an old man in a boat fishing. He looked pale and sad and as grey as the mists. Percival asked if there was anywhere nearby he might find food and shelter for the night, and the fisherman told him that if

The Fisher King

he followed the shore of the lake, he would find a castle and that he would be treated kindly there.

Perceval set off in the direction the fisherman had indicated. The castle was a long way away, and it was dark when he arrived, but the servants there seemed be expecting him. They took his horse off to be fed and watered, and led Perceval into a great brightly lit hall.

Four hundred knights were already at table. They were all bearded and wearing white hauberks displaying the emblem of the red cross. They watched solemn-faced and in silence as Perceval was led by the servants to the top table by the fire. Here a man sat on a wooden throne, wrapped in sable.

When Percival was near enough he was surprised to discover that this lord of the castle was the fisherman he had spoken to earlier. Now he was shivering, obviously cold even though he was sitting right next to the fire. In fact he looked as if he was suffering from a wasting disease.

'You have been long expected,' he said, and gestured for young Perceval to sit down next to him.

Perceval now noticed that there was a stench of illness in the hall.

At that moment a servant entered at the far end, carrying a lance. All watched in silence as he walked around the hall, and when he approached the top table Perceval could see that there was a drop of blood on the tip of the lance.

He was on the point of asking his host the meaning of this ceremony, but then, as the servant with the lance left the hall, a procession entered and the sight of it awed him into silence. Two nobly dressed women carried golden candelabras, each with seven candles, around the hall. Then a third woman, also nobly dressed, appeared, carrying a golden bowl. She too walked around the hall.

Percival was impressed by the solemnity of the occasion but also slightly worried. Everyone else seemed to understand the significance of the ceremony and he began to wonder if he ought to know too? Everyone now seemed to be looking at him expectantly, but he didn't know what he was supposed to do. He wanted to ask, but felt overawed and thought that perhaps he should remain silent, like the 400 knights.

When the bowl had been carried from the room, dinner was served and eaten, again in hushed silence.

Afterwards, Perceval's host turned to him and looked at him eagerly. Still Perceval didn't know what to say. His host turned away in disappointment and, supported by two servants, dragged himself to his feet and left.

Two more servants arrived to escort Perceval to his chamber. Before leaving the hall, they opened a door and showed him a room off to the side. There, in front of a large tapestry of a battle scene, an extremely old man lay on a low couch. His still handsome face was wreathed in white curls. He lay semi-conscious it seemed, lips quivering, mouthing words Perceval could not quite make out.

That night Percival had disturbing, even demonic dreams. He was attacked by beaks and talons. He awoke bleary-eyed.

To his surprise no servants came to help him get ready in the morning and when he emerged from his room he could find no signs of life. He called out. No reply. The place seemed completely deserted.

He tried various doors, which turned out to be locked.

It took a while before he found one that was unlocked. It opened into another chamber, where again all the doors were locked except one. By this means Perceval found himself ushered into the main court-yard, where his horse was saddled and waiting.

He crossed the drawbridge and immediately it was drawn up behind him. He heard a voice: 'Cursed be he who was chosen to do great work and has not done it. Go and return no more.'

He looked up and saw a flash of green eyes between the battlements.

As he rode away it began to snow. He rode on with a crushing feeling of failure and disappointment.

Five years later, following a series of desultory adventures, he at last fell in with a knight who invited him to join his fellowship of knights. Perceval had been wishing for this ever since the day when, as a boy dressed in rabbit skins, he had seen the three knights riding in the woods.

But as the heralds blew their trumpets to announce Perceval's initiation into the fellowship, a veiled figure arrived at court on a donkey.

She threw back her veil. Her nose was hooked like a beak, her skin was withered brown like a leaf in winter and her eyes were a fiendish green. She said, 'Perceval is unworthy of the honour you intend to bestow upon him. He was chosen for the greatest quest of any knight and he failed.' She also told the assembled company that while still an unbearded boy he had callously left his mother to die, and that she had died cursing him.

Perceval hung his head and the ladies of the court sniggered at his new humiliation.

So yet again the young fool set out on his travels, alone once more. He wanted above all to return to the Grail Castle, but could not seem to retrace his steps. It was as if he was playing a game of chess with a mind infinitely greater than his own.

In those days the winters were becoming harsher and longer, until they seemed to take up most of the year. Crops were failing and the people were desperately hungry.

Wandering through the cold grey wasteland at dusk, Perceval met a group of barefoot pilgrims, praying for forgiveness and for the end of the bad times. They rebuked him for carrying arms on a holy day. He said he was truly sorry, that he'd lost track of time and hadn't real-ized what day it was. Seeing that he was feverish, they smiled kindly at him and forgave him.

Merlin – the enchanter enchanted
(fragment of a medieval book binding from Limoges).

Then he remembered what his mother had told him about going inside every church. He asked to be directed to the hermitage. He wanted to pray.

He found a small white thatched building in a grove of firethorn trees. Its berries shone like fairy lights in the setting sun.

Frozen to the bone and exhausted, Perceval dragged himself to the door and knocked. It was opened and, stooping to enter, he was surprised to find a hermit of tall, noble bearing. The hermit helped him over to a bed of moss and Percival gratefully lay down on it. He was so tired that he fell asleep immediately.

In the morning he noticed a sword with an elaborate golden hilt hanging on the wall and asked to whom it belonged. The hermit explained that he had once been a knight and led a wild and pleasure-seeking life, fighting for fame and riches and to win the love of many women. He said that he was the brother of a man called Amfortas and that they had been partners in crime until his brother had been wounded in the genitals by a poisoned spear. Amfortas, he said, was now in such pain that he wished only to die, but could not. He was too ill to live, but not ill enough to die.

They were the grandsons of a king called Titurel, the hermit explained, and he went on to tell his story . . .

One spring morning, Titurel, just home from fighting against the Saracens, was walking in the woods. He felt as if God was speaking to him in the songs of the birds, the rustling of the foliage and the murmur of the brook. He noticed that there was one soft fleecy cloud in the clear blue sky – and was surprised to see it coming towards him with astonishing speed.

Suddenly the voice of an angel came out of the cloud, telling Titurel that he had been chosen to build a castle on Montsalvaat to guard the Holy Grail . . .

Thus Titurel and his family became guardians of the Grail. But they fell into bad ways, and as a result, Titurel's grandson, Amfortas, and the land itself were now wasting away with illness.

Titurel prayed continually. He had been told of a prophecy that a chosen one, a pure fool, would come. He would come with compassion and an enquiring mind – and if he asked the right question before nightfall, the evil spell afflicting the family and the land would be broken. Amfortas would be cured of his wound, the wild blood would be purified and spring would come to the wasteland once again.

The hermit went on to tell Perceval that a man could not find the Grail castle by *intending* to find it. The castle had to find him.

Perceval did not perhaps understand completely with his intellect, but in his heart of hearts he did.

'The All-merciful only speaks to those who have received Him into their hearts,' said the hermit, and he told Perceval that his mother had died not long after he had left their home in the woods and that she had died blessing him. Perceval wept.[2]

In no time at all he found himself at the gates of the castle. Again
he was expected. Amfortas and the 400 knights were in the same places
as before. The squire came in with the lance again, then the maidens
with the candelabras and finally the queen carrying the Grail.[3]

Perceval prayed: 'Merciful Father, and our sweet Lord and Saviour,
teach me what I must do!' and it seemed to him then that angels spoke
in his ear, saying just one world: 'Ask!'

Turning to Amfortas, he said, 'What ails you, great king?'

Immediately the Grail shone with a light that eclipsed everything
else in the hall, and Perceval suddenly found that Titurel was standing
beside him holding a crown over his head. A beam of sunlight came
in through a hole in the roof and struck the crown, illuminating it so
that it seemed to open up like a flower.

The name 'Perceval' means 'coming through the vale'. Perceval had
journeyed beyond pain and humiliation until he finally found the kingly
part of himself.

In Perceval's story we are beginning to see the stirrings of a
distinctively Islamic wisdom in the soul of Europe. Sufi ideas on the
inner life were spreading, and transforming European culture and
consciousness. According to Ibn Arabi, the great teacher of Sufism, we
may know the constant changing of the Absolute and the changing of
the world by scanning our own hearts. If we see with our inner eye
how our own heart in all its myriad states and dimensions is mutating,
transforming and evolving at every fleeing moment, then we may also
begin to understand the operations of the divine.

Perceval's great quest is also an inner journey, and finding the Grail
is arriving at an understanding of his own evolving consciousness. He
is learning a new questing spirituality and compassion. He discovers a
new direction of the heart which is also a direction for humanity.

Tales of the Arabian Nights

The sands' amount, the measures of the sea,
Tho' vast in number, are well known to me.
I know the thoughts within the dumb conceal'd,
And words I hear by language unrevealed.

Oracle of Apollo, given to Croesus

Tales of the Arabian Nights combines glittering descriptions of the material world with magical thinking. The story of the City of Brass is a mirror image of Perceval's quest for the Grail.

Three explorers – an emir, a wazir and a sheikh – and their servants set off across unknown territory to find the fabled City of Brass.

After nearly two years they came to a high hill where they found a brass statue of a horseman carrying a glistening spear. On the spear was an inscription: 'O you who come to me, if you do not know the way that leads to the City of Brass, rub the hand of the horseman and he will turn and then will stop, and in whatsoever direction he stops, thither proceed.'

Emir Musa rubbed the hand and the automaton turned and pointed the way with his spear.

The explorers continued their journey until in the middle of a vast and desolate plain they came across a pillar of stone from which protruded two stone wings and four stone legs like the legs of lions. There were also two eyes high up in the pillar that burned like coals and a third eye in the middle, green like a lynx's eye. A voice seemed to speak to them, telling them he was a *jinn* trapped in the pillar by Solomon. When they asked him the way to the City of Brass, he directed them and they set off again.

Then one evening they saw on the horizon between two hills a black object with what looked like two fires on either side of it, and one of them remembered that *The Book of Hidden Treasures* described the City of Brass as having black walls with two great brass pillars. The pillars they were staring at looked like fire in the light of the setting sun. They had found the City of Brass!

As they approached, it rose high in the air above them. The walls were some eighty cubits tall, beautifully and smoothly constructed. *The Book of Hidden Treasures* claimed it had twenty-five gates, they remembered, but they could find no trace of any of them. They called out, but there was no reply.

They climbed a nearby hill and looked down into the city. They could see shining domes, pavilions and palaces and treetops. They strained their ears, but could hear nothing except the sound of running water, as of a river, and the flapping of tents.

The wazir proposed they construct a ladder. The servants set to and made a stout ladder of wood and iron, which they placed against the wall.

One of the servants volunteered. He climbed to the top and stood on the wall gazing down on the city. He clapped his hands, cried out, 'How beautiful you are!' and threw himself down into the city and certain death.

A second servant volunteered and exactly the same thing happened.

The sheikh insisted he would try himself 'in the name of God, the Compassionate, the Merciful'. He ascended the ladder, and when he reached the top he too clapped his hands.

The emir called out, 'Don't do it, don't do it!'

The sheikh laughed and said, 'God has saved me from the artifice of the Devil because I recite "in the name of God, the Compassionate, the Merciful".'

'What can you see, sheikh?'

'When I reached the top of the wall I saw ten damsels, beautiful like the moon, who were beckoning me as if to say "Come to us." I looked and I thought I saw a river I could dive into to be with them, but as I continued to recite, the river faded away and I saw the mashed bodies of our servants.'

The sheikh now walked along the top of the wall until he came to one of the brass towers. He found himself facing two golden gates set in the tower, but apparently without knob or lock. Looking more closely, he saw moulded onto the gate the small figure of a horseman with his hand pointing out of the surface. On the hand was an inscription: 'Turn the pin in the middle of the horseman's body twelve times and the gates will open.'

He couldn't see the pin at first, but he kept looking until he found it, strong, firm and fixed. When he turned it twelve times, the gates ground open with a sound like thunder.

The sheikh went in and found himself in a long passage, at the end of which was a staircase.

At the bottom he found a room with benches on which were lying men with shields over their heads. They were dressed as guards and armed with swords, bows and arrows. They turned out to be stone cold – dead.

The sheikh wondered if they might have on them the keys to the city. He found the oldest man, lifted up his garments, and yes, there was a bunch of keys hanging from his belt.

With a spring in his step, the sheikh made his way to a gate at the foot of the brass tower. He inserted the largest, brass, key into the fine, delicate and very complex mechanism. It whirred and clicked and suddenly and noiselessly the great brass gates slid open.

The emir, the wazir and the others who had been waiting outside greeted the sheikh with a cheer. They entered the city, passing chamberlains and lieutenants lying dead on beds of silk, then went into the marketplace. There were shops on all sides and on many levels, some projecting over the walkways. All the shops were open, with rows of brass utensils ranged in order of size. The merchants were in their shops, too, fallen as if they were sleeping, but they were all dead.

On the other side of the market the explorers came to a magnificent ultramarine palace. Venturing inside, they found a large hall decorated with gold and silver. In the midst of the hall, surrounded by smaller fountains, was a great fountain of alabaster over which hung a canopy of brocade. Channels of water flowed along the floor – four streams

Illustration to an 1870 edition of *Tales of the Arabian Nights*.

like the four rivers of Paradise meeting in a great tank lined with marble.

They noticed a door inlaid with ivory and ebony and adorned with plates of gold. Over it hung a curtain of silk, and there was a delicate lock on it made of white silver. The sheikh made quick work of it and they found themselves in a passage paved with marble and with curtains running along both sides on which wild beasts and birds were embroidered in gold and silver thread.

At the end of the passage, they arrived in a room made of marble so polished that the floor looked as if it were made of running water. In the middle of the ceiling was a giant golden dome, and entering it, they discovered a pavilion. It was raised on columns of red gold and inside were birds made of gold and emeralds arranged around a fountain. By the fountain was a couch on which lay a girl whose beauty shone like the sun. Her hair was black, her cheeks were rosy and her eyes danced with light. She was wearing a dress of brilliant pearls and a crown of red gold and on her forehead were two shining yellow gems.

The emir and his friends had never seen a girl so beautiful. They looked at one another, each with the same question burning in his heart: was this the sole living person in the City of Brass?

Or were there more? On either side of her, it looked as if there was a slave standing stock still, one white and the other black, one carrying a steel spear and the other a bejewelled sword. Their weapons were raised, but they were as still as statues . . .

'Peace be to thee, O damsel!' said the emir.

But the wazir said, 'You should know that this damsel is dead! There is no life in her.'

'She looked at me with love! Her eyes flashed with joy! I've never seen anyone so full of life!'

'She has been skilfully embalmed,' said the wazir, 'and her eyes have been taken out and quicksilver has been put beneath them, then they've been put back in place so that they gleam.'

The sheikh stepped up and read an inscription on a gold tablet beneath the girl's feet:

All the world's things are borrowed, and what you borrow
from it, it will take back. The world is like the confused

visions of the sleeper and the dream of the dreamer. Where is Adam, father of mankind? Where are Noah and his descendants? Where are the kings of India and Iraq? Where are the Caesars?

I am Tedmur, daughter of the king of the Amalekites. I ruled justly and acted impartially to all my subjects, so that they enjoyed happy and easy lives. I built an impregnable city of brass to make sure that we were all safe and I laid up such stores of wealth that we could be sure we would never run out.

Then there alighted among us the Terminator of Delights and the Separator of Companions, the Desolator of Abodes, the Destroyer of all Creatures Great and Small.

Child of Adam, let not hope make game of thee.

The emir tried to hold him back, but the wazir mounted the steps to where the princess lay and reached out to take one of the jewels from her forehead. At that moment the slaves revealed they were not statues but automata, one plunging the spear into his back and the other decapitating him with a swift sweep of his sword.

The story of Perceval is about how at the heart of the cosmos you may find your true self, the Self, the creative principle of the cosmos. The story of the City of Brass is about how at the centre of everything is death.[1]

The mustard seed and the seed of death.

*　　　　*　　　　*

Omar was a wealthy merchant in Cairo. When he died it turned out he had divided his fortune four ways – between his three sons and his wife. But the two elder sons quickly ran through their portions and then tried to get their hands on their brother Judar's, pursuing the case through court after court until they were all destitute. So Judar took his mother to live with him and every day he went fishing on the banks of the Nile to try to earn a few coppers. The brothers soon became wretched naked beggars, so Judar took them in too. They did nothing to help and yet they resented living on their younger brother's charity.

Then Judar happened to go through a very lean patch. For several days he caught nothing, not even a single sprat. He decided to go further afield and fish in Lake Karun, and it was here that a rich merchant called Abdul came to find him.

Abdul explained that his own father had been a student of magic and that his prized possession had been a book called *The Fables of the Ancients*. This contained details of all the great hidden treasures of the world – and how to find them. The greatest treasure trove of all was the one belonging to an enchanter called Al-Shamardal. The treasure consisted of a celestial planisphere, a ring with a seal on it and a phial of ointment. If you pasted that ointment on your eyes, you could see where all the other treasures of the Earth were buried! His father had tried to find this treasure, but the red *jinn* who controlled it had got wind of this and hidden themselves at the bottom of Lake Karun. Before he died his father had consulted an astrologer who had told him that the treasure of Al-Shamardal could only be seized with the help of a young fisherman of Cairo called Judar, son of Omar.

Judar explained he could not possibly leave his mother to fend for herself, so Abdul gave him plenty of money to go and leave with her.

When Judar returned, Abdul said, 'Mount behind me,' and together they rode until mid-afternoon prayer, when they stopped to eat.

They rode like this for four days, and Judar noticed that there always seemed to be plenty to eat and drink in the saddlebags, though he never saw Abdul replenish them.

Then one morning Abdul said, 'Judar, this is the day the astrologer said was appointed for the retrieving of the treasure.'

They rode until midday again, when they came to a river. Abdul brought from out of his saddlebags a hollow wand and three tablets of red carnelian, which he placed on the wand. Next he brought out a dish, some charcoal and some incense, and said to Judar, 'I am about to begin the necessary conjurations and fumigations, but once I have begun I cannot speak or the charm will be broken. So listen very carefully to what I am going to say.'

'Teach me,' said Judar.

Abdul gave him the instructions from *The Fables of the Ancients*:

'When I have recited the spell and thrown the incense on the fire, the water will dry up from the riverbed and you will be able to see a golden door there with two metal rings on it. Give three knocks in rapid succession and you will hear a voice ask, "Who knocks at the door of the treasure, unknowing how to solve the secrets?" You must answer: "I am Judar, the son of Omar." And the door will open and there will come towards you a figure with a burning sword in his hand. He will say to you, "If you be that man, stretch forth thy neck, that I may strike off your head." Then stretch forth your neck and fear not, for when he lifts his hand and smites you with his sword, he will fall down before you, and you will see in him a body *sans* soul. But if you gainsay him, he will slay you.

'When you have done this, go down the tunnel until you see another door. This door will fly open and you will see two dragons, which will open their mouths and fly at you. Put forth both hands and they will each bite each a hand and fall down dead, but if you resist them, they will slay you.

'Then go to the next door and knock, whereupon your mother will come forth and say "Welcome, O my boy! Come that I may greet you!" But you must reply, "Keep back from me and take off your dress." And she will answer, "O my son, I am your mother – why would you strip me naked?" Then you must take your sword and brandish it, saying, "Strip!" whereupon she will wheedle and humble herself, but do not be beguiled, nor cease to threaten her with death till she doffs all that is on her and falls down. Whereupon the enchantment will be dissolved and the charms undone and you will be safe as to your life.

'Then enter the hall of treasure, where you will see gold lying in heaps. Pay no heed, but look for a curtain at the end of the hall. Draw back the curtain and there you will see the enchanter Al-Shamardal.'

'How will I be able to endure these terrors?' said Judar.

'Fear not, for they are semblances without life.'

Judar did as he was told, and it all went as Abdul had said until he came to the last door and his mother.

'I'm glad to see you, my boy.'

'What are you?'

'O my son, I am your mother who carried you for nine months and suckled you and reared you.'

'Take off your clothes.'

'You are my son. Why would you strip me naked?'

'Strip or I will strike off your head with this sword.'

As he redoubled his threats, she took off some of her clothes.

'Take off the rest!'

She removed each article very slowly, all the while pleading, until she had nothing left on but her last undergarment.

'Will you dishonour me and shame me? This is unlawful, my boy.'

At this point he could not go on. 'What you are saying is right. Leave that last garment on.'

'He has failed!' she cried. 'He is no real man. Beat him!'

And demons rushed on him, covering him with blows and thrusting him back up the corridors and through the doors until he was ejected out into the daylight and the waters closed over the riverbed and the door.

'Didn't I warn you not to swerve from my directions?' said Abdul. 'Now you must abide with me till this day next year.'

He told Judar that although he had escaped with his life this time, if he tripped up a second time he would certainly be killed.

A year later Judar went through the same process until his mother appeared before him again, saying, 'Welcome, O my boy!'

But this time it was different. 'How am I your son, you accursed spirit?' said Judar, and he made her take off all her clothes, at which point she fell down dead.

Then Judar entered the hall of treasures. The enchanter Al-Shamardal lay on a couch of gold with the ring on his finger, the celestial planisphere hanging over his head and the phial on his breast. Judar took them from the sleeping form and was swept up above the ground.

Abdul embraced him. 'Ask what you will and be not ashamed, for you are deserving.'

'I ask first of Allah and then of you that you give me yonder saddlebags.'

Abdul gladly gave Judar his saddlebags, and two more filled with gold and jewels. Then he sent Judar off on a mule with a slave to guide him.

Judar travelled day and night until he entered Cairo by the Gate of Victory. There he saw his mother sitting and begging. He almost lost his wits with pain as she explained that his brothers had cheated her of all she possessed and sent her out to beg.

Judar took her home and took food out of the saddlebags and laid out a meal for her. It is worth detailing: they had roast chicken and peppered rice, sausages and stuffed cucumbers and stuffed lamb and stuffed ribs of mutton and vermicelli with broken almonds and nuts and honey and sugar and fritters and almond cakes.

Later he built a fine palace and said to his mother, 'Tell me, will you live with me in this palace?'

Later still, he saw the king's daughter. He looked fixedly at her and said, 'Ah!' and his limbs were loosened, for love and longing and passion and pining were upon him, and soon he married her.

Then Judar and his wife and mother lived together in their palace. A eunuch sat on a golden throne at the front. He was more than capable of seeing off Judar's brothers or anyone else who wanted to cause trouble.

*   *   *

In *The Arabian Nights: A Companion*, the scholar and novelist Robert Irwin describes how entertainments like the story of Judar and his brothers had parallels in descriptions of real-life adventures. Treasure-hunting was a popular way of making a living in Egypt in the Middle Ages, as it is today. Manuals detailed the elaborate precautions set up to guard the treasures hidden in the pyramids. A thirteenth-century treatise on treasure-hunting described passageways lined with sword-wielding statues. The treasure-hunters were advised to beat the ground in front of them with a long stick to activate trip wires, so that the swords would fall harmlessly in front of them. There were trapdoors, revolving doors, collapsing staircases and sudden firestorms. The treatise also warned that spells were needed to ward off attacks by demons.

In the fifteenth century a sultan was visited by a Sufi saint called Sheikh al-Dashuti. They argued about whether Mohammed really had journeyed through the heavens and the sultan said he was a bit sceptical. The sheikh told him that if he plunged his head into a bowl of water just for an instant, he would understand. When the sheikh raised his head from the bowl, he said that in that instant he had experienced many lifetimes.

From childhood onwards the nineteenth-century essayist Thomas de Quincey often had experiences that felt to him like omniscience. Later in life these were enhanced by drugs. Were they delusions?

De Quincey's writings are full of visions of the interconnectedness of everything. He wrote that walking endlessly round the streets of

London he had the sense that all had been laid out for him as in a game. As he walked, it seemed to him that there was a spider somewhere in London sending invisible threads across the globe.

Borges was intrigued by another passage in de Quincey with a similar theme. In his *Autobiographical Sketches*, de Quincey wrote that he remained fascinated all his life by a mysterious, unfathomable and sublime passage in *Tales of the Arabian Nights*. Its grandeur, he said, had made him restless all his life.[2]

At the opening of the tale, a magician living in the central depths of Africa is introduced to us as one who has been made aware of an enchanted lamp endowed with supernatural powers that are available to any man who should take it into his keeping. But the lamp is imprisoned in subterraneous chambers, and from these it can be released only by the hands of an innocent child. But this is not enough: the child must have a special horoscope written in the stars, or else a peculiar destiny written in his constitution, entitling him to take possession of the lamp. Where shall such a child be found? Where shall he be sought?

The magician knows: he applies his ear to the earth, he listens to the innumerable sounds of footsteps that at the moment of his experiment are tormenting the surface of the globe, and amongst them all, at a distance of 6,000 miles, playing in the streets of Bagdad, he distinguishes the peculiar steps of the child Aladdin. Through this mighty labyrinth of sounds, one solitary infant's feet are distinctly recognized on the banks of the Tigris, distant by 440 days' march of an army or a caravan. These feet, these steps, the sorcerer knows, and challenges in his heart as the feet, as the steps of that innocent boy, through whose hands only he could have a chance for reaching the lamp.

The wicked magician, having laid aside as useless many billions of earthly sounds, and having fastened his murderous attention upon one insulated tread, has the power, still more unsearchable, of reading in that hasty movement an alphabet of new and infinite symbols; for, in order that the sound of the child's feet should be significant and intelligible, the pulses of the heart, the motions of the will, the phantoms of the brain must repeat themselves in secret hieroglyphics uttered by the flying footsteps. Even the inarticulate or brutal sounds of the globe must be all so many languages and ciphers that somewhere have their corresponding keys, their own grammar and syntax, and thus the least things in the universe must be secret mirrors to the greatest.

Part of what intrigued Borges was that this episode appeared in no known version of the *Arabian Nights*, but it was nevertheless an accurate account of the mystical beliefs of the age when these stories originated.

A sense of the interweaving of everything, however far away in space and time, is integral to idealism and its mind-before-matter account of the cosmos. According to this mystical view, the entire material universe is held together by a unifying force, which is the great Cosmic Mind. In Jewish tradition God spoke the cosmos into existence and therefore everything in it is connected in the same way that language is connected – by meaning and intention. The sequence of letters by which God called the cosmos into existence is the sequence of the Hebrew letters in the Torah.

Mystical ideas on how to tune into the creative powers of the cosmos were preserved in secret societies, and members of these societies sometimes allude to such ideas in their published writings. The nineteenth-century French novelist Honoré de Balzac had one of the most energetically creative imaginations in human history, and in his titanic sequence of novels *La Comédie Humaine* he tried to create a cosmos grand and varied enough to rival the material cosmos. He also wrote about a quality he called 'specialism'. He described it as 'the formula of God' and a path to the infinite known to the people of greatest genius. He was, of course, thinking in the first instance of himself:

Specialism . . . consists of seeing the things of the material universe and the things of the spiritual universe in all their ramifications, original and causative. Jesus had the gift of Specialism. He saw in each fact its root and results, in the past where it had its rise, and in the future where it would grow and spread. His sight pierced into the understanding of others. The perfection of the inner eye gives rise to the gift of specialism.

*　　　　　*　　　　　*

Because we are so far removed from idealism and its way of thinking about the world, there is a danger that our impression of it and its claims becomes caricatured – especially with regard to the ontological status of the material world. Is idealism *really* suggesting that the world is totally unreal? Does an apple or a table *really* cease to exist the instant you stop looking at it? This extreme, unlikely proposition might seem to be one of the implications of idealism and part of its baggage.

I am not denying that there have been world-denying and also world-hating impulses in the history of religion, but idealism encompasses some extremely sophisticated thinking about the different orders of reality and the ontological status of the objects and contents of different types of experience – and no more so than in Islamic mysticism.

According to the medieval poet and philosopher Al-Kashani, everything intelligible, everything that comes from the world of the unseen into the world of sense experience, is a communication from God. Everything in the outer world is a creation of God's mind, of His imagination. To put it another way, the physical world is not a subjective illusion – you and I are not subjectively hallucinating it. It is rather an objective illusion.

The material world is not therefore *sheer* illusion. It is not something that exists nowhere or has no ontological status. It has a level of reality because everything that exists on the material plane has a corresponding existence in the higher, more spiritual planes. In this sense the whole world is a forest of symbols, although the meaning of these symbols maybe hidden from everyday human intelligence.

Knowers are mystics and visionaries with powers of imagination beyond the ordinary. They have what Sufis call 'veridical dreams', which are visions of a higher, more real, reality. These dreams may then be interpreted by reason so that reason and imagination work together in harmony.

Knowers also have waking veridical dreams in which the symbolic structure and meaning of the material world – what God intends to communicate through it – become clear to them.

We have all experienced the difference between ordinary, banal dreams and significant dreams in which we sense we are being told something important. Similarly in our waking lives all – or most of us – have had experiences where life seems to be trying to tell us something. Among Sufi mystics, these experiences and the distinctions they give rise to are the focus of a great deal of attention and thought.

*   *   *

Arabian ideals and ideas of the interconnectedness of the cosmos would eventually give birth to their shadow. Scientific materialism would come to see the whole cosmos as interconnected, with every part connected to every other part, no matter how far away – not by the intentions of a Cosmic Mind but by impersonal forces like gravity.

We will see later that science can now give us experimental proof that we can affect the behaviour of subatomic particles just by thinking about them. We will see, too, that it can show us that the movement of one electron can affect the movement of another electron on the other side of the cosmos.

Could it be that the *Tales of the Arabian Nights* are more than just entertainment, and that the esoteric lore that underlies them is an accurate description of the cosmos?

The Arabian garden as Paradise (from *The Pictorial Gallery of Fine Arts*, 1847)

St Francis Takes the Gospels Seriously

A large part of this history of the world according to idealism has been concerned with a great cosmic plan to help humankind develop a narrow head consciousness, a capacity for reflection, for abstract intellectual thought that is denied to other creatures.

In the last few chapters we have seen hints of a new development, the seeds of a new heart consciousness.

*   *   *

Francis was born in Assisi in 1182. His father was a rich cloth-merchant. His mother came from Provence and told Francis stories of Arthur and Lancelot, of Charlemagne and Roland, which lit up his imagination. Troubadours from his mother's native land were also wandering through Italy by this time, singing new songs of love.

Francis was a lighthearted boy, full of happiness, always playing the fool. As a young man he dressed extravagantly, as a gorgeous, gallant knight like Roland. Many laughed at him, but he was sweet and everyone excused his eccentricity, though he suspected that some were perhaps laughing more at him than with him. 'You'll see,' he said. 'One day I'll be adored by the whole world.'

He was setting off on horseback on a road leading out of Assisi one day when he experienced a vision. We don't know what it was but it changed him. He turned back to Assisi and spent the days that followed in long walks in the countryside. Finally he went into a cave hidden amongst the olive trees and emerged pale and seemingly distraught.

At the end of a stony path on the outskirts of Assisi, amid lavender and rosemary bushes there was a small dilapidated chapel called St Damiano. One day Francis prayed there for an hour, then looked up at the simple wooden crucifix over the altar. On it there was a painting of Jesus Christ, surrounded by angels and the two Marys, and he distinctly heard it speak to him, saying, 'Go, Francis, repair my church, which, as you see, is falling into ruin.'

The little church he was kneeling in was in need of repair, and Francis immediately set to work. After a while, though, he began to understand the wider picture; in the thousand years or so since it had been established the Church had also made its compromises with the world. The Italian countryside looked beautiful, but most who lived in it were serfs, struggling to scratch a meagre living and at the mercy of the weather and their landlords. The impact of bishops was as local administrators taking tithes from the poverty–stricken. The elderly, the handicapped, the mad, lepers and those who couldn't work all suffered neglect and cruelty.

A *trouveur* or troubadour, a singer of songs of courtly love. (Sculpture on the portico of the Abbey of St Denis, twelfth century.)

The Papacy was dogmatic and intolerant, persecuting groups whose ideas threatened its authority. Movements like the Waldenses in Germany, the Cathars in France and the Bogomils in Bosnia renounced property and marriage and tried to live lives of complete purity, but were accused of indecency and promiscuity.

There were rumours of great changes coming, wild prophecies. A Calabrian hermit, Joachim de Fiore, retreated higher and higher into the mountains, where he worked on his mystical theory of world history. He said that an age was coming when humankind would live consumed with love. In Germany, Elizabeth of Schönau was told by her guardian angel, 'Cry with a loud voice! Shepherds of my Church, you are sleeping, but I shall awake you!', while Hildegard of Bingen said, 'A nation of prophets shall appear illumined from on high, living in poverty and solitude . . . and the angels will return with confidence to dwell amongst men.'

On another journey out of Assisi, Francis came across a leper. He couldn't suppress a reflex reaction of disgust, but then he was angry with himself. He leapt from his horse, gave the leper all the money he had on him and kissed his hand. It felt like the hand of a corpse. Later he realized that in the person of the leper he had met Christ.

Francis started to appear in the streets in rags, white-faced and distracted. The children of the town mimicked him and mobbed him. He was *pazzo* – mad. But Francis didn't shrink from crowds – he sought them out. He was charged with love, sang of it, and he was full of laughter too, because he had thought of an amusing idea. *Why not take the message of the gospels literally?* Why not consider the lilies? Why not give away all your material possessions and devote your life to loving your neighbour?

This upside-down inside-out sort of thinking was highly threatening to the Church. It made a mockery of authority.

Francis' father, too, was furious, and decided to disinherit him. This legal process was to take place in the town square at a formal hearing in front of the bishop. During the solemn proceedings Francis disappeared into the bishop's palace and returned stark naked. He rolled his clothes into a bundle which, together with the last of his money, he put on the ground in front of the bishop. 'God is my father now,' he said.

Then he left the town and wandered the countryside wearing a tattered old cloak that the bishop's gardener gave him. He stayed in a leper-house, lavishing love upon the lepers, wiping and washing their sores.

Soon he began to appear in the town again, going to the squares and singing hymns, begging for food from door to door. He realized that to take the gospels seriously is to look like a fool in the eyes of the world, which is why his followers became known as *jongleurs* – God's jesters.

Francis liked to compare himself with the lark – happy only when free under an open sky. A handful of companions left their homes and built shelters of branches which were open to the winds. They lived in the same

St Francis preaching to the birds (miniature from a thirteenth-century psalter).

poverty as the people of the countryside and preached in the common tongue. Francis asked to sow love where there was hatred and unity where there was discord, but whenever he said this sort of thing, it just made people angrier.

There was a playful, almost surreal side to Francis. Once, after a heavy snowfall, he rushed out and made a row of snowmen: 'See, here is my wife, and behind her are my two sons and two daughters, with the servant and the maid carrying all the baggage.' Was this a regret for a life he might have chosen?

Women joined Francis, led by his kindred spirit, Sister Clara. He often depended on her for support and advice.

Francis spoke of 'having nothing but possessing all things'. By possessing nothing, by wishing for nothing, he and his companions were really free, he said. For them, what was important in life was *experience of life itself*. As we shall see, this marked a major shift. Francis represented an affront to authority and dogmatism – but also the coming of individualism and inspiration.

Francis had an unusual quality which one of his biographers described as the 'tact of heart which divines the secrets of others and anticipates their desires'. The poor felt they had found someone who cared for them and would look after them.

This empathy extended beyond humanity to all living things. Another biographer said of Francis that 'he discerned the hidden things of nature with his sensitive heart'.

Turning off the road one day, he approached a flock of birds. Rather than taking flight, they gathered around him. 'Brother birds, you ought to praise and love your Creator very much,' he said. 'He has given you feathers for clothes, wings for flying and all you need. He has made you the noblest of his creatures. He lets you live in the pure air. You need neither sow nor reap, yet he takes care of you, watches you and guides you.' He stroked them.

Later, when he tried to speak to people, swallows were chirping so loudly that he couldn't make himself heard.

'It's my turn to speak now, little sister swallows,' he told them.

Francis took joy in the fecundity of nature, making homes for doves and telling them to breed and multiply. He had a pet crow that ate with the brothers and accompanied him when he visited the sick.

The countryside around the nearby town of Gubbio was being terrorized by a large wolf. One day Francis encountered this wolf on the road. He walked towards it and it came at him slavering. But he made the sign of the cross and said, 'Brother wolf, in the name of Christ, I command you not to harm me or anyone.' At this the wolf lay down at his feet, then began to walk alongside Francis like a tame dog.[1]

Francis' famous canticle, 'Brother Sun, Sister Moon', is a blazing vision of the cosmos as idealism conceives it. The heavenly bodies and

The wolf of Gubbio

the natural world are shown as expressing the care that the Cosmic Mind has for humanity:

O most high, almighty, good Lord God, to thee belong praise, glory, honour and all blessing.
    Praise be, my Lord God, with all his creatures and especially our brother the Sun, who brings us the day and who brings us the light; fair is he and shines with a very great splendour . . .
Praise be, my Lord, for our sister the Moon, and for the stars, the which he has set clear and lovely in heaven.[2]

Francis brought to Christianity the same compassion for all living things that we saw earlier in the teachings of the Buddha and 'miracles burst forth under his footsteps' as they had under the Buddha's. He practised what we might call a 'transcendental idealism'. By uniting his spirit with the divine in prayer, he transformed himself and enabled himself to perform miracles. What the stories of Francis are saying with all possible clarity is that *being good, being spiritually minded, bends the laws of nature.*

Francis also performed exorcisms. One eyewitness report described a possessed brother 'rolling on the ground, hitting himself against whatever lay in his way, contorting, becoming rigid, leaping high in the air. Francis came to see him and healed him.'

Francis said that he fought with the Devil many times. He heard strange, troubling voices in the night, and on one occasion he reported that demons had beaten him violently and left him trembling.

He also felt a painful process of transformation beginning to take place in humanity.

Guided by his dreams, he travelled to the upper valley of the Arno. He and his companions journeyed high above the wheat fields, past the chestnut trees and oaks to the pines and firs, and the bare rocks on the higher ground.

By now Francis was ageing fast, and because he was too frail to walk any further, the brothers went to look for an ass. Francis stopped to rest on a smooth rock, and a gruff old peasant came by and asked if it was true that he was Francis of Assisi. When Francis said that he was, the peasant frowned and said sternly, 'Well, my advice to you is to really apply yourself to try to make sure you really are as good as people say you are, so that people aren't disappointed when they meet you.'

Francis laughed and thanked him warmly.

Francis and the brothers travelled on. Then, when they were near the peak of Mount Verna, they stopped to rest under a great oak. Flocks of birds gathered round them singing and settling on Francis' arms and shoulders.

'I see that it's pleasing to our Lord Jesus that we have come to this mountain,' he said, 'as our brothers and sisters the birds are so pleased to see us!'

That evening, as they were constructing a rough shelter of branches and leaves, Francis told his companions that he did not have long to live.

A few days later, on 13th September, he spent the night alone, praying. As the first rays of the sun began to warm his body, he saw something in the sky on the horizon. An angel, one of the Seraphim, was flying towards him. In the centre of the vision was a cross, and the Seraph, with six flaming wings, was nailed to it. Francis was suffused with ecstasy.

Then the vision suddenly disappeared and he felt sharp pains. Trying to work out what it all meant, he looked down and saw on his hands and feet marks with the form and colour of the piercings that Jesus suffered on the cross – and there was a wound in his side, too. From time to time a little blood would seep out of this and stain his tunic.

Like the Christ event, what we might call the Francis event was momentous, and likewise we have not perhaps yet fully understood it . . .

As the small group of brothers left Mount Verna, Francis turned to speak: 'Adieu, Monte Verna – we shall never see one another again.'

The next day they arrived at Monte Casale, where Francis healed a friar who was possessed.

In one of the villages people took a bridle that had been touched by Francis and brought it to a woman who was having difficulty giving birth. She gave birth immediately and without the slightest pain.

People were already quarrelling over Francis' clothes, strands of his hair – even his nail parings.

When Francis arrived back at Assisi and his beloved church of St Damiano, he told the brothers, 'Never abandon it, for this place is sacred, the house of God.'

Francis lost his sight for two weeks, and nights were painful. One night angels sang for him, which eased his pain. When a doctor told him his disease was incurable, he cried out with great joy, 'Welcome, Sister Death!' Then he began to sing.

He died on 3rd October 1226, as night fell and larks were alighting on the thatch of his cell.

After his death Francis appeared to his companions and told them that Jesus Christ had given him the stigmata so that he could pursue a divine mission to the departed, helping to lead them to God. The dead had found someone to help them.[3]

The New Arabian Way of Loving

*'I am his hearing with which he hears, his sight
with which he sees, his hand with which he seizes,
his foot with which he walks.'*

God describing His relationship to one he loves in a *hadith*.[1]

*'The eye with which I see God and the eye with
which God sees me is the same eye.'*

Meister Eckhart

Sooner or later humans would have to learn about sexual love.

Ibn Arabi was a Spanish Arab who would be called the greatest sheikh – or teacher – of Sufism, the main mystical impulse within Islam.

When he was seven, his family moved from Murcia to Seville. He grew up to become an able and successful administrator. He married and settled down. But then he fell ill and began to have visions. He gave up working, gave away his possessions and went to live in solitude, to pray and meditate. He went on pilgrimages.

He met Khdir several times. One encounter took place at night in the port at Tunis. Ibn Arabi was on a boat when he was startled to see a man coming towards him over the surface of the water, walking in an extravagant style, raising each foot high in turn, as if to demonstrate that the soles were not wet. He drew near enough for Ibin Arabi to talk to him. Afterwards, he turned and set off in the direction of a lighthouse, seeming to cover a distance of about two miles in three steps.

On another occasion Ibn Arabi saw Khdir performing his prayers on a magic carpet.

Rather as Elijah had passed his mantle on to Elisha, Ibn Arabi chose a disciple and passed on to him the mantle, or *khirqa*, he had received from Khdir – a symbol of 'a chain of transmission' whereby a teacher has the ability to pass on the gift of intense spiritual experience. The method of transmission may appear magical, for example the master touching the pupil's forehead with his finger to awaken the inner, spiritual eye, or it may involve spiritual exercises or *work*, including imaginative re-enactments of the experiences of Enoch and Elijah of the type we engaged in earlier in this book.[2]

Sufism emphasizes personal experience over doctrine. Sufis talk of seeing a higher reality denied to those who try to understand everything by rational thinking alone. This 'unveiling' can happen as a result of mystical vision.

*   *   *

In 1202, at the age of thirty, Ibn Arabi went to Mecca to be warmly welcomed into the home of an eminent sheikh, his sister and his beautiful niece called Nizam. He spent many happy evenings with them in cultured discussion of the great questions of life and death. Then one night he was performing the ritual walk around the Ka'bah. A few verses came into his head and he began reciting them, just loudly enough to be heard. Suddenly he felt the touch of a hand on his shoulder. That touch was softer than silk. He turned round and found himself looking into the eyes of Nizam – and now he was startled by her flashing eyes and her warm, scintillating beauty. When she smiled, he felt as if the sun was rising. Later he would write of her dark tresses and honeyed tongue. 'She is one of the girls with swelling breasts, tender, virgin and beautiful. Full moons over branches, they fear no waning . . . In a garden of my body's country a dove is perched on a bough, dying of desire, melting with passion.'

He was enchanted by Nizam's blazingly erotic presence but also by her secret and mysterious *otherness*. Remember the amazement that you feel when you are *with* someone really exceptionally beautiful? You can hardly believe that this wonderful being, this otherness, is next to you. From now on Ibn Arabi's nights would be radiant with Nizam's face, 'my day dark with her hair' ... He had fallen in love, and he yearned for Nizam, ached for her. 'My heart is love-sick,' he wrote. 'Thy gardens are wet with dew and thy roses are blooming, thy flowers are smiling and thy boughs are fresh.'

But there was an element of challenge contained in her gaze too: 'Her looks are drawn swords.' Ibn Arabi felt challenged to 'cross the desert', just as Christian knights were challenged to perform noble deeds by their romantic love for the ladies of the court.[3] However, Ibn Arabi's love for Nizam also filled him with a great generous energy to help meet this challenge.

Life is an enigma and a paradox. It is mysterious – and never more so than when we are in love. Falling in love gives us a heightened state of consciousness. When we fall in love we have an enhanced sense of the guiding forces in the world that have brought us to this place. We feel that great secrets and mysteries, new dimensions of the world, are opening themselves up to us – mysteries that transcend the ordinary and the everyday.

And the experience of falling in love can also challenge the intellect. Because what is the source of this love? For Ibn Arabi, the love that moves the whole universe also moves through him, so that when he is in love he is experiencing, *tasting*, directly something of that universal love.

*   *   *

Since the time of Abraham humanity had been developing a faculty for conceptual thinking and intellectual reasoning. In medieval times in the first European universities, these faculties were developed to an exceptional degree. A monkish pursuit of refining and defending dogma, called Scholasticism, was pursued on what we might today call an industrial scale. But by the thirteenth century new ideas from Islam were filtering into Europe, bringing new ways of feeling alive in the world.

We saw that Mohammed refused to perform miracles because, he said, the material world, the world revealed by the senses, was miraculous enough. There is a *hadith*, a saying traditionally attributed to Mohammed, which has God talking about someone He loves: 'I am his hearing with which he hears, his sight with which he sees, his hand with which he seizes, his foot with which he walks.' Here then is an awareness of the whole human body as an organ of perception. Different ways of perceiving are talked about as centred in different organs of the body. This impulse, these ideas, were developed by the writers, philosophers and poets of Sufism.

Ibn Arabi's contemporary, the poet Rumi, talked about intense sensual experience in glowing terms. He wrote poems about the joys of sex and drunkenness. This beguiling sensuality, this recommendation of the joys of drinking and free love by Rumi, Omar Khayyam and others, might seem outrageous, but here was a delight in the material world that inspired the troubadours and planted the seeds of the flowering, the light, colour and magnificence of the Renaissance. As early as the thirteenth century, the opening up of new forms of consciousness can be seen in the inventions of harmony in music and of perspective in painting, in the inner illumination of not only St Francis but also of his friend Giotto, the prophet Joachim, Thomas Aquinas, Bernard of Clairvaux and Dante.[4]

As idealists, Sufis like Ibn Arabi naturally believed that the cosmos came into existence as the result of a mental act. What was new was their fast-growing appreciation of the variety, richness and beauty of the different types and dimensions of mental acts. As this grew, so too did their understanding of God.

Another saying that Islamic tradition put in the mouth of God was 'I was a hidden treasure, and I *loved* to be known.' For Sufi mystics, love was the great mental act which moved the great comic mind in the act of creating. Love was the great primal event, and He was looking for lovers to seek him out and to respond to his loving with a love of their own. A spirituality which had grown cold and intellectual now warmed and became more heartfelt.

For the Sufis the heart is the organ of the perception of life's values. As an organ of perception, it shows us some things that the brain cannot: love, happiness and beauty. It is above all love, the Sufis say, that awakens us both to the reality of God and to the greater reality of ourselves. According to Rumi, we love when we see our innermost nature in the one we love. When we are in love we see new goodness in the one we love and also in ourselves, and we are inspired, too, with a new willingness to do good. Love is a transformative experience in all these ways. It takes us over and transforms all other feelings. We feel an inpouring of sweetness.

The Sufis held up intensity of experience as an ideal in a way that has had an almost universal influence. We may all have the experience of making love with such intensity that afterwards it feels as if the very fabric of the universe has been changed, as if the atoms inside us have been dancing then settled back down into a better place. We have been re-made. 'Divide your stone into the four elements,' says Hermes Trismegistus, 'then join them together again as one, and you will have the whole *magisterium*.'

St Bernard of Clairvaux's famous and highly influential sermons on the Song of Songs adopted the same language of erotic love, of the bride yearning for the groom. He talked of the kisses of contemplation, the mystic kiss, sweet embraces and rapt joys. This could have been written by Rumi or Ibn Arabi: 'When he has entered into me he has brought my soul alive . . . He has set fire to my heart and softened it too. He is living and powerful.'

Brutality, cruelty, poverty, plague, serfdom, ignorance, fear – we are familiar with the grim outer aspects of the Middle Ages, but the lives of the wise, such as Hildegard of Bingen, Ibn Arabi, St Francis and St Bernard, were not directed to exterior things. They were illuminated on the inside by a new love.[5]

*   *   *

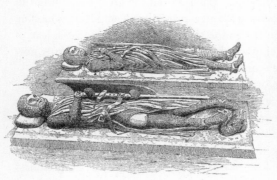

Tombs in the Temple Church in London. St Bernard wrote the Rule of the Knights Templar, who were also influenced by Islamic mysticism. Their degrees of initiation were influenced by Islamic initiatic secret societies. (For more on this, see *The Secret History of the World*.)

A bishop is present at the forging of a bell, giving it his blessing (from a French fourteenth-century manuscript). Brass bells had been used since ancient times in sacred rites, at lunar eclipses and following a death, because brass's sonorous, shrill and penetrating sound was thought to be best for the expiation of pollutions – and for preventing spells from reaching the moon, where demons lay in wait for such summonses.

We saw how people fought over St Francis's hair and fingernails even before he died. In Europe in the Middle Ages, it was not only great individuals who had a strong sense of spiritual manifestations in their everyday lives – most people did too.

The Church exercised power through bell, book and candle. Church bells would be rung to drive away demons. Bells were rung, too, at the founding of a church, when holy water was also sprinkled and prayers were said, asking a saint or angel to protect it.

Cripples hoping to be healed by the beneficent influence of relics. (Drawing attributed to Matthew Paris, early thirteenth century.)

The Church published books with rituals for blessing cattle, boats and armour, for curing infertility and illness in humans and animals, for ensuring success in battle, protection on journeys and the retrieval of lost possessions. A patient might write 'Jesus Christ, for mercy's sake, take away this toothache', recite it, then burn the paper on which it was written.[6] Amulets, called the *agnus dei,* were made out of the wax of church candles. They were popularly used to ward off demons, fire, storms and diseases. You might pray overnight in a church for healing, as in ancient Greece the sick had stayed in the temple of Asclepius to be cured by the 'temple sleep'. Today we still go on demonstrations, following in the footsteps of the great processions once organized by the Church in medieval times. These helped ward off plague or famine, and the pilgrim's staff had a wand-like power to fend off demons.[7]

But the biggest generator of supernatural power was the Mass. Consecrated bread was a universal medicine, a protection against plague, curing blindness and other afflictions. It could be scattered on the garden to eradicate pests or on fields to make them fertile, or to encourage bees to make more honey. It was at the heart of Christian life.

Ibn Arabi's contemporary Thomas Aquinas, a Dominican priest known as 'the Angelic Doctor', was Christianity's great theologian

Angels farming (from Cotton MS, Nero, C iv).

of angels. His collected works were the monumental achievement of Scholasticism. His *Summa Theologica* elaborated on Dionysius's account of the heavenly hierarchies and described in intimate detail, for example, how angels work on human physiology, playing on the nerves so that someone might see a vision and stimulating the intellect to understand it. Thomas Aquinas worked to marry the spiritual and the intellectual, and in 1215 he formulated Church doctrine regarding the Mass, describing what really happened during the ritual by his doctrine of Transubstantiation.

In the Middle Ages most practising alchemists were clerics. Aquinas himself had a well-developed interest in alchemy, and several alchemical texts are attributed to him. In his account of the Mass, the substances at the centre of the work – bread and wine – are transformed in

A monk making astrological calculations (by Jacquemin Grigonneur).

their inner essence, and the people *doing the work* – celebrating the Mass – are similarly transformed. 'The Eucharist is the Sacrament of Love,' he wrote. 'It signifies Love and produces Love.' He is here thinking of love as Sufis described it, of a love that doesn't only transform our mind but also has the power to transform our body, so that a real physiological change takes place.

The cult of the Holy Grail spread through Europe at the time when the doctrine of Transubstantiation was being formulated by Thomas Aquinas. Both grew out of an alchemical tradition of thinking. Both were concerned with spiritualization of matter by mind.

We have been building up a picture of the way that, according to esoteric and mystical idealism, the human mind plays a crucial part in the transforming and spiritualizing of the whole material universe. According to this account, the human mind starts the work of transformation by working first on the material to which it is closest – the human body.

In the Mass the greatest creative forces of the universe were brought to bear, energizing and directing this change. For the idealists of the Middle Ages, the unleashing of cosmic power that took place in the Mass was as powerful and dangerous as the secrets of nuclear fission are to us today. It was partly for this reason that the Church tried to insist that this spiritual experience only takes place under its aegis.

But, independently of the Church, a new science of love, a wisdom that came from direct personal experience of the divine and bodily transformation, had been filtering into Europe through Spain and up into southern France.

The *jinn* was out of the bottle.

*   *   *

The Church's second crusade was not against Muslims but against Christians.

Like St Francis, the Cathars took Jesus' teachings on how to live seriously. In the south of France communities of Cathars renounced property and lived simply. They also sought spiritual experiences outside the Church's control. Access to the spiritual realms, strictly regulated and in some senses minimized by the Church, was thin gruel when set against the cosmic consciousness of the Cathars, their heaving visions of a world woven together by great angels.

The Inquisition was the Church's instrument for shutting these perspectives down. Having slaughtered many hundreds of thousands of heretics at Béziers, Bram, Lavaur and Minerve in the south of France, the soldiers of the Inquisition surrounded and besieged the surviving Cathars in the mountain-top castle of Montségur. Eleven months later, in 1244, 200 Cathars walked singing down the mountain and into the fire the Crusaders had prepared for their execution.

They were singing because, despite appearances, they believed they had accomplished their mission. Shortly before the town fell, four initiates had shimmied down the near-vertical rockfaces and spirited away a secret – something the Cathars believed to be crucial for the future of humankind.

There has long been speculation about what they smuggled out. Was it secret scrolls? Was it the cup of the Last Supper? Was it a treasure trove that suddenly made a priest at Rennes-le-Château wealthy, as proposed in *The Holy Blood and the Holy Grail*?

In fact they were smuggling out something much more precious . . . A baby.

The four Cathars took their precious cargo to a Cistercian monastery, where he was cared for by twelve wise men. These men together were able to raise the child's soul out of his body and impress on it the ancient primeval wisdom. They worked in the same way that hierophants had worked on the souls of candidates for initiation in the King's Chamber of the Great Pyramid.

The incarnation of great spirits is often problematic. Such a spirit is often attached to the body in a different way from the usual. It may be attached more loosely to enable it to float free of the body and communicate more easily with the spiritual worlds. The configuration of body-soul-spirit is delicate in these rare individuals, and they are often sickly and live perilously close to death.

The child in the monastery *was* sickly, sometimes so sickly his skin seemed transparent, and sometimes the skin seemed to glow with a deep inward love. He died young.[8]

*   *   *

While I was writing this book, Lorna Byrne told me that she was seeing what she called 'glowing babies'. Only she could see their glow, but everyone was drawn to them by their remarkable, spiritual emanations. Passers-by would often long to hold them, for instance. I am certain that Lorna was unaware of the history of the glowing baby born in Montségur in the thirteenth century, which is known to us because of the researches of Rudolf Steiner.

The forces of good and evil, Lorna says, are gathering for a great battle, and these glowing babies are on the side of the good. They are often sickly and sometimes physically retarded. Often they do not live long. But they are harbingers of a new stage in human evolution.

Later we will return to the glowing babies and to this gathering.

Dante, the Templars and the Road Less Travelled

It was in 1260, in the middle of his life, that Brunetto Latini was returning to Florence from Spain. Passing through the Valley of Thorns, he met an Italian student riding a mule in the opposite direction. Brunetto asked if he had any news of Florence. What the student told him was deeply troubling: the Guelph party, to which Latini belonged, had been expelled.

Walking along alone and brooding on this news, Brunetto unwittingly left the main road and took the road less travelled. He found himself lost in the middle of a forest he did not recognize. He walked on and eventually saw a mountain looming above the trees.

Then a strange thing happened. Rabbits, mice, hares, deer, foxes, wolves, bears, birds and some creatures he didn't recognize came towards him. They were all together, not minding one another. Then, stranger still, he saw why – they were all in a loose procession accompanying a giantess.

She smiled down on him and said, 'I am Nature, and by the Sovereign Creator was I created. I make whatever He wills.'

Was this the divine guidance he had so long looked for? Had he finally broken through the material veil to the other side?

Brunetto knelt before this great visionary creature and begged her to tell him her story.

She told him she was going to explain to him the subtle genius and power of the human mind. She told him that God had first created the world out of His own nature, but that it then fell 'through the pride of the mad angel'.

She went on to tell Brunetto a sort of Miltonic history of the world. She showed him a vision of the creation of the planets and of the four rivers running out of Eden, made out of the purest water and running over the brightest, most precious stones. He saw the generation of the animals – tigers, lions, camels, panthers, hyenas, griffons and some he had never heard of, including Ethiopian insects as big as dogs that dug up gold with their feet. This history of the world encompassed the temptation of Eve by the serpent, the murder of Abel, the Tower of Babel and the siege of Troy.

Dame Philosophy (illustration to Brunetto Latini's *Li Livres duo Trésor*, from a fifteenth-century manuscript).

The goddess explained that humankind stood above all created things and pulled all the best strands of creation together to form the crown of the work, and that the crown of the human mind was the ability to discern good and evil.

She then told him to dive down deep inside himself.

In modern, materialist terms we might describe this as a diving down into the subconscious, but in terms of the idealism of the day this would not have been a mental event sectioned off from material reality. According to the mystical philosophy espoused by Brunetto Latini, it is because humanity is the crown of creation that we can learn about all creation by examining ourselves. We are a book, and if we learn to read that book, we can read everything.

Brunetto was able to observe the action of the divine powers on his life functions. He swam amongst the forces of the soul, able to see the separate workings of the four temperaments – the choleric, melancholic, phlegmatic and sanguinary principles. He understood how these principles also worked outside the human body and in the wider world as fire, air, water, earth.

He encountered the four virtues, Prudence, Temperance, Bravery and Justice, not as abstract ideas but as living spiritual principles.

He slipped in through the portals of the senses, diving down inside his own body to see how the movements of the planets worked inside us – how we were moved to desire by Venus, to anger by Mars, to reflect by the moon.

He flew up through the heavenly hierarchies and finally found himself swimming in a great sleepy ocean.

Then he awoke to find himself still in front the goddess. He kissed her feet and she vanished.

Brunetto resumed his journey 'through the narrow road seeking to see, to touch, to know whatever is fated'.

Brunetto Latini had also been taught a profound lesson: how knowledge of the workings of the physical world could be discovered through spiritual experience. It was a lesson that would not be lost on Isaac Newton and other leaders of the scientific revolution.

Brunetto had also had his taste for direct spiritual experience sharpened. He later had a vision of a young child standing naked with a bow and arrow, winged but blind. The boy's name was Piacere – sensual love. He was accompanied by four helpers: Fear and Longing, Love and Hope.

Brunetto was shown how they work on people, so that when someone falls in love they also yearn, fear, hope and love, and that although all four work in different ways, they also work to one common end.

Then the Ovid, the great Afro-Roman poet and initiate of the Mystery schools, appeared to Brunetto and told him to search his own heart for the goodness and the delight that were born of love, but also the evil and error that it spawned.

Again, there is in Brunetto's visions an emphasis on personal experience and the importance of being attentive to it.

*   *   *

Because he had met the Italian student riding in the opposite direction, Brunetto knew it would be dangerous for him to return home to Florence, so he turned around and went instead to live in exile in Paris.

Perhaps because he was trying to make sense of his visions and place them in a wider intellectual context, he met Thomas Aquinas there and was initiated into a lay brotherhood affiliated to the Knights Templar. To those in the know, he was now a *Frater Templarius*, a member of a secret order dedicated to the pursuit of Sapientia, the goddess or angel of wisdom.

We do not know the exact form of Brunetto's initiation or the ceremony he underwent, but there are clues . . .

By the time Brunetto Latini made contact with the Templars in Paris, they were a massively rich, powerful and influential organization, the centre of European finance. The Temple in Paris was a self-regulating and largely closed city within a city, like the Vatican in Rome today.

The Templars had been founded in 1118, partly to protect Christian pilgrims to Jerusalem from attacks by Muslims, and in 1128 Bernard of Clairvaux had written their Rule, recognizing this fighting élite as a monastic order. We have seen that Bernard was influenced by Sufi philosophy and much has been written about the influence of Islam, and Sufism in particular, on the Templars. At that time Islamic civilization was far more advanced than European civilization in

Portrait of Brunetto Latini, Corso Donati and Dante by Giotto (taken from the Chapel of the Podesta in Florence).

science, technology, philosophy and spirituality. To the Muslims, the Europeans must have seemed barbarians, and to the Templars the Muslims must have seemed the source of all that was new and cutting edge.

The Templars operated something like an early secret service and may have learned much that helped them become rich and powerful. While in charge of the Dome of the Rock in Jerusalem, they studied Islamic traditions and made an early treaty with the much-feared secret society the Order of Assassins, the followers of the Old Man of the Mountains. They remained respectful of Islamic traditions and practices for as long as they managed to keep control of Jerusalem, allowing Muslims in their charge to continue to pray to Mecca. Later Templar architecture would be much in the Islamic style. The white wool loincloth of the Templars may have been derived from the white woollen garments of the Sufis – the word 'Sufi' coming from an Arabic word for wool because of the robes they wore as symbols of their purity. The Templars wore a cord similar to the one worn by initiates of the Order of Assassins – and by the dervish followers of Rumi. One of the accusations that would be made against the Templars was that this had been consecrated in a vast artificial underground cave in front of an idol called Baphomet – a name which was interpreted as a corruption of Mohammed.

In 1266 there was another political upheaval in Florence that allowed Brunetto Latini to return home. By now he was one of the foremost scholars in Europe, a renowned authority on, among other things, the occult properties of stones. He befriended Dante's family and took the young man under his wing.

Like Francis of Assisi, Dante came from a mercantile family, but he had intellectual and spiritual aspirations that would lead him down a different road. He was initiated into the Templar brotherhood by Brunetto and taught by him to have mystical visions like the one that he himself had experienced in the Valley of Thorns.

In 1301 the politics of Florence underwent another reversal, and with his property confiscated and under threat of execution, Dante too went into exile and lived for a while in Paris. In 1307, the French king, Philip the Fair, suddenly arrested the Templars. Dante was probably there to witness the burning of the Grand Master of the Templars, Jacques du Molay. So, by the time he began to write *The Divine Comedy*, he had learned well the dangers of heresy and knew not to show a support for the Templars that was too open. Ancient mystery wisdom, astrology and Kabbalistic number mysticism and the Sufi philosophy of ecstatic love are woven into his poem – but encoded. In the *Commedia* Philip the Fair has a

The boatman Charon
(from an Attic vase).

Luciferic beauty, and suffers in the lowest rings of hell for his crime against the Templars.

*   *   *

Dante's guide at the beginning of his great visionary poem, the figure who leads him down into the Underworld, is not Brunetto Latini but an earlier initiate, Vergil. The Roman poet's epic poem the *Aeneid* contains an account of a journey to the Underworld by its hero, Aeneas. Vergil describes his hero being sent to find a golden bough that flowers and grows on a tree like mistletoe. This 'wand of destiny' will enable him to pass through various tests and dangers underground.

Aeneas later meets the boatman, Charon, who rows him across the underground river, the Styx, the three-headed dog Cerberus, and he arrives at the parting of the ways (one way leading to the Elysian Fields and the other to the torments of hell).

The way downwards spirals nine times. Aeneas witnesses the horrible punishments of famous wrongdoers and then at the end enters a place of brilliant light and bright spirits, where all are full of joy. At last he is given a vision of the Divine Mind sustaining and working through everything in the universe, and he understands the fates of individuals within the greater destiny of the cosmos. All this is described with astonishing realism, just as Dante in his account of his vision is at pains to convey that these are real rocks he is slipping and stumbling over in the half-light. Both poets want us to know that what we are reading is not mere fantasy. Both are describing a real journey taken in a trance state.

Vergil was an initiate of the ancient schools. Reconstructions from the *Aeneid* and other scattered literary references show that after a long period of preparation which might have involved long periods of fasting, sensory deprivation, meditation, prolonged solitude, bathing in highly scented water that may have been drugged (the 'Waters of Forgetfulness' and the 'Waters of Memory'), the disoriented candidate for initiation would have been led by priests wearing masks into, it seemed, the very bowels of the Earth. The candidate witnessed a sacrifice, was dragged through small holes in a wall, propelled into pits and finally taken to an inner sanctum where they had an experience that was partly an experience of a physical place and partly visionary – an experience not totally unlike a modern séance but much more elaborate and conceived on a much larger scale. The candidate might spend days underground, typically three days, though Apollonius is reported to have spent seven, before being led upwards again to the heavens.

The great initiates of the ancient world describe this as a profoundly moving experience which fundamentally altered their understanding of the world.

The site of Vergil's initiation was rediscovered in the late 1950s by an English engineer called Robert Paget. My friends Robert and Olivia Temple recently excavated the site at Baia in southern Italy. They found a network of long, narrowing passages full of volcanic fumes, an underground river, the place where Cerberus was tethered and a dividing of the ways. There were false doorways and trapdoors, through which a candidate might have been pitched into a snake pit, and an inner sanctum, where the candidate for initiation would have met the spirits of their ancestors and the gods. It was exactly as Vergil had described it.

*   *   *

Some people are born with a visionary consciousness. Others may be initiated into it by the ceremonies of secret societies. The techniques for

Illustration to Dante's *Divine Comedy* (by the initiate artist John Flaxman, described by William Blake as his 'dearest friend').

inducing higher states of consciousness and contacting higher intelligence are among the most closely guarded secrets of the secret societies.

Brunetto Latini was a great teacher, who had a greater pupil. He taught Dante to take the road less travelled. He guided him down the dark and dim passageways of an as yet undiscovered initiation centre somewhere under the streets of Florence in order to lead him into higher states of consciousness. There he would experience visions like the visions he himself had experienced in the Valley of Thorns and meet the same goddess. 'Oh happy those few,' he would write later, 'who sit at that table where the bread of angels is eaten.'[1]

*   *   *

Dante's *Inferno* is a vision of the whole universe powered by love, of love working in every little intricate part of it. His vision of angels in heaven forming a white rose looks forward to the techniques of meditation taught by the Rosicrucians. (Illustration by Gustave Doré.)

After the destruction of the Templars, the Temple in Paris was raided. Lurid rumours had led people to expect devilish idols and other instruments of sexual perversion and blasphemy in the underground chambers. In the event, they only found a reliquary in the shape of a woman's head.

The Jewish scholar of the Dead Sea Scrolls, Hugh Schonfield, applied the ATBASH cipher, in which the first letter of an alphabet is substituted for the last, to the name 'Baphomet' which, under torture, the Templars gave out as the name of the idol they worshipped. He discovered that Baphomet was code for 'wisdom'.

The Sufis, the Cathars, the Knights Templar, Brunetto Latini and Dante worshipped the angel-goddess Sapientia, the Wisdom of higher, visionary intelligence. They reached a place where the eyesight has another sight, the hearing another hearing and the voice another voice.

*   *   *

Dante's vision is greater than Latini's partly because of the more powerful way he envisions love . . .

We live in two universes – one held together by gravity and the other, the one Dante described, by 'the Love that moves the Sun and the other stars'. By the end

of the medieval age a chorus was singing new songs full of the joys of love, singing that no greater happiness could be wished or hoped for by any mortal. There were many voices with one message: the heart is the hinge on which the world turns.

Fra Angelico's figures reveal an inward light. He believed his brush strokes were directed by the will of God. (Engraving from a detail of *The Last Judgement*.)

Christian Rosencreutz and the Birth of Yoga

Later we will see how in the late nineteenth century a small group of British Freemasons went on a journey to hold meetings with their German brethren. They were looking for evidence of a genuine Rosicrucian tradition, and they discovered that Christian Rosencreutz was not, as many had assumed, the hero of an allegorical fiction but a historical character.

Born to a poor family in Germany in 1378, Christian Rosencreutz was orphaned at the age of five and put in the care of a convent, where he was well educated. At sixteen, he set out to travel the world in search of wisdom.

He knew that wisdom was there to be discovered because it had been imprinted on his soul in his previous incarnation. As a baby he had been smuggled out of Montségur and later initiated by twelve men, representatives of the great spiritual impulses that guide world history.

Now Christian Rosencreutz travelled the world trying to wake up to the wisdom he sensed lay somewhere inside him. He knew he would recognize it, that his soul would respond to it, if he managed to track down the real thing.

He spent five years in Arabia, and it was said that during this time he was initiated into a secret Sufi brotherhood and that on the road to Damascus he was carried up into the heavens like Saul.

Christian Rosencreutz's intellectual mission was focused on the gifts of the Holy Spirit, such as prophecy and healing. Anyone who prays sincerely in any religion is working on the assumption that mind is in some sense prior to matter and able to move it. The gifts of the Holy Spirit, enumerated in the New Testament seem to promise that under certain circumstances this kind of prayerful activity can be more effective. Christian Rosencreutz asked: 'Under what conditions?' If mind could move matter, then how and in what circumstances? It was the beginning of what we might call a science of the spirit.

Christian Rosencreutz developed a form of meditation that involved visualizing a wreath of seven roses resting on the cross. In the course of meditation these white roses turned red as a sign that the spirit of Christ was transmuting not only the spirit, but also the soul and body. Mind was moving matter by enlivening and activating the seven chakras.

The wisdom and spiritual practice of Christian Rosencreutz saw the life, work and crucifixion of Jesus Christ as being central and unique, but the teachings of other great world religions were valued too. Christian claimed that teachings on reincarnation, astrology and the chakras had always been a part of Judaism and Christianity and could be found, encoded or otherwise, in their sacred texts.

But when Christian returned to Europe and tried to talk to Christians about these ideas, he met with incomprehension and incredulity. So, with seven friends from Germany he founded an underground movement called the Brotherhood of the Rosy Cross, known later as the Rosicrucians.

The brothers' secret mission was to reform the world. They vowed that as they sowed the seeds of their secret teachings, they would also heal the sick.

They adopted the clothes and customs of the countries they visited so as to remain a secret organization, but their fame as healers and wonder-workers meant they were in constant danger of being discovered. In a world obsessed with eradicating heresy, to teach reincarnation, for instance, would be to invite conflict and persecution. The brothers decided to meet in secret once a year, and that each brother would nominate a successor shortly before his death.

*　　　　　*　　　　　*

Matysendranath was one of the great gurus of the Middle Ages in India. It was said that he had overheard the secrets of the gods. The founder of Hatha yoga, he taught new ways to purify the body in order to reach greater spiritual heights.[1]

Sometimes he would sit in the forest in solitude, and at others he would wander from town to town and go begging from house to house.

One day he stood in front of the house of a merchant and called out. The wife of the merchant came to the door.

'If you have anything to give me, give it to me at once,' Matysendranath said.

She saw before her a god-like form, perfected by yoga, earrings shining like constellations. Matysendranath had rubbed sacred ashes all over his body, wore a beautiful waist cord and his eyes were shining.

Recognizing that this was no ordinary human being, she told him her sadness. Though she and her husband enjoyed every kind of wealth, because they had no child, their home seemed empty – empty like a garden without water, like wisdom without luck.

Matysendranath took some of his sacred ash, blessed it and gave it to her, telling her that if she ate it, she would certainly have a son. There was only one condition: 'Tell no one.'

But the moment the holy man had departed, the merchant's wife called all her friends to come round and of course she told them everything.

One of her friends advised her not to trust holy men, warning her that they used magic ash to seduce women and that if she swallowed it, she would be unable to stop herself from chasing after Matysendranath in the night. So the merchant's wife threw the ashes into the fire.

Twelve years later Matysendranath called at the house again. He asked the merchant's wife if he could see her son.

The moment she saw him, she remembered what had happened. She was afraid to say anything. *If I tell him the truth, he will curse me*, she thought.

Matysendranath said, 'Tell me at once whether you ate the ashes or whether you threw them away.'

She confessed that she'd had doubts and had thrown the ashes on the fire.

'Tell me quickly where you put the cinders from your fire.'

She explained that they always threw the cinders on the dunghill.

The yogi took her to the dunghill. He called out and there was an answering muffled cry from within the mound. He told the woman to have her servants open up the dunghill, which they did – and a beautiful twelve-year-old boy emerged.

This boy was Goraksha, who became Matysendranath's famous disciple.

The temptations of a holy man are many and great, and years later Matysendranath was visiting Ceylon when he fell under the spell of a queen. Living in her palace, surrounded by 1,600 beautiful women, he forgot who he was and all about his life outside the palace.

Goraksha feared his master was doomed, and set out to rescue him. A woman on the island told him where his master was being kept, but warned him that yogis were not permitted to enter the palace under threat of death. She said that only female dancers were allowed near Matysendranath.

So Goraksha disguised himself as a dancing girl, and managed to gain entrance to the palace and find his way to the wing where Matysendranath was living. He began playing a drum, softly at first, and dancing in front of him, singing beautiful songs about their former life together and the things they had seen and done, until gradually something began to stir deep in Matysendranath.

And then he looked into his pupil's eyes and remembered who he was.

When the queen and her helpers tried to seize them and stop them leaving, Matysendranath turned these sirens, who had bewitched him, into bats.[2]

*   *   *

At the age of eighty Christian Rosencreutz had a vision. It was Easter Saturday, 1458. Christian was sitting at a table in his cottage on the top of a hill when a tremendous storm arose, so fierce he feared the winds would carry his house off into the sky. Suddenly he felt someone tug at his coat and there standing behind him was a beautiful woman with wings that were covered with eyes. She was wearing a blue robe decorated with stars and was carrying a trumpet of beaten gold.

She handed him an invitation to a royal wedding. On it was written a verse with the message asserting that those who weren't pure wouldn't be able to survive the ceremony!

Christian's hair stood on end and he broke out into a cold sweat. Before going to sleep he asked his guardian angel for help – should he accept the invitation?

That night he had dreams of escaping from a dungeon. He took this to be an encouraging sign, and so in the morning he set off. He was wearing a white linen coat with a red cross on it in the form of a ribbon and he had four red roses on his hat.[3]

He was walking through a forest, singing, when he found himself faced with a choice of paths to follow. He was wondering which to take when he saw in the distance the gateway to a castle on the top of a hill. He hurried off along the path that led that way, hoping to reach it before nightfall.

Arriving, he was greeted by a man who introduced himself as the Guardian of the Portal. Seeing Christian's invitation, the Guardian welcomed him inside and gave him a token he would need to pass through the castle's inner gateway.

Now things turned strange. Christian had to find his way past a chained lion which was barring the way and which leapt up roaring when it saw him.

Next he had to hurry to reach the inner gate of the castle before it shut and when he succeeded, he was given new shoes to enable him to walk on the very shiny and slippery marble floor on the other side of the gate.

Finally two pages arrived and led him up winding staircases to a great, brightly lit hall, where he saw rows of men seated at long tables and a great feast about to take place.

The same beautiful winged woman who had appeared in his cottage now arrived, gliding into the chamber on a gilded throne. She welcomed everyone on behalf of the Bride and Bridegroom and told them that the next day they would all be tested to see if they were worthy to attend the wedding.

In the morning the Virgin, as Christian now knew the winged lady, appeared carrying a pair of golden scales, like the scales St Michael uses to weigh the souls of the dead. The men from the feast were weighed in it one by one. Those found wanting were given the Draught of Forgetfulness. They would return to the everyday world with no memory of what they had seen.

The Virgin was pleased to see the four roses which Christian had with him and he was chosen as one of the few worthy to attend the wedding. As a sign of this he was made a Knight of the Golden Fleece.

In Rosicrucian and other esoteric thought, the Golden Fleece is a symbol of the vegetative or 'etheric' part of human nature once it has been transformed by spiritual practice. Once we have thoroughly worked on and tamed the animal side of ourselves, we start to work on the vegetable side of ourselves, charging it with the golden spirit of the Sun god. This work brings great spiritual gifts, including dreams that aren't muddled like ordinary dreams but bring messages from the

The alchemist (after an engraving by Vriese). In alchemical practice the athanor is bounded by the two subtle tubes called *nadi* in Hatha yoga, one of which carries the spiritual energy of the sun and the other the spiritual energy of the moon. When these are worked on by means of breathing exercises, the fire of the athanor is lit and the third eye opens.

spiritual world – the sort of messages Christian Rosencreutz is here delivering.

Some extraordinary things were revealed to those who had been chosen to attend the wedding, the newly made Knights of the Golden Fleece. The Virgin summoned a lion carrying a sword and a snow-white unicorn with a golden collar.[4] If there was any expectation of a fight, it was thwarted. The Virgin broke her wand and the lion broke its sword in a gesture of peace. The knights were also shown a phoenix and a giant astrolabe which they could climb inside to view the motions of the planets.

The following day they were told to bathe in a healing fountain belonging to Mercury.[5] Then they ascended 365 steps to a great hall where, it seemed, the wedding was to take place. They found an altar, on top of which was a turning globe, a skull with a white snake winding in and out of it and a crystal fountain spouting red water. A laughing, chattering cupid was clowning around and tormenting the birds in the sky. The mood of Christian's vision is celebratory – but with a sinister undertow.

The knights were now shown six thrones. Three kings and three queens took their places on them. Then the Virgin brought six black scarves to cover their eyes and coffins were laid before them. A coal-black Moor arrived and beheaded them all in an instant. Then he himself was beheaded and his head was laid in a little chest.

This seems to be a very bloody wedding, thought Christian.

That night Christian could not sleep. Rising from his bed, he looked out of the window and saw seven ships sailing on the sea with a flame hovering over each one, and he understood that these were the spirits of the seven who had been beheaded.

In the morning the Virgin invited the knights to sail with her to an island where they were to assist in preparing salves to bring the beheaded back to life.

During their voyage a mermaid swam up to the ship and handed the ship's company a magnificent pearl that had been lost.[6] They were told that this was the wedding gift of the goddesses of the sea.

On the island was a tower that turned out to be part laboratory, part shrine. The knights took part in an elaborate procedure in which a golden globe, suspended from the ceiling, was split into halves to reveal a white egg. This was then gently warmed in a copper vessel until it cracked open and a black bird freed itself. When this bird shed its black feathers, it immediately grew white ones, and these then took on all the colours of the rainbow. Later the bird was bathed in milk and stepped out of the bath as if newborn. A clock chimed, and when one of the knights chopped the head off the bird, its blood was collected in a golden bowl and its body was burned.

The knights were ushered up steps to higher chambers in the tower and when they reached the seventh floor, musicians arrived and merrily told them to climb onto the roof. There they were met by one of the kings who had been beheaded. He laughed until he was fit to burst when he saw how frightened the wedding guests were to see he had risen from the dead.

'From now on, my sons,' he said, 'learn that humans never know how well God provides for them.'

Finally the Virgin fetched the bird's ashes, which were made into a paste and pressed into two moulds. From these emerged two forms of babies about four inches long. Bright, glowing, almost transparent, they

The king about to swallow his son. This 'Merz picture' (by Tabitha Booth), combining elements from John Tenniel and Lambspinck's *De Lapide Philosophico*, shows an interesting continuum of sensibility.

were placed on satin cushions and fed with blood from the golden bowl, drop by drop into their tiny mouths. They seemed to grow little by little until they seemed life-sized, and so lifelike that Christian could almost imagine they were breathing. At last, by now sporting full heads of golden curly hair, they were laid on a bed.

A great trumpet was taken and positioned so that the top end of it opened onto a hole in the ceiling and the other end was in the mouths of the two moulded forms, one after another. Christian was amazed to see two souls streak like lightning down through the trumpets into the two figures. He thought he saw a twinkle in their eyes, and indeed they now seemed to warm, stir and awake. Christian understood that they were the royal couple who were to wed, and now they were here in bed together on this their wedding day. A curtain was tactfully drawn in front of the wedding bed.

The following morning Christian Rosencreutz was to sail back to the castle. The king he had met on the top of the tower embraced him. He informed Christian that this would be the last time he would see him in this form.

Christian returned to the real world. But he brought with him first-hand knowledge of processes of generation within the body that normally lie far below the threshold of consciousness. He had seen, too, how the process of incarnation and reincarnation might look to beings living in the spirit worlds, with the souls descending into the physical bodies via the trumpets. He had also been shown something of the chakras and the secrets of alchemy.

*   *

In the West knowledge of reincarnation and the chakras had been suppressed since Mani. Now, as the authority of the Church was questioned more and more keenly, and as many began to feel that it was failing to satisfy people's needs, a new stream of spirituality arose which didn't deny the great central truth of Christianity but also embraced the truths of other world religions.

The visions of Latini and Dante have a certain medieval starkness to them. The vision of Christian Rosencreutz has a richness, a colour and a gorgeousness that looks forward to the High Renaissance. One dimension opens up to reveal another and then another, and they are

An alchemical depiction of putrefaction and rebirth (from *Practica* by Basilius Valentinus, the pseudonym of a fifteenth-century alchemist).

all continually mutating. The narrative unfolds on different levels – for example the seven days of the week are also the seven days of creation – and in different dimensions. There is a material dimension, the dimension we encounter in dreams and the spiritual dimension we encounter in between Earth lives. *The Chymical Wedding* alludes to the physiological changes that accompany spiritual changes, the place of these physiological changes in the history of the world and their development in the history of an individual over several incarnations.[7]

Christian Rosencreutz died at the age of 107 and was buried in a mausoleum which was to be discovered more than 100 years later, in 1604. Lying inside was his uncorrupted body.[8]

Like Enoch, Elijah and the Hidden Imam, Christian Rosencreutz would be able to incarnate at will.

Joan and the Key to the Small Door

'He who is near me is near the fire.'

The Gospel of Thomas, saying 82

*'I was born under a star. No one has ever done, nor will
ever be able to do what I have done.'*

Gilles de Rais

Joan lived with her parents and brothers and sister in a small village called Domrémy.

The village girls liked to go to the Lady's Tree. There were stories about fairies appearing near this large and ancient beech and Joan's godmother said she had seen a fairy woman there. Joan would go with the other girls and hang garlands of flowers and herbs on the tree in May and dance around it. Next to the tree was a fountain that the villagers believed had healing powers.

As she grew older, Joan didn't play with the other girls so often. 'When I was thirteen I heard a Voice from God. I was petrified at first. It was nearly midday when the Voice came to me. It was summer and I was in my father's garden next to the graveyard.'

After that, voices came to her perhaps two or three times per week. Sometimes she heard them in the ringing of the church bells. Sometimes a particular voice spoke out of a dazzling cloud of mist, and after a while she recognized the form of the Archangel Michael within this mist. He told Joan she would have to leave home, that she had a mission.

He told her, too, that she should be guided by St Catherine and St Margaret, and soon they too appeared to her by the Lady's Tree. She would say later that she could see them as clearly as if they were made of flesh and blood.

Joan promised she would keep her virginity – or at least until she had completed her mission – but now her father was urging her to marry a local man.

There was once a girl whose father wanted her to marry a fine local gentleman. He was rich and wore dazzling clothes embroidered with gold, but he had a bristling bestial black beard – so black that it looked blue. The girl was frightened of the man they called Bluebeard, and when she saw him in the woods, she shrank from him and hid.

When Michael, Catherine and Margaret told Joan she must go to fight for the Dauphin and help him reclaim his kingdom from the English, she resisted. She didn't know how to ride a horse, let alone fight a war. But her heavenly guides persisted, giving her precise instructions. They said she must go to the nearby town of Vaucouleurs and there meet a certain Captain Baudricourt. He would give her the help and guidance she needed to reach the Dauphin. So, at the age of sixteen she deserted her family and left behind the young suitor her father favoured.

But when one of Captain Baudricourt's soldiers took her to see him, he said, 'Take her back to her father for a bloody good spanking!'

All the soldiers laughed, but Joan stood her ground and reminded him of a prophecy of Merlin's: a maid from their region would come to 'throw down citadels' and confound the British.

The captain had second thoughts, and after a while Joan arrived at the castle at Chinon. The Dauphin was holed up there, indecisive and ineffectual.

As Joan was led across a courtyard a horseman pulled up beside her and said, 'So this is the maid! Let me spend a night with her alone and she won't stay a maid for long!'

Then, in the hall, the Dauphin tried to play a trick on her. He dressed one of the courtiers as a king, hoping Joan would be fooled, but, guided

Joan of Arc before the Dauphin at Chinon (from a Flemish late fifteenth-century manuscript MS.Roy.20D.viii).

by the light of her guides, she went straight to the Dauphin and fell at his feet.

Behind the Dauphin stood Gilles de Rais, his right-hand man, the richest man in the kingdom and Marshal of France, in command of its military might. He was eight years older than Joan, strikingly dark and handsome, with glittering black eyes and a bushy black beard. He also had an insatiable desire for knowledge. He wanted to know the secret of life and was prepared to do anything to find it.

Joan told the Dauphin that God had told her to lay siege to the English stronghold at Orléans and then to lead the Dauphin to Reims, where he was to be crowned king. She was able to convince him that she was divinely inspired, amazing him by telling him what he had said alone in silent prayer, and she reassured him about his deepest, darkest secret, which he had never told anyone: that he was illegitimate.

So the Dauphin had a suit of armour and a banner made for Joan and presented her with a white horse.

Joan's voices meanwhile told her about an ancient sword, the sword of the great French champion Charles Martel, who had defended France against Moslem invasion. The voices told her it was marked with five crosses and was hidden beneath the altar of the nearby church of St Catherine. The Dauphin sent his armourers to the church. The stone slabs were removed and they found the sword with five crosses where Joan had said it would be. As they pulled it out of its dark hiding-place, its rust seemed to melt like snow in the sun.

Not himself a fighting man, the Dauphin entrusted Joan to the protection of Gilles de Rais. She rode out with Gilles at her side.

Bluebeard turned out to be far richer than anyone had imagined. He was very generous and charming, and soon the girl was persuaded to marry him.

A depiction of heavenly help in battle (probably sixteenth century, collected by Conrad Lycosthenes in *The Book of Prodigies*, 1557).

Joan and Gilles led a small French army and, guided by Joan's voices, they turned back the English at Orléans and Les Tourelles. Nearly 1,200 Englishmen died at Jargeau, where the French lost only 20. Against odds that should have been overwhelming, Joan's banner and sword carried all before them.

The English believed Joan's invincibility could only be witchcraft. Gilles de Rais, meanwhile, was in as good a position as anyone has ever been to observe at first hand how miraculous spiritual power can change the course of history.

And twice Joan was wounded in battle and twice Gilles acted heroically to protect her.

Gilles was there when a Constable Richemont, meeting her for the first time, said, 'I don't know if you come from God or from the Devil' and made the sign of the cross.

'Whenever I am sad,' said Joan, 'when people will not believe that God tells me to say these things, I go off by myself and pray. And he says to me, "Child of God, go, go, go! I shall be there to help you!" When I hear *Messire* speak, I am happy.'

Joan continued to urge the hesitant Dauphin onwards to his coronation at Reims.

At the fulfilment of the mission that St Michael had given Joan just eighteen months previously, it was Gilles de Rais, in magnificent gold and bejewelled livery, who headed the procession to the cathedral, carrying a reliquary shaped like a golden dove. It contained holy oil that had been used to anoint the kings of France since ancient times.

Joan stood waiting by the altar, her banner in her hand. 'Now at last,' she said, 'the will of *Messire* is fulfilled.'

She saw an angel place a crown on the new king's head.

She had completed her mission, but she was determined to build on her victories, to drive the English out of France completely.

But now she found that her voices no longer gave her such precise instructions on how to lead her troops.

The girl was married to Bluebeard happily enough. She grew accustomed to his bristling beard and was a little less horrified by it. But her husband was not a constant presence. There were many unexplained absences.

Bluebeard (illustration to Perrault's *Fairy Tales* by Gustave Doré).

One day he said he was going away for several days and he handed her the keys to the house. It was a great big bunch of keys because they lived in a very large house, more like a castle. In fact it was so big that the girl had never even visited some parts of it. Bluebeard explained which keys opened which rooms and which closets and wardrobes, containing furniture, clothes and jewellery. He said she was free to explore all of these. But, he said, very sternly, that there was one small key which opened a door at the bottom of a flight of stairs leading down from the ground floor. She was absolutely forbidden to open that door, and if she did, he would know.
And with that he left her all alone.

Fighting now without the guidance of her voices and also without the protection of Gilles de Rais, Joan was surrounded by French allies of the English. She was dragged down from her horse by a giant from Picardy. Then she was handed over to the English, imprisoned and kept in irons at Rouen. She was sexually assaulted and once she was saved from rape by the intervention of the Earl of Warwick.

Her interrogators tried to find the source of her magic. They asked her if her voices had told her that she would lose her all-conquering powers if she lost her virginity. She replied that she had been given no revelation on that matter.

Her voices returned to tell her she would be saved. But when the Inquisitors showed her their instruments of torture – the rack, the pincers, the needles – her courage began to fail her.

At her trial, the judge said, 'Abjure – or you will burn.'

'Abjure! Abjure! Abjure!' chanted the crowd, until Joan was heard to assent. But then it emerged that the judge had been lying – and she was to burn anyway.

Her head was shaved and a Friar Martin heard her last confession. She told him she had been beaten and sexually molested and that an English lord had raped her.

On the morning of her execution a Father Pierre came to her cell. He said her voices had been evil spirits. Good spirits would not have lied to her by telling her that she would be freed.

She was dressed in a robe and a mitre which had the words 'Heretic, apostate, idolater' painted on it.

A hundred soldiers with swords and battleaxes escorted the cart that carried Joan to the marketplace. There were two stages for courtiers and dignitaries of the Church on either side of the stake, set high on a platform, and beside the stake stood the executioner in his red uniform.

Joan called out to Catherine, Margaret and Michael as the flames began to rise from the pyre. Then she let out a long agonized scream. Her robe burned away and when the smoke parted the spectators could see her naked. The executioners rebuilt the fire until finally she was reduced to ashes.

An English soldier was heard to say, 'We have murdered a saint.'

Gilles de Rais wasn't there that day, though he heard detailed accounts of what had taken place. He left the service of the king and retreated to his ancestral lands. From there he sent out for holy relics, alchemists, the rarest books and the most erudite scholars.

Was he trying to make sense of what he had seen? Joan had undoubtedly exercised miraculous powers – but had those powers betrayed her in the end?

Gilles had a splinter of the True Cross sewn into his arm. He endowed a college and church dedicated to the Holy Innocents. He was famous for giving away treasures to servants and strangers. But a number of children in the region began to go missing – and some of them were last seen in the company of employees of Gilles de Rais.

One day he went to stay in a hotel in the small town of Rochebernat. In a house opposite lived a family with a ten-year-old son. One of Gilles de Rais's servants, called Poitu, asked the mother of the boy if she would hire her son to them as a page. He said she would be well paid and the boy would be well looked after and educated for a better life. The mother agreed. When the boy was taken over to meet Gilles, the lord apparently said he was as fair as an angel. The last time the mother saw her son he was on a pony Poitu had bought him, riding away with the lord. Two or three weeks later she went to Nantes, where she saw the same pony carrying another little boy.

Of course it would have been quite impossible for any commoner to make a complaint or institute any investigations into the affairs of a great lord like Gilles de Rais. If worried parents asked, they were merely told that their child was 'doing well'.

Bluebeard's young wife roamed through the castle, opening room after room, marvelling at all the fabulous, glittering riches she found there. She tried on some of the clothes, playing games by herself and wishing she had people to play with. But the thought of the little key and the room she was forbidden to enter was glowing in her mind.

Suddenly she set off towards it. By the time she reached the stairs leading underground she was moving so fast that she almost tripped. She picked out the key from the bunch and opened the little door. Beyond it was pitch black.

She walked inside. The stone floor felt cold and sticky through her silk slippers. After a while, as her eyes became accustomed to the dim light filtering in through the door behind her, she made out dead and mutilated bodies – the bodies of children her own age. They were propped up against the walls on either side. She dropped the key in fright, then snatched it up again and ran from the room. As she locked the door, she noticed that the key was sticky with blood.

Upstairs she tried to wash the blood from the key, but it was impossible. It was evidently a magic key, and now she understood why Bluebeard had said he would know if she had disobeyed him.

At that moment she heard him ride in through the main gates.

She imagined her brothers riding over the horizon to rescue her.

Gilles de Rais had been the richest man in France, but because of his extravagance he became nearly bankrupt and his downfall came about as a result of a dispute about money. He surrounded a church with a troop of armed men and demanded that a man he believed had swindled him come out of the church, where he was claiming sanctuary. If he didn't, Gilles said, he would kill him.

When the man emerged, he was violently beaten, then thrown in prison. In this way Gilles made an enemy of the Church. He was arrested and his houses were searched. They found first a child's shirt stained with blood, then the charred remains of what looked like human bones.

In the end the remains of approximately 140 children were discovered. Tried by the Inquisition, as Joan had been tried, Gilles was accused of sorcery, invoking evil spirits, sodomy and the murder of children. The alchemists he had summoned to help him and also his servants testified against him. It seems he had hung children up on iron hooks, then kept them lingering, hanging on to life while he sexually assaulted them. Poitu testified that after a child's head had been cut off, Gilles de Rais would often sit on their stomach and take pleasure in watching the last signs of life fade away. The body parts of children were also used in magic ceremonies.

Was all this an attempt to replicate a power to bend the world to the will that Gilles had seen in his friend Joan? Or was it an expression of rage against the cosmos or against God, who had betrayed her?

It was October 1440. On the gibbet and with the noose about his neck, Gilles de Rais implored the watching crowd to pray to God for his forgiveness, as they themselves would wish to be forgiven, and in a strange echo of Joan's power to move people to do good things, they did pray. As the stool was kicked out from underneath his feet, Gilles called out to St Michael . . .

The focus of this nineteenth-century engraving is a symbol current in some highly secretive Masonic fraternities that preserves Rosicrucian traditions. A variation of the symbol of the related compasses is a symbol of Luca, the divine light, and points to a high level of initiation, involving Christ-like qualities. The painting from which this engraving was taken was attributed to Leonardo da Vinci in the nineteenth century and held pride of place in the National Gallery in London. Now it is attributed to Luini and is not on public display. It is said to be a depiction of Jesus disputing with the doctors in the Temple, though of course he was a child when he did that.

OPPOSITE: *Laokoon. (Engraving by Marco Dente).* The artists of Renaissance Italy believed that by working with great spirits, angels, the gods of the stars and the planets, they could themselves become divine co-creators. They were inspired in this belief by the newly translated Hermetic texts: '. . . when a Daemon flows into an Humane Soul, he sprinkles in it Seeds of his own Notions, whence such a Soul, sprinkled with Seeds, raised in a Fury, brings forth wonderful things.' As this engraving illustrates, the process was not without risks. (There is contrast and comparison to be made here with sacred Hindu art. The Hindu artist raises himself to a higher level of consciousness and contemplates the divine archetypes, then reproduces them as nearly as he can. Originality is not prized.)

The Fairies Want our Juice

'There's always a kind of unspoken contract between a book's author and its reader . . . the subliminal contract for nonfiction is very different from the one for fiction.'

David Foster Wallace

The far west of Cornwall is a misty place, much of it wild and still resisting attempts to farm it. There are islands of rocky banks overgrown with furze and brambles, swarming with adders and surrounded by miles of bog, with springs, streams and deep, dangerous pools. Before tarmac, much of it was impassable except for rough causeways.

One afternoon William Noy, a farmer, was staying at a neighbouring farm, helping bring in the harvest. As more hands were required for the following day, the day of the harvest supper, he rode to the local village, Church-town, to recruit them, and also to invite the parson and his sexton to the supper. The latter would be particularly welcome, as he was a good fiddler.

Soon after 'day-down', Mr Noy, followed by his dogs, left the Church-town pub to return to the neighbouring farm. But he didn't arrive that night. Some thought that he might have enjoyed himself too much at the inn and gone back to his own house. But next day when people from all around asked after him and no one had seen or heard of him, they began to get a bit uneasy.

With all the corn safely stowed under thatch before suppertime, the farm workers and their helpers forgot about Mr Noy for a while. They enjoyed roast and boiled beef, mutton, rabbit and hare pies, followed by pudding, then there was drinking, singing and dancing through the night. At daybreak, though, many volunteered to search for Mr Noy. They spread out, some on horseback, others on foot – but there was no sign of him anywhere.

The search parties returned at night, and next morning horsemen were dispatched to neighbouring parishes, where everyone joined in the search.

On the third day, in the grey of the morning, a horse was heard to neigh and dogs to bark among thickets on an island of dry ground near the edge of Selena Moor. A group of men found a passable wooden track leading on to the island, and there they found Mr Noy's horse and hounds. The dogs led the way through thorns, furze, and brambles till they came to the ruins of what looked like a roofless old cottage or some sort of storage building. Inside they found Mr Noy lying on the ground fast asleep. He seemed groggy and disoriented when they woke him and said he was very glad they'd come as he didn't want to miss the harvest supper. When they told him that the corn had all been gathered in three days earlier, he said they must be joking. In fact he refused to believe it till later that day he saw with his own eyes all the mown hay under thatch and roped down.

Then, seated on a chimney-stool by a blazing fire, he told his neighbours what had happened.

The night being clear, he had decided he might as well take a short cut across the moor instead of going round by the stony bridleway. But after a while he found himself lost in a part of the moor that was unknown to him, even though he thought he knew every inch of that area.

After wandering for miles, he heard strains of lively music and spied the lights of a large house glimmering through the trees. There were people moving about and this made him hope he had found a farm.

His dogs slunk back and the horse wasn't willing to go on, so he tied him to a tree and took a path through an orchard towards the lights. He came to a meadow where he saw scores of people, some seated at tables eating and drinking with great enjoyment. Others were dancing reels to the beat of a tambourine. This was played by a girl dressed all in white, standing only a few paces from him.

The revellers were smartly dressed, but they seemed, at least most of them, to be very small, the size of infants or even smaller. The tables and the drinking cups were all in proportion to the size of these people. The dancers moved so fast that he couldn't count the number, and it made him giddy to look at their quick and intricate whirling movements as they danced jigs and reels.

He noticed that the girl who was playing the tambourine was more like ordinary folk in her stature. He thought she cast a side-glance towards him, and the music was so charming and lively, he decided to take her by the hand and join the dancing.

But as he approached, she frowned and, looking alarmed, made a motion with her head for him to withdraw round a corner of the house out of sight. Then she moved towards the orchard he had just come through, signalling to him to follow.

In a pool of moonlight, she waited for him. He approached and was surprised to see that she was none other than a farmer's daughter, one Grace Hutchens, who had once been his sweetheart. She had died three or four years earlier and been buried in Buryan churchyard.

'Thank the stars, my dear William,' she whispered, 'that I was on the lookout to stop you, or you would this minute have been changed like me.'

He went to kiss her.

'Oh, beware!' she said. 'Don't touch me, don't touch any flower or fruit. Eating a plum in this orchard was my undoing. What was buried in the churchyard was only a sham body. With my real body I feel much the same as when being your sweetheart was all I lived for.'

As she said this, several little voices squeaked in the night, 'Grace, Grace, bring us more beer and cider! Be quick about it!'

She looked scared. 'Stay behind the house. Be sure you keep out of sight, and if you value your life, don't touch fruit or flower.'

Again he wanted to kiss her.

'No, my love, not for the world,' she whispered. 'Wait for me here, I'll soon return. My sad lot is to be stolen from the living to be a slave.'

She left him in the garden and a few minutes later she returned, leading him further away from the house and the dancing and into a bowery walk, where the music and noise of merriment faded. She said,

'You know, my dear Willy, that I loved you, but you can never know how dearly.' She pointed to a stone, 'Take that seat.'

Mr Noy seated himself and Grace told him how one evening, about dusk, she had been out on Selena Moor looking for stray sheep. She had missed her way among ferns higher than her head, then wandered on for hours, completely lost. After many miles, as it seemed to her, she had waded through a brook and entered an orchard where she had heard music. Walking towards it, she had entered a beautiful garden with alleys bordered by roses. Apples and other fruit, ripe and bursting, had hung low around her head.

Feeling tired and thirsty, she had plucked a plum that looked like gold in the clear starlight. But no sooner had her lips closed on the fruit than it dissolved to bitter liquid that made her sick and faint, and she fell to the ground in a fit. She couldn't say how long she lay there, but she woke to find herself surrounded by dozens of small people, who seemed very pleased to see her. They said they very much wanted a tidy girl who knew how to bake and brew and who would keep their habitation decent, and nurse the children they stole.

At first Grace felt entranced and dazzled, but gradually she got used to living with them. She said she believed they had no hearts and little sense or feeling. She thought they were very ancient and had lived there since the olden times. What appeared to be plums and apples in their gardens were only the wild berries that grew naturally on the moors. Grace said that at first their food of berries and honeydew had made her sick, and though she had grown used to it, she often longed for a bit of salt fish.

She said that one of the elderly men had grown attached to her and was especially kind to her. Then, seeing Mr Noy glowering, she added, 'Oh, my dear Willy, don't be such a noddy as to be jealous! He's no more than vapour and what he is pleased to call love is no more substantial than fancy.'

Mr Noy asked if there were any children among them besides those they stole.

'Very few,' she said, 'though they are fond of babies and there is great rejoicing when one happens to be born amongst them. They are not of our religion, but star-worshippers. They don't live together like Christians and turtle doves. Considering how long they live, perhaps that would be tiresome for them. And the old withered men – well, one can almost see through them, like puffs of smoke. And indeed they often yearn for the time when they will be altogether dissolved in air and end their wearisome existence.'

Grace assured Mr Noy of her everlasting love but said she would rather see him in flesh and blood than changed to her state. She told him that if he wished to join her when he died, they could then be united and dwell together in the fairyland of the moors.

Mr Noy wanted to know much more about these strange beings and was about to ask when they called, 'Grace, Grace, where art thou so long? Bring us some drink quickly.'

The music stopped and Mr Noy heard tiny feet coming towards them. He remembered being told as a child that any garment turned inside out and cast among the piskies – which is what the small people are called in Cornwall – would make them flee. He put his hand into his coat pocket and felt there the gloves that he wore for binding hay. Quick as thought, he turned one inside out and put a small stone into it, and as a group of the piskies came round the corner, he threw it among them.

In an instant they vanished, along with the house, the orchard and Grace. He just had time to glance round, seeing nothing but thickets and a roofless old cottage, before he received a blow on his forehead that knocked him out.

From that night on, Mr Noy was a changed man. He talked of little else but what he had seen and heard. Often at dusk and on moonlit nights he wandered the moors in hopes of meeting Grace. He became melancholy, neglected his farm, grew tired of hunting and departed this life before the next harvest. But whether he really died or passed into fairyland, no one knows.[1]

*　　　　*　　　　*

A woman lived in a cottage with a garden in front with two rose trees in it. One bore white roses and the other red roses. When she had two girls, she called one Snow White and the other Rose Red. They were good and happy, busy and cheerful, but Snow White was quieter and gentler than Rose Red. Rose Red liked to run about in the meadows and fields, pinching flowers and catching butterflies, while Snow White liked to sit at home with her mother and help her with her housework.

Piskies (drawn from life by Tabby Booth).

It was winter, and Snow White lit the fire and hung the brass kettle on the hob. It shone like gold, so brightly was it polished. In the evenings that winter a lamb lay upon the floor beside them, and behind them upon a perch a white dove sat with its head hidden beneath its wings.

As they were all sitting comfortably together enjoying the fire, someone knocked at the door. The mother said, 'Quick, Rose Red, open the door. It must be one of the travelling people seeking shelter.'

Rose Red went and pushed back the bolt. A bear pushed his broad, black head inside.

Rose Red screamed and sprang back. The lamb bleated, the dove fluttered, and Snow White hid herself behind her mother's chair.

But the bear began to speak in a deep and gentle voice. He said, 'Don't be afraid, I will do you no harm! I am half frozen, and only want to warm myself a little.'

'Poor bear,' said the mother, 'lie down by the fire – only take care that you do not burn your coat.' Then she said, 'Snow White, Rose Red, come out from hiding. The bear means well, I'm sure.'

So they both came out, and by and by the lamb and dove came nearer too and were not afraid of the bear.

The bear said, 'Here, children, knock the snow out of my coat a little.'

So they brought the broom and beat the bear's hide clean. Then he stretched himself by the fire and growled contentedly and comfortably.

Later the girls relaxed completely and began to play tricks on their clumsy guest. They tugged his hair, put their feet upon his back and rolled him about. Once they took a hazel-switch and softly beat him, and when he growled, they laughed. Only when they became a little too rough, he protested, 'Leave me alive!'

When it was bedtime and the others went to bed, the mother said to the bear, 'You can lie there by the hearth, then you will be safe from the cold and the bad weather.'

As soon as day dawned, the two children let the bear out, and he trotted across the snow into the forest.

For the next four months the bear came every evening, laid himself down by the hearth and let the children amuse themselves with him as much as they liked. They got so used to him that the door was never fastened for the night until after their black friend had arrived.

But when spring arrived and all outside was turning green, one morning the bear said to Snow White, 'Now I must go away and cannot come back for the whole summer.'

'Where are you going then, dear bear?' asked Snow White.

'I must go into the forest and guard my treasures from the wicked dwarves. In the winter, when the earth is frozen hard, they are obliged to stay below and cannot work their way through. But now, when the sun has thawed the earth, they come out to pry and steal. And what gets into their hands or their caves does not easily see daylight again.'

Snow White was sad as she unbolted the door for the bear.

As he was hurrying out, he caught himself against the bolt and a piece of his hairy coat was torn off. It seemed to Snow White that she saw gold shining through it, but she wasn't sure.

The bear ran away quickly and was soon out of sight amidst the trees.

A short time afterwards the mother sent the children into the forest to get firewood. There they found a big tree lying felled on the ground, and close by the trunk something was jumping backwards and forwards in the grass. They couldn't make out immediately what it was, but when they came nearer they saw a dwarf with an old withered face and a snow-white beard a yard long. The end of the beard was caught in a crevice of the tree and the little fellow was jumping about like a dog tied to a rope, and clearly didn't know how to free himself.

He glared at the girls with fiery red eyes. 'Why are you just standing there?' he said, angrily. 'Come here immediately and help me!'

'What are you up to, little man?' asked Rose Red.

'You stupid, prying goose!' answered the dwarf. 'I was going to split the tree to get a little wood for cooking. I had just driven the wedge safely in and everything was going as I wished when the wedge suddenly sprang out and the tree closed so quickly that I couldn't pull my beautiful white beard out in time. So now it's stuck and all you silly, sleek milk-faced things can do is laugh!'

It was true – the girls were having a fit of the giggles. They pulled themselves together and tried very hard, but they couldn't pull the beard out. It was caught fast and the little man roared with pain and anger.

'I'll run and fetch someone,' said Rose Red.

'Don't do that, you stupid girl!' the dwarf snarled quickly.

'There, there, don't worry,' said Snow White. 'I'll help you,' and she pulled her scissors out of her pocket, and in an instant she had cut off the end of the beard.

'You wicked girl! Why did you do that? You ruined my beautiful white beard!' cried the dwarf.

Then he grabbed a bag which lay amongst the roots of the tree and which they could see was full of gold. Continuing to curse the girls, he swung the bag upon his back, and without once looking back, he trudged off.

Twice more the girls saved the dwarf and twice more he was ungrateful and angry.

Then one evening as they were crossing the heath on the way home after a day's shopping, they came upon him once more. He had emptied out his bag of precious stones on a patch of bare earth and the evening sun was shining upon the brilliant stones. They glittered and sparkled so beautifully that the children stood still and stared at them.

The dwarf's expression hardened when he saw the girls. 'Why do you stand there gaping?' he cried, and his face became copper-red with rage.

He was still cursing them when there was a loud growling and a black bear came trotting towards them.

The dwarf sprang up in fright, but he couldn't reach his hole in time and he cried out in dread: 'Dear Mr Bear, spare me, I will give you all my treasures. Look at the beautiful jewels lying there! Grant me my life. What do you want with a slender little fellow like me? You wouldn't even feel me between your teeth or as you swallowed. Come, take these two wicked girls instead. They are tender morsels for you, fat as young quails!'

The bear took no notice of his words, but gave the dwarf a single blow with his paw.

The girls turned to run away, but the bear said, 'Snow White and Rose Red, don't be afraid.'

They looked back and saw the dwarf lying still on the ground.

'Wait, I will come with you,' continued the bear.

They recognized the kindness in his voice, and when he came up to them his bearskin fell off, and there stood a handsome young man, clothed all in gold.

'I am a king's son,' he said. 'I was bewitched by that wicked dwarf, who stole my treasures. I have had to run about the forest in the form of a bear until I could be freed by his death.'

Snow White was married to the prince and Rose Red to his brother. The two couples divided between them the great treasure which the dwarf had gathered together in his underground cave.

Two rose-trees still stood before their mother's window and every year bore the most beautiful roses, white and red.

*   *   *

Is the story of Rose Red and Snow White sheer fantasy? We have touched on Sufi teachings regarding the level of reality in fantasy – its ontological status – and we have also touched on the mystical meaning of roses in the visionary life of Christian Rosencreutz.

The story of Rose Red and Snow White is about the mystery of the purified blood. Rose Red is red blood and the life of feeling, of the

Mr Bear

animal spirit that it carries, running around the woods full of joy, active and impatient. Snow White is the life of thought. She is quieter, more reflective. They play together and the inspirations of the heart are carried up to the mind, bringing to life the higher spiritual realities that are reflected there, a little thinly and anaemically at first.

The fairy story of Rose Red and Snow White is also historical in the sense that it is an account of an alchemical form of meditation developed by a historical personage, Christian Rosencreutz, adapting forms of meditation practised in the East to make them suitable for people living in the West.

Physiological transformation is brought about by spiritual exercises, by disciplines of sacred thinking, called Mercury in alchemical texts. These exercises are intended to engender encounters with living spiritual beings, and the bear in the story is of course Christ. Blood, the carrier of spirit, our animal consciousness, is called Sulphur in alchemy. Our blood may be purified by a sacred marriage to Christ and made ready to carry the Christ spirit.

And what of Mr Noy's experiences? Is there any way of even beginning to view these in a scientific light?

Paracelsus and the Mysteries of Spiritual Healing

A few years ago I had the pleasure of working on a book with the renowned botanist David Bellamy. He told me that one of the ways that large drug companies prospered was by seeing which traditional folk remedies were working and selling well in healthfood stores, then researching and refining dosages and finally slapping a patent on them so that they were no longer freely available. He predicted that something like this would happen to the traditional folk remedy St John's Wort in a few years.

The question arises how were these folk remedies discovered in the first place? Is it plausible to think it was by trial and error? Or are there other ways of knowing?

*   *   *

An Iroquois warrior called Nekumonta married Shanewis. He was a great hunter and warrior and she was beautiful and they were much in love. But shortly after they married, the snows came and kept coming. It was an exceptionally severe winter, food became short and members of the tribe began to fall sick. Nekumonta watched as one by one, his father, mother, brothers and sisters and his wider family in the village all fell sick and died. Was the whole tribe going to be wiped out?

Then Shanewis began to feel ill. Nekumonta cried out to the heavens in pain. He prayed to the Great Spirit for help. Where could he find the herbs to save his beautiful wife whom he loved so much?

Covering her with as many layers of furs as he could find and placing water within easy reach, he set off in the snow. He climbed over huge drifts and tried to find places where the snow was less deep, so that he could dig for herbs. But he found nothing.

That night he fell asleep exhausted and woke up to find a rabbit looking at him.

He said, 'Tell me where to find the herbs planted by the Great Spirit that will heal my wife.'

But the rabbit just twitched its nose, turned and hopped off amongst the trees.

Nekumonta prayed again to the Great Spirit as he pressed on into the depths of the forest.

On the second day he found the cave of a bear. He asked the bear the same question, but it turned its back on him and resumed hibernating.

On the third day Nekumonta saw no animals at all. *Perhaps*, he thought to himself miserably, *I don't know how to pray?* He kept walking and digging until finally he collapsed at the foot of a great rock.

Then he had a dream. Animals, birds, trees and plants were gathering around him. They were remembering that he had always treated them with respect. He had never killed animals except for food and clothing. Moreover he had never killed a deer, for instance, without asking permission from the Great Spirit of the deer, and he saw and loved the sacred life running through the trees and plants as well. Now all prayed with him and for him, and helped carry his prayers up to the Great Spirit.

His dream changed. He saw his wife, still lying sick but murmuring. Then she started singing a beautiful song. The sound rippled outwards and Nekumonta realized it was the sound of a spring. He listened more intently and he could hear the words of the song. The spirit of the water was saying, 'Find me, and beautiful Shanewis shall live.'

Nekumonta awoke. He stood up and looked around him. No spring.

He went back to where he had been lying and began to dig. It was hard, because the ground was frozen, and he also had to pull out rocks and old roots. He was just about to give up when he saw a glint in the bottom of the hole and a small spring of water started up.

It grew stronger and soon the hole was full up. Nekumonta sprang up with joy and drank some of the water. Immediately he felt his strength flooding back. He ran back to his village, carefully carrying some of this spring water.

He found his wife lying still, her eyes closed. He poured a few drops through her lips. She opened her eyes. They were just as beautiful as he remembered.

*   *   *

'I am a rough man, born in a rough country,' said Paracelsus. 'I have no desire to live comfortably, nor do I wish to be rich. To be happy is to wander freely, possessing nothing that needs my care, to study the book of nature with my feet over its leaves.'

Born in the countryside near Zurich in 1493, he travelled in his teens to study under a famous mystic and esoteric scholar called Trithemius, abbot of Sponheim, but Paracelsus didn't stay long in the abbey library. He wanted to learn directly from life. Like St Francis, he was more interested in personal experience than in dogma.[1]

Between 1517 and 1523 Paracelsus travelled to Ireland, Portugal, Spain, Egypt, Lithuania, Poland, Hungary and Croatia. It was said that he underwent a shamanic initiation among the Tartars. As he travelled, he researched folklore and folk cures. A healer and a listener, while curing the common people he was also learning from them.

There can be few more miraculous worlds than the world of Paracelsus. Believing that this world is a product of a great universal mind, he looked at the stars and saw them as the great slow-moving thoughts of God, and below these great thoughts he saw a hierarchy of lesser thoughts, faster moving, more intimately concerned with the details of everyday life. These, he said, were angels and spirits.

We have seen similar ideas in ancient teachings – and in the teachings of mystics in all ages. What is strange and startling in Paracelsus is his vivid account of these teachings not just as doctrine but as *lived experience*. He was a visionary who didn't just leave us with visions of the heavens, but of heavenly and spirit creatures working in many different areas of human experience and in the natural world.

Paracelsus saw directly how the stars acted on human beings, exerting an influence at a distance on the 'constellations of the stars' within the human body. In other words, parts of the human body have a special relationship with particular stars and planets, and these parts of the body are directly affected by the corresponding stars and planets in the sky. Mars has a connection with the blood, for example, and the sun with the heart.

Like Brunetto Latini, Paracelsus saw that the intelligent principles and essences that make up a human being also make up the universe. Humanity is the quintessence of the cosmos. To Paracelsus, as to a Sufi knower, this means that we can find out all there is to know about the universe by examining ourselves. In fact this seemed entirely natural to him. He wrote: 'If man in his waking state knows nothing of such things, the cause of this ignorance is that he does not understand how to search in himself for the powers that were given him by God.'

Paracelsus's world has regions in it that are very strange indeed. He was the great biologist of the spiritual world, describing, naming and classifying its fauna and flora. He wrote: 'There are certain localities where large numbers of elementals live together, and occasionally a man has been admitted to live with them for a while and they have become visible and tangible to him.' Knowing how to look for these localities, he was able to find and describe the different types of elementals. According to him, their behaviour is not unlike that of humans. In fact they like to mimic humans, and even dress like them, but they have only animal intelligence and, like animals, are incapable, he said, of spiritual development.

Different groups of elementals are responsible for different dimensions of the natural world. The Athnici, as Paracelsus called them, are the elemental spirits of fire. They might sometimes appear as shining globes or fiery tongues. The Cobalo are little men who work underground. They are about two feet tall and they like to laugh and muck about.[2] Paracelsus described them as dressing as miners did then, wearing leather aprons. The Gigantes are another type of elemental with a human form, living in the Earth but of great size. The Pygmaei are the class of elemental belonging to the earth. These tiny beings are perpetually at war with the dwarves. Durdales are what Paracelsus called invisible beings living in trees – called the dryads by the Greeks. The elementals of the air are called Lemures, those of water Melinosinae, those of water plants Nymphae, those of fire Salamanders.[3] Sylphes are elementals living in mountainous regions.

Paracelsus also wrote of another order of beings which may be created by humans. Aquastors are given life by the power of the human imagination. They may obtain life and form. They may become visible and even tangible. Succubi, incubi and vampires are of this type.

Homunculi are artificially made human beings, and Paracelsus's writings include instructions on how to make one!

These descriptions of elementals may remind us of Puck, Ariel and Titania and the variety of spiritual life forms in Shakespeare's woods:

> . . . I serve the fairy queen . . .
> I must go seek some dewdrops here
> And hang a pearl in every cowslip's ear . . .
> Where the bee sucks, there suck I . . .
> On the bat's back I do fly.

You might think Paracelsus's visions of elementals are imaginary, and he might have agreed – with the proviso that Paracelsus, of course, had an exalted view of the imagination. For him, it was the creative power of man: 'The imagination is a sun in the soul of man, acting in his own sphere as the sun of the earth acts in him.' Similarly, he wrote: 'Wherever the sun shines, germs planted in the soil grow and vegetation grows up, and the sun of the soul acts in a similar manner and calls the forms of the soul into existence . . .'[4] The great world is a product of the imagination of the universal mind, and a human being is a little world of its own that also creates by a similar power of imagination. If our imagination is strong enough to penetrate every corner of our interior world, it will be able to create in those corners.[5]

Imagination is a mental force with power to create matter and also to move it like a magnet. God imagined the world into existence, and through our imagination we become co-creators. Of course the imagination of an individual human being is not as powerful as the imagination of God, but an individual's imagination plays a crucial role in moulding the world around that individual. It exerts a pressure on the fabric of space-time, pushing or pulling it so that ripples start locally before spreading out across the universe.

By these doctrines Paracelsus pioneered notions of what would later be called the subconscious and its power to cause and also to heal disease. He wrote about diseases arising because of children dwelling on fantasies they had heard – what we would today call psychosomatic illness.

To take another obvious example of the power of an individual human imagination to affect the material world and generate matter, semen is born from imagination. Less obviously, Paracelsus writes that if during coition the desire or passion of the female is stronger than that of the male, male children will be produced – and vice versa. As the power of the imagination ripples outwards from one body, it invades first the mind and then the body of the next closest person.

'All the imagination of man comes from the heart, and by imagination we may perfect the will,' Paracelsus writes. Imaginative pictures can awake the impulses of will, and willpower can in turn be brought to bear directing imagination. The creative power of perfected imagination lay at the heart of Paracelsus's practice of alchemy.[6]

Paracelsus also had a strong sense of the power of the eye to change what it was looking at. Leading scientists since the quantum revolution, including John Wheeler and Roger Penrose, have speculated that something like the quantum effect – whereby the way we look at

There is a strong Hermetic dimension to the thought of Paracelsus, which is to say it concerns wisdom derived ultimately from ancient Egypt. The ability of the third eye to reach out and strike, to change what it sees, is depicted in this carved head. (Wall carving of Amenerdas, wife of Shabaka, Egypt's second Nubian ruler, 721–707 BC).

Portrait of Paracelsus rubbing the sleep out of his third eye (from *Astronomica et astrologica opuscula*, 1576).

Woodcut of the 1530s illustrating the world of Paracelsus, showing how an initiate of a low degree of initiation may appear to someone with 'eyes of fire'.

something changes it – known to be a feature of the microcosmic world, must also be a feature of the human-scaled world of our senses. Paracelsus says that we all have the power to affect things in this way. In fact we all do it through our imagination, even if most of us do it unwittingly. But if we are prepared to work on our imagination, we can do it in a more focused, more effective way.[7] Just as training for athletes may involve visualizations that stimulate the will to win, so alchemical images in the works of Paracelsus are designed to help and train the imagination so that it can move and morph objects in the material world effectively.

In 1527 Paracelsus set up as a doctor in Basle. However he arrived at his cures, they were so successful that they enraged the local doctors, and he was forced to set out on his travels again. Throughout his life

A sun tree and a moon tree (from *Livres des Merveilles*, a fourteenth-century manuscript). Paracelsus called plants 'growing water' and described how plants as well as humans – columns of water – are affected by the movements of the stars and planets. The water in a plant or body responds particularly by means of the small traces of salts that have an affinity to a particular heavenly body. For example, the iron in our blood responds to Mars, and traces of copper and mercury respond to Venus and Mercury. Paracelsus believed that disease arose because of a lack of harmony between the cosmos and the microcosm of the human body.

he was driven from pillar to post. He would enjoy a little local success, become too successful, have a row and be forced to flee. He was naturally boastful about his discoveries and our word 'bombast' is derived from his full name Theophrastus Bombastus. He died alone and unrecognized in rented accommodation. He had, however, succeeded in achieving one of his wishes – not being rich.

*   *   *

Paracelsus's influence on civilization after his death was immense, in many different fields. He would be highly influential both on mainstream and alternative medicine, as well as the development of the scientific method. He is accredited with devising the principles that lie behind homoeopathy and with introducing an emphasis on hygiene into medicine. He has been called both the father of toxicology and of experimental medicine, and his focus on the chemical constituents of cures led to his identifying zinc – the name of which he also coined. His books were studied by both Francis Bacon and Isaac Newton.

How did the folk remedies that Paracelsus collected – many of them the basis for today's industrialized medicine – come to be discovered? Was it really a process of trial and error or pure accident? Or was it, as the Iroquois and Paracelsus believed, because healers are guided by spirits and angels?[8]

According to idealism, we are all connected to a great Cosmic Mind via our own individual minds. So, if you believe in idealism, you are more likely to set greater store by the role of the imagination – to think that it has something 'magic' in it – than you are if you are a materialist seeing each individual mind as closed off. And, as we shall see shortly, many great scientific discoveries have been made by people who cultivated states of consciousness in which they were receptive to the thoughts of the great Cosmic Mind.

The Cobbler Has Another Way of Knowing

You and I could sit together and by a series of spiritual exercises work ourselves into an altered state of consciousness, perhaps even a visionary state of consciousness in which the world seems a mysterious place, a place of unfolding dimensions, a place controlled by unseen intelligences, where everything that happens is meant to be.

People often *do* experience the world in these alternative states, and if you want to you can experience the universe in this way too. But the important question is this: when you are in this altered state, seeing things in the world you don't normally see and understanding the world working in ways you don't normally perceive or understand, are you seeing anything real? Are your perceptions true insights that can help you live better in the world or are they simply delusions? Are you able to see real things that you couldn't see before, as if you had suddenly acquired something like X-ray vision, or are you indulging in an exercise in wilful gullibility, like watching a good stage magician?

*　　　　　*　　　　　*

Among the Zulus, the soul is said to assume a shape that is part beast and part human after death. This is in a sense our true shape, the Zulus say, because while we are on Earth we have a bestial nature. But a short while after death this animal shape is thrown aside and our human part moves on back up through the heavens to its place of origin.

In tribal life all boys are initiated into adulthood, but then for a chosen few there is a further initiation. In the Australian outback this later initiation makes a young man a *karadji*, a shaman, chosen by the All-father and the tribal ancestors to travel between this world and Dreamland.

The chosen boy is woken in the night by elders wearing animal masks. He is not allowed to utter a sound or raise his eyes from the ground. His body is painted and buried in a shallow grave. He is dead to the world in a symbolic sense, but he also fears that he really will die.

His first night's journey will become even more terrifying and almost unbearably painful. He might be led into a snake pit and made to commune with a giant snake. He might be attacked by animals with human heads. These are evil spirits. He might see the dead walk towards him and hear the rattle of their bones. Like Enoch or Daniel, he may see fiery, thunderous storms tearing the whole world apart.

The elders then take him to another dark place and begin to make incisions in his skin. They take rock crystals and press them inside him. They push them gradually, gratingly, up his legs and up his abdomen to his breastbone. A hole is cut into the first finger of his right hand and a crystal inserted. More crystals are rubbed into his scalp and he is also forced to eat food containing crystals. This is repeated for three days until a large hole is gouged in his tongue, a sign that the power of the crystals is within him.

In esoteric doctrines that see the Earth as a living being, crystals are its eyes. With crystals inside him, the *karadji* will begin to see everything that lives in the spirit worlds and be able to tell the people what he sees.

There follows a long period spent mostly alone in the desert. Elders will come to him from time to time and teach him breathing techniques and postures that will help him to see the spirit worlds at will, both when he is awake and when he is sleeping. He is taught telepathy, how to see spirits and how to see inside human bodies to diagnose and heal illnesses, how to exorcise, how identify murderers and the art of astral travelling so that he can see what is happening over long distances. He may begin to grow the stumps that are the signs of feathers beginning to sprout on the tops of the arms.

He will perhaps be able to invent new stories, new songs and dances.

The land was devastated by drought and a *karadji* was asked by his people to intercede for them.

For four days he climbed the steps cut into the rock of the mountain Ooobi-Oobi. Finally he reached a spring. He drank from it and felt wonderfully refreshed.

Then he saw a circle made of columns of stones. Inside the circle he heard a terrible roar and he knew the great god was near. He prayed for the drought to end and suddenly he was lifted into the presence of the All-Father seated on a throne made of quartz crystal. He was told to gather as many blossoms as he could manage and take them back down the side of Ooobi-Oobi to his tribe.

Travellers in Lapland at the end of the seventeenth century encountered tribes who still worshipped Thor. Olaus Rudbeck was deputed by the king of Sweden to travel to write a natural history of these people. At the centre of what Rudbeck called Laplanders' 'Magick Art' was a drum made out of a hollow piece of wood, either pine, fir or birch, but it had to be from a tree that turned 'directly according to the Sun's course', so that the grain of the wood turned from the bottom to the top of the tree, winding from the right hand to the left. The Laplanders sewed reindeer skin over the hollow and painted pictures on it in a red colour that was made by staining the skin with the bark of an alder tree. They also attached a bunch of brass rings to the drum. The hammer they used to beat the drum was made of reindeer horn and was called Thor's Hammer.

The beating of the drum with Thor's Hammer caused the brass rings to move across the pictures, telling the Laplanders what they needed to know, so that, for example, if a ring leapt onto the image of a wolf, they should hunt wolves that day. The drummer knelt beside the drum and drummed softly at first, then faster and louder, and began to reel and dance in a circle until finally he fell down in a dead faint. He would remain unconscious for hours, maybe for as long as twenty-four hours, and meanwhile the others attending the ceremony would continue to sing and would make every effort to keep the flies off him.

While the drummer was unconscious his spirit was free to travel either in the realm of the dead – to consult ancestors – or over large distances on the surface of the Earth, or to see the past or the future, or to travel to meet the gods. Sometimes in seeking the counsel of the gods the drummer would take a golden apple in one hand and Thor's Hammer in the other – and sometimes, too, a serpent made of copper. Shamans might also carry pouches containing blue flies, which they could send off to do their bidding.

Rudbeck noted that by the time he went on his trip, in 1695, the magical uses of the drum were already being forgotten by the Laplanders.

The Laplanders' shamanic search for cures brings us back to Paracelsus's search for folk remedies in Switzerland and Germany and his own shamanic initiation among the Tartars, and it raises again the question how were these cures discovered?

There is no doubt that people in all times and in all places have entered altered states hoping to learn things closed to them in ordinary everyday consciousness.

Are there other ways of knowing?

*   *   *

Jacob Boehme was born in 1575 in a small village. His parents were pious but illiterate Lutheran peasants. Jacob was a sweet-natured dreamy child who never questioned the stories of miracles he heard in church or the fairy tales his parents told him. His parents put him to work as a shepherd, but he was too delicate and sensitive for farm work and was later sent to work as an apprentice to a cobbler in the nearby town of Görlitz.

One day when his boss had left him temporarily in charge of the shop, a stranger came in. He looked poor and his eyes seemed to burn with an otherworldly light. He told Jacob he wanted to buy a pair of shoes. Jacob wasn't sure he actually had the authority to sell anything, so he quoted an unreasonably high price. The man bought the shoes anyway and left the shop. Then from the road he called Jacob out in the street to talk to him.

'Jacob, you are little as yet, but you will become great, and a man so uncommon that the world will marvel. Be dutiful to God and reverence Him.' He told Jacob to read the scriptures, where he would find 'consolation for the poverty and trials you will endure and for the persecution you will suffer. Be brave, be persevering. God holds you in his love and will be gracious to you.'

Then the stranger took Jacob's hand, gave him another piercing stare and was gone.

After that, Jacob began to experience visions. This was initially a problem. He had never really fitted in at the shop and soon his increasingly distracted behaviour led to his dismissal. He became an itinerant shoemaker, but he was anxious and depressed.

In 1599 he returned to Görlitz, set up as a cobbler with a stall of his own and married the local butcher's daughter. It proved to be a happy marriage and they would have six children.

Jacob was small, lean and plain, a bit hawk-nosed, with grey eyes and high temples. He had a thin beard and a small, low voice. He was amiable, modest, humble and meek in conversation – but in spite of all this he was destined to make a deadly enemy.

In 1600 his eye was caught by the sun's reflection in a burnished pewter dish. As he watched he seemed to be 'admitted into a world transformed'. This was a vision of another order. His inner mind became pulsing and radiant and, it seemed to him, divine.

Taken aback, he tried to snap out of this trance by leaving the building and going out into the fresh air, but there he was amazed that he seemed to see into the heart and essence of nature, perceiving directly the harmonious forces pushing up through the herbs and grasses. He believed he was seeing and feeling creation at work.

He began to keep a journal of his mystical experiences. 'Sometimes the gate of His mystery was opened to me,' he wrote. 'Then in a quarter of an hour I understood more than if I had been many years at university.'

Once he had a vision of the creation in which he seemed to be present in the beginning:

> Let no man wonder if I write about the creation of the world, as I have been there and witnessed it . . . As a human mind acts and moves the thoughts and senses from the highest to the lowest, and comprehends and commands by the thoughts from the highest to the lowest, so the eternal mind has

manifested itself from the highest majesty, even to the lowest, to the greatest darkness. And this world, with the sun, stars, and elements, and with every creaturely being, is nothing else but a manifestation of the eternity of the eternal will and mind. And as it was in the beginning, so it still stands in its seething and vegetation . . . I saw and comprehended the Being of all Beings, the Byss and the Abyss . . . I saw the original and primal existence of this world and of all creatures. Within myself I perceived creation entire, in its order and movement: I saw first the divine world, of the angels and of Paradise, second, the darkened world, the fiery realm and third, the world all around us, visible and tangible, as an issue and expression of the inner, eternal, hidden worlds.[1]

There can be few clearer statements anywhere of idealism's account of how the Cosmic Mind creates by thinking.

Jacob Boehme wrote a commentary on Genesis which, with a nod to Paracelsus, he titled the *Mysterium Magnum*:

The angels are God's instruments in governing the world, and as such they not only glorify the celestial nature where they rule, but they also dominate over the terrestrial world and its individual regions.

Each country has its princely guardian spirit.

Whenever the celestial melody of the angels begins to sound, there arise various growths, figures and magnificent colours . . . The celestial powers, by their interaction, generate trees and bushes, whereon grows the beautiful and lovely fruit of life. Likewise by means of these powers there arise various flowers of beautiful celestial colours and exquisite odour.[2]

Boehme gave detailed descriptions of how spiritual powers worked in nature:

Behold a tree. Outwardly it has a hard and rough shell, appearing dead and encrusted, but the body of the tree has a living power, which breaks through the hard and dry bark and generates many young bodies, branches, and leaves, which, however, all are rooted in the body of the tree. Thus it is with the whole house of this world, wherein the holy light of God appears to have died out, because it has withdrawn and seems dead. But love ever again and again breaks through this very house of death and generates holy and celestial branches in this great tree, and which root in the light.[3]

In *On the Signature of All Things*, written in 1622, he also gave a unique account of how the angels he elsewhere called the 'spirits of the celestial bodies' gave form, colour and taste to different types of plants. 'The Sun draws the power out of the root in the earth, and the joyful Mercury ascends up along with it . . .'

He understood that the information needed to enable a plant to grow into its proper form wasn't contained solely in the plant itself but in the universe as a whole – and in particular in the relationship of the plant to the sun and the planets with which it interacted in the growing process:

> The Sun reaches towards the oil in the centre of the fruit, and fervently longs after it, and gives itself freely into the fruit, and the fruit's inner Sun sucks the virtue into itself, and gives it forth in its joy into the austere property of the fruit, and meekens and sweetens all with love.

He also gave a comprehensive account of how the moon and planets exerted their influences:

> Jupiter inclines to blue and helps make a pleasant taste . . . Mars causes hardness, and makes for a bitter taste, by reason of his anxious nature . . . Venus makes for green and a sweet taste . . . The Sun makes the yellow colour, and gives the right sweetness in the salt . . . Saturn inclines to black, and makes for astringent and sour tastes . . . The Moon has an affinity with tubers which swell and shrink with its waxing and waning.

Boehme used these planetary 'signatures' of plants as a guide to their medicinal properties: 'A herb which grows not high, that is somewhat rough in the touch; the rougher it is, the stronger is Mars therein. It is better to be used outwardly to bind wounds and sores, than take inwardly.'

Though it may be enclosed and hidden, the intelligence that comes from the great spiritual sun is in everything: 'We recognize that the whole world is all Sun and the locality of the Sun would be everywhere, the power of the Sun *is* everywhere – but hidden.'

Boehme had such a strong sense of this sunny inner world that he described the material world as the Outworld.

A local nobleman read *Aurora*, Boehme's collection of his early writings, and was immediately fascinated. He had it copied and circulated among his influential friends.

The local clergyman, Pastor Richter, was at first alarmed to find a visionary mystic in his flock, then stirred to bitter hatred and envy when Jacob was invited to courts and universities. He began to denounce 'false prophets' from the pulpit. When a copy of *Aurora* found its way into his hands, he branded it 'a tool of Satan'. He called on the town to banish Jacob, causing him to be escorted out of town and left to wander among the fields alone.

When Jacob returned, windows in his house were smashed and he and his family were threatened with violence. He was made to promise not to write any more books.

However he did start to write again. His scripts were smuggled out of town in sacks of grain, and the seeds of his thoughts were carried to the wider world.

At the age of fifty he lay in bed. It was a Sunday night and it seemed to him that he heard sweet music. He asked his son Tobias if he could hear it too. Tobias couldn't. Jacob then asked for the door to be opened so the music could be heard more clearly.

At six in the morning he asked to be turned so that he was facing away from his family, because their love was binding his spirit to the Earth. He said, 'It is time to go into Paradise.'

Like *Aurora*, the later scripts smuggled out of Görlitz were enthusiastically copied and shared. Jacob Boehme's ideas would cause a revolution in the history of human thought. The revival of idealism among German philosophers, the romantic revolt against materialism and the rise of

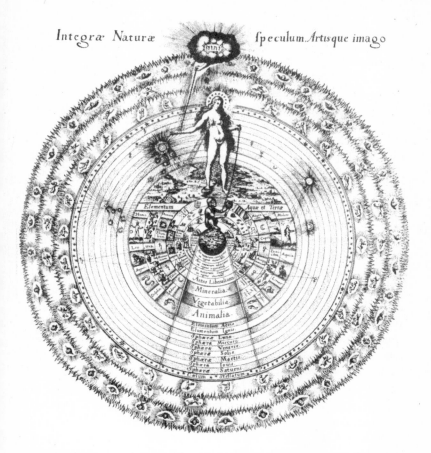

Illustration from *The History of the Macrocosm and the Microcosm* (1617) by Robert Fludd, a defender of the Rosicrucians and closely associated with them. This illustration shows the integration of heavenly bodies with natural processes. The doctrine of signatures was first outlined by Bolus of Mendes in about 200 BC. He gave many examples of it. But Boehme's exposition is the first practical and philosophical account. His and Paracelsus's ideas would underlie Culpeper's celebrated *Herbal*. There is perhaps an echo of these ideas in Rupert Sheldrake's theory of morphic resonance in at least one respect. Sheldrake asserts that the genetic code of living beings has not turned out to provide all the information needed for them to fully generate themselves, as its discoverers initially supposed, but only a small percentage of it. The rest must be 'out there' in the cosmos, and the plant or animal must be formed out of the interaction between the information described by the code and these external forces – perhaps the influence of the stars and planets as described by Boehme.

Nonconformism all have roots in Boehme. Milton's cosmic visions were inspired by Boehme's, as were Swedenborg's and Blake's. Novalis and Coleridge called themselves his disciples. Rubens called him a 'blessed instrument in the hands of the spirit of God'. Hegel found in his writings the inspirations for his way of looking at the world and called him 'the father of German philosophy'.

Unlike St Francis or Paracelsus, Boehme did not perform miracles or make scientific discoveries. No one else could see his visions. But he had a detailed, comprehensive imaginative vision of the cosmos as idealism conceives it. He showed how idealism worked in practice, how the thoughts of God unfolded to create the species of plants and trees and our individual selves – and he showed all of this in extraordinary, convincing detail. His was a harmonious vision and it rang true. Many great men and women have recognized it as an account of origins and workings of the world as they experience of it.

At the beginning of this book I said that it would be reasonable to expect our experience of a world emanating from a Cosmic Mind to be very different from our experience of a world that had been created by chance alone. Reading other people's accounts of their experiences can, of course, help us to focus on elements of our own experience which we might not otherwise be conscious of. We may recognize in the work of some writers something we have never seen described before and say, 'Yes, my experience of life is like that too!'

I think there may be much greater differences between people's temperaments than we generally assume.[4] In fact, to put it more strongly, I think the idea that we all share the same form of consciousness is a polite fiction and that in fact there is a broad spectrum of consciousness ranging from, say, Jacob Boehme or Rudolf Steiner at one end to, say, Richard Dawkins at the other. Some of us experience the world in a way that accords with idealism, while others experience it in a way that accords more with materialism. Those who are more inward looking, intuitive and imaginative are more likely to notice what we think of as meaningful coincidences and other mystical patterns, to experience otherworldly promptings, to feel sometimes that what is happening to us was meant to happen and perhaps even to experience visions.[5]

People who experience life in this way, who are closer to this end of the spectrum, are more likely, like Hegel, to read Jacob Boehme and

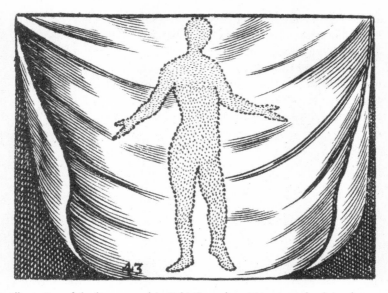

Illustration of the human soul in *Orbis Sensualium Pictus*, a textbook by the Czech Rosicrucian and pioneer of education John Amos Comenius.

say, 'Yes, this is an accurate and insightful account of the way the world works in all its mysterious aspects.'

*   *   *

When I studied philosophy as an undergraduate I found that idealism was not a position that any serious academic wished to defend. History is written by the victors, and idealism was seen as of only historical interest and only ever raised to be knocked down.[6]

Yet the work of idealists such as Paracelsus and Boehme is not all airy-fairy. It has had demonstrable detailed practical applications. We touched on Paracelsus's innovations in science and medicine earlier, and the work of both men on the influence of the stars and planets was revived and elaborated on by Rudolph Steiner in the twentieth century. In his book *Harmony: A New Way of Looking at our World*, Prince Charles recommended a system of agriculture geared to 'the miraculous ingenuity of Nature', taking farming closer to the Earth's life cycles. In the biodynamic farming practised on his farms on Cornwall, these cycles are not just the cycles of the sun and the seasons, but the cycles of the moon, the planets and the stars. Their influence on the growth of plants, as described by Boehme, is used to grow better, healthier crops.

Prince Charles writes, too, of 'the depths of human consciousness, where human nature is rooted in Nature herself'. In idealism there is a sense of the intelligence that underlies all being, and that we can engage that intelligence in intelligent conversation.

Shakespeare and the Rosicrucians

In 1614 a pamphlet called the *Fama Fraternitatis* ('Rumour of the Brotherhood') announcing the existence of an underground fraternity called the Rosicrucians, was anonymously published in Kassel in Germany. The *Fama* claimed that the seven-sided sepulchre of the fraternity's founder, Christian Rosencreutz, had recently been discovered, that his body was perfectly preserved and that lying next to him were a copy of the Bible and works by Paracelsus. A year after that another pamphlet, called the *Confessio*, also mysteriously appeared. A year after that came Christian Rosencreutz's *Chemical Wedding*, and in 1623 posters appeared on the streets of Paris, causing a fever of excitement and speculation.

In science matter is just what it *is*. Look for definitions online and you will find lists of its constituents, which is like defining a house by saying it is made up of bricks, cement, glass, etc.

In idealism, on the other hand, there is a higher order definition of matter. It is 'what forms a barrier to spirit'. For example, it encloses the spirit of an individual human being so it is blocked off from God, angels and other spirits. This is what it is *for*.

When humans lived without interruption in the love of God, when they 'walked with God', when there was no barrier between them and they stood in the full flow of God's love, they were overwhelmed. Filled with the sublime and all-powerful thoughts of God, they were unable to think for themselves. Later, when matter hardened, they would have to forge a new form of consciousness. They would develop a new way of thinking that focused on material things.

We have been following a change of consciousness, as humanity shifted from an ideas-based form of consciousness to an object-based form. In the seventeenth century this became a conscious project, culminating in the scientific method of Francis Bacon and the rationalism of Descartes. Humanity would have to get to grips with objects, understand them inside out and learn to manipulate them.

Underlying these schools of thought was the development of what we might call binary thinking – the assumption that something must be either true or false. Something cannot be the case and also not be the case. This is what logicians sometimes call 'the law of excluded middle'. If we are to discover the truth about the world, it is surely crucial that we are quite clear whether something is true or not – and surely determining whether it is true or not is of the utmost importance?

That something is either true or false is, you might think, undeniably true. And it *is* true in that it works as a way for us to navigate our way through our lives . . .

Francis Bacon, Vicount St Alban
(by William Marshall, after Simon de Passe, 1640)

. . . up to a point.

At the very moment Francis Bacon was forging the scientific method, a man with whom he rubbed shoulders and shared many inspirations was importing the contrary impulse into the world.[1]

Shakespeare had fairy blood. His plays turn on the supernatural, and the supernatural element in his writing still quickens our blood. He gives such vivid expression to the experience of the supernatural and such a compelling account of the way that it shapes our lives that it has illuminated the world through the darkest days of materialism. The underground visions of Paracelsus, of Christian Rosencreutz, of Jacob Boehme, of the country folk who told each other fairy stories in the long winter evenings were brought up and out into the world in *A Midsummer Night's Dream*, *A Winter's Tale* and *The Tempest*. In the character of Ariel, a Paracelsian sylph speaks to us. *Macbeth* has an occult power that frightens actors today.

In *A Midsummer Night's Dream* Titania says to Bottom:

'Sleep thou, and I will wind thee in my arms . . .
So doth the woodbines the sweet honeysuckles gently entwist, the female ivy so enrings the barky fingers of the elm.'

There are clues to a secret and sacred philosophy here. In ancient times an elm was sacred to the moon, and in Vergil's account of initiation an elm tree stands on the threshold of the otherworldly realm. The ivy was associated with Bacchus. Ivy is the emblem of passion unpruned: 'The predominant passion of the mind throws itself like the ivy round all human actions, entwines all our resolutions and perpetually adheres to, and mixes itself among, or even overtops them.'[2]

Bottom is being initiated according to rites that had been described in the second century by Apuleius. His sleep – 'more dead than common sleep' – is the trance of the candidate for initiation, induced while his material body is being refined and purified of its bestial appetites and while he is losing the asinine stupidity of the uninitiated. Titania says to Bottom, 'And I will purge thy mortal grossness so that thou shalt like an airy spirit go.' His spirit is to be freed like an initiate's to fly up through the spheres.

Afterwards, when Titania places roses on Bottom's head, he will be reborn and restored to waking consciousness. Coronets of roses were worn at Bacchanalian orgies, and in Apuleius' *Golden Ass*, it is roses that restore the ass to human shape. Rosicrucian spiritual practice symbolizes work on the chakras in the image of a garland of seven red roses on a cross. Seven roses also appear, of course, on the tomb of William Shakespeare.

Shakespeare's account of human history is a story of invisible events and improbable facts, but he is nevertheless asserting that this dimension is real and that his account of what happened there is accurate. In this respect, his mystical thought is Sufi in flavour.

In his comedies, characters stray into the greenwood, where weird things begin to happen to them and their lives are transformed and put right. In Sufi terms, the greenwood is what has been called the *mundus imaginalis*.

Henry Corbin was a twentieth century French writer and philosopher responsible for explaining Sufi wisdom to a wider Western audience. He described the *mundus imaginalis* as a world between the worlds, a place that is 'No place'. We should not try to find out where it is, he said, because '*Where is inside this realm.*' For the most part we cannot perceive this world, because when we reach out to the physical world with our senses, we tuck away this other world with a will that lies far below the threshold of consciousness – what Corbin calls the 'agnostic reflex'. In order to undo this and enter the *mundus imaginalis* we need to develop what Corbin calls the faculty of 'active imagination'. By developing this faculty, adepts have perceived and even visited this realm. It has a consistent topography, including cities that all who enter may visit.

Because this realm lies in between the physical world and the world of the higher spiritual beings, if you can enter it and imagine what you desire with enough intensity, you can bring it to you in the material world.

Ibn Arabi advised on the development and practice of what today is sometimes called 'lucid dreaming'. He wrote that if you discipline yourself to control your thoughts while dreaming, the alertness that this brings will enable you to become aware of the intermediate dimension, 'which brings great benefits for everyone'.

The Taming of the Shrew is based on a Sufi parable about waking to higher states of consciousness. Katharina – the shrew – represents the unquiet part of ourselves that must be stilled before we can achieve higher consciousness.[3] Access to the higher states of consciousness is then achieved by developing the powers of the imagination that the Sufi's described. A powerful imagination can effect changes in the material world. Theseus in *A Midsummer Night's Dream* talks of 'the poet's pen which turns the forms of things unknown . . . and gives to airy nothing a local habitation and name. Such tricks hath strong imagination.' Prospero calls forth spirits to enact his 'present fancies'.

Sufi wisdom offered practical methods for directing the power of mind over matter. *Himmah* is a concentrated spiritual energy that brings with it extraordinary power. A knower can affect any object by concentrating all their spiritual and imaginative energy in a certain definite direction. The highest knower can even bring physical objects into existence by exercising their *himmah*.

Symbols can play an important part in concentrating spiritual energy in Sufi teaching stories, in the Shakespeare's poetry and indeed in the stories in this book, devised by minds far greater than my own. Symbolism has a different function in idealism than it does in the world according to materialism, where symbols move only the mind. In the world according to idealism, you can, by contemplating symbols that strike a deep chord in the human psyche, send out vibrations that affect the very fabric of the material world.

It is of course widely speculated that Prospero in *The Tempest* is in part modelled on the famous Elizabethan magus Dr Dee. Many com-

Two rose images (from Harold Bayley's *The Lost Language of Symbolism,* 1912). Bayley says that the rose garden may represent either the enclosed garden in the Song of Solomon or the one in *The Romance of the Rose.* He associates roses with an awakening out of the forehead. The rose is the flower of love in Shakespeare, in *Romeo and Juliet* and the sonnets. It has come to seem a universal symbol of love and also very English, but in fact the glorious red roses referred to are probably Damask roses – from Damascus. Like the whole idea of falling in love, roses were a recent import from Arabia. I am indebted to my friend Roderick Brown for his original research into the importation of different types of roses. (See also Henry Nicholson Ellacombe, *The Plant-Lore and Garden-Craft of Shakespeare,* 1878, p.252.)

mentators have also noted that when a statue seems to come back to life at the end of *A Winter's Tale*, Shakespeare has clearly been influenced by Christian Rosencreutz's *Chymical Wedding*. The *Chymical Wedding* was published in 1616 and *A Winter's Tale* was produced 1609–10, but Rosencreutz's text was written and circulated privately before the writing of the play, and it's hard not see the influence of Rosencreutz's imagery of the statues coming to life on Shakespeare's descriptions of Hermione coming back to life and the play's themes of magic, rebirth and transformation:

> See, my lord, Would you not deem it breathed? and that those veins did verily bear blood? . . . The very life seems warm upon her lip . . . The fixture of her eye has motion in't . . . There is an air comes from her: what fine chisel could ever yet cut breath? . . . the ruddiness upon her lip is wet . . . Shall I draw the curtain?

Hamlet stands at the dawn of the modern age and sees it going out of joint, going wrong, growing darker. Hamlet is learning how to live both in the newly dark material world and also in the giddy world opening up inside time. Earlier generations had almost no way of thinking about their internal life except using the narrow language of the sermon. Every human being would now be able to develop a sense of an internal mental space that was as wide as the cosmos, and Shakespeare peopled that cosmos with a new race of characters – Lear, Falstaff, Romeo and Juliet, Puck, Prospero and Oberon.[4]

Ariel (by Robert Anning Bell).

'There is more in heaven and earth than is dreamed of in your philosophy,' says Horatio. Our lives in the material world are relatively unreal and insubstantial. We are such stuff as dreams are made on. Our little life is bounded by a sleep. Shakespeare's great philosophical thrust and the great impulse behind the Rosicrucians were to show that the invisible and spiritual is

The White Hart Inn, Scole, Norfolk, built 1655 (from C. J. Richardson, *Studies from Old English Mansions*, 1851). It is possible to catch in this old pub gateway the wild fairy riot of Shakespeare's England, brought back to life so beautifully and poignantly in Jez Butterworth's play *Jerusalem* (2009).

greater than the visible. To put it in Rosicrucian terms, Shakespeare gave shape, form and colour to God's great world-weaving thoughts, so that the human imagination could grasp them.[5]

Hamlet raises questions about different states of consciousness. Hamlet feigns madness, Ophelia goes mad, Hamlet may really be mad too. He suffers from the seventeenth century version of Plato's divine madness, famously depicted by Dürer in *Melencolia* I (1514) and called 'divine melancholia' or 'melancholic genius'.

This melancholia was said to afflict philosophers and writers of genius. Like them, Hamlet lives in an uncanny twilight, an alternative state of consciousness in which he sees great truths that the other characters in the play cannot see.[6]

Ted Hughes, the most prominent British poet of his generation, had a well-developed interest in esoteric and mystical thought. He wrote that in *Venus and Adonis* and then in *Measure for Measure* Shakespeare was describing a shift in society, a crisis caused by the rise of Puritanism. Shakespeare has Adonis shrinking from the goddess's desires. In

Measure for Measure, the Puritan Angelo is overcome by lust and tries to abuse his position to force Isabella to have sex with him, again with dire consequences. The Puritan is committing a crime against humanity, but this crime is not simply that he is repressing the sex drive, it's that he is repressing the sex drive as part of a drive to close down consciousness, to reduce it to a very narrow point of literal-mindedness, to materialism. What Shakespeare is depicting, then, is not just narrow attitudes to sex, but also narrow attitudes to consciousness.

Neither *Venus and Adonis* nor *Measure for Measure* are simply accounts of how a Puritanical attitude to sex causes problems in society,

In esoteric philosophy we are enabled to think because we direct life forces to power our thoughts. Thinking makes us a little less alive, leeches our life force – 'the pale overcast hue of thought' – and is in this sense a Saturnine process. (Albrecht Dürer, *Melencolia* I, 1514.)

because they work on many different levels. Some critics have tried to identify contemporaries of Shakespeare who might have been the model for Angelo, but Angelo's temptations are universal. We may all recognize the *Venus and Adonis* impulses working within us, and we may recognize Angelo and Isabella in ourselves too.

Venus and Adonis is historical in the sense that this story was enacted as sacred drama in the Mystery centres of the ancient world, and these dramas were reconstructed in the nineteenth and early twentieth century by scholars, including Sabine Baring-Gould and Sir James George Frazer. The story of Venus and Adonis depicts a religious ceremony which is a way of achieving higher states of consciousness. In this story Venus's interest in Adonis is not narrowly sexual. The mental *furore* she induces is a form of the divine madness.

Shakespeare writes with the multi-dimensional thinking characteristic of idealism. The truth of a line in Shakespeare cannot be determined by the law of excluded middle, a simple true or false test of the sort that binary thinking demands. It is true or false on many different levels, because it emanates from a consciousness that operates on many different levels.

So we should never say, 'I've discovered the real meaning of this story,' implying that it follows that previous accounts are false. According to Sufism's sophisticated ontologies, it is unwise to apply the law of the excluded middle to any sacred story. According to idealism, what we see with our senses is not reality but *virtuality*. What's important, valuable, meaningful and real lies somewhere else.

According to mystical teachings, we all have the potential for a multi-dimensional consciousness capable of these sorts of perceptions. Though we have forged a sense-oriented consciousness that is usually focused on the material world, our minds are still connected and in communication with the great Cosmic Mind with its limitless knowledge of past and future and other people's minds. According to Lorna Byrne, we are all capable of tuning into other dimensions, but habitually close our minds to them.

According to Ibn Arabi, our heart is continually changing, and this is because of the many different divine influences it feels. If we shut out the material world for a while and are attentive instead to the innermost part of ourselves, we may become of aware of the changing

The Soul of Shakespeare (by George Romney).

It is thought that free access to the *mundus imaginalis* confers immense power – for good or evil. When David Bowie wrote 'The Man Who Sold the World' the occultist Aleister Crowley was much on his mind. Crowley had been called 'the wickedest man in the world' and was certainly very influential in the rise of the counterculture of the 1960s and also on the fashion for using occult lore for personal gain. David Bowie might also be said to have used his imagination to change the world. In the drab, recession-hit 1970s his musical landscapes and lyrics opened up other possible universes and ways of being.

and metamorphosing of forms there, and this is the beginning of a mystical view of life.

Shakespeare illuminated the ever-changing, infinitely various and beautiful inner life of humankind perhaps more than any other writer. His contemporary John Baptista von Helmont was likewise influenced by Sufism and intrigued by the Rosicrucians. Helmont wrote of the magic power that lies hidden in the inner life of humankind. For the most part, he wrote, it keeps sleeping, but it can be awakened either through divine illumination or by the spiritual exercises of the adept, who can awaken this power at will.

'Such are called the makers of gold . . .'

The roof of Milan cathedral (engraving published in 1900). Churches have traditionally been oriented to planetary bodies. Robert Temple recently discovered that there is a lodestone built into the roof of Milan cathedral with no possible practical function. The metals of the planets are also involved in drawing down or warding off planetary influences.

Altar of the chapel of St Ignatius Loyola, by Andrea Pozzo, in the church of the Gesù in Rome, the mother church of the Society of Jesus, or Jesuits. Pozzo's original statue of the saint in beatific vision was made of solid silver, but it was melted down to pay Napoleon. *The Spiritual Exercises of Ignatius Loyola* (1548) were on one level the Catholic Church's response to the spiritual exercises taught by the Rosicrucians. Disciples of Ignatius Loyola, like Francis Xavier, were enabled to experience encounters with angels and other spiritual beings by the practice of these exercises.

The Holy Family (by Esteban Murillo, 1665–70). Mystical traditions around the world talk of a baby choosing to be born to its parents, in its particular body and situation. 'A man is born into a world he has made,' *Satapatha Brahmana* vi.2.2.2.27. 'Entering into the state of existence the living being builds its own appropriate body,' *Panchastikaya-sara* 136 *Treatise on Five Universal Components*, in the Jain scriptures. In Western art the esoteric symbol of this belief is the cherub.

Supernatural Stories in the Age of Science

'Millions of spiritual Creatures walk the earth,
both when we wake, and when we sleep.'

John Milton

'The illustrious Sir Isaac ploughed with
Jacob Behmen's heifer.'

William Law

From its beginnings in 1660, the men of the Royal Society who would forge the scientific method and unleash industrialization on the world took note of the experiments of Paracelsus. They applied the new scientific method to the material world – but they also applied it to spiritual and religious experience.

Isaac Newton's alchemical experiments are famous. When someone mocked his interest in astrology, he retorted, 'Sir, I have studied it – you have not!'

Newton believed that God had set humankind a series of tests in the forms of messages encoded in ancient monuments like the Great Pyramid, in ancient texts like Genesis and in the very fabric of nature itself. God's plan was that humanity would be intrigued by these mysteries and continue to develop the faculty of intelligence until the time came when it would be able to crack these codes. Gottfried Wilhelm Leibniz, Newton's rival in the devising of the calculus, made

Frontispiece to *Novum Organum Scientiarum*, the 'New Instrument of Science' (1620), by Francis Bacon, mystic and instigator of the scientific method.

his advances while studying the Jewish numerical mysticism of the Kabbalah.

Isaac Newton drew deeply on the philosophical approach of Jacob Boehme. Boehme's idealism had led him to look for a unifying principle that held the universe together and put everything within it in place. For Boehme, it was a law of love or desire which he called the *lubet*. Newton carried the search for a universal principle over from idealism into materialism and called it gravity.

Among Newton's peers in the Royal Society were a number of remarkable men with both scientific and esoteric, spiritual interests. Sir Robert

Moray published the first ever scientific journal. He was a fervent researcher into Rosicrucian lore. Founding member Elias Ashmole was an alchemist. Robert Boyle's law of thermodynamics paved the way for the internal combustion engine, and he too was a practising alchemist. So was William Harvey, discoverer of the circulation of the blood. Robert Hooke believed that new instruments, like the microscope he was developing, would recover for humanity the ability to see into the world of spirits and angels that it had enjoyed before the Fall.

Robert Kirk studied under Boyle. While living in the Highlands of Scotland he decided to conduct a scientific survey of his parishioners' experiences of what they called 'second sight' – the ability to see into a world of spiritual beings. It seemed to Kirk that he could discern in their stories the outlines of a cogent and coherent world picture, and he set out to collect, classify and categorize their data in order to determine the rules governing this other world.[1]

In 1691 he started to write a book noting that the spirits he classified as 'the Subterraneans' had bodies of 'congealed air', which easily changed shape and were best seen at twilight. People with second sight routinely saw them at funerals; it was because the Subterraneans were sometimes seen to eat at funeral banquets, he said, that people with second sight generally declined to eat at those occasions.

Subterraneans appeared much more frequently at the four great astronomical and spiritual turning points of the year, the equinoxes and the solstices. Tribes of Subterraneans were seen to walk the surface of the Earth then, and people with second sight would not leave the house at these times, except to go to church to pray for protection for themselves, their cattle and crops.

The houses of the Subterraneans were said to be large and fair and brightly lit with lamps and fires. The Subterraneans liked to eat and drink, make music and dance, and they held 'convocations'. They also protected 'the privacy of their mysteries' and if an outsider chanced upon them they would 'smite them with a puff of wind and bereave them of their sights and memories in the twinkling of an eye'. Anyone visiting one of their houses should not eat any food, or they would be trapped there forever.

Kirk recorded the stories of babies abducted, with a shrivelled substitute left in the cot. (Titania in *A Midsummer Night's Dream* has abducted a baby.) Highlanders often left iron overnight next to a child to ward off the Subterraneans, who were said to be scared by it.

The Subterraneans were said to live longer than humans but to vanish eventually. Then a funeral would take place. Their world-view was that nothing, great or small, ever died or disappeared completely, but transmuted into another state, and that everything went round in circles. They believed that every living thing had a smaller thing living on it.[2]

Kirk recorded that when men of second sight wished to enable someone else to see temporarily what they could see all the time, they'd put their head and hand in a certain posture.

This early attempt to collect and categorize spiritual data using scientific methods is remarkably consistent in its details with the accounts of Paracelsus and folk tales from other places, for example, the Cornish story of William Noy retold in Chapter 34. As suggested earlier, different people in different parts of the world at different times visit this same region of the *mundus imaginalis* and encounter the same species of disembodied beings there.

Similarly, we may tend to think of poltergeists as a modern phenomenon, but there were well-attested cases centuries earlier, including one recorded shortly before Kirk wrote his book and another not long after it was published.

The affair which became known as the Drummer of Tedworth began in 1661 after a gentleman called Mr Momposson seized the drum of a vagrant musician who had been annoying him. Subsequently, in Momposson's house and in the presence of a clergyman, chairs walked about the room by themselves and a staff was thrown at the local minister. Over the following months the children of the house often heard a jingling of money and saw lights wandering about the house, 'blue and glimmering'. A knocking noise persisted in the woodwork of the children's beds and sometimes knocks answered knocks made by visitors.

Disturbances began in the house at Epworth of Samuel Wesley, father of John and Charles Wesley, the founders of Methodism, in December 1715 and continued until January the following year. The case was recorded in some detail in Samuel Wesley's journal and corroborated by contemporary letters from members of the family and later reminiscences. The disturbances began with a groaning, then came knockings which flitted about the house. The noises used to follow one of the daughters, Hetty, and to thump under her feet. Sometimes the knocks replied to those made by the family. Mrs Wesley and her other daughter, Emily, saw an object 'like a badger' run from under a bed and vanish. Robin, a servant, saw a hand-mill work violently. Robin called this invisible 'old Jeffries', after a gentleman lately deceased, while the family called it 'Jeffrey'. Samuel Wesley himself heard nothing till 21st December, but afterwards he was 'thrice pushed by invisible power' and once his plate 'danced before him on the table a pretty while, without anybody's stirring the table'.

A similar study to Kirk's was published in 1705 by a gentleman called John Beaumont and comprehensively titled *An historical, physiological and theological treatise of spirits: apparitions, witchcrafts, and other magical practices. Containing an account of the genii . . . With a refutation of Dr. Bekker's World bewitch'd; and other authors . . .* Beaumont includes in his paper accounts given by several witnesses called upon in Manningtree in Essex in 1645 to observe and test the claims of one Elizabeth Clarke that she was regularly attended by imps. The witnesses swore on oath that they saw her play with a white imp on her lap and that a quarter of an hour later another imp appeared, very plump and with very short legs, white with some sandy spots. It vanished, then another appeared called Vinegar Tom, in the shape of a greyhound with legs as long as a stag's. There was also an imp like a polecat but with an outsize head. On another occasion a white imp with red spots was seen, and on another eight imps were gathered together, including one in the shape of a ferret, another in the form of a rabbit and another like a black toad.[3]

A contemporary, John Pordage, wrote in 1655 of his experiences of second sight:

Were but the eyes of men open to see the kingdom of the Dragon in this world, with the multitudes of evil angels, which are every where tempting and ensnaring men, they would be amazed, and not dare to be by themselves without good consciences, and a great assurance of the love and favour of God in protecting them by the ministration of the holy angels.

Elementals. In 1670 a book was published called *Comte de Gabalis*. Written by a priest called the Abbé de Montfaucon de Villars, and purporting to be based on meetings with a mysterious count, The book was a series of dialogues or discourses on the inner life, where the teacher, this count, was presented as a Rosicrucian adept. It was originally published with illustrative work by Rembrandt, and various candidates have been suggested as the author, including the Comte de St Germain. At one point the adept promises this to the candidate for initiation: 'When you have been enrolled among the Children of the Philosophers, and when your eyes have been strength- ened by the use of the very Holy Medicine, you will straightway discover that the Elements are inhabited by most perfect beings. The immense space which lies between Earth and Heaven has inhabitants far nobler than the   birds and insects . . . they die only after several centuries; but what is time in comparison with eternity? They must return for ever into nothingness.' The book influenced Alexander Pope, who played with ideas from it in *The Rape of the Lock*.

He described what he would himself see: 'Those tho' all in the shapes of men, yet represented themselves monstrously misshapen, and with ears like those of cats, cloven feet, ugly legs and bodies, eyes fiery, sharp, and piercing.'

This is dark stuff, and might remind us of the warnings of hellfire preachers like Jonathan Edwards:

> The manifold and continual experience of the world in all ages shows this is no evidence that a man is not on the very brink of eternity, and that the next step will not be into another world. The unseen, unthought ways and means of persons going suddenly out of the world are innumerable and inconceivable. Unconverted men walk over the pit of Hell on a rotten covering, and there are innumerable places in this covering so weak that they will not bear their weight, and these places are not seen. The arrows of death fly unseen at noon-day; the sharpest sight cannot discern them.

At the dawn of the age of materialism many people's experience of the spirit worlds was dark and darkening.

*   *   *

Science does what it says on the tin. It has been successful in large measure because scientists and philosophers developed an efficient set of criteria for modelling the way the world works. A good scientific theory, they decided, should account for a defined set of phenomena in a way which was:

materially adequate (in that it accounts for them all)

consistent

simple and elegant (in that you don't have clumsy and inelegant exceptions to the rule)

repeatable and testable, so that you can use it to predict future examples of the same set of phenomena.

This way of describing the world was initiated by the Scottish philosopher David Hume in the middle of the eighteenth century and continues to evolve.[4]

Hume focused on how we could reasonably talk about things that happened in the world – what he called 'matters of fact', as distinct from 'relations of ideas'. Today we call this process 'inductive reasoning', as distinct from 'deductive reasoning'. Hume noticed that while we could *prove* whether or not a sum in maths or a logical formula – 'closed-circuit' types of reasoning – was right and true, the same could not be said about statements about what was happening in the world. The claims we make about these events can't be certain in the same way. Hume realized that there was exciting philosophical work to be done. He noted that this 'part of philosophy has been little attended by the ancients or moderns'. He was right. He was on to something big, and the attempt to shore up statements about the world that followed gave rise to the philosophy of science.[5]

Hume's breakthrough books were *An Enquiry Concerning Human Understanding* (1748) and *An Enquiry Concerning the Principles of Morals* (1751), which contained a section called *of miracles*, that has become the great Ur-text of atheism. Hume argued that while claims about cause and effect could not be certain, like closed-circuit reasoning, we could reasonably claim that a particular cause gave rise to a particular effect if they were always seen to be 'contiguous', by which he meant if they were next to each other and one was always seen to follow the other. If the letting go of an apple is always followed by its falling, if two events like these have been constantly conjoined together in all countries and all ages, if this is universally the evidence of the senses, then that is how a law of nature is established.

Therefore, Hume argued, if a miracle is defined as a violation of one of these laws, yet someone reports seeing a miracle, we should ask ourselves what is more likely – that the weight of evidence of the senses in all ages and all countries is misleading, or that the person is either lying or deluded?

*　　　　　*　　　　　*

Science works because of its narrow focus. Science concentrates on the evidence of the senses. Hume wrenched attention away from an appreciation of the texture and subtleties of our inner life and focused on objectivity and the measuring of sense data.

The trouble is that spiritual experiences – experiences of meaning, divine promptings and visions – tend to be highly subjective and resist measurement.

And if what can be measured becomes the epitome of what is real, the danger is that all spiritual experience, including religious experience, comes to be seen as unreal. Indeed, some scientists have moved to the extreme position that only what can be accounted for by a scientific theory is real. So religious and spiritual phenomena have been attacked on the grounds that in order to count as real, a phenomenon has to be repeatable. If a healer cannot perform miracles on demand, for example, then those miracles never happened, no matter how well-attested they might otherwise be.

But if you switch focus from the evidence of the senses to the subtleties of the inner life, a very different picture arises, suggesting a very different model of reality. You might say, for example, that the great preponderance of evidence in all times and in all places has been that prayer is answered. Humanity has always had a deep-seated intuition that there is something in the universe that responds to its deepest needs – that the relation between mind and matter isn't all one way.

An astrological medal made for Albrecht von Wallenstein by Johannes Kepler.

The observatory at Delhi built by Maharaja Jai Singh II in 1710 in a 19th century engraving. Jai Singh built five giant observatories, enabling him to measure the movements of the heavenly bodies more accurately than Copernicus, Galileo or Kepler, the better to make his astrological calculations.

Insisting on repeatability is loading the dice, and fails to take account of the sort of phenomena we are dealing with here, even though these phenomena are universally a part of human experience.

'The Christian religion not only was at first attended with miracles, but even at this day cannot be believed by any reasonable person without one.' We can see in Hume's mocking tone the beginnings of the intolerance of religion and spirituality that would end in the militant atheism of philosopher Daniel Dennett and biologists Richard Dawkins and Lewis Wolpert.[6] What Hume means to say is that the patterns of the supernatural that we have seen in this book so far do not happen today because they have never happened.

In the rest of this book we will ask whether these sorts of experiences and pattern have also happened in the age of science.

Have there been demi-gods like Theseus in modern times?

Have people been guided by their daemons like Socrates?

Have supernatural forces guided people to fulfil their destiny as they did Mohammed?

Have there been visionaries whose visions have proved to be true and useful like the visions of Paracelsus?

Have there been inspired human teachers sent by heaven to guide humanity?

Do people still visit the realm of the dead like Dante and report back on what is in store for all of us?

Do angels visit us as they visited Abraham?

Have there been large-scale miracles witnessed by thousands like the ones that attended Moses?

Napoleon – the Great Magnet of the Age

'I know it by the Light in his eyes . . . I regard him as the Magnetic Centre of the Age.'

Chief Sardar

'I have shown myself to you so often and you have not seen me.'

Ibn Arabi, *The Book of Theophanies*

On 13th October 1806, the German philosopher Georg Wilhelm Friedrich Hegel saw Napoleon ride by on his way to seal a great victory. He wrote in a letter to a friend: 'I saw the Emperor – this soul of the world – go out from the city to survey his reign. It is a truly wonderful sensation to see such an individual, who, concentrating on one point, while seated on a horse, stretches over the world and dominates it.'

Hegel believed he was seeing the realization, the unfolding of the great Cosmic Mind – 'the Absolute' – before his eyes. He would write that certain individuals stood at the forefront of all great historical movements and could 'cause the ideal to stand before the real'. In his eyes, Napoleon was a man of action who revealed to humankind its creative possibilities. Napoleon knew what he had to do, and because he was unfolding the history of the world, the divine plan, he could break moral codes, infringe rights and trample over others and destroy.

The Little Red Man (illustration to *Chansons de P-J de Béranger*, 1869). A little gnome-like man dressed in blood-red clothes is said to have appeared to Catherine de Medici and others, usually presaging a massacre, assassination or defeat in battle. He apparently appeared several times to Napoleon, first during the Egyptian campaign and for the last – and best-attested – time on 1st January 1814. Napoleon had left instructions not to be disturbed, but on being told by Councillor of State Mole that a small man dressed all in red was insisting on seeing him, he gave instructions that he should be admitted immediately. His abdication followed shortly afterwards.

Napoleon depicted in death and in bas-relief in Les Invalides as he saw himself in life – as a god. (Engraving published in 1854.)

Others would always let him, because on some level they recognized he was an agency of the divine. He had, said Hegel, the right to make laws and found states. He was 'the new Theseus'.

But Hegel read and reread Shakespeare all his life, and also saw Napoleon as a tragic figure. Denied the quiet pleasures of an ordinary life, he was never free from sorrow and conflicts which led to eventual disaster and ruin. Napoleon himself said, 'I feel myself driven towards an end I do not know. As soon as I have reached it, I will become unnecessary, an atom will be enough to destroy me.'

Powerful leaders, artists and scientists of genius, tend to have a visionary consciousness. The people who make history tend to be inspired, if you are looking at it from the point of view of idealism, or mad if you are looking at it from the point of view of materialism.

We saw how Francis Bacon's forging of the scientific method was accompanied by the contrary impulse in Shakespeare's wild imaginings. Similarly, David Hume's philosophy of science was attended by a rebirth of idealism. As the empiricism, the materialism, the emphasis on objectivity that Hume initiated took root and spread, the opposing impulse arose in Germany – an idealism alive to the varieties, the subtleties and the anomalies of human experience.

The great tradition of idealism in German philosophy includes Johann Georg Hamann, known as 'the Magus in the North', Fichte, Schelling and later Rudolf Steiner, but the dominant figure was Hegel. His starting point was Jacob Boehme's exact and detailed account of his own spiritual experiences. He took the imaginative vision of Boehme and translated it into an academic philosophy.[1]

For Hegel, as for Boehme, the whole cosmos is an expression of a great cosmic mind which is, he says, 'a friend to all life's feelings'. It is supportive of the great undertakings of a Napoleon, but also initiates and encourages, engenders and nurtures us all in the apparently poor and unimportant activities of everyday life.

* * *

Napoleon was, of course, a hero to the Romantics. Goethe wrote of him that he was 'always illuminated, always clear and decided, and endowed at every hour with enough energy to carry out whatever he considered necessary. His life was the stride of a demi-god, from battle to battle, and from victory to victory. It might be said that he was in a state of continual illumination.' Goethe also mused on daemons, in the Socratic sense: 'The higher a man is, the more he is under the influence of daemons and he must take heed.' In the *Conversations with Eckermann* he is reported to have said that Napoleon was 'of the daemonic sort': 'He was so and so thoroughly and in the highest degree. He was a daemonic being of the sort Greeks reckoned demi-gods.'

To militant materialists and people of a down-to-earth temperament, this kind of talk may seem high-flown nonsense. Hegel wrote about people with a certain temperament, people who have 'no feeling whatsoever for the more tender representations of love . . . the organs with which they feel are rather more blunt . . . the chords of their hearts do not resonate to the gentle stroke of love'. They respond to fear, to violence, he explained. They are greedy for food, sex, fame. The fabric of their feelings is not so finely woven, and their hearts may be too cold to empathize with deeper feelings. When these people rise to positions of power and influence and their ideas become influential, they are 'in the habit of replacing the fullness and warmth of faith with cold cognitions and deft displays of verbal dexterity'. If they have a higher spiritual nature, they don't have access to it.[2]

Illustrations by William Blake to *Night Thoughts* by Edward Young (1797). The opposition of the two philosophies is depicted in the art and poetry of the Romantic poet William Blake: '. . . a Robin Red breast in a Cage/Puts all Heaven in a Rage . . .': the cage is science and the robin is our own personal experience.

As I have already suggested, there may be a much greater range of forms of consciousness among people than is generally assumed. This is Goethe's account of his own experience of the world: 'We all walk in mysteries . . . So much is certain – that at times we can put out the feelers of our soul beyond its bodily limits so that a presentiment, an actual insight into the immediate future is accorded to it.' He also wrote about the decided influence that one soul might have on another. For instance, by holding an image of something in his own mind, he could cause a companion to start talking about it. He wrote that this magnet-like power was especially strong between lovers. As a young man, he said, he had been able to draw his lover to him over long distances.

Happy to walk in mysteries, Goethe was adept at what John Keats called 'negative capability'. This is 'when a man is capable of being in uncertainties, mysteries, doubts, without any irritable reaching after fact and reason'. Poets like Goethe, Coleridge and Keats do not rush to impose a pattern on experiences. They prefer instead to let consciousness expand and to continue scanning their experience to see if it yields anything that lies outside the bounds of what is currently understood.

The nineteenth-century German philosopher Schopenhauer said, 'As soon as you put a thought into words it ceases to be true.' He recognized that experience is far too varied, subtle and elusive to ever be constrained by language – let alone by scientific materialism.

German idealism was diffused through the world in the form of Romantic poetry. What these philosophers and poets are saying is that if your account of human experience is 'materially adequate', as philosophers of science expect a good theory to be, then it will take account of the full richness and subtlety of human experience. You will then see that your account has many things in it that cannot be accounted for by scientific materialism.[3]

The Education of Achilles (drawing by Eugene Delacroix, approx. 1862). Romantic poetry and romantic music aim to induce *furore*, the form of consciousness that accords with idealism. Belief in idealism brings many benefits, not least feelings of belonging in the world and life's having meaning in the context of a meaningful universe – and much art, music and literature is, consciously or unconsciously, a yearning to return to it.

The response of scientific materialism to the 'anomalous' experiences described by Goethe is to say that we can't really be having them. Scientific materialism seeks to define them out of existence. In the course of this book we are gathering evidence to show that there is a problem with this, which is that many people believe they have spiritual experiences all the time. You may pray and sense your prayers are heard. You may have premonitions or meaningful dreams or other forms of otherworldly prompting. You may encounter coincidences which you sense are meaningful. You may fall in love and feel that it is *meant to be*. You may have all of these experiences with all the vividness and immediacy that human life has to offer and you may bring to bear on them the most subtle, delicate, heartfelt and deep-thinking powers of discernment of which you are capable – but scientific materialism will tell you that *you are not really having these experiences at all*. And if you believe you are having them, you are kidding yourself.

Abraham and Bernadette

'The Almighty has His own purposes.'

Abraham Lincoln

Lourdes was small town hidden in the shadow of the Pyrenees, its houses grouped around an isolated rock where legend had it that Charlemagne had once fought.

It was 11th February 1858, the feast of St Genevieve. In a house in the rue Petits-Fosses lived François Soubirous, his wife Louise and their four children, two boys and two girls, the eldest child being Bernadette. The father had been the owner of a mill, but now he had to take casual labouring jobs to provide for his family.

Bernadette's mother had persuaded a peasant neighbour to be Bernadette's wet nurse, and she remained there after weaning. Then, when she was old enough to be useful, the peasants, who were fond of her, kept her, and she helped by looking after their sheep on the hillsides.

In February 1858 she was fourteen, though she looked like a child of eleven. She suffered from severe asthma. A fortnight before the 11th she had returned to her parents to prepare for her first communion. Her mother was unusually anxious for her. She was fragile and her chest hurt alarmingly at times.

'It was a Thursday,' Bernadette recalled later:

> . . . and a cold dark day. After we had finished dinner, mother
> told us that there was no more firewood. My sister Toinette

and I offered to go and gather some. My mother said that the weather was too bad, but then Jeanne Abadie, who lived next door, came in, and said she would like to go with us. We begged my mother and now that there were three of us she gave us permission.

We reached the end of the meadows, almost opposite the grotto at Massabielle. We stopped when we came to the canal. There was not much water in it, but I was afraid of wading across because it was so cold. Jeanne Abadie and my sister took their clogs in their hands and went over. I was sure that if I stepped into the water my asthma would come on again. I asked Jeanne, who was bigger and stronger than I was, to come back and carry me over. 'No,' she said, 'if you can't come over by yourself, then stay where you are.'

With this they gathered a few sticks below the grotto and then disappeared along the banks of the canal.

After they had gone, I threw some stones into the water to see if I could use them to step on, but it was no use. So I decided to take off my clogs and stockings and wade across. I had just taken off one of my stockings when I suddenly heard a great noise like a storm coming. I looked to the right and the left, at the trees beside the river, but not a thing moved. I thought I must have been mistaken and went on pulling off my stockings when I heard another noise just like the first. I was frightened and stood up. I tried to shout, but found I couldn't make a noise. I did not know what to think. Then I looked across the water at the grotto and saw that a wild briar bush in one of the openings was waving about as if in a strong wind.

Almost at the same time a golden cloud came out of the grotto, and soon after it came a young, beautiful lady, more beautiful than anyone I had ever seen. She came out and stood in the opening above the bush. She looked straight at me and smiled, and beckoned to me to come over to her as if she were my mother. I wasn't frightened any longer. I rubbed my eyes, I shut them and opened them again, but the Lady was still there . . .

This is how Bernadette would later describe her appearance:

> The Lady looks like a girl of about sixteen or seventeen. She wears a white dress. Round her waist is a blue ribbon which falls the length of the dress almost to the ground. Her hair can hardly be seen, because of a white veil which falls behind, over her shoulders and below the waist. On her naked feet, which are almost hidden by the folds of the dress, are golden-coloured rosettes. In her right hand she holds a rosary with white beads, and a golden chain which glitters like the rosettes on her feet.

On that first appearance she 'was smiling and trying to make me understand that I was not dreaming. Without really knowing what I was doing, I took my rosary out of my pocket and knelt down. I wanted to put my hand up to my forehead to make the sign of the cross, but my arm seemed paralysed and I could not do it until the Lady had crossed herself.'[1]

When the rosary had been said, the Lady withdrew into the back of the grotto and the golden cloud disappeared with her.

> As soon as she had gone, Jeanne and my sister came back to the grotto and found me kneeling there. They laughed and asked if I was coming home with them or not. I waded through the brook without any trouble now, as the water seemed to me to be lukewarm, like water for washing dishes.
>
> We carried three bundles of branches and driftwood back with us. On the way I asked Jeanne and Toinette, my sister, if they had noticed anything at the grotto.
>
> 'No – why do you ask?'
>
> 'Oh, never mind. It doesn't matter.'
>
> But later I couldn't help telling my sister about the strange thing that had happened. I asked her not to tell anyone. But

all that day I thought of the Lady, and in the evening, when we were all saying our prayers, I began to cry. Mother asked what the matter was, and Toinette's hints meant I had to explain.

'It's all just something you have imagined,' mother said. 'Put those fantasies out of your head. And don't go to Massabielle anymore!'

Then we went to bed, but I did not sleep. No matter what my mother had said, I could not believe that I had been mistaken.

The next day Bernadette's mother saw her little girl had changed. She looked sad. She was evidently longing to go to see the Lady again.

Friday and Saturday passed, but on Sunday afternoon her mother gave permission for another visit in the company of the two girls who were already in on the secret.

'Go along, then,' she said. 'But don't worry me about it again! And be back in time for Vespers, or you know what's in store for you!'

The girls took a bottle of holy water to protect them from the Evil One. Bernadette knelt and prayed, with eyes fixed on the niche where the first vision had appeared. The others stood nearby, watching expectantly.

Suddenly Bernadette exclaimed: 'There she is, there she is!'

The bottle of holy water was handed to her and she flung some towards the vision.

After a moment's pause she said, 'The Lady is not at all angry. She is nodding and smiling at us.'

Then she went into an ecstasy and remained immovable and very pale, entirely unconscious of her surroundings, with a radiant, transfigured face.

By now the other girls were on their knees too. One of them cried out, 'Oh, what if Bernadette dies!' They went closer to her, talking to her, but she didn't seem to hear them. Her eyes remained fixed on the niche behind the bush and she seemed lost in the contemplation of a heavenly spectacle visible to her alone.

At that moment, the mother and sister of a local miller arrived. They spoke to her gently and insistently, but still she didn't seem to hear.

The miller's mother ran off to find her son. After a while the adults led Bernadette away and took her back to the mill.

Meanwhile the news had spread and Mme Soubirous suddenly appeared at the mill, very angry. Birch in hand, she went straight up to her daughter, saying, 'You little hussy, do you want to make us a laughing stock! I'll give you what for with your tall tales about ladies.'

She was on the point of striking her daughter when the miller's wife interposed. 'What are you doing? What has your daughter done that you should punish her?'

Lourdes filled with rumours and on Wednesday evening two devout women, anxious to know more, visited the Soubirous home. A trip to the grotto was arranged for them for early the following morning.

A candle was lit at dawn and the three knelt before the grotto and prayed. Soon Bernadette cried out with joy, 'She is coming! There she is!'

The ladies had brought pen and paper and they asked Bernadette to beg the Lady to write down her message. This was refused, and instead the following message was given to Bernadette: 'What I have to tell you, I do not need to write. Come here every day for two weeks. I do not promise to make you happy in this world, but in the next.'

And so began fourteen days – 18th February to 4th March – when Bernadette went to the grotto every morning.

By the fifth day, hundreds were accompanying her. Some among the townspeople asked her to ask the Lady her name, but Bernadette did not receive a reply.

The whole town was talking about the strange events. Some said they were miraculous. Others, especially the better educated, smiled knowingly, some saying it was merely a nervous phenomenon well-known to science.

On the morning of 21st February, the mayor of the town, the procurator and the superintendent of police met at the town hall and cooked up a plan to try to prevent any further manifestations. Order must be preserved, superstition must be repressed, fanatics must be corralled and morbid fancies checked. The best means to do this seemed to them to persuade Bernadette not to return to the cave. They were sure the young girl would be unable to resist their authority.

The procurator had Bernadette brought to his office.

'Will you promise me not to return to Massabielle?'

'No, sir, I will not promise you.'

'Is that all you have to say?'

'Yes, sir.'

'Well, then, go – we will see about this.'

In the evening the police superintendent tried to see what he could do. He ordered Bernadette to come to his office, and he too asked Bernadette not to return to the cave.

'Sir,' she replied very simply, 'I promised the Lady to go back.'

'If you will not immediately promise not to return to Massabielle, I will send for the police and put you in prison.'

But Bernadette remained firm, even when the superintendent threatened her father with prison too.

The next day she was again at the heavenly meeting-place. Two policemen followed her, as did a considerable and curious crowd. She went to her usual spot, but her face showed no sign of ecstasy and when she rose she said that the Lady had not appeared.

The sceptics were triumphant. 'The Lady fears the police,' said someone, and many in the crowd laughed.

Before dawn on the following day, nearly 200 people had already arrived when Bernadette knelt down, and while she began to tell her rosary beads she looked at the rock longingly and enquiringly. Suddenly, as if struck by lightning, she gave a start. Her eyes brightened and glittered. Heavenly smiles hovered round her lips and, as an eyewitness put it, 'An indefinable grace filled her whole person. Bernadette was no longer Bernadette.'

Spontaneously, all the men present uncovered their heads and bowed.

Now and again Bernadette nodded approval or seemed to be mouthing questions.

The following day there were dramatic developments. When Bernadette approached the cave, she moved aside the branches of the briar bush and stooped to kiss the earth just beyond it. Then she fell once more into an ecstasy. At the end of two or three decades of her rosary, she rose again – and seemed to become embarrassed. She hesitated, took two or three steps, then stopped, looked behind her like one who is called and seemed to listen to words which seemed to come from the direction of the rock. She made a sign in the affirmative, then moved to the left-hand corner of the cave. Three-quarters of the way up the slope she halted, stooped down and began to scratch the ground with her hands. The little hole she managed to scoop out filled with water. She waited a moment, drank some of it, then washed her face with it, after which she took a blade of grass which was growing at her feet and put it in her mouth.

When she rose again, her face was dirty with muddy water. Was the poor child going mad?

She didn't seem to notice the exclamations on all sides. After her face had been wiped, she returned to her celestial vision, apparently happier than ever.

Later she would explain what had happened:

> While I was praying, the Lady said to me: 'Go and drink and wash yourself in the cave.' I went to obey, but I couldn't see any water. Not knowing what to do, I raked up the earth and some water came. I let it settle a little, and then I drank some and washed myself.

As for eating the grass, 'I felt inwardly that the Lady wanted me to do it.'

At first the water was hardly enough to make a muddy puddle. But a local doctor called Dozous decided he would not leave the cave without having carefully explored all the different parts of the ground. He later said: 'I found that it was dry everywhere except where Bernadette had hollowed a little hole with her hands. That was where the spring had immediately flowed.'

The water went on increasing in volume for the rest of the day, continuing after most people had left.

The next day, when the people returned to the spot, the jet of water was as big as a finger.

The Lady had asked Bernadette to go to the cave for fourteen days. On the last day there was a feeling of expectation that some miracle would take place. The crowd was immense – 15,000 people at least.

The Lady came, the ecstasy lasted more than an hour, but no miraculous sign was given to the crowd. As they went away disappointed,

Bernadette was asked if she would return to the cave.

'Oh yes,' she replied, 'I shall come back, but I do not know whether the Lady will reappear. Only that she smiled at me when she went away, and that she did not bid me goodbye.'

In the days that followed she often went back, but the mysterious being did not show herself.

Then, after twenty days, on 25th March, the Feast of the Annunciation, the Lady arrived once more. Later Bernadette would remember:

> After I had knelt down before the Lady, I told her how glad I was to be allowed to see her again, and after I had unburdened myself to her, I took up my rosary. While I was praying, the thought came to me that I should now ask her what her name was, and after a little time I could think of nothing else. I was afraid that she might be angry if I again asked a question which she had always refused to answer, and yet there was something that seemed to force me to speak. At last I could not keep the words back any longer, and I asked the Lady to be so kind as to tell me who she was.
>
> As she had always done before, the Lady bent her head and smiled, but did not answer. I don't know how it was, but I was brave and asked her again if she would not trust me with her name. Again she smiled and bent her head. Still she said nothing. Then I folded my hands, and while I admitted to her that I was unworthy of so great a favour, I repeated my request the third time.
>
> The Lady was standing above the rose-bush. When I made my request the third time, she looked grave and then she lifted up her hands, laid them against each other on her breast and looked up to heaven. After that she slowly moved her hands apart again and as she bent forward towards me she said in a voice that trembled, 'I am the Immaculate Conception.'

Afterwards Bernadette turned to a bystander and asked: 'But, *mademoiselle*, what do those words mean? "*Que soy er Immaculada Councepcion?*"'

(Her dialect was closer to Spanish than French.)

The doctrine of the Immaculate Conception had been given to the faithful by the Vatican only three years earlier. When the spectators learned of the Lady's name, they were transported by religious enthusiasm. Some workmen constructed a wooden conduit in order to carry water from the spring to a little basin, and soon the sick and infirm began to drink the water.

Later in 1858 a stone-cutter from Lourdes called Louis Bourriette, who had been blinded in one eye by a stone splint twenty years earlier and was now in danger of losing the sight in the other eye, sent his daughter for some water from the mysterious spring, and although it was muddy he applied it to his eye. His sight improved with each application and the following day he went to see his doctor, Dr Duzous. His cure proved to be permanent and in a record of this on 17th November 1858, at the request of the Bishop of Tarbes, Dr Duzous wrote:

> I have examined both of Bourriette's eyes and found them quite equal both in shape and in the organization of the individual parts. Both pupils reacted normally when subjected to rays of light. In the right eye a scar was still visible. Otherwise there was no trace of the injury that had once damaged it.

Bernadette would live for another twenty years, but the visions never returned.

After a while the nuns who ran the local school took her in to live with them as an invalid. It was here that, between the ages of eighteen and nineteen, she finished learning how to read and write. Eventually she decided to make the life of a religious community her own, and at twenty-two she left the school for a convent in Nevers. She never returned to Lourdes.

Over time her asthma developed into tuberculosis and on 16th April 1879, she died with the crucifix in her hands saying, 'I saw her. Yes, I saw her.'[2]

*   *   *

Abraham Lincoln was born in a log cabin and raised in the wild fron-
tier country of Kentucky and Indiana. He had no formal schooling. He
rose from working as a shopkeeper and postmaster to becoming a
surveyor, then a lawyer, and all the while he was developing a sense of
justice that led him to assert that the nation could not be 'half slave,
half free'.

Lincoln was as committed to religious freedom as much as to political
freedom. His wife was Episcopalian and attended a Presbyterian church,
and Abraham would accompany her now and then. He would explain
that he had never joined any church or attended regularly, because he
found it hard to commit himself to dogma. But, as his friend Isaac
Britton explained, there was another reason and 'very few knew why'.

Britton was a prominent devotee of the great eighteenth-century
Swedish scientist and philosopher Emanuel Swedenborg, as were
several of Abraham Lincoln's friends. 'Swedenborg enables us to
understand why we were created, why we are alive, and what happens
to us after our bodies die. Swedenborg enables us to have the best
possible understanding of God's message as it exists in those Bible
books which constitute God's Word.' So said Martin Luther King.

Abraham Lincoln also sometimes echoed Swedenborg's teachings,
holding that religious conviction was a matter of individual conscience,
and quoting 'Conscience is God's presence with man.'[3]

*   *   *

It was 1860. Abraham Lincoln received the news of his election victory
via the telegraph and celebrated with his friends. He returned home
and collapsed exhausted on the sofa. In the morning he awoke and
found himself looking at his reflection in a mirror on a bureau:

> Looking in that glass, I saw myself reflected nearly full length,
> but my face, I noticed, had two separate and distinct images,
> the tip of the nose being about three inches from the tip of
> the other. I was a little bothered, perhaps startled, and got
> up and looked in the glass, but the illusion vanished. On
> lying down again, I saw it a second time – plainer, if possible,
> than before; and then I noticed that one of the faces was a
> little paler, say five shades, than the other. I got up and the

thing melted away, and I went off, and in the excitement of the hour, forgot all about it – nearly but not quite, for the thing would once in a while come up, and give me a little pang, as though something uncomfortable had happened.

Lincoln tried to replicate the vision, as if it were just an optical illusion, but he couldn't, and the weirdness of the experience stayed with him.

His wife, Mary, was very worried by it all.[6] 'She thought it was a sign that I was to be elected a second term of office, and that the paleness of one of the faces was an omen that I should not see life through the last term.'

An article on the vision appeared in *Harper's Monthly* magazine in July 1865. How would its readers have reacted to their President talking about this spooky experience? Didn't they think it odd?

It is perhaps helpful to see these events in the context of the rise of Spiritualism.

Lincoln's wife may have been interested in Spiritualism as early as the late 1840s and by the time the Lincolns arrived in Washington in 1860, séances had become fashionable among the ruling élite. Mary attended them frequently and Abraham accompanied her at least once. In 1862 she even invited mediums to hold séances in the Red Room in the White House.

On 11th April 1865 Abraham Lincoln told his wife and a small gathering of friends about a dream he had had about ten days earlier. One of the friends, Ward Hill Lamon, later recorded in a biography what he had said:

I retired very late. I had been up waiting for important dispatches from the front. I could not have been long in bed when I fell into a slumber, for I was weary. I soon began to dream. There seemed to be a death-like stillness about me. Then I heard subdued sobs, as if a number of people were weeping. I thought I left my bed and wandered downstairs. There the silence was broken by the same pitiful sobbing, but the mourners were invisible. I went from room to room; no living person was in sight, but the same mournful sounds of distress met me as I passed along. I saw light in all the rooms; every object was familiar to me; but where were all the people who were grieving as if their hearts would break? I was puzzled and alarmed. What could be the meaning of all this? Determined to find the cause of a state of things so mysterious and so shocking, I kept on until I arrived at the East Room, which I entered. There I met with a sickening surprise. Before me was a catafalque, on which rested a corpse wrapped in funeral vestments. Around it were stationed soldiers who were acting as guards; and there was a throng of people gazing mournfully upon the corpse, whose face was covered, others weeping pitifully. 'Who is dead in the White House?' I demanded of one of the soldiers. 'The President,' was his answer; 'he was killed by an assassin.' Then came a loud burst of grief from the crowd, which woke me from my dream. I slept no more that night; and although it was only a dream, I have been strangely annoyed by it ever since.

Earlier that month Robert E. Lee, the commanding general of the Confederate Army, had surrendered to General Ulysses Grant. An actor called Robert Wilkes Booth, who was a Confederate sympathizer, hoped to rally Confederate troops and inspire them to carry on the fight. On 14th April 1865, while Lincoln was with his wife watching a play called *Our American Cousin* at Ford's Theatre in Washington, DC, Booth shot him in the back of the head.

The Nabob of Odd[1]

'Praise the Lord, all cedars' (from *The Child's Bible*, nineteenth century).

The phenomenon which would become known as Spiritualism began in 1848 in Hydesville in New York when the Fox sisters, Margaret and Kate, began to hear furniture being moved about the house and strange knockings. They said that when they challenged the spirits to respond to the snapping of their fingers, a mimicking rapping was heard on a table. When they made this known, they achieved instant fame. Later they would confess to being frauds, but here was an idea whose time had come and soon others exhibiting more impressive powers came forward.

Zephaniah Eddy was working on the farm one day when he saw his two sons playing with feral children he had never seen before. When he went after these strange children, they seemed to vanish in mid-air.[2] The old man hauled the brothers over to the barn and beat them with a rawhide whip; he had long worried about a history of witchcraft in his wife's family and now wanted to do everything he could to stamp it out.

But as the boys grew older weird things continued to happen – slates, tables and inkwells flying around the house, strange pounding noises and disembodied voices. Spirits appeared, including a creature with white fur that the boys said sniffed at their faces when they were in bed, then grew larger until it turned into a luminous cloud with a human shape.

Zephaniah grew increasingly alarmed and when the boys fell into trances he would sometimes beat them, even pour boiling water on them or singe them with burning coals – anything to try to make them snap out of it. The Eddy brothers left home as soon as they could, but then they were stoned, stabbed, manacled, tortured and even shot at by angry mobs, and they returned home, to the small, basic farm in Vermont, when their father died. They remained scarred, sullen, suspicious of the world, but news that the farm was infested with spirits began to spread.

Henry Steel Olcott was a successful attorney. He had been a colonel in the Union army, where he had been responsible for investigating fraud and corruption in arsenals and military shipyards. He was also a prominent Freemason and one of a panel of three men charged with investigating the assassination of Lincoln. Later he would become editor of the *New York Tribune*. In 1874 he was sent to investigate events at the Eddys' farm and he travelled there, accompanied by an artist called Kappas, whose illustrations he would use in a remarkable book, *People from the Other World*.[3]

On his first day he attended a séance led by the Eddys at a local cave, Honto's Cave. Beforehand he investigated the location to make sure there were no hidden entrances or passageways. When the séance started, he was amazed to see a gigantic Native American emerge from the cave. Then another appeared, silhouetted on the top of the cave, then a squaw. Afterwards Olcott could find no trace of footprints.

He was hooked. He stayed for two and a half months, recording some 400 spiritual manifestations. During his stay he virtually took the farmhouse apart, plank by plank, to prove to himself that he wasn't being duped by trapdoors or other contrivances.

The phenomena at the farm included prophecy, speaking in tongues, healing, levitation, the appearance of free-floating hands, messages appearing on paper floating in mid-air, psychometry, the materialization of *apports* (objects that appear through paranormal means, usually in séances) and the production of phantom beings that became visible, tangible and sometimes even audible to everyone present. One of the brothers was talented at producing these material manifestations, and Olcott was permitted to measure and even weigh some of them. He reported

Honto's Cave (from *People from the Other World* by Henry S. Olcott, 1875) .

in his book that the body of a materialized being felt cold, unlike the flesh of a living person, and that there was a rhythmical but feeble pulse.

Sometimes the spirits of hundreds of men, women and children, more than could be numbered precisely, appeared all at once and in front of a large audience. These spirits were bathed in a moon-like glow, some hovering over the medium and showering brilliant sparks upon him. Some spirits were bluish, some greyish, some pure white with shining raiment and faces 'like Moses when he descended from Sinai'. Some spirits laid crowns of flowers on the heads of members of the audience. Some seemed to kneel and gaze up at people as if they were old friends. Then suddenly a candle was lit and all the spirits instantly disappeared.

Afterwards Olcott collected sworn statements from many dignitaries.

A few weeks after Olcott's arrival, another visitor came to the farm-house. This was Madame de Blavatsky, an eccentric Russian traveller with a well-developed interest in esoteric teachings and a magnetic personality. When she attended séances, some of the beings manifested

An evening when hundreds of spirits appeared at once to a large audience (from *People from the Other World* by Henry S. Olcott).

by the Eddy brothers began to speak and write in Russian. New spirits manifested themselves before Olcott and the rest of the company, some of whom Madame Blavatsky claimed to have met earlier on her travels, including a Kurdish warrior and the leader of a band of jugglers from North Africa.

Olcott tried to make sense of the exercises of power he was witnessing and to discern universal principles underlying them:

What is this insensible something that envelops us like an inner atmosphere, and saturates all whom we meet? What subtle power made the mere touch of an Apostle's robe efficacious to cure disease, and the laying on of a royal hand effect the same result? What human lightning darting from Napoleon's eye converted every soldier into a hero as it fell upon him? What potent spell lurked in the presence of Florence Nightingale, and made the wounded men at Scutari better, if they could barely kiss her shadow as it flitted across their beds?[4]

There are other early historical parallels. It is perhaps unlikely that the Eddys or even an educated man like Olcott would have known of the writings of the Neoplatonists, as they were only patchily translated into

English then and known only to a handful of scholars. But we have already mentioned that Plotinus attended a séance in the temple of Isis. He and some of his followers witnessed mediums being thrown into trances for the purposes of delivering messages on several occasions. Apuleius described mediums being induced to sleep. Proclus and Psellus wrote that in some cases the medium's own personality was completely eclipsed by the spirit, but in others the medium was conscious of communicating with the spirit. According to Iamblichus, some mediums had convulsions, while others become completely rigid. Iamblichus himself was seen by his pupils to levitate. Sometimes false or unwelcome spirits intruded. Sometimes a medium's body elongated. Usually only the medium could hear the voice of the spirit, but on other occasions the other sitters heard disembodied voices too. Sometimes the spirits left material traces – *apports*. Sometimes luminous forms were seen exuding from the body of a medium – what in modern times has been called ectoplasm. Clearly we are dealing with exactly the same set of phenomena appearing to Greek philosophers, then nearly two millennia later to illiterate American farmers.

It was in the mid-nineteenth century that the sacred texts of oriental religions were translated into European languages. Amidst a growing sense that the established Church was no longer able to provide people with satisfying spiritual experience, many of Europe's cultural and intellectual leaders, including Nietzsche, Schopenhauer and Wagner, became curious about oriental spirituality. The new translations also naturally led to renewed attempts to delineate universal truths – a perennial philosophy. As we have seen, ideas concerning a universal and perennial philosophy had been a part of heretical groups driven underground since the time of Mani, and now within secret societies that traced their roots back to the Rosicrucians there arose a debate about whether to make public its own cosmic wisdom.[5]

In 1875 Blavatsky and Olcott co-founded the Theosophical Society, with the aim of promoting a universal brotherhood, regardless of race or creed, based on a free-thinking study of world religions. In 1887 Madame Blavatsky published *Isis Unveiled*, a vast compendium of Rosicrucian lore. She outlined a theology intended to make sense of the explosion of spiritual activity in the second half of the nineteenth century, much of it under the umbrella of Spiritualism.

Master Koot Hoomi, one of
the spiritual masters who
guided Madame Blavatsky
to found the Theosophical
Society (from *Through the Eyes of
the Masters* by David Anrias,
1932).

Olcott was a Freemason and Madame Blavatsky, though she never took any of the regular degrees of Freemasonry, was a close ally.[6]

Freemasonry has been an important influence for the good in ways which are routinely overlooked. Masonic rituals enjoin initiates to explore 'the hidden mysteries of science and nature'. The roots of the Royal Society lay in Freemasonry and it also looked to the Masonic ideals of brotherhood, equality and freedom – above all, freedom from fanaticism and prejudice. Freemasonry and the Royal Society provided a space which was tolerant. Here the hidden mysteries could be explored in a sympathetic, thoughtful way in a place where everyone would behave equably and well.

This tolerance was equally important when it came to exploration of spiritual mysteries and to considering the great questions of life and death, the beginning and end of the universe. The human condition has been constructed in an odd way. When we are considering ordinary and practical matters, the trivia of day-to-day life – how many sweets are left in the bag, how much petrol in the tank – we can generally be pretty clear about what the truth is. There tends to be a preponderance of evidence. On the other hand, when we come to consider the great questions of life and death, the evidence is never so clear and there is usually far less of it.

As I pointed out in the introduction, when we come to consider the beginning of the universe and ask whether it was a Big Bang as science describes or whether it was in some way meant to be, whether there was some Cosmic Mind behind it all, the evidence is extremely sparse. In fact there is almost no evidence at all. What you get is the tiniest and most ambiguous scrap of evidence and on it there balances a huge inverted pyramid of speculation.

How curious then that it's on the basis of beliefs in this area, where we are unable to assert anything with certainty, where the evidence is most faint and open to interpretation, where any hypothesis is bound to be highly tenuous, that our opinions tend to be fiercest, most fanatical and intolerant, and failing to show the equanimity and generosity that ought to be the mark of a happy and mature quest for the truth.[7]

Is there any way of bringing order to this debate? Criteria both sides can agree on? In the nineteenth century, Freemasons asked if it would be possible to apply the refinements of Hume's thinking, which was even then making science so successful, to spiritual matters. Could there be a science of the spirit? It was necessary first to gather as much data as possible . . .

Sponsored by Freemasons, Spiritualism quickly became an international phenomenon in the late nineteenth century, as more and more people with extraordinary gifts made themselves known. The leading scientists of the day were fascinated and asked if these phenomena could be investigated scientifically. They included the famous French astronomer Flammarion and William Crookes, discoverer of thallium and identifier of helium, who also pioneered vacuum tubes as a means of studying the properties of electricity. Crookes wrote *Researches into the Phenomena of Spiritualism* (1874), in which he complained that hostile scientists tried to disprove Spiritualist phenomena by imposing conditions unsuitable to the phenomena under investigation. As we have already seen, Alfred Russel Wallace, the co-discoverer of natural selection, believed that this process is guided by creative intelligences, which he identified with angels. Marie Curie attended séances. Both Thomas Edison, the godfather of recorded sound, and Alexander Graham Bell, inventor of the telephone, made their discoveries while researching into the spirit worlds. Edison tried to make a radio that would tune into the spirit worlds. Television was invented as a result of trying to capture psychic influences on gases fluctuating in front of a cathode ray tube.

Today Spiritualism is often seen as nutty fringe, a hole in the wall activity, but from the mid-nineteenth to the early twentieth century it was seen as a progressive movement, allied to the campaign against slavery and the suffragette movement.[8] Queen Victoria, Prime Minister William Gladstone and Charles Dickens consulted mediums. Co-founders of the Labour party Keir Hardie and Ramsay Macdonald were respectively a Spiritualist and an avowed follower of the work of Swedenborg. Prime Minister Arthur Balfour and Air Chief Marshal Lord Hugh Dowding, who was in charge of the Battle of Britain, were Spiritualists, and Winston Churchill consulted the medium Helen Duncan.

One of the most famous mediums was Daniel Dunglas Home. This Scot demonstrated his gifts to many of the crowned heads of Europe as well as many intellectuals, including sceptics. Whereas most mediums worked in darkness, he worked in full light. Despite the best efforts of sceptics, he was never caught out in any fraud. He would go into a trance state, sometimes shivering and seeming distressed, at other times calm and peaceful with what was described as an angelic expression. His ability to elongate his body while in trance state was well attested. 'The one who is to protect you,' he said, addressing Lord Adare, 'is as tall as this.'

And upon so saying, Mr Home – and in order to demonstrate – grew taller; as I stood next to him (my height is six feet) I hardly reached up to his shoulder, and in the glass opposite he appeared a full head taller than myself. The extension appeared to take place from the waist . . . Walking to and fro, Mr Home specially called our attention to the fact of his feet being firmly planted on the ground. Next he grew shorter and shorter, until he only reached my shoulder.

This account was by a well-known barrister of the day, H. D. Jencken.[9]

Home's most famous supernatural feat took place in front of three witnesses, two of whom wrote detailed accounts. He levitated out of a window in one room, three storeys above ground. He then floated six inches above the sill of the neighbouring window for a few seconds before raising the window some eighteen inches and gliding in through the gap, feet foremost.

'One side will make you grow taller.'
(From *Alice's Adventures in Wonderland* by Lewis Carroll, 1865.)

*   *   *

Have civilizations always been founded on violence? It's been said many times and with a great deal of justification that many of the founders of the European empires in Africa and Asia were pirates and adventurers, but it is equally true to say that they brought in their wake the values of the Freemasonic lodge – tolerance and equality before the law. There is also at the heart of Freemasonry a genuine spiritual impulse, a quest to understand mysteries. Yet any large organization will ossify, and in the mid-nineteenth century what had already happened to Christianity began to happen to Freemasonry too.

Freemasonic initiation ceremony (from *A Ritual and Illustrations of Freemasonry* by Avery Allyn, 1831).

English Freemasonry is still cagey about its spiritual and esoteric interests. Lodges engaged in spiritual pursuits keep these activities well hidden, even from other Freemasons, leaving high-ranking spokesmen free to rubbish in public any claims that outsiders make regarding Freemasonry and the occult.

While writing this book I found in a second-hand bookshop in Tunbridge Wells a Freemasonic book published in 1860, called *The Mysteries of Freemasonry* by J. Fellows. This gives an account of a mystical history of the world that is very similar to the history of the world given by Madame Blavatsky and her Theosophical followers. This account was then elaborated on by Rudolf Steiner, but it is essentially the same history: Osiris, initiations in ancient Egypt, Zoroaster, Orpheus, Cadmus, Enoch, Moses, Solomon, the Buddha, Solon, Pythagoras, the mysteries of Eleusis, Socrates, Mani (here called Scythianus), the Templars, Dante and Christian Rosencreutz.

I say this not to denigrate Theosophy or Rudolf Steiner. Maintaining a genuine tradition is at a premium here, not originality. My point is that there is a secret and mystical history of the world that is very old indeed – and that Freemasonry seems to have played a large part in preserving it.

The connections between Freemasonry and Rosicrucians go back at least as far as 1638, and in 1676 there is a record of 'the Company of accepted Masons' and 'the Ancient Brotherhood of the Rosy-Cross' dining together. The journals of Elias Ashmole, the founder of English Freemasonry according to United Grand Lodge, record his successful research for the great secret of alchemy – the alchemy of attaining access to higher spiritual realms described in *The Chymical Wedding* of Christian Rosencreutz.[10]

However by the mid-nineteenth century the spiritual trail seems to have gone cold. Some Freemasons perhaps thought their brotherhood was ossifying and becoming cut off from genuine spiritual streams, because the 1860 book records as a fact of great significance that 'German Freemasons maintain that Christian Rosencreutz was a real person':

> . . . In Germany, it is related that one Christian Rosy Cross was born in 1387, and making a voyage to the Holy Land he had at Damascus some conferences with the wise Chaldeans from whom he learned the occult sciences; after which he perfected himself in the lodges of Egypt, Libya and Constantinople. Returning to Germany, he established an order, of which the substance descended to the Freemasons of Britain and Germany by different channels.

In 1906 another British Freemason, Dr Robert Felkin, was concerned to discover the truth about the origins of the Degree of the Rose Croix within British Freemasonry and, perhaps hoping to find a genuine, spiritual source, went to Germany. He travelled through Cologne, Ulm, Stuttgart, Munich, Vienna, Passau, Regensburg, Nuremberg and Berlin, visiting lodges and five 'Rosicrucian' temples, taking part in ceremonies, some lasting five and a half hours, during which the candidate was placed in a coffin and the lid was screwed down. He heard loud organ music and shouts, saw fire in the darkness and was shown an adept hovering high up in a cloud of incense. There were references to Ahriman and Lucifer, and the Germans demonstrated to him their powers of clairvoyance.

Felkin was keen above all to meet one of their 'Secret Chiefs', the source of their occult power. However, the leading lights among occultists in British Freemasonry and affiliated organizations at that time were very grand upper-class gentlemen, and when Felkin did eventually meet one of the Secret Chiefs, he did not like his manner, reporting that he found him uncouth. His name was Rudolf Steiner.

In 1913 Rudolf Steiner severed all links with Theosophy and in 1914 also with Freemasonry.

Like Jacob Boehme before him and Lorna Byrne today, Steiner would write about his vivid experiences of spiritual realms and beings and their interaction with the material world with great clarity. Despite the work of the Spiritualists and more recent researchers, almost none of this interaction – perhaps none of it – is verifiable by science, but reading these writers (and as we are about to see, quite different types of writers) may encourage the rest of us to bring into full consciousness spiritual and mystical experiences that we might otherwise pay little attention to or fail to recognize altogether.

The Great Secret of This World

My story is set in Spain, in Seville, in the time of the Inquisition, when fires were lit every day to the glory of God, and the wicked heretics were burnt in the splendour of an *auto da fé*. In His infinite mercy He came once more among men in that human shape in which He had walked among men fifteen centuries earlier. He came down to the hot pavements of a southern town.

He came softly, unobserved, and yet, strange to say, everyone recognized Him. The people are irresistibly drawn to Him, they surround Him, they flock about Him, follow Him. He moves silently in their midst with a gentle smile of infinite compassion. The sun of love burns in His heart, light and power shine from His eyes, and their radiance, shed on the people, stirs their hearts.

He stops at the steps of the Seville cathedral at the moment when the weeping mourners are taking in a little open white coffin. In it lies a child of seven, the only daughter of a prominent citizen. The dead child lies among clusters of flowers. 'He will raise your child,' the crowd shouts to the weeping mother. The priest coming out to meet the coffin, looks perplexed, and frowns, but the mother of the dead child throws herself at His feet with a wail. The procession halts, the coffin is laid on the steps at His feet. He looks with compassion, and His lips softly pronounce, 'Maiden, arise!' and the maiden arises. The little girl sits up in the coffin and looks round, smiling with wide-open wondering eyes, holding a bunch of white roses they have put in her hand.

There are cries, sobs, confusion among the people, but at that moment the Grand Inquisitor passes by the cathedral. He is an old man, almost ninety, tall and erect with a withered face and sunken eyes, in which there is nevertheless a gleam of light. He stops at the sight of the crowd and watches. He knits his thick grey brows and his eyes gleam with a newly sinister fire. He holds out his finger and bids the guards arrest Him. The crowd instantly bows as one before the old Inquisitor. He blesses the people in silence and passes on.

The guards lead their prisoner to the close, gloomy vaulted prison in the ancient palace of the Holy Inquisition and shut Him in it. The rest of the day passes and is followed by the dark, burning, breathless night of Seville. The air is fragrant with laurel and lemon. Then in the pitch darkness the iron door of the prison is suddenly opened and the Grand Inquisitor himself comes in with a light in his hand. He is alone. He stands in the doorway and for a minute or two gazes into His face. At last he sets the light on the table and speaks.

'Is it you?' but receiving no answer, he adds at once, 'Don't answer, be silent.' There is silence.

'Have you the right to reveal to us one of the mysteries of that world from which you have come?' the old man continues, and answers the question for Him. 'No, you have not; that you may not add to what has been said of old, and may not take from men the freedom which you exalted when you were on earth. Whatsoever you reveal anew will encroach on men's freedom of faith.

'You promised them the bread of Heaven, but can that really compare with earthly bread in the eyes of the weak, ignoble race of man? And if for the sake of the bread of Heaven thousands shall follow you, what is to become of the millions and tens of thousands of millions of creatures who will not have the strength to forgo the earthly bread for the sake of the heavenly? Or dost you care only for the tens of thousands of the great and strong, while the millions, numerous as the sands of the sea, who are weak, must exist only for the sake of the great and strong? In that question lies the great secret of the world.

'We on the other hand care for the weak too. They are sinful and rebellious, but in the end they too will become obedient . . .We have corrected your work and have founded it upon *miracle*, *mystery* and *authority*. And men rejoiced that they were again led like sheep.

Oh, ages are yet to come of the confusion of free thought, of their science and cannibalism. For having begun to build their tower of Babel without us, they will end, of course, with cannibalism. Freedom, free thought and science, will lead them into such straits and will bring them face to face with such marvels and insoluble mysteries, that some of them, the fierce and rebellious, will destroy themselves, others, rebellious but weak, will destroy one another, while the rest, weak and unhappy, will crawl fawning to our feet and whine to us: "Yes, you were right, you alone possess His mystery, and we come back to you, save us from ourselves!"

'We shall show them that childlike happiness is the sweetest of all. They will become timid and will look to us and huddle close to us in fear, as chicks to the hen. Yes, we shall set them to work, but in their leisure hours we shall make their life like a child's game, with children's songs and innocent dance. And they will have no secrets from us. We shall allow or forbid them to live with their wives and lovers, to have or not to have children and they will submit to us gladly and cheerfully. The most painful secrets of their conscience, all, all they will bring to us, and we shall have an answer for all. And all will be happy, all the millions of creatures except the hundred thousand who rule over them. For only we, we who guard the mystery, shall be unhappy . . .

'What I say to you will come to pass, and our dominion will be built up. Tomorrow you will see that obedient flock who at a sign from me will hasten to heap up the hot cinders. For if anyone has ever deserved our fires, it is you. To-morrow I shall burn you.'

When the Inquisitor ceased speaking he waited some time for his Prisoner to answer him. The old man longed for Him to say something, however bitter and terrible. But He suddenly approached the old man in silence and softly kissed him on his bloodless lips.

*   *   *

The story of the Grand Inquisitor, taken from Dostoyevsky's *The Brothers Karamazov*, is on one level about the Catholic Church.[1] In its early days the Church had been a protective carapace around the growing tip of humanity's evolving consciousness, but after a time it had begun to harden and restrict. Where once it had sought to spread spiritual experience, it now sought to control and restrict it. When the Inquisitor argues with eloquence that humanity does not want freedom, we are meant to understand that the better part of us *does* want it. The Inquisitor uses the language of morality and spirituality, but what he says is double-dealing and oleaginous. It drips with evil.

But the Inquisitor's critique of human nature and the human condition is devastating, even if we may feel it is not the whole truth. He is suggesting that there is a fundamental mismatch between human nature and the human condition, that the terms and conditions of our existence are too harsh for us, that we are too weak. We have all probably thought at some time, *Couldn't life be easier?* Yes, we appreciate that life has to be hard in some ways so that we may evolve and develop free will and exercise it – but, *still*, couldn't life sometimes be just a *little bit* easier? Who is to say it couldn't be? Dostoyevsky himself had these disturbing thoughts, and one of the other Karamazov brothers says to Ivan, who has told the story of the Grand Inquisitor, 'How can you live with such Hell in your heart and your head?'

The Inquisitor says that if the Church won't provide the miraculous, science will bring the rebellious face to face with marvels and mysteries that will destroy them. The Grand Inquisitor brackets science and cannibalism together in a prophecy that is consonant with the prophecies of Dostoyevsky's friend Soloviev concerning the Antichrist.[2]

Dostoyevsky's fiction is prophetic on many levels. He anticipates both Nietzsche and Freud in his account of the frenzied, dark, irrational forces that were working their way out of the depths of the human psyche in the second half of the nineteenth century, forces that would grow and cause havoc and destruction in the twentieth century. But there is a deep ambiguity in Dostoyevsky. He *loves* the irrational and believes that rationalist theories of utopianism of the sort his country would adopt are doomed – and fatal. '"Twice times two is four" is not life, gentleman, but the beginning of death.' Implicit in his fiction is the belief that these dark, mysterious forces in the human psyche cannot be reasoned away, cannot be denied. They must be embraced and in some way, transmuted.

*   *   *

Herman Melville also spent his life wrestling with the great questions of life and death. He died without finishing a short novel called *Billy Budd*, set on a ship in Napoleonic times.

Billy Budd is an orphan, perhaps not very bright and certainly not very articulate, partly because he has a speech impediment. But he is wholly good, innocent and handsome – and very popular with the rest of the crew, which arouses hatred in the ship's master of arms, John Claggart.

> The ship at noon, going large before the wind, was rolling on her course, and Billy, below at dinner and engaged in some sportful talk with the members of his mess, chanced in a sudden lurch to spill the entire contents of his soup-pan upon the newly scrubbed deck. Claggart, the Master-at-arms, happened to be passing along, and the greasy liquid streamed just across his path. Stepping over it, he was proceeding on his way without comment, since the matter was nothing to take notice of under the circumstances, when he happened to observe who it was that had done the spilling. His countenance changed. Pausing, he was about to ejaculate something hasty at the sailor, but checked himself, and pointing down to the streaming soup, playfully tapped him from behind with his rattan,[3] saying in a low musical voice peculiar to him at times, 'Handsomely done, my lad! And handsome is as handsome did it too!' And with that passed on. Not noted by Billy, as not coming within his view, was the involuntary smile, or rather grimace, that accompanied Claggart's equivocal words. Aridly it drew down the thin corners of his mouth. But everybody taking his remark as meant for humorous, and at which therefore as coming from a superior they were bound to laugh 'with counterfeited glee', acted accordingly; and Billy tickled, it may be, by the allusion to his being the handsome sailor, merrily joined in . . .

Claggart is overcome by malice and falsely accuses Billy of planning a mutiny. When he repeats these charges in front of the captain, Billy is

too inarticulate to defend himself and strikes out at Claggart, accidentally killing him.

'Struck dead by an angel of God! Yet the angel must hang!' cries the
captain.

Any enlisted sailor who kills an officer is subject to the death penalty.
The captain is bound by this, and Billy is duly hanged on the yardarm
the next morning.

The soup-spilling incident on which the whole novel turns and which
leads to Billy's 'crucifixion' could hardly be smaller or seem less
significant. It is hard to imagine a more trivial accident. It seems so
unnecessary. Yet it *is* necessary to Billy's story, to the shape of his life,
to its meaning. Melville's wider point is that the great events of all our
lives often turn on the most trivial events – that the things that are
meant to be, and which are the result of otherworldly prompting, may
seem insignificant.

We saw battles in heaven refought in epic battles on earth in the
stories of Charlemagne and Roland. These were stories of armies
commanded by the most powerful, the most obviously extraordinary
people on the planet. In modern times the battle between the forces
of evil and the angelic forces is seen on the level of the more mundane
events in the lives of ordinary people.

*   *   *

Sometimes thinking in straight lines, in categories, in abstract terms
is not enough. There are parts of experience that don't fit any categories,
experiences that elude conceptual and rational thinking. But where
discursive language reaches its limits, we can give expression to these
experiences, deal with them and try to come to terms with them by
telling each other stories.

So, what makes a story? Attempts to define what is essential to a
story have tended to centre on conflict: maximum desire encounters
maximum obstacle for maximum drama. That is the Hollywood
formula.

But I think that in addition to conflict there is another essential
element.

A man goes up to another man in the street and hits him.

Is that a story? Does it *work* as a story and give us the satisfaction we expect from a story? I don't think it does.

A man goes up to another man in the street and hits him for no apparent reason.
'Why on Earth did you just hit me?'
'You don't remember? You used to bully me at school.'

That *is* a story, I think, and the additional element that makes it a story is the element of mystery. Stories address our sense that there is more to understand, more than meets the eye. In stories the cosmos responds to a character's life decisions – to be a bully or to be bullied – by mysteriously presenting that character with a situation that gives him the chance to learn the meaning of that life-decision and to change it.

In the universe of scientific materialism it would be extremely unlikely that we would ever encounter situations tailored to the life decisions we made earlier. In the universe that stories describe, on the other hand, we are constantly caught up in this kind of meaningful interaction with our circumstances. We may try to block out this kind of meaning or remain oblivious to it, but then something will happen to bring us face to face with what, to put it in more elevated terms, we might call our destiny. Melville was writing at the dawn of psychological realism in fiction. He does not show an angel or a demon nudging Billy's elbow, but he is nevertheless showing a turn of events that would not be happening if materialistic science accounted for everything. Stories emphasize the operations of divine immanence in the world.

So, in order for a story to be a story and not a random sequence of events, it has to obey a set of laws. The big question is: does life obey this same set of laws? Are stories an accurate reflection of our experience of life? Or are they just entertainment? I suspect that militant materialists are not big readers of fiction. Deep down they may be suspicious of stories. They may see them as seductive and utterly contradictory to an atheistic world-view. And they are right.

*   *   *

Our fates are tied to the fates of other people and we do not know how or why. There is an ante-room somewhere containing all the people who shape our life and give it meaning by their configuration. There are our parents and our children and our siblings and partners, and also that boy who bullied us at school and that girl on a bike we knocked over, but also that old woman we befriended and looked after and that man whose life we saved with a kind and thoughtful word, though we didn't know we were saving it. They live on in our life even when they are not physically present. They are what gives our life depth and meaning.

The Story of Life after Death

Freemasons were working behind the scenes, and as we have seen, many leading Theosophists were Freemasons too. But if Madame Blavatsky and Theosophy had originally been inspired by a Rosicrucian impulse to bring together Western and Eastern religions in a transcendental unity, some in the movement felt that her work had become unbalanced in favour of the Eastern. In 1914 Rudolf Steiner left Theosophy to found his own movement, Anthroposophy, with the aim of righting the balance.

How does this relate to the story of life after death? Beliefs about what happens after death have changed through history. Primordial beliefs about the heavens such as we saw in Enoch's antediluvian account had become clouded by the time of Homer and the Psalms. They describe the spirit wandering in 'the Pit' in a kind of half-life. Following the life and death of Jesus Christ and his descent into hell, there were new visions of a glorious afterlife. Steiner explained that people's ideas about what happened to human spirits after death changed *because what actually happened after death changed.* What follows is his account of the after-death journey.

In modern times the soul and the spirit have been confused and conflated, but traditional religious thinking distinguished between the two and in order to understand the after-death experience it is necessary first to understand the different components of a human being according to mystical idealism. There are four.

1. First, there is of course the physical body.
2. Then there is the animating principle that gives the material body organic life. This is the soul. Mystics like Lorna Byrne see it filling the material body. In the Kabbalah it is called the *nephesch* and in Theosophy it is known as the etheric body. Some mystics, including Jacob Boehme and William Blake, have called it the vegetative body, because it gives us the life we share with plants.[1]
3. Nestling in this vegetative body is the animal body – the spirit – which gives the animal form of consciousness which plants do not have. This is called the *tzelem* in the Kabbalah and the astral body in Theosophy.[2]
4. This in turn contains the self, which is a spark of the divine nature. The self gives us the sense of individual consciousness that an animal does not have and that enables us to enjoy free will and free thinking.[3]

In order to stay alive we need our vegetative body to stay inside our physical body. In sleep we are alive but not conscious. When some clairvoyants watch someone go to sleep, they see the vegetative body stay within the material body, but they also see the animal body, carrying the divine spark, rise above the physical body. Under normal circumstances it does not float freely upwards towards the ceiling, as is sometimes imagined, but stays just above the physical body or, in some accounts, emerges partially from it.[4]

Paracelsus said that during sleep the spirit became freer in its movements and could sometimes rise out of the body and converse with ancestors or angels. Usually when we awake we have 'drunk the Draught of Forgetfulness' and forget our meetings with angels, but sometimes when we are in a terrible predicament, ministering spirits may speak to us with such intensity that we will remember what they have told us in the morning.[5]

In other words, because the animal body and self may emerge from the physical body, which screens out spiritual influences, we may during sleep have experiences of the spiritual worlds. This is what dreams are: jumbled up experiences of the spiritual realms. In death, on the other hand, the other three bodies leave the material body. The vegetative body leaves the physical body carrying with it the animal body and self. As they rise up from the physical body, the vegetative body begins to dissipate. And then so too does the animal body or spirit.

This rising up and dissipating accounts for the first after-death experiences in modern times as they are described by Rudolf Steiner.

There is a popular belief that someone who is in grave danger of dying, by drowning for example, sees their whole life flash before them. According to Steiner, an important physiological reality lies behind this popular belief. This brief memory 'rewind' is the effect of the vegetative body becoming loosened from the physical body.

If you do in fact die, says Steiner, you experience a clarity and a brightness, which is a sort of awakening.[6]

The life review that appears as we feel we may be about to die is brief and mechanical, a rapid, visual summary, such as we might see on a screen. It is not *involving*, though. On the other hand, if we do die, if our animal body frees itself from the dissolving vegetative body, then we experience another life review, but this one is much longer and we feel it deeply. While we were alive it was our animal body that enabled us to feel emotions and experience desires. Now, because our self is still nestling within our animal body, we still feel desire, but because we are no longer contained in a physical body, we have no means of satisfying these desires.

This second life review may last perhaps a third of the time we spent on Earth – so maybe twenty to thirty years. It is what is known as *Kamaloca* (literally, 'the place of desire') in Hinduism, and is the Purgatory of Christian tradition. Our desires, which we can no longer satisfy, must be purged before we can enter the higher heavens (what Hindus call *Devachan*). To put it another way, we must shake off attachments to earthly existence. At the lowest level, these attachments might be bestial or depraved appetites or greed for material possessions. They might also be more elevated attachments, for example, a love of art for art's sake (and so art devoid of spiritual content) or, indeed, attachment to materialistic philosophy, however well-meant.

While we experience the pain of desires which cannot be fulfilled and which must be torn from us, we also realize that the desires that attached themselves to us during our lifetime were really beings. They may now appear to us as evil hybrids, half human, half animal.[7]

The sight of demons is painful and horrifying. But there are other

Hermes leading the spirit upwards, from an archaic onyx gemstone carving (from *Antique Gems*, by the Rev. C. W. King, 1866).

pains too. As well as our own emotions, if we have caused others pain, we now feel that pain as if it were our own. Something of this is captured in *A Christmas Carol* by Charles Dickens, but after death spirit has no opportunity to make amends. After death it is too late.

When we have travelled through this realm and been purged of every element of the animal body, we shed our astral corpse. (Steiner said that mediums who promote themselves as being in contact with the dead are sometimes only in contact with these astral corpses, containing traces of memory and language but no living intelligence.)

Then we experience this burst of light and enlightenment as we move from the sphere of the moon – the sphere of desire or purgatory in all religious traditions – to the next sphere. As messenger of the gods, Mercury is there to guide us, to light the way upwards.[8]

In the fourth century, Emperor Julian wrote about the capacity of starlight raying down upon him to send him into a state of higher consciousness.[9] A sense of awe inspired by the stars in someone walking on the surface of the Earth is increased many times as we emerge into higher heavens. We see the great angelic beings that lie behind the physical bodies of the planets and stars. We understand how what we saw on Earth – the physical objects and the events – was created for us by these spiritual beings working together.

In the sphere of Mercury we may be reunited with those we knew on Earth, including friends and family. This will be a happy reunion if we acted well towards them in life, if we have a good conscience. If not, we will feel isolated and distant from them.

In the sphere of Mercury we will understand, too, that the spiritual beings who worked to create the physical circumstances we experienced during life on Earth were also working within us, cradling us and gently educating us in what we ought to do. How did we respond to these beings? In the sphere of Mercury we ask questions like these: Didn't I love enough? Did I fail in love? Was I jealous? Did I harden my heart? Did I throw away my chances of leading a happy and fulfilled life casually on that rainy day in April? Did I pass up a chance to do good, pretending to myself I didn't recognize the opportunity? The danger is that in this realm the might-have-been may turn out to have been the greater part of our life.

Earlier in this history we saw that the mission of Jesus Christ was as much to the dead as to the living. An individual who has absorbed Christ's loving wisdom will understand the journey through the spheres, will communicate better with higher spiritual beings between lives, and as a result will return to Earth with greater blessings, greater gifts.

After Mercury we pass through the spheres of Venus, Mars, the Sun and Saturn, and then on until finally we are in the presence of God.

You have perhaps been picturing a small disembodied self rising up through vast cosmic spheres – which is how it is conventionally depicted. But according to Steiner, the true picture shows the spirit expanding to fill first the vast sphere enclosed within the moon's orbit, then the Mercury sphere and so on until the self stretches to fill the entire cosmos, as depicted in Leonardo da Vinci's famous drawing of cosmic man. The self is stretched out over the Self. The entire cosmos is then in a sense the body of that self. The planets are the organs in that body, Saturn being the spleen, for example, the sun being the heart and the moon being the brain. At that moment the entire cosmos is encapsulated with it. The self then begins to shrink back down again and into a new physical body. And when we do shrink back down into a human body, the heavenly bodies we have encompassed remain inside us in essence. The Church father Origen wrote: 'Understand that you are a small cosmos within yourself, and that the sun, the moon and the stars are within you.'[10]

To someone like myself, brought up in the Church of England, Steiner's descriptions of the spiritual life and the spiritual worlds are surprising because of their boldness and precision. There is in Steiner no compromise with materialism. He worked out the implications of idealism in every sphere of life – and here also in death.

Jung and his Daemon

All his life Carl Gustav Jung was attuned to the mysterious. As a child he scanned his inner life and his dreams were often more vivid than his waking experiences. Later it seemed to him that the discipline of psychiatry he was helping to devise was in danger of becoming too focused on assessing mental illness from the outside, on categorizing behavioural data. What it lacked, he believed, was a way of talking about inner experience such as he found in reading Emmanuel Swedenborg. Prompted by this reading, Jung began to forge a language based on his own subjective experience and, like Swedenborg, he would come to believe that part of our psyche existed outside time and space.[1]

In 1914, when he was in his thirties and had moved out of Freud's shadow, he began a series of experiments on himself. He was influenced by Ludwig Staudenmaier, a professor of experimental chemistry who published *Magic as an Experimental Science*, based on various self-experiments, including automatic writing.[2]

Jung would describe his project as 'plunging into the darkness of the unknown'. Part of this involved working on his dreams. In one dream he saw the mighty Germanic hero Siegfried appear on the top of a mountain with the first rays of the morning sun. Siegfried then charged down the mountain on a chariot made of human bones. In the dream Jung took a rifle and shot him dead.[3]

At the time, the worst slaughter in human history was taking place on the battlefields of the First World War, almost within earshot of Jung's villa on Lake Lucerne. If Jung had intended to try to block this out while he performed thought experiments, he did not succeed. His house became haunted. His younger daughter saw a ghostly white figure moving through the upstairs rooms, while the elder daughter had her blanket snatched from her bed in the night and on one occasion everyone heard the doorbell ringing when they could all see quite plainly that no one was near it.

In another dream Jung found himself in a dreary sunless land that seemed to him like the land of the dead. He encountered an old man with a long white beard, who identified himself as Elijah. Accompanying the elderly prophet was Salome, a beautiful young woman. Jung was surprised to see these two personalities together. *An odd couple*, he thought. He might have been less surprised if he'd been familiar with the work of his contemporary Rudolf Steiner, who wrote extensively about John the Baptist as the reincarnation of Elijah.

Both Jung and Steiner were hugely influenced by Goethe's mysticism. Jung saw Goethe's *Faust* as being, like the Siegfried legend, prophetic of Germany's fate – a country and a people aspiring, striving idealistically, but doomed to become murderous. In *Faust*, he said, the people of Germany were unconsciously preparing for future catastrophe.

In Goethe's play, Faust causes the murders of Philemon and Baucis, an elderly loving couple. In Greek mythology they are kind and hospitable to gods who visit in disguise. Even though they don't have enough to eat themselves, they sacrifice their only goose. When the gods leave, their humble cottage is transformed into a golden temple, and when they die, they are transformed into two trees lovingly intertwined.

Sometime after he encountered Elijah and Salome, Jung also encountered Philemon. This old man was to step outside his dreams into his waking life and become his mentor, his daemon. As an embodiment of wisdom Philemon surpassed even Elijah.

When he first encountered Philemon in a dream, he saw him sailing through the sky on wings like a kingfisher's. Like Elijah, he was an old bearded man, but he had the horns of a bull and was lame in one leg. He was carrying a bunch of four keys and holding one of them as if ready to open something.

Jung began a painting of Philemon and on one of the days he was engaged in this he was out walking in his garden when he found a

Philemon in profile

dead kingfisher. Kingfishers are rare in that part of the country – Jung wouldn't see another one for another fifty years – and this occurrence was to him an example of what he would later call 'synchronicity'. It was a coincidence by means of which the cosmos was trying to tell him something important.

He came to realize that although he had originally encountered Philemon as part of an inner experience, Philemon had an independent existence and knew many things that he did not. Jung would pace up and down the garden with him, deep in conversation.

When Jung later met a friend of Gandhi's and asked about his guru, the Indian replied that his own guru was Shankaracharya. Jung asked in some astonishment if he meant the eighth-century reformer of Hinduism. The man replied that was indeed who he meant and went on to explain that some gurus lived and taught in spirit form, which helped Jung understand Philemon.

The name, as we have seen, comes from the Greek myths, and Philemon's appearance also suggests Egyptian and Gnostic traditions. Jung would later say he came from Alexandria, where East meets West, and also that he had been mentor to the Buddha, Mani, Jesus Christ and Mohammed – to all who had truly communed with God. Philemon's kingfisher wings also recall the Holy Grail, because Perceval was directed to the Grail Castle by the fishing king who turned out to be its guardian, and Jung would later have a dream in which he crossed the sea to bring back the Holy Grail.

Jung's explorations of the subconscious led him to believe that although Christianity was central to any understanding of the cosmos and its history, Church doctrine had become too narrow to cover the varieties of religious experience. He wrote about 'Paracelsus as a Spiritual Phenomenon'[4] and also explored the Paracelsus-flavoured alchemy of the Rosicrucians. He studied the life of Jesus Christ in terms of the Church's suppressed teachings on astrology, and he explored, too, the chakras of oriental religious practice. He was perhaps as influential as Rudolf Steiner on the flowering of the New Age movement in the twentieth century.

In *The Red Book*, Jung's journals of his dream experiments, he describes coming across Philemon watering the tulips in his garden.[5] He meets Baucis too. She is standing at the kitchen window calmly watching Philemon and his watering can.

The couple are extremely elderly and slow and seem exhausted. Their horizons don't seem to extend beyond the tulips. Then Jung notices a wand and a few books of Kabbalistic and Hermetic magic on the shelves of a cupboard. He calls out to Philemon.

Philemon appears deaf at first but then turns, trembling and asks Jung what he is doing there.

Jung replies that people have told him he knows about magic and asks what Philemon will tell him about it.

The old man says that really there's nothing to tell. When Jung presses him, he replies that he only helps the sick and the poor by exercising some sympathy. That's all it amounts to.

When Jung presses him further, Philemon tells him not to be so impertinent. But Jung persists in trying to draw him out and eventually Philemon says that 'magic is the negative of what one can know', that is 'precisely everything that eludes understanding'.

Still Jung insists on questioning him more closely, but Philemon warns him that he's not really listening. Jung is still trying to use his reason – and that's no good.

Jung begins to feel dizzy and moves down the street, away from the house and garden. There he overhears neighbours say that they have noted that he's been talking with Philemon a long time and so believe that he must know the mysteries . . .

Later Jung has a vision of the old man laughing in his garden at midday. The blue shades of the dead are sighing in the shadows of the house and the trees. Jung sees Philemon talking to a blue shade that is set apart from the other shades, a shade that seems darkened by torment and has blood on its forehead. This, he realizes, is Jesus Christ.

'If you stare into the abyss long enough,' said Nietzsche, 'the abyss stares back at you.' The dialogues of *The Red Book* are clearly influenced by Nietzsche's *Also Sprach Zarathustra*. Jung not only explores the different dimensions of religious experience revealed in different traditions, he wants to confront its dark and difficult sides. He wants to be part of a tradition of thinking about life and the world that is, as he put it himself, 'unpopular, ambiguous and dangerous'.

He wrote: 'The meaning of my existence is that existence has posed a question to me.'

Some people experience life that way. Others choose not to dwell on the mystery. They just accept life and get on with it. I don't suppose those two groups of people will ever learn to see eye to eye.

*   *   *

Jung awoke in his bed. He was in a hotel room. He had retired there after a lecture. He felt a strong pain in his forehead and had an intuition that a patient of his had committed suicide.

Later he investigated and had it confirmed that his patient had indeed shot himself at precisely the moment that he had woken up.

On 11th February 1944, when he was sixty-eight, Jung fell and broke his leg. Complications set in. He had a heart attack and lost consciousness.

He had a dream or a vision in which he found himself floating out of his body over the Arabian desert and the snowy peaks of the Himalayas. Then he descended again and saw a Hindu temple. He understood that all the answers to his questions, his life's work, were to be found in that temple. Then his doctor appeared to him and told him that it was not yet his time to die. He had been sent to bring him back.

On 4th April Jung felt well enough to sit up in bed, but he felt a great burden. He knew from his dream that his friend the doctor had sacrificed himself so that Jung might recover and live to complete his work.

That very day the doctor took to his bed with septicaemia and a few days later he died.

*   *   *

Before I began the research for this book I had been persuaded by a casual reading of several accounts that the apparent sightings of angels in the First World War, such as the angels of Mons, had been inspired by a short story by the occult author Arthur Machen published in the *Evening News*, which many mistakenly read as reportage. But recent reading has convinced me that this cannot be true.

French, Belgian and British troops were being swept aside by the Germans near the town of Mons. With defeat looking likely, a national day of prayer was called, and the churches in Britain were packed. On the field of battle the Germans seemed to have the British at their mercy. As the British retreated, the German cavalry bore down on them, but suddenly the German horses turned, refusing to go any further – like Balaam's ass. Firing stopped on both sides and afterwards many soldiers reported seeing three, four or perhaps five shining white-robed beings floating in the sky, their backs towards the British and facing the Germans.[6]

It was a hot and clear evening, between eight and nine o'clock. The strange lights in mid-air were quite clearly outlined and could not have been a reflection of the moon, as there were no clouds. Officers and soldiers stood watching them for about forty-five minutes.

Key witness statements of these events were recorded and published before 14th September, when Machen's story was published. Besides which, the apparitions in Machen's story are ghostly bowmen, recalling the longbow men who defeated the French knights at Agincourt – very different from the angelic creatures reported by men in the trenches on both sides.

In March 1918 British and Portuguese troops fighting north of Bethune in northern France were again in danger of being wiped out by the Germans. Paris was endangered. Remembering what had happened at Mons, there was another national day of prayer. The Americans, who had in May the previous year decided to send troops, joined in too.

First World War angels

Again the line of advancing German troops suddenly halted and ceased fire. Someone heard a lark sing. What on Earth was going on?

Later German soldiers who had been taken prisoner reported that they had seen a brigade of cavalry advancing towards them, wearing white uniforms and riding white horses. Because of the strange white uniforms, they assumed these must be some colonial forces they had never encountered before. At first they also thought that these cavalrymen were acting very foolishly, charging German positions over open ground. The Germans fired shells and turned their machine guns onto them, but the white cavalry kept coming towards them without one man being taken down, a great and overwhelming tide.

Fátima and the Secrets of the Guardian Angel

Named after Mohammed's daughter, the town of Fátima is situated in central Portugal.

In 1915 an eight year old called Lucia dos Santos was looking after her family's flock of sheep in fields near the town with some friends. After lunch they were saying the rosary when Lucia saw a figure hovering above a tree in the valley some distance away. She would later describe it as whiter than snow and at the same time transparent. The figure hovered over the tree and didn't come any closer or try to communicate with her.

In the next few days Lucia saw the figure twice more. When she told her sisters back home about it, they teased her, saying it must have been a man wrapped up in a sheet pretending to be a ghost.

The following year her cousins, Francisco, then nine years old, and Jacinta, then seven, were allowed to help Lucia look after the flock. One spring morning it started to rain and the three children took shelter in a cave. Afterwards they emerged, had lunch and were playing games when suddenly there was a very strong wind. They looked up and all three saw a figure approaching them over the trees. It was, again, whiter than snow, and in the light of the sun it looked transparent, like a crystal. As it drew closer, they saw that it had the appearance of a boy of about fourteen or fifteen.

'Do not fear!' he said. 'I am the Angel of Peace. Pray with me.'

He knelt and put his forehead on the ground.

The three children followed his example and also repeated his prayer: 'My God, I believe, I adore, I hope, and I love you! I ask for your pardon for those who do not believe, do not adore, do not hope and do not love you.'

(Unlike his cousins, Francisco could not hear what the angel was saying, but he joined in by repeating what the girls said.)

Later that year on a hot summer's day the children were playing in the shade. They were by a well at the bottom of a garden when they suddenly looked up and saw the angel. 'What are you doing?' he asked. He told them to pray constantly and that the Hearts of Jesus and Mary had plans for them. He also told them that he was the guardian angel of Portugal.

In the autumn after the harvest they were again looking after the sheep. They had eaten lunch and were praying in the way the angel had taught them. While they had their foreheads to the ground they suddenly became aware of a great light shining all around them. They looked up and the angel was holding a chalice. Over it a host was suspended, and blood was dropping down into the chalice. They stayed praying after the angel had gone and until it grew dark, when they returned home.

The following year after Mass on Sunday 13th May the three children were once more guarding their flocks when they saw what they at first took to be a flash of lightning. They rounded up their sheep and prepared to return home. Then it occurred to them that there wasn't a cloud in the sky. They saw a second flash and then a lady dressed in white and surrounded by a bright light hovering over a small oak tree. They were only a few feet from her and felt themselves bathed in the light.

'Do not be afraid,' she said. 'I will do you no harm.'

'Where do you come from?' asked Lucia.

'I come from Heaven.'

'What do you want from me?'

The Lady asked her and the other children to return to the same oak tree for seven months in succession, always on the thirteenth day of the month.

'Will I go to heaven too?'

'Yes, you will.'

'And Jacinta?'

'Yes, she also.'

'And Francisco?'

'He will go to heaven too, but he must say many rosaries.'

She asked about a friend called Amelia.

'She will be in Purgatory until the end of the world.' (The implication was, I think, that at the end of the world Amelia would be set free to go to heaven.)

The Lady asked the children if they were willing to offer themselves to God and to bear all the suffering He would send them. They said they were willing and the Lady replied: 'Then you are to have much to suffer, but the grace of God will be your comfort.'

With this last phrase she opened her arms and a light streamed from her which seemed to the children to penetrate to the innermost depths of their being. They fell to their knees and began praying again.

Then as the Lady began to rise in an easterly direction, her way across the sky lit up so that they thought they saw heaven open.

The children decided not to tell anyone what they had seen, but Jacinta couldn't help herself and the news quickly spread. Lucia's family mocked her at first, and then, when she wouldn't be kidded out of her claims, they became worried and tried to make her admit she was lying.

On 13th June the children arrived at the site of the oak, as the Lady had instructed. A small crowd of about fifty gathered too. The Lady appeared and told Lucia that she should learn to read. Lucia asked for a sick boy she knew to be cured and the Lady told her he would be if he converted within the year. She also told Lucia that she would soon take her sister and brother from her.

'Am I to remain here all alone?'

The Lady told her no, she would never forsake her and 'my Immaculate Heart will be your refuge'. She showed Lucia a vision of her heart encircled by thorns.

On 13th July witnesses heard Lucia cry out. The Lady was showing the children a vision of hell and terrifying demons in the shape of unknown animals. She said that if people did not cease offending God, then although the present war would end, a worse war would break out in the pontificate of Pius XI. She also called for 'the consecration of Russia to my Immaculate Heart', warning that if this did not happen, errors would be spread throughout the world. (This has been widely interpreted as a reference to the spread of communism and atheism.)

The local Church authorities were at first hostile, suggesting that the phenomena might be work of the Devil. City officials threatened the children with prison. Adults were by turns threatening and then flattering when they became anxious to learn any secrets that might have been revealed.

On 13th July the Lady also gave Lucia what later came to be known as the Third Secret of Fátima.

The Vatican's report on this secret was published in 1984, carrying a commentary by Cardinal Ratzinger, who later became pope. According to this report, the secret seemed to foretell the assassination of a pope. There have always been rumours that there are other elements of the Third Secret that have been held back, however, including revelations about the imminent incarnation of the Antichrist.[1]

After she had been told the secrets, Lucia asked for a miracle to help people believe.

The children were unable to keep their appointment with the Lady on 13th August, because the authorities briefly imprisoned them and even subjected them to threats of torture and death by boiling oil.

It is estimated that on 13th October between 70,000 and 100,000 people arrived hoping to see a miracle. Expectation had reached fever pitch and Lucia's mother said she was worried the children might be attacked if no miracle took place.

It was a day of torrential rain, and photos show a sea of umbrellas. The Lady appeared to the children and told them that the war was going to end and that the soldiers would soon be returning to their homes. In Lucia's account, the muddy conditions did not prevent people from kneeling. She asked people to close their umbrellas. Then the children saw a vision of the Lady with St Joseph and the child Jesus, both of whom traced the sign of the cross, blessing the world.

Suddenly this vision disappeared and Lucia felt impelled to cry out, 'Look at the sun!'

People found they were able to look directly at the sun, which was at that moment appearing from behind the clouds. They found they could continue to do so as it grew brighter and brighter and suddenly began to spin round like a coin spun on its edge. This was seen as many as seventy miles away, with some witnesses describing it as looking like a Catherine wheel. Photographs show crowds gazing up at this miracle, their faces and bodies bathed in an intense light. When they looked at one another they saw that they were bathed in the colours of the rainbow, constantly shifting and morphing. There were cries of 'Miracle!'

Suddenly the sun seemed to hurtle towards the Earth. A cry went up. Was this the end of the world?

But then 'the dance of the sun' suddenly stopped and it returned to its normal place in the sky. People discovered that though they had been soaked a few moments previously, they were now bone dry, and so too were the trees, the plants and the earth.

Dr José Maria de Almeida Garrett, a professor at the Faculty of Sciences of Coimbra in Portugal, witnessed the phenomena that day and later wrote an account of them. He described how three times a thin column of bluish smoke rose two metres above the children's heads then dissolved. Then there was uproar. Like everyone else, he turned away from the children to look at the sun, which he described as a clear sharp-edged disc, neither veiled nor dim as it would have been if seen through mist or clouds. It was spinning round on itself. He thought it remarkable that he could look at it without damaging the retina.

Then suddenly there was another cry from the crowd as the sun turned red, seemed to 'loosen itself from the firmament' and descend as if it was going to 'rush us with its huge and fiery weight'.

Here then we have a miracle witnessed by thousands, a miracle on the scale of the miracles in the story of Moses.

For non-Catholics, there may be uncomfortable elements in these events. The Lady's aim seems to be promoting Catholic dogma. At Lourdes, this does not seem to have been the Lady's main aim in appearing to Bernadette, but at Fátima, the Lady emphasizes the saying of the rosary and the importance of evading hell, as well as the doctrine of the Immaculate Heart. We may be reminded of Catherine of Siena, a great and very holy saint, surrounded by miracles, who was also a political player. Catherine believed that an important part of her divinely inspired mission was to push for another crusade – which, from a modern perspective, was an enterprise fraught with moral ambiguities. Perhaps it's helpful to remember that however extraordinary the individuals who are the mediators of these spiritual messages may be, they are human.

Some writers have seen in the Marian appearances of the late nineteenth and early twentieth century an impulse which is more sympathetic to modern sensibility – as a spiritual source of the feminist movement.

*　　　　*　　　　*

The boy who would become known as Padre Pio was born in 1887 into a large family of illiterate peasant farmers in southern Italy.

He began to experience visions early. He would later refer to his guardian angel as 'the companion of my infancy' and explain that as an infant he had assumed everyone could see angels as clearly as he could. At the age of five he promised to devote his life to St Francis of Assisi.

In 1910 he was ordained as a priest and in the same year he received the stigmata, as St Francis had done, the wounds of Jesus Christ on the cross appearing in his hands and feet. Some witnesses said that these wounds, the width of a coin, went all the way through his hands and feet and that light could sometimes be seen through them. Later Padre Pio prayed, not for the pain of his wounds to be taken away, but for them to be made invisible, because he was embarrassed by the marks and felt ashamed. When his prayers weren't answered, he took to wearing gloves on his hands and stockings on his feet.

During the time of the visions of the children at Fátima, he was called up for military service. In 1916 an Italian general called Cadorna was relieved of his command after a catastrophic defeat. He was in his tent, holding a gun to his head, when he had a vision of a priest, who told him to put his gun down. After the war the old soldier was visiting a monastery where he recognized Padre Pio as the priest who had appeared in his tent.

Padre Pio was discharged from the army in 1918. In August of that year he was hearing confessions when he had a vision in which Jesus Christ appeared to him with a wound in his side – and at the same time he received the supernatural gift called the transverberation. He would later write about the terror and pain he felt as a long sharp metal blade was thrown into him. He thought he was dying. For two days it felt as if his entrails were being ripped apart.

Some of his supporters said that he lost about a cupful of blood every day from the wound in his side. Some said later that his blood smelled of violets and roses.

Not only this, but he was often attacked by demons during the night. In the morning he would appear severely beaten, sometimes bleeding from the mouth, nose or forehead. Sometimes the Devil appeared to him as a black cat, and sometimes a sensuous young woman who would dance.

'If the Devil is making an uproar,' said Padre Pio, 'that is an excellent sign.' He believed that his path to God was through suffering.

The Devil also appeared to him as a tall, thin, elegant man who said he had come to confess but kept equivocating. Eventually Padre Pio challenged him to say 'Live Jesus, Live Mary!' and at this point the thin man vanished in a flash of fire.

Padre Pio later wrote of the dangers warned of by St Paul: that 'the Artificer' may appear in the guise of an Angel of Light (Corinthians 11.14).[2]

He quickly became famous as a confessor because he demonstrated on many occasions that he could read the minds of those who came to him. If he saw that people were being dishonest or insincere, perhaps holding sins back or not intending to reform, he would become angry and insult them, sometimes even strike them.

He was seen to levitate and performed many healing miracles, including curing a girl of blindness. He also exorcised demons. He said that his most important work would begin after his death and that he would not enter Paradise until he had 'seen the last of my spiritual children enter'.

By the time he died in 1968, he had made many enemies, even within the Church, and was accused of being both a fraud and a psychopath. In 2002, however, he was canonized by Pope John Paul II, who had visited him as a young man.

*　　　　　*　　　　　*

Padre Pio advised people to send their guardian angels to him if they had a message or a petition for him. A lawyer called Antilio de Sanctis told him of a wonderful thing that had happened. He had fallen asleep at the wheel yet managed to drive his car for twenty-seven miles without accident. Padre Pio told him, 'Your guardian angel drove your car.'

Padre Pio talked about his own guardian angel, saying that it would often help relieve his pain. We have seen that Christians have talked about their guardian angels since *The Shepherd of Hermas*, written in the first or second century. There was a revival of appreciation and understanding of guardian angels in the twentieth century, when their qualities and deeds began to be described in new ways.

Pius XI told a group of visitors that he prayed to his guardian angel every morning and evening, and often again during the day if his work became hard. He told a diplomatic envoy for the Vatican about a 'marvellous secret':

Send your guardian angel ahead of you to smooth the way, to sort out difficulties, and help establish an understanding before you get there. Ask your angel to speak to your interlocutor's guardian angel, to ask them to put the other person at ease, to understand. By this means we can establish communication with anyone at any time . . .

When you arrive in a new neighbourhood, ask your angel to talk to the guardian angels of your new neighbours . . .

Our guardian angel can also help us in our relationship with God, teach us to be more intimate.

*   *   *

The most detailed information on the qualities and role of the guardian angel are given by Lorna Byrne. According to Lorna, your guardian angel never leaves you during your life on Earth. It is attracted to you and bound to you by the spark of divinity that resides within you. 'Your angel is the gatekeeper of your soul,' Lorna says, and sometimes it allows other angels and loved ones in heaven in to help you.

Hitler and the Hungarian Angels

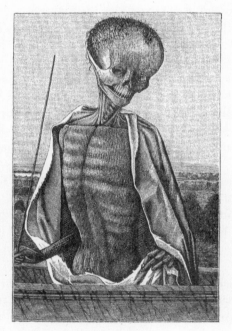

Doctor Death (miniature from a sixteenth-century Book of Hours).

When the tribes of northern Europe saw Odin leading the wild hunt across the sky and heard the deafening clamour of the ride of the dead, the snorting black horses and the baying of black hounds, it was to them a bad omen. In the late nineteenth century Richard Wagner revived the spirit of the wild hunt in the Ride of the Valkyries. He said, 'I am convinced there are Universal Currents of thought . . .' He believed that those who knew how to tune into these currents would receive cosmic inspiration.[1]

Hitler's table talk shows that he too was charged with a sense of destiny. He believed he had miraculously escaped death on many occasions during the First World War because he was being protected by higher powers. He reported that once he had been eating dinner with comrades when a voice told him to get up and walk twenty yards along the trench, which he did, carrying his mess tin with him. As he sat down, there was massive flash and a bang. A shell had hit the spot where he had been sitting and all his comrades had been killed.

'I carry out the commands that providence commanded me to do.' He said he would do nothing unless a voice – which he believed to be the voice of providence – told him what to do. He would procrastinate, spend hours walking alone, waiting to hear this inner voice, and in the days of his rise his opponents considered the timing and effectiveness of his decisions uncanny.

'The Superman is living amongst us now!' he said in private. 'He is here . . . intrepid and cruel.' In public he proclaimed: 'Providence has given me a mission to reunite the German Peoples . . . to restore my homeland to the German Reich.' His studies in occultism, the philosophy of Nietzsche and the music of Wagner deepened this sense of destiny. The English occult writer Houston Stewart Chamberlain, Wagner's son-in-law, acclaimed him as the German Messiah. Dark-side idealism was leading to expectations of a Hegelian hero who could bend the world to his will.[2]

There are many accounts of Hitler's charisma. It seems that ordinarily the atmosphere surrounding him was surreptitious, insincere. Herman Rauschning, a supporter who later turned against him, described it as 'a reeking miasma of furtive, unnatural sexuality . . . false sentiments and hidden lusts. Nothing in this man's surroundings is natural and genuine.' But it is clear from other witnesses that when Hitler spoke in public something extraordinary happened. 'Listen to Hitler,' said Gregor Strasser, another supporter, '. . . a gentleman with a comic moustache turns into an archangel.' Joseph Goebbels wrote excitedly of his first encounter with Hitler the orator that he felt as if he were newly born, that he knew where his life was leading him, that he was intoxicated and that Hitler's eyes were 'two great blue stars'.

Meanwhile Rudolf Steiner was criticizing the appropriation of an ancient symbol, the swastika, for political purposes: 'Be certain that these people who are now bringing this sign to Central Europe – *they know exactly what they are doing. This sign works.*' If there was one man alive capable of understanding the spiritual realities behind Hitler's charisma – the identity of the beings behind him – it was Rudolf Steiner.

Steiner spoke out repeatedly against the rising tide of anti-Semitism, calling it an 'expression of spiritual inferiority' that showed contempt for the whole world's cultural achievement, in which the Jews had played such a central role, and 'the opposite of a sound way of thinking'.

Hitler attacked Steiner in the press as a friend of the Jews, and his supporters called for a war on him. When a lecture was disrupted by right-wing thugs, Steiner cancelled the rest of his tour, and shortly afterwards stopped giving public lectures altogether. Libellous statements circulated, accusing him of black magic involving the sexual abuse of his supporters. It was in this atmosphere that his headquarters, his architectural masterpiece the Goethaneum, was burned to the ground in an arson attack.

In 1938 Germany annexed Austria and Hitler was driven into Vienna to the acclaim of ecstatic crowds. That night would come to be known as 'the night of the terror', as a brutal round-up of the city's large Jewish population began. Some 70,000 would be arrested and a new concentration camp, Mauthausen, was founded on the banks of the Danube.

Later Hitler would have the Spear of Longinus, which had been in the treasure house of the Hofburg Museum in Vienna, transported back to Germany, amid great celebrations at its return to the Fatherland. It remained on proud display in St Catherine's church in Nuremberg until the spirits that had been empowering Hitler deserted him and he faced defeat.

*　　　　*　　　　*

Gitta was the daughter of a Hungarian army officer and an Austrian mother. She worked in a graphic art studio with a married couple called Hanna and Joseph. When the Second World War broke out and Budapest became a dangerous place for Jews, all three moved to a house in a village not far from the city, together with Lilli, who was Jewish, like Hanna and Joseph.

On 25th June 1943, Hanna began receiving messages. When she began to relay these to Gitta, she explained, 'It is not I who will speak to you.'

It became clear that Hanna was hearing angels. Later Gitta began to sense the presence of her own inner guide, who helped her to understand the messages and ask the right questions.

The teachings they were given were often harsh. The two young women were reproved for the depth of their ignorance by the angels. Humans, said Hanna's angel, don't even *know* a single cell of their bodies. Later the women were told how every tiny cell in our bodies can join in the process of prayer.

A theology emerged from these angelic messages that seemed to look back to Mani and Christian Rosencreutz. The women were told that ecstasy was a presentiment of the weightlessness that would come when our bodily matter was transformed. As in *The Chymical Wedding,* they were told to look forward to the sacred wedding of heaven and Earth. When that happened, the angels told them, death itself would die.

The angels talked about transformation in terms of seven spheres and seven inner gates – again like ancient mystical teachings. New light, they said, could only come when the seven flames were lit inside us, one after the other.

Some of the teachings are extraordinary:

'Only when given to the hungry does bread become bread. Matter is only meaningful in relation to human desires.'
'If we listen in the right way, even a stone will speak to us.'

The angels gave the friends a perspective that took in wide sweeps of cosmic history, explaining that each of us has a self that had been in the process of being formed since the beginning of time.

There were warnings of a storm approaching, too. The city was described as a place of cursed dust. A cry of anguish was coming from the cosmos.

In March 1944 Hungary was overrun by German troops. In April apartments in Budapest belonging to Jews were confiscated and their inhabitants herded into the ghetto. By May Jews were required to wear the yellow star.

'Each of you will be given exactly what is needed,' said Hanna's angel. But in June her husband Joseph was packed into a cattle truck and deported.

With the help of a Catholic priest, Gitta requisitioned an old cloister, turning it into a factory for making military uniforms. She pretended that her aim was to help the army in which her father had served with great distinction, but really the cloister was intended as a shelter for approximately a hundred Jewish women and their children. The gamble was that because of the patriotic nature of the enterprise, the increasingly powerful anti-Semitic factions would not realize that the women making the uniforms were Jews.

Gitta and Hanna continued to meet after work for their dialogues with the angels, but the sound of gunfire was heard as local Nazis grew in confidence. Gangs stalked the streets. Women were at risk. There were rumours of Jew-hunts and torture chambers.

Rescuing angel

In one of the last messages, the angels spoke of gathering in the old stars and sowing new ones.

The local Nazis were beginning to voice suspicions that something subversive was going on at the cloister. Thanks to her Austrian mother, Gitta was fluent in German and she used this to persuade German soldiers to protect them from the locals. She claimed she had authority from a local German commander and something in her upper-class manner was persuasive for a while. But on 5th November 1944, 'Father' Kun, an infamous former priest, called her bluff. He arrived at the head of a mob, dressed in black priest's robes with guns and knives stuffed into a red belt. His followers broke down the gates at the front of the factory. Some of the women took advantage of a temporary confusion to flee into the nearby forest, but seventy-two women remained. They were lined up and marched away. Gitta was knocked down, kicked and spat upon. Father Kun said he would arrange for her to have 'special treatment'.

Hanna had always told Gitta that she must be the one to survive in order to take the angels' message to the world. Now Gitta found out that Hanna and Lilli had not been among those who had taken the chance to flee into the forest. They were being taken to Ravensbrück concentration camp.

After the war Gitta was told by a witness that one of the SS guards, while shaving Hanna's head, noticed her Aryan blonde hair and her blue eyes, and asked, 'What are *you* doing here?'

'I'm a Jew,' she replied.

Gitta did manage to keep her black notebooks containing the descriptions of the angelic conversations with her and intact. In 1983 she was asked by the C. G. Jung Institute in Zurich to talk about her experiences in public. She said she was persuaded because she had been very moved to read about Jung's own experiences with his spiritual guide Philemon.[3]

We may perhaps catch an echo of different spiritual guardians working with people in different countries and different cultural traditions and religions – but with a common aim.

The That Without Which

There are certain similarities between the lives of Presidents Lincoln and Kennedy, and certain strange coincidences in the circumstances of their assassinations. Both were athletic men, over six feet tall. Both were boat captains, and of course both were concerned with what today we call race relations. Lincoln was elected to Congress in 1846, Kennedy in 1946. Lincoln was elected President in 1860, Kennedy in 1960 – and in both cases the legality of their election was contested. Both were friends with Illinois Democrats called Adlai E. Stevenson, both knew a Doctor Charles Taft and both had friends and advisers called Billy Graham. Both remarked several times on how easy it would be to shoot a president. Both were shot in the head on a Friday and were cradled by their wives. Both their killers were detained by officers called Baker, and both killers were themselves killed by a single shot from a Colt revolver before they could be brought to trial. John Wilkes Booth was born in 1839, and Lee Harvey Oswald was born in 1939. Lincoln and Kennedy were both succeeded by southern Democrats named Johnson.

The two great scientists of the soul in the twentieth century were Jung and Rudolf Steiner. What would they have said?

Coincidences are not properties of events in the material world but of human observations of those events. If you looked at the two sequences of events stripped of any human descriptions of them, including for example the way we choose to measure time, there would be no meaningful similarities.

So these two sequences of historical events show remarkable coincidences only when looked at in a *mindful* way. In order for a coincidence to occur, a mind has to *make* the connection. In other words, coincidences happen in the interweaving textures of mental lives over time. To narrow the focus further, coincidences also depend on linguistic connections. A coincidence would not occur in isolation from language and only achieves meaning by its place in a net of other words.

Like many of the phenomena described in this book, coincidences are much easier to account for from the point of view of idealism than they are from the point of view of materialism. If unembodied but intelligent beings such as the angels of the planets and constellations are gradually helping to shape history, if great world-weaving thoughts move through many minds at once, as idealism proposes, then it is no surprise that these patterns are traced or that we find ourselves drawn by a sense of cosmic interconnectedness.

We see circular patterns in the great patterns of history and we see them too in our own lives. Most people have had the experience of ducking out of one of life's challenges only to see it come round again in a different form. We can see these patterns in the great events of our lives and also in small everyday ways. I recommend the films of the Thai director Apichatpong Weerasethakul as beautifully informed by idealism as a philosophy of life. In *Syndromes and a Century* the camera moves with a circular movement around a statue of the Buddha in the grounds of a hospital, then we see a group of nurses walking down a corridor and one pauses to tie up a shoelace. Now we see a group of interns, one of whom also pauses to tie a shoelace, and afterwards we return to circling the Buddha. In this apparently trivial coincidence we are being shown something magical: the same thought moving through different bodies.

*   *   *

Earlier we saw spiritual traditions stream down from the mountains of Tibet and flow all over the world. Historically, Tibet's leaders have been spiritual leaders. The most famous is, of course, the Dalai Lama, but there are others, including the Panchen Lama and the Karmapa. The Karmapa is the leader of the oldest of the four main schools of

Tibetan Buddhism, whilst the Dalai Lama and the Panchen Lamas are the leaders of the newer and more prominent reforming schools.

All these leaders are said to be *bodhisattvas*. This means that they have achieved enlightenment but chosen to return to Earth to help the rest of humanity awaken too. They are also so spiritually evolved that they can *choose* their next incarnation. A Karmapa leaves instructions on how the child who is to be his next incarnation is to be found, how he is to be recognized. Then, when he dies, his followers set off in accordance with those instructions, wise men in search of a divine child. The chosen children are always precocious, often learning to read and write early and showing remarkable understanding of Buddhist doctrine. They often have memories of their previous incarnation, recognizing people and places they used to know.

The supernatural abilities that come with spiritual development are called *siddhis* (parallel to 'the gifts of the spirit' in the New Testament or the signs of a 'friend of God', according to Mohammed).

There seems to be much more emphasis on such abilities in Tibetan Buddhism than in most streams of Christianity. If the Dalai Lama has become the foremost political figure among the Tibetan leaders, the Karmapa has traditionally been the leader most closely associated with miraculous powers. Traditionally, Karmapas were able not only to heal the sick, exorcise demons, prophesy, fly through the air and read minds, but could also summon great spiritual beings to appear in the sky in front of vast crowds and cause the heavens to rain petals. They could also sometimes leave footprints and handprints in solid rock.[1]

In the fifteenth century the Chinese emperor gave the Karmapa as a gift the Vajra Crown – the Black Hat – as a symbol of his authority. Adorned with rubies and sapphires, the Black Hat was a physical representation of a spiritual crown that those with 'second sight' could see adorning the Karmapa's head.

The sixteenth Karmapa was heard reciting *om mani padme hung* in his mother's womb. Born in 1923, he took seven steps and spoke as soon as he had left the womb, like the Buddha. As a youth he rushed into a nest of deadly snakes and danced with them wrapped around his body. On another occasion he tied a knot in a guard's sword as easily as if it were string.

In 1950 Tibet was invaded by China. The intention, according to China, was to sweep away the old feudal, theocratic regime that had kept the peasants in ignorance, superstition and poverty since the Middle Ages. Accompanied by the Karmapa, the Dalai Lama went to see Mao Tse-Tung. 'Religion is poison,' said Mao. At least they knew where they stood . . .

In 1959 the Dalai Lama fled Tibet disguised as a soldier, and the Karmapa followed a few months later. At first the Karmapa stayed in India. His host, the king of Bhutan, was unable to have children. He complained of this to the Karmapa, who casually replied that his wish would soon be granted, and he was proved right, much to the king's delight.

Pilgrims began to come from Europe and America to visit the Karmapa. They reported that they had seen his third eye shining, that he could induce a mystical experience in other people with just a click of fingers, or that he could open a pilgrim's third eye by the touching of a forehead.

The Karmapa began to travel more widely. At a gathering in London when he ceremonially adorned himself with the Black Hat, it seemed to everyone there that he shone with such a bright light that it filled the whole hall. This light only ceased when he put the Black Hat back in its box. He travelled to New York, too, and there were rumours that he was occasionally drunk at speaking engagements and that he slept with some of his female disciples.

When he fell ill with cancer in 1976 and was hospitalized, the doctors were amazed by measurements which seemed to show that he was able to control his metabolism at will.

People in the West were becoming increasingly fascinated by Eastern religion. Tibetan Buddhism of the school of the Karmapa promised an open access to the supernatural which was attractive to many at a time when Christianity seemed boring by comparison. Apologetic, prevaricating and lukewarm, Christianity seemed to offer only a very limited experience of the supernatural, either within the confines of a conservative Catholic Church or in extreme evangelical groups, which from the outside at least looked equally narrow and controlling.[2]

The cutting-edge thinkers in liberal Christianity – elements within the Anglican and Episcopal Churches in particular – were part of a movement called Christian-realists or 'Christian atheists'. They conceded that the scientific materialist view of the cosmos must be right and that therefore there is no such thing as the supernatural. Religious language in the Bible and elsewhere that appears to be describing supernatural events is symbolic, they said, poetic expressions of psychological states or assertions of moral attitudes, or even descriptions of events in a parallel universe that have no effect at all on the material universe. They talked a lot about the value and importance of 'spiritual experience', but tended to use this phrase to mean a warm fuzzy feeling of at-oneness with the universe, rather than in its original and more useful meaning of an experience of spirits, of unembodied intelligence. More and more well-meaning clergymen admitted that if they were honest, they didn't really believe in very much at all. These thinkers included John Robinson, an Anglican bishop and author of *Honest to God*, Don Cupitt and David Jenkins, then Bishop of Durham, who hit the headlines when he said he didn't believe in the physical resurrection of Jesus Christ.

I have written this book to show that while we should try to reconcile religion with reason, what it cannot be reconciled with is materialism. If you concede that matter came before mind, then you have conceded so much that there is nothing left worth defending. Idealism is the *sine qua non*, the 'that without which' religion cannot survive. If matter came first, if matter is not *meant*, if the only meanings the cosmos has are the ones we invent for it, then the great claims of religion are false. If we came from nothing, the world religions are worth nothing.

The irony here is that the version of science that Robinson, Cupitt and the others gave way to – what I sometimes think of as the Meccano model of the universe – is, well, very 1950s. It is no longer the version that cutting-edge scientists believe in.[3] The universe that leading physicists are exploring today has uncertainty as its major principle. Objects in it can be in two places at the same time, affect each other's movements at opposite ends of the cosmos and interact with the human mind.

Quantum mechanics describes what happens at the smallest level. We now know that conscious observation affects the behaviour of subatomic particles. Posited in Schrödinger's famous 'Cat in a box' thought experiment, it was demonstrated experimentally by the 'delayed choice experiment' proposed by John Wheeler, the father of the hydrogen bomb, in 1978 and carried out in practice in an experiment devised at Maryland University in 1984.[4]

So there is a cat in the box, but there is also an elephant in the room. If we can affect the behaviour of matter at a subatomic level, then why can't we affect it at a human level, or even at a cosmic level? If at the level of an electron, why not at the level of a football or of a star? Or the universe as a whole? This, says the physicist Roger Penrose, is a profound question to which science does not yet have an answer. 'Quantum mechanics,' he says, 'makes no distinction between single particles and complicated systems of particles.'

Experiments conducted on Apollo 11 have demonstrated that in certain circumstances human senses are fine-tuned enough to register a single subatomic particle.[5] Since we also now know that 'entangled particles' have partners whose behaviour they may influence instantly over intergalactic distances, we can begin to see how it might be possible to envisage the human mind exercising a power over matter over vast distances *in terms which are acceptable to science*. Perhaps intelligent observation had, or has, a role in the formation of the universe? Perhaps the universe suits us so well because our intelligence has helped to form it? Perhaps the cosmos is ordered and continues to run according to natural laws because of human observations?

John Wheeler put it like this: 'If the universe is necessary to the creation of life, could it be that life is necessary to the creation of the universe? Do acts of observership, in the quantum sense, have anything to do with bringing about that which appears before us?'

*   *   *

Imprisoned by the Chinese for his outspoken criticisms of their policies, the tenth Panchen Lama was released in 1977 and in January the following year he was allowed to return home, where he lived under house arrest. But in 1989 he again protested about the Chinese occupation of Tibet. A week later he mysteriously fell ill and died.

The sixteenth Karmapa had died a few years earlier, in 1981, and the reincarnations of both the Panchen Lama and the Karmapa have been disputed. The seventeenth Karmapa was found by following instructions that the sixteenth Karmapa had left, according to custom. He was a boy from a nomadic community – herders of yaks, sheep and goats. His mother had dreamt of three cranes the night before his birth. The sound of a conch shell had filled the valley to herald his arrival on Earth, as the sixteenth Karmapa had predicted. The boy had told his parents that men were going to arrive to take him away the day before they appeared on the horizon. They took him to a monastery to be educated, and he was enthroned as the seventeenth Karmapa in 1992. But meanwhile some of the sixteenth Karmapa's former supporters claimed that the notes that had been used to iden-tify his reincarnation were a forgery, and in 1994 they put forward a rival candidate.

As for the Panchen Lama, it is the sacred duty of the Dalai Lama to find the boy in whom the next Panchen Lama will incarnate. In 1995 the Dalai Lama declared that he had found the eleventh incarnation, a six-year-old boy called Gedhun Choaekyi Nymai: 'I am fully con-vinced of the unanimous outcome of all these recognition procedures performed strictly in accordance with our tradition.'

But the Chinese government repudiated this identification, calling it arbitrary and illegal. They put forward a new candidate, and the child identified by the Dalai Lama was arrested and, together with his family, flown to Beijing. There they disappeared.

The Dalai Lama has expressed anxiety that the boy may have been 'killed, drugged or put in some asylum where he will be rendered use-less'. The Chinese government has refused to answer questions about the boy asked by the United Nations, Amnesty International and Human Rights Watch, only affirming that he is being held at a secret location 'for his own safety'. Meanwhile the Chinese government has enthroned their own choice as the eleventh Panchen Lama.[6]

In 2002 the seventeenth Karmapa went to sit under the tree where the Buddha had achieved enlightenment and spoke to the crowd who had gathered to greet him. 'A lot of you were fortunate enough to meet the sixteenth Karmapa,' he said. Then he added, with a gentle smile, 'Unfortunately I didn't meet him . . .'

When Mao said he was rescuing the people of Tibet from religion, from medieval superstition, he was harking back to the Marxist theory of religion: that it is a ruse invented by ruling élites to frighten the people into submission. I like to think of this as the 'Scooby Do' theory of religion. Marx took Hegel's philosophy of a Cosmic Mind working its purpose out by dialectically refining itself in its encounters with opposing forces and adapted it to materialistic ends. Stalin and Mao were titans of materialism, and scientific materialism is itself a machine that has had a deadening effect on humanity in this life and also in the next. Entering the spirit worlds with little idea of what to expect, spirits do not realize where they are. Their souls are slow to dissolve. We are surrounded by shades as never before.[7]

According to Lorna Byrne, on the other hand, more and more people are developing the ability to see and hear spiritual beings of light.

*   *   *

In the 1960s Christian missionaries reported seeing shining white beings in the African jungle. Then, during the Jeunesse Rebellion in the Congo, armed rebels were menacing a missionary school containing some 200 pupils. The school was protected by only a couple of soldiers and a flimsy fence. The teachers knew that rebels intended to massacre them all – children as well as teachers. There were several hundred in the approaching rebel army, and their only defence against them, the teachers believed, was prayer.

But as the rebel soldiers advanced on the compound, the missionaries suddenly saw them turn round and run away. The same thing happened on three successive days, and then the danger passed.

Sometime later, one of the rebels was injured and brought to the hospital attached to the school. Asked why the rebel soldiers had run away, he explained that they had seen the compound surrounded and protected by an army of soldiers in white uniforms.

What would well-meaning clergymen like John Robinson and Don Cupitt make of this?

In 1991 a committed Christian called Hope Price was at a conference when she heard God speaking in her heart, telling her to write a book about angels. She began by inserting requests for people to send her accounts of their experiences in Christian magazines. Local radio and a local newspaper picked up on this and soon she was receiving hundreds of letters through the post. They were collected in a book called *Angels: True Stories of How They Touch Our Lives* (Guidepost Books, 1993). The following two stories are typical:

In the 1960s Joan Thomassen was driving from Lowestoft to Ipswich when suddenly she heard a loud voice shout 'Put your foot on the brake!' As a result she avoided a lorry coming round the next bend in the middle of the road.

In 1986 Kerry Cole was with a friend out shopping with her pram and as she stopped to look in a shop window she inadvertently let go of the pram. She turned round horrified to see the pram rolling off the kerb into a busy road. As she threw herself towards it a tall man in a coat suddenly appeared and blocked the pram.

'O praise the Lord!'

She turned to look at her friend, and when a moment later she looked back the man had vanished into thin air.

At the height of the Troubles in Northern Ireland a young soldier was on patrol in the notoriously dangerous Falls Road area of Belfast. At 2.45 in the morning he was in a courtyard adjacent to a Catholic church when he saw a light above it that gradually took on the shape of the Virgin Mary, her arms stretched out lovingly towards him. His mate came into the courtyard and saw the apparition too, and the first young man became convinced that Mary had appeared to him in this way to save him from Hell.[8]

*　　　　　*　　　　　*

In the later chapters of this book we have seen a modern demi-god in the figure of Napoleon, a thinker who, like Socrates, was guided by his daemon in Jung, and people who, like Lot, were guided by angels in times of extreme peril in Gitta and Hanna. Great spiritual beings intervened in the First World War as they did at the siege of Troy, and they appeared to Bernadette Soubirous as they once appeared to St Francis. Prophetic vision came to Abraham Lincoln as it earlier came to Constantine the Great. In the miracle of the sun at Fátima a large-scale miracle was witnessed by thousands, like the miracles attending Moses. In Rudolf Steiner and Lorna Byrne we have modern-day mystics who share a vision of the way the world works that is the same as the visions recorded by Ibn Arabi, Paracelsus and Jacob Boehme.

Not many people today see angels and other great spiritual beings continuously as Lorna Byrne sees them. It maybe that no one else has her abilities. But large numbers of people have had some spiritual experience. A survey conducted in Britain in 1987 by David Hay and Gordon Heald showed that 55 per cent of people had recognized meaningful patterning in their experience, 37 per cent had experienced prayers being answered, 25 per cent had been aware of the presence of the dead, 25 per cent had been aware of an evil presence and 38 per cent had been aware of the presence of God. No questions about angels were asked.[9]

An online survey conducted by the Bible Society and ICM in the UK in 2010 reported that 31 per cent believed in angels, 29 per cent believed in guardian angels and 5 per cent believed they had personally seen or heard an angel.[10]

In America the statistics are much higher. In 2008, *Time* magazine reported a survey showing that 69 per cent of Americans believed in angels, 46 per cent believed in guardian angels and 32 per cent claimed to have had a direct encounter with an angel.[11]

According to sociologists Christopher Bader, Cason Mencken and Joseph Baker, following a survey of 1,700 respondents in 2008, 55 per cent of Americans claimed they had been personally saved from harm by their guardian angel, while a 2007 survey showed that the percentage of people in America who claimed direct personal experience of an angel varied according to variety of faith: 57 per cent of Catholics, 66 per cent of Evangelical Protestants and 10 per cent of Jews![12]

Modern history is secular history. We have been brought up to believe that there have been no great eruptions of spiritual power, no 'supernatural' events in modern times. I have written this book partly to show that isn't true.

More important, perhaps, we have been brought up to screen out our own personal experience of manifestations of spiritual power.

In the war between idealism and materialism, is materialism about to carry the day?

Lorna Byrne and the Mysticism of Everyday Life

'Let him who seeks continue seeking until he finds.
When he finds, he will become troubled. When he
becomes troubled, he will be astonished, and
he will rule over All.'

Jesus, The Gospel of Thomas

'The earth will become sun.'

Tommaso Campanella

'God is revealed in the deep feelings of sensitive souls.'

Abraham Isaac Kook

Biting winds from the North will cover everything with ice, and the frost
giants will rejoice. The Earth will become wild and barren, and the sky will
darken. The World Tree will grow rotten, gnawed by maggots. Wolves will
emerge from the Iron Wood, becoming braver and preying on humans, and
starving mothers will eat their babies. The Sun and Moon will be seen no
more and then at the sound of the cock's crow the World Tree will tremble
and Heimarr, watchman of the gods, will sound his horn for the last time.
The great serpent will break free and arise from the deep, and slither towards
the field of battle, and guided by Loki the giants will come over the moun-
tains.

There was a time long, long ago when Loki used to take nothing seriously, but evil grew in him until now he is nothing but evil. The other gods realized too late, and the world is full of his evil. Hela, Queen of Hell, will spring out of the ground, leading the hounds of hell on a leash, and behind them the hosts of hell will march and assemble on the plains where the last battle will take place. The whole of creation will shake with the marching of the giants.

The giant Fenris wolf will break free of the magic chain.

Wearing a golden helmet, Odin will lead the gods out of Asgard and over the rainbow bridge, which will crumble and fall once they have passed over it. On the field of battle Fenris will open his mouth so wide that it encompasses the sky and the earth and the All-devourer will swallow the All-father, the first god to die. Thor will slay the great serpent, but the red-bearded one will then stagger nine paces and fall, dying from the venom that has flooded out of the serpent's wounds. The leader of the Fire giants will send flames all around the World Tree so that it will be consumed and darkness will come like a thief in the night.

Lorna Byrne was born to a poor family in Dublin in the early 1950s. Their house, which also served as her father's bicycle repair shop, was ramshackle enough to collapse when she was a child, and it left them homeless.

But right from the start, Lorna was able to see disembodied beings. Her brother, Christopher, died in infancy, and yet he became her playmate. She also saw angels. They tended to have a human appearance and look as if they were dressed in a variety of radiant colours. They had a bright light shining inside them and wings. Their feet did not touch the ground.[1] She assumed everyone could see them too and says now that all children see spiritual beings, at least up until about the time they learn to talk.

Perhaps because Lorna was continually distracted by otherworldly beings and not focusing on everyday material things in the normal way, her family came to believe she was retarded.

She saw a guardian angel accompanying every single person, usually about three paces behind, sometimes leaning forward to wrap themselves lovingly around that person. The attitude of these angels, she says now, is always loving, never angry. They tend to look youthful. They don't really have a gender, but may take on a masculine or feminine appearance, and indeed may vary their appearance. They only very rarely acknowledge other guardian angels, focusing instead on the person they are guarding.

After a while Lorna stopped seeing these guardian angels in all their glory all the time. Instead she would see a column of light moving behind each person and stretching up above them. This beam would open up to enable Lorna to see the guardian angel when it had something important to communicate. She says that if the angels showed themselves fully to her all the time she so would not be able to cope with everyday life at all. As it is, she grew up with what today we would call 'learning difficulties' and to this day she has not read a single book all the way through.

This is important, I think. So much of what has been revealed to her by the angels chimes in with the traditional mystical and esoteric teaching we have been exploring in this book, and she has not found out about these things from books but has had a direct vision of them.

Early on an angel appeared to her who was different. She first saw him in the corner of her bedroom and he said simply, 'Lorna.' He was a commanding, masculine presence. They soon became firm friends and he told her his name was Michael.

One day she was out in the countryside when she saw an angel with the appearance of an older man coming towards her across a river. He looked as if he was walking, but his feet weren't touching the water. This angel would become another companion, but he wasn't warm and friendly like Michael. He was always serious and high-minded, sometimes fierce and angry, sometimes even a little strange and disconcerting. Once when he'd finished talking to her he blew in her face and suddenly disappeared. This was the angel Elijah, who would have an important part to play in teaching Lorna how to fulfil her mission.

When I was editing Lorna's first book, *Angels in My Hair* (she writes for the most part by dictating into a computer voice box), I pointed out to her something she did not know: that Elijah is a character in the Old Testament. (To someone from a Protestant background it might seem odd that anyone could go through the school system and not be aware of the biblical Elijah, but I've been told that Catholic Ireland places much less emphasis on the Old Testament.) Lorna asked the angels about this, and the answer came back that yes, this was the same Elijah, and the

Elijah in the Old Testament had been a man with an angel dwelling in his soul. As Lorna describes him arriving over the water he is also strikingly reminiscent of Khdir, who in Islamic mysticism is sometimes identified with Elijah, as we have seen. (It is interesting that intellectuals in the Islamic community, including John Esposito and Tariq Ramadan, have been so quick to recognize and endorse Lorna's gifts.)

Lorna also encountered an extremely bright figure with a smiling face, whom she knew as the queen of the angels. She also met an angel called Elisha. This angel had a female appearance, unlike the prophet in the Old Testament.

Over time Lorna began to learn about the different orders and types of angels, such as the healing angels and the angels of the nations. She encountered a tree angel, the group spirit of the foxes (who showed himself to her in the body of an individual fox) and a river angel, perhaps what the Greeks would have called a river goddess.

I have spent many happy hours with Lorna in Ireland and in England, in the area around Glastonbury, while she has tried to teach me to see nature spirits and the energies around plants and animals. Her vision is essentially Christian, but it is not exclusively Christian in the sense of denying the spiritual reality of other faiths and traditions.

When she was in America to promote *Angels in My Hair*, she visited the Metropolitan Museum in New York, and the spirit of the temple of Dendur, which has been reconstructed there, appeared to her, telling her that this temple should be returned to Egypt. This tall thin being that she describes as the angel of that temple is perhaps what the ancient Egyptians would have called a *neter*, which is to say a god.

Michael continued to appear regularly to Lorna, assuming different forms. He often appeared in the form of a man with short black hair and black clothes like a priest's.

On one occasion she was walking along a gravel path in the grounds of a theological college in Maynooth, just outside Dublin, deep in conversation with Michael, when a pair of priests came walking towards them. One of them said, 'Good morning, father.' On this and other occasions it seemed that when Michael took on a human form, other people were able to see him too. In her second book, *Stairways to Heaven*, Lorna gives an instance where an angel dimmed its inner light to play with children in a park.

Eventually, when Lorna was fourteen, Michael revealed himself as the Archangel Michael. She saw him then with long hair and radiant sapphire eyes, wearing a golden crown, a robe of white and gold, and sandals which each bore a golden crucifix. He was gleaming like the sun, and Lorna understood that he was the Archangel of the Sun. Later she would see him carrying a shield and an enormous sword with a golden handle.

On another occasion she was in a junk yard. She had been playing with a friend, but then she saw a light coming towards her through a wall. For a split-second she thought that the moon was coming towards her, then she saw it was a giant angel with a beautiful face like a full moon. He announced himself as the Archangel Gabriel. Later she would see a book deep within his eyes, its pages permanently turning, and she would come to think of him as the angel of the book.

As we saw earlier, the tradition that Michael is the Archangel of the Sun and Gabriel is the Archangel of the Moon is not widely advertised in mainstream Christianity. The Church likes to play down the connection between spiritual beings and heavenly bodies. However, it is a part of various mystical and esoteric traditions, the mystical history gathered together in this book.

In *Stairways to Heaven* Lorna recalls when she first saw the angel Jimazen. She was about five years old, gazing over a garden wall at some apple trees, when she suddenly looked upwards and saw a gigantic angel stretching up into the sky as far as the eye could see. He had no wings, but was wearing armour tinged with black and carrying a massive staff. When he struck the earth with it, she felt the whole Earth move and she was terrified. She came to understand that Jimazen was the guardian angel of the Earth.

Later she was also shown a vision of Mother Earth, who was curled in on herself in the core of the planet, beautiful, female, emerald-green, blue and gold and moving her arms gently, like sails. Lorna understood that Jimazen's role was to control Mother Earth, to stop her convulsing with pain at times of ecological crisis, and she would learn to dread seeing Jimazen because she knew that his appearances heralded floods, earthquakes and other disasters.

We see here a modern and spontaneous vision of the ancient myth of Mother Earth and Saturn retold in Chapter 2.

The fact that so many different people in so many different times and different cultures have had visions of what are clearly the same beings doing the same things is a strong argument for saying that there is a spiritual realm that has an important level and degree of reality. As we have seen, Sufi mystics say that travellers may go to the same locales within this place and meet the same beings there.

It is possible to draw from Lorna's writings a complete picture of the 'ecosystem' of this spiritual realm in its many different levels and dimensions, at least in relation to life on Earth. Lorna has talked about the dark side, though she does so infrequently because she believes it is dangerous to dwell on it.

In *Angels in My Hair* she describes the occasion she went fishing with her father and they sheltered from the cold in an old ruined house. But the inside of the house felt freezing to Lorna, and when her father lit a match, it exploded and an old chair flew across the room. Before they fled, Lorna just had time to see a poltergeist, which was about three feet long, as wide as a human chest and looked like melted wax, without a clear mouth or eyes. She says it looked horrible, and that these Satanic creatures without souls are brought into being when people experiment with ouija boards or black magic.

Many years later a businessman came to see her for advice. He had behaved ruthlessly in order to amass his wealth and he was continuing to behave badly towards his wife and son. He somehow knew he should feel remorse, but said he didn't know how to go about it. Lorna could see he was under Satan's influence, and as he sat at her kitchen table she saw an evil face rise out of his chest, as if from his depths, and smirk at her. She said later it was as if the evil spirit was gloating because she hadn't seen him earlier – but of course in this very act of boasting he was revealing himself!

I have asked her how people become possessed and she has said it can happen because of 'meddling' in the occult. Sometimes if someone plays dangerous games as a child, this can leave the forces of evil poised to take possession and then that individual needn't do anything very terrible in adulthood – casually curse someone, for instance – to let them in.

We each of us have within us a small portion of the divine, sometimes called the self. This nestles within the spirit, which in turn nestles in the soul. Ordinarily the soul is enclosed within the material body, and as a result we also have limited perceptions of the spiritual realms. Lorna says that sometimes the soul 'moves forward' partially out of the body, and that is when we may experience visions. The soul moves forward, for instance, when we are very ill, when we are close to death.

Lorna has experienced agonizing and frightening jolts, but been ecstatic at the same time. In this state she had some of her most extraordinary and revelatory visions, including the vision of God's heavenly library mentioned earlier. (My personal speculation is that this library is in some way connected to Enoch.) In this disembodied state she has been allowed to be present in some way at the Nativity and on another occasion to be there during the childhood of Jesus. Both these visions are recounted in *Stairways to Heaven*.

With regard to her experiences of being raised to heaven, Lorna will say that she never wanted to come back, even though this would have meant separation from the family she loves very much. She was not allowed to die, she was told, because she had a mission to fulfil. In the course of her life Michael and Elijah have helped her to understand what this mission is.

Because of Lorna's great goodness and her pure, loving quality, many people benefit from a connection with her, even a brief, passing one. I believe she takes on other people's pain and lessens it for them. Perhaps the most important part of Lorna's mission is to tell as many people as possible about these spiritual realities, particularly the role of guardian angels.

It was one summer's afternoon when she was pushing a pram that Michael appeared to her and told her that the angels needed her to write a book. At the time that seemed an impossible task. The story of how she was guided to find me through an Irishman living in Italy who was a friend of her agent, Jean Callanan, is told in Chapters 20 and 22 of *Stairways to Heaven*. From my perspective, I was very reluctant to get involved. The publishing list I was responsible for was already very full, I felt overworked and did not want to take on any more projects. I also knew how sceptical my colleagues would be. As a fallback position I thought that if I felt we really had to take it on, I would pass it on to another editor. But gradually it was borne in on me that I must play my part.

What decided me was meeting Lorna. I was impressed by her integrity and by her advice, which, although it comes from an otherworldly source, is reassuringly sensible. It is extraordinary to spend time with someone who has a mode of consciousness which is so different, who is permanently seeing many things that the rest of us cannot see but which 'check out'. I discovered later that one of Lorna's gifts is that she can see the flow of the life force around the body, much as it is conceived in Chinese medicine and which they call *chi*. She saw a blockage in my energy flow and indicated a part of my abdomen that I should have examined by a doctor. I forgot all about this – as I say, I was busy – until a few months later I began to feel uncomfortable. It turned out I had a hernia and needed an operation.

The angels wanted Lorna to write books to inform people that each one of us has a guardian angel, who was chosen for us when we were conceived. Before we incarnate, the guardian angel is with us, preparing us for the joys and challenges we will experience. It never leaves our side during our time on Earth – unlike, say, an archangel, which is never a constant presence and can be in more than one place at the same time – and finally the guardian angel helps us to pass over to the other side. Even after death it stays with us for a while.

Guardian angels have very long names of about a hundred letters. Lorna may tell you a shortened version of your angel's name, which is easier to cope with and which may seem familiar to you.

The voice of your conscience or other promptings to do good may be your guardian angel speaking to you. You can ask your guardian angel to help you and the angel may in turn 'invite other angels in' to help you – for example, healing angels or angels to help you with a particular skill or task. Like Pope Pius XI, Lorna says that you can ask your guardian angel to talk to another guardian angel, if for example, you are in conflict and you want it resolved for the best, or are simply going to a meeting which you worry may be difficult. Your angel also prays with you and, together with other angels, strengthens your prayers.

No one who has read Lorna's autobiography, *Angels in My Hair*, will expect angels to give you everything you ask for. In her childhood and for much of her life afterwards Lorna lived in grinding poverty and with the stigma of being thought retarded. After years of marriage, which, despite poverty and illness, were very happy years, her husband Joe died young, and it was then she would say to Michael, 'Why can't you make it a little easier?' And yet she had great things to achieve and has achieved many of them already, and she has also had many blessings in her life that she perhaps would not have had without the help of the angels.

Lorna's message is a very important message for our times, she says. People need to develop awareness of spiritual realities, because the forces of good and evil are gathering. In *Stairways to Heaven* she writes of the incarnation of the Antichrist and of his outriders, who are already here, preparing the way. On the side of God, the glowing babies are physically imperfect, many diseased or disabled so that few survive childhood, but they are perfect in love and wisdom, forerunners of a newly evolved humanity. Lorna has seen, too, a boy in Ireland who has an angel dwelling in his soul like Elijah. If he survives, he will have an important part to play in the history of the world. The queen of the angels has promised that at the right time she will show herself to all in the same way she has shown herself to Lorna, and as our physical bodies and our souls work into each other over time, we will develop greater spiritual gifts.

Lorna has asked me to add that she has no doubt that good will prevail in the end.

Conclusion

Angel sounding the trumpet (engraving of a detail in the frescoes in the Duomo, Orvieto, by Luca Signorelli).

In the debate between idealism and materialism, materialism holds the upper hand, in fact so much so that it may be hard for us even to begin to understand why anyone ever believed what in earlier ages *everyone* believed – that thoughts and ideas are more real than objects, that objects are the shadows of thoughts rather than the other way around. But my purpose has been to suggest that idealism is a more comprehensive account of human experience.

Throughout the book we have been gathering the sorts of experience that are hard to account for in terms of materialism, not only large-scale well-attested miracles that have changed the course of history, but ordinary, ever-day experiences. Here again are just some of them. We feel a special connection with some people when we meet them.

We may meet someone and feel we have met that person before, even though we know we haven't met them in this life at least. We have premonitions. We have dreams that we believe are trying to tell us something. We sense that someone is looking at us. We sense that a place is evil or sacred. We know quite clearly and without a shadow of a doubt what someone else is thinking. We act badly and events seem to conspire to give us our comeuppance. In the end good-heartedness is rewarded and our prayers are answered. At the third attempt we succeed. We feel someone send us loving impulses over a large distance. We try to duck out of a challenge and it comes round to meet us in a different guise. Circumstances come together to test our deepest fears, where we are weakest. We fall in love and we feel it is meant to be. In these sorts of ways we may experience communion with an intelligence that is guiding us towards experiences that demand a response, and also with a love that looks out for us and responds to our innermost thoughts in a caring way.

I believe that deep down we all have an instinct that the relationship between mind and matter is not all one way, from matter to mind. We sometimes intuit that we are engaged in a battle of wits. 'The seeker desires one thing but receives another,' said Bernard of Clairvaux. 'The spirit tricks us, the spirit plans behind our backs, the spirit lies,' said Hegel. And there is another, gentler side to our intelligent interaction with the cosmos that is alluded to in the Lord's Prayer. 'Forgive us our trespasses as we forgive those who trespass against us' refers to a dynamic process, a flow like the flow in a pump. Forgive others and we will leave a space in ourselves into which healing forces of forgiveness may flow.

Idealism is the philosophy that underpins all religion, and looked at through the lens of idealism, all these experiences, instincts and intuitions make sense. If we define the power of the mind to move matter as 'supernatural', then according to idealism we live in a super-natural universe. Mind underlies everything and informs everything. It lives just below the material surface of things, directing and moving them according to a divine plan and in response to our prayers.

Religion and idealism like to dwell on what is unclear and unknown, on life's great mysteries. They dwell on the sleep, the darkness, that bounds us on every side – on either side of individual lives, either side of the history of the human race and either side of the entire material cosmos too. Religion and idealism look at this darkness, the unknown bearing in on us, and ask what is emanating from it.

Religion tries to take in the whole of human experience, including some experiences that are odd, anomalous and on the edge – what sociologists call the numinous – and to give an account that makes sense of it all.

Scientific materialism produces a clear, bright and very useful account of what is left when you take the shadowy part of life away. One of the problems with it is that it yields a narrow account of what the good things in life are. If the only things worth valuing are the ones that are suitable for measuring and testing, then we are pushed in the direction of materialism in the lower sense, being too interested in money, possessions, commodities, white goods, the sexy and the thrilling. All humanity's finer, higher feelings, all subtlety, may be filtered out. We saw earlier that idealism in the philosophical sense encouraged idealism in the popular sense. So also materialism in the philosophical sense encourages materialism in the lower sense.

The trouble is that, as I say, materialism has the upper hand. We have so lost sight of idealism and its way of understanding the world that the greater part of religion and spiritual thinking, indeed the greater part of human thought and culture, is a closed book to us now.

And that is one of the reasons why stories of the type retold in this book are so important. As we have seen, stories show the immanence of the divine in everyday life. When we read Dickens, for example, we enter a place where we are much more warm-hearted and determined to do good.

Dickens is an extreme case, but all stories do something along these lines. They open up a universe structured according to questions of *quality*, a universe which has values intrinsic to it that it would not have unless an outside agency put them there. Stories portray *a personal universe*, in the sense that it is concerned with the lives of individuals. Stories show the universe interacting with, sometimes playing with an individual's hopes for happiness, for good, for love, for truth. A storyteller creates a dialogue between an individual, yearning for happiness, for beauty, for the good, for meaning, and a series of events which frustrate that yearning, that hope or perhaps fulfil it in an unexpected way. Stories reflect back to us evanescent aspects of our own experience.

They can help us to think about fate, destiny and the promptings of providence in an age when we no longer have a language to talk about them in the abstract, except perhaps in the language of the personal horoscope. (Yes, astrology may sometimes seem shallow. Astrology has perhaps been intellectually orphaned in an age when the sharpest minds are no longer idealists.[1]) Beginning his enquiry into how we can justify talking about causality in matters of fact, Hume noted that it was 'a question hardly considered'. The same might be said now about questions of the meaning of life.

I have tried to show that there isn't a simple choice between reason and faith. Religion is reasonable, based on the assumptions of idealism, just as science is reasonable, based on the assumptions of materialism. Objective testing is the touchstone of science, while subjectivity, the test of human experience, is the touchstone of religion.

*   *   *

Is mind an accident of matter? Or was the material cosmos precipitated out of a great Cosmic Mind?

In Switzerland the Large Hadron Collider, a machine 27 miles in circumference that has taken 30 years to plan and build and cost billions of dollars, attempts to replicate the conditions that existed less than a nanosecond after the Big Bang some 13.7 billion years ago. Arrays of detectors are being used to try to register the smallest trace of subatomic rubble spewed out from the collisions that the machine creates, with the aim of learning more about the forces that shaped the cosmos at the beginning of time.

The Large Hadron Collider has been built, then, to try to find evidence in support of the theory of the origins of the cosmos according to materialism.[2]

What machine would you need in order to find evidence in support of the opposing view – idealism? Where could you find evidence that the material universe is dependent on mind and responsive to it? Is it possible to detect traces of the Mind of God?

The human brain is still the most subtle, complex, altogether most mysterious machine in the known universe. I am suggesting that we can make a more informed judgement as to what happened at the beginning of the cosmos by contemplating certain aspects of our everyday experience than we can by examining data from the Large Hadron Collider.

If you look at life as objectively as possible, you will get exciting and useful results. Science opens the gates to the wonders of living – but only in the realm of quantity.

But what happens if you look at life as subjectively as possible? What if you focus on your innermost responses, your highest hopes and deepest fears and ask yourself, 'Does the cosmos respond?'

To track such things needs attentiveness to the most evanescent, subtle movements of the human spirits, the subtlest shadings of the heart.

To ask these questions of our own experience, we need to apply the ways of looking that can be found in the writings of Dostoyevsky, George Eliot, Hermann Melville, David Foster Wallace – storytellers who have risked peace of mind, perhaps even sanity, to wrestle with the trickiest and most shadowy of all philosophical problems.

Is the cosmos responding to our deepest, most subtle, our innermost desires, our deepest fears, our most heartfelt prayers? Were we brushed by the wing of an angel? Only we can be the judge of that. What were our intentions towards our lover? Were they good-hearted and true? What in our heart of hearts do we wish for? What, finally, are we going to trust – our own experience or the opinions of the latest crop of experts?

Death and Immortality (by William Blake).

Notes

PREFACE

1. In the world according to materialism, imagination is a faculty to be suspicious of, and it is often equated with mere fantasy. In the world according to idealism, the philosophy where mind is in a sense more real than matter, human imagination has a much more exalted role. It can tap into the great creative forces of the cosmos and enable us to become conscious co-creators. See Chapters 30 and 38 for an account of imagination as it is understood in idealism, in the world-view of Ibn Arabi, Henry Corbin and William Shakespeare among others.

2. As a narrative of creation, the first part of the book is 'creationist' in the sense that it sees Genesis as giving a true account of the creating of the human condition by God and by angelic beings helping to work out His plan. But I shall be suggesting that because this is an account of *inner* history, rather than one pieced together from the outside using scraps of data, it is not necessarily inconsistent with the objective findings of modern science.

3. A note on vocabulary: I have generally been cautious about using the word 'supernatural'. The question 'Are there supernatural events in the world?' is a question of the order of 'When did you stop beating your wife?' Both contain a hostile assumption. As we shall see in Chapter 38, the word 'supernatural' arose with scientific materialism and contains the assumption that there are universally established laws of nature that are extremely unlikely ever to be broken. If you start from materialism, supernatural events are improbable in the extreme. However, as we shall see in the course of this book, if you start from idealism, you may learn to expect them and to look out for them.

4. The Neoplatonist philosopher Plotinus put the case for idealism and I don't know if it has ever been put more succinctly and clearly: 'External objects present only appearances. The world of ideas is not to be investigated as a thing external to us, and so only imperfectly known. It is within us. The world of ideas lies within our intelligence. Consciousness, therefore, is the sole basis of certainty. The mind is its own witness.' (*Letter to Flaccus*)

5. With a nod to Hegel and his *On the Prospects for a Folk Religion* (1793).

6. Whether or not they have ever expressed it in precisely these terms, most religious people have believed in idealism implicitly. I will argue that you can't really call yourself religious or spiritual without being on the side of idealism against materialism. (See Chapter 39.)

7. To be certain here in the face of the evidence is, I suggest, inappropriate to its scant nature, though fanatics on both sides – religious fundamentalists and militant atheists – do profess certainty. The appropriate response, I suggest, is genial, tolerant and open-minded.

8. Alvin Plantinga, *Where the Conflict Really Lies: Science, Religion and Naturalism*, Oxford University Press Inc., 2011

9. George Eliot, *Scenes of Clerical Life*, Blackwood and Sons, 1858

10. David Foster Wallace, *Infinite Jest*, Little, Brown, 1996

INTRODUCTION

1. St Thomas Aquinas, the great theologian of angels, defined a mystic as 'someone who has experienced a taste of God's sweetness' which he also says is 'beyond speculation' (*Summa Theologiae* II/IIq97a.2.re2).

2. Henry Maudsley, founder of the famous psychiatric hospital in Camberwell, south London, believed that many spiritual leaders, including St Paul, Mohammed, Mother Ann Lee, founder of the Shakers, Swedenborg, Ignatius Loyola, George Fox and Charles Wesley, suffered from epilepsy. For an account of altered states of consciousness as a battleground between religious belief and psychiatry, see Ivan Leudar and Philip Thomas, *Voices of Reason, Voices of Insanity: Studies of Verbal Hallucinations* (Routledge, 2000). There was a poignant moment during one of Lorna Byrne's public

events at the Quaker Hall in London in November 2012, when she admitted that one of the reasons why she didn't talk about her visions of angels when she was a child was because she would have been locked away in an institution and her message would never have reached the wider world.

3. To be so transported that you lose all awareness of the material world is to experience the 'Beatific Vision'. It is not always a wholly blissful or pain-free experience. Lorna Byrne reports that for her it is preceded by an angel reaching into her chest. Her soul is pulled from her body with a terrible jolt.

4. There is a brilliant scene in Woody Allen's *Annie Hall* where he is waiting in line at a cinema with Diane Keaton and is irritated by a man behind them who is showing off to his date by expostulating on the subject of Marshall McLuhan. Woody has an argument with this guy, telling him he doesn't know what he's talking about. Then out of nowhere he produces Marshall McLuhan, who duly agrees that this guy completely misunderstands his thought. Woody turns to the camera and says, 'Wouldn't it be great if life were like that?' I have been asked by my agent, Jonny Geller, why I accept Lorna Byrne as an authority. Great mystics have a natural authority, something *like* a force of personality. It is not derived from books or other authorities, though it may be consistent with the visions of other mystics and religious traditions. St Francis's biographer, St Bonaventure, described him as 'filled with knowledge', and, when dying, pointed to a crucifix saying 'This is the source of all my knowledge'.

5. Job 38.6: '... the morning stars sang together and all the angels shouted for joy'; see also Genesis, 3.24: where Cherubim bar the way back to Eden. But there is another, more esoteric layer of interpretation regarding the role of angels in creation, which is explained in *The Secret History of the World* (Quercus, 2008). The word 'Elohim', translated into English versions of Genesis as 'God', is in fact a plural noun, referring to seven angels acting in concert as the Word of God. They are God in the act of creation. The accounts in Genesis and in the Gospel of St John are consistent. It was through the Word – through the Elohim – that everything was made.

6. *The Book of Jubilees* 2.2: 'For on the first day He created the heavens which are above and the earth and the waters and all the spirits which

serve before Him – the angels of the presence, and the angels of sanctification, and the angels [of the spirit of fire and the angels] of the spirit of the winds, and the angels of the spirit of the clouds, and of darkness, and of snow and of hail and of hoar frost, and the angels of the voices and of the thunder and of the lightning, and the angels of the spirits of cold and of heat, and of winter and of spring and of autumn and of summer and of all the spirits of his creatures which are in the heavens and on the earth.'

The Book of Jubilees is an ancient Jewish text which was regarded as authoritative by the early Christian Church. Some scholars believe that some of its source documents are as old as the source documents of the early books of the Old Testament. Similarly the *Hermetica*, writings of Egyptian origin which were to be influential on the thought and art of the Renaissance, and the surviving fragments by the Egyptian historian Manetho writing about the generations of the gods, are all older than some parts of the Bible, and some of the sources of these texts are perhaps as old as anything in the Bible. Moreover, the different orders of spiritual beings which these texts describe are also depicted in the pyramids and temples of the ancient world, suggesting that they were part of a universally accepted cosmology long before they were written down in the texts that have survived.

The description of the different orders of angels is typical of theosophical thinking. Today the word 'theosophy' is perhaps associated in most people's minds with Theosophy, the movement founded in the nineteenth century by Madame Blavatsky, but in fact, as we have just seen, the roots of this way of thinking go back at least as far as late antiquity in Greece and probably much, much earlier. Theosophy is the attempt to think systematically about human experience of the divine – the geography of the spiritual realms, the different orders of spiritual being and their characteristics, the divine plan for the cosmos and its various stages of unfolding, the divine plan for individual humans before birth, during life and after death. If theology as taught in universities has tended to be narrowly Christian, theosophy aspires to be universal and tends to focus on what the world religions have in common. It has a long and august, if sometimes shadowy tradition. I have found tracks of this tradition in (usually very long) Victorian books, often written by clergymen of the type satirized by George Eliot in the figure of Casaubon. It's a joy to find these books in second-hand bookshops, or these days on Abebooks, because of the extensive, punctilious scholarship that notes the similarities of pattern and exchanges between the great religious traditions. Casaubon has perched on my shoulder during the writing of this book.

CHAPTER 1

1. The great conflict of the twentieth century can be seen as the battle between Communism and the forces of atheism on the one hand and Christian democracies and theocracies like Tibet on the other.

2. 'With this field-dew consecrate every fairy take his gait ...' Oberon in *A Midsummer Night's Dream* (Act V. Scene III). We will examine the immersion of Shakespeare and other great writers in this realm of thought in later chapters.

3. Idealism's account of different orders of spiritual beings emanating from the great Cosmic Mind in order to form the material universe is called emanationism. It can be traced back at least as far as early Egyptian religion. The ancient Egyptians saw their gods – or *neteru* – as personifications of the generating principles of nature working together to lend it form.

   One of the earlier accounts of emanationism comes in Hermeticism. Hermeticism presented cosmos as a living emanation of the divine, woven together by complicated and finely distinguished layers of emanation. It is widely accepted now that these writings, or at least the ideas behind them, probably originated in priestly circles in Egypt, and the documents that we have may have been written by Egyptian priests in exile after the Mystery schools were closed down.

   Other forms of emanationism include the Kabbalah's account of the *sepiroth* and the account of different orders of spiritual beings by the Neoplatonist Plotinus. It can be seen, too, in the account of the different orders of angels alluded to by St Paul and given in full by his follower Dionysius the Areopagite, which is the classical account of the orders of angels in the Christian tradition. For a parallel account of different orders gleaned from the wise men of the Zulus in the twentieth century, see 'The Ancient Wisdom in Africa' by Patrick Bowen in *Studies in Comparative Religion*, volume 3, no.2, Spring 1969, pp.113–121. For an account of the account of the 'drama in Heaven' as it appears in parallel in Christian-Gnostic traditions, the Kabbalah of Isaac Luria and Shi'ite Ismalian Gnosis, see 'The Dramatic Element Common to the Gnostic Cosmogonies of the Religions of the Book' by Henry Corbin, from *Cahiers de l'Universite Saint Jean de Jerusalem*.

4. Corinthians 4.18: 'The things that are seen are transient, but the things that are unseen are eternal.'

CHAPTER 2

1. There is a strong metaphysical dimension to the film, typical of Terrence Malick's work. He doesn't mean to talk here merely about a clash caused by the mere knocking of atoms against atoms; he is talking about a clash of values at the heart of nature. I have worked for many years editing and publishing SAS hero Chris Ryan, who tells me that *The Thin Red Line* is one of two movies that best conveys the sense of what it's really like to be in battle.

2. The Neoplatonist Proclus wrote that according to Orphic theology 'the divinity who is the cause of stable power and sameness and the first principle to conversion of all things is of a male characteristic, but the divinity which emits from itself all growths and powers is feminine, and a communication between the two was denominated by the theology of the sacred marriage . . . the theologists called it the marriage of Heaven and Earth, Saturn and Rhea.' Quoted in *The Works* of Plotinus with a commentary by G.R.S. Mead, 1929.

3. It is in the nature of minerals to fragment and break up. 'The self is made manifest in the opposites and the conflicts between them; it is a *coincidentia oppositorium*,' Carl Gustav Jung, *Psychology and Alchemy* (Routledge, 1944).

4. The development of the concept of 'the Word' as the organizing principle of the cosmos may be traced through Heraclitus, the Stoics and the Greek-educated Philo, who was probably influential on the author of John's gospel. In Greek tradition Apollo was the divine

representation of this ordering principle. See *Jesus Christ, Sun of God: Ancient Cosmology and Early Christian Symbolism* by David Fideler (Quest Books, 1996). See also *The Popol Vuh*, 1,1: 'All was in suspense, all was calm and silent, all was motionless, all was peaceful, and empty was the immensity of the heavens. Behold then the first word.'

5. Plotinus, one of the followers of Plato, who took his idealism in the direction of practical mysticism, wrote: 'In this intelligible world everything is transparent. No shadow limits vision. All the essences see each other and interpenetrate each other in the most intimate depth of their nature.' (*The Enneads V.8*)

6. In mystical philosophy the vegetable dimension embodied by Adam and Eve lives on in us as the vital principle that gives life and organization to our material bodies. As the Sufi poet Rumi puts it, 'You and I were with Adam and Eve in the beginning.' This is a theme we will return to repeatedly. *Mathnawi*, vi.735

CHAPTER 3

1. Apart from the sun and the moon, Venus is the only heavenly body that shines strongly enough to cast shadows.

2. The emerald was the precious stone sacred to Hathor, the Egyptian Venus. A medieval poem called 'The Wartburg War' preserved the tradition of an emerald stone falling from Lucifer's crown, and we shall see later why this became an important element in the Grail story.

3. All humans crave happiness. Death is the blacking on the back of the mirror that enables us to see ourselves.

4. Where Genesis says that Adam and Eve knew they were naked, it means to say that as animals they became conscious that they had bodies in a way that plants were not conscious. With this realization came the potential for 'sin'.

5. We acknowledge this duality – the way that evil attacks us from two directions – in the Lord's Prayer: 'Lead us not into temptation [Venus] and deliver us from evil [Saturn].'

6. For instance, Michael has traditionally been depicted as the Archangel of the Sun and Gabriel as the Archangel of the Moon. For a fuller

account of how astronomical lore is both explicit but overlooked and encoded in the Bible and church architecture and Christian art, see *The Secret History of the World*.

7. Tamil inscription noted by the renowned scholar of traditional religion Ananda K. Coomaraswamy.

CHAPTER 4

1. Compare *The Yoga Sutras of Pantanjali*, for instance:
'Meditate on the elephant to gain the strength of an elephant.
Meditate on the ear to be able hear over great distances.
Meditate on the lightness of cotton to be able to pass through space.'
2. Taught by the Spider Woman, the little girl was able to go back home and show the Navaho people how to weave the beautiful patterns for which they are famous.

CHAPTER 5

1. Cinderella's glass slipper is an obvious echo of this 'perfect fit'. Lots of stories we know from childhood – *Sleeping Beauty, Jack the Giant Killer, Cinderella* – are stories about what happened to angels.
2. *Poimandres,* the 'knowledge of Ra', a chapter in the *Corpus Hermeticum*, describes how the spirit of a man mounts upwards through the heavens, casting off different bad qualities in different spheres, for example discarding the machinations of cunning in the Mercury sphere, lust in the Venus sphere, rashness in Mars, greed for wealth in Jupiter and falsehood in Saturn.
3. Novalis: 'A birth on earth means a death in the spirit worlds.'
4. Esdras describes a primeval spirit world which humanity inhabited before the creation of the material world (Second Book of Esdras, 3.4–7).
5. The myths show gods – angels – doing things so that humans will be able to do them. They are forging a path for us. The story of Isis and Osiris is about how we come to be born and live in the material world for a certain limited time, measured by the sun and the moon, and how we will be tested, undergo certain trials according to the

gifts we have been blessed with. How we will be given divine help if we ask for it and then die to the material world and continue in the angelic realms for a while.

We live just long enough to be tested, and be tested again and again. We each have our own encounter with Seth, and the Egyptian priests promise that after death we will meet Osiris and see clearly by his light what is happening.

CHAPTER 6

1. The main source of these stories of metamorphosis is, of course, Ovid, but some of the language is Shakespeare's.
2. There is a saying attributed Baal Shem Tov, the founder of Hasidic Judaism: 'Every blade of grass has an angel next to it saying, "Grow! Grow!"'
3. Milton described spirit bodies as 'soft and uncompounded ... their essence pure, not tied or manacled with joint or limb – nor founded on the brittle strength of bones' and angels as able to metamorphose in pursuit of their 'airy purposes'. *Paradise Lost* Book 1.425–30.
4. In another Celtic story, *Cormac's Adventures in the Land of Promise*, the king is travelling through the Land of Promise and finds a well which is the source of five streams. He is told that each stream is one of the five senses.

    This is a startling instance of a narrative twist which suddenly brings home that the perspective of the storyteller is otherworldly – in other words, looking from the point of view of the otherworld at how the everyday material world is formed. In this it is like the scene in the film *The Matrix*, based on the esoteric and mystical novels of Philip K. Dick, when the viewer is suddenly shown that the characters in the film are strapped into machines that are making them experience a virtual world that they have been mistaking for the real world.

    On one level, stories like this and the story of Taliesin describe what happens in initiation, showing the reader or listener the otherworldly perspective. Insofar as they accustom the reader to this perspective, they can be described as initiatory in themselves.

CHAPTER 7

1. Odin's mission was to combat the possibility of evil that had been allowed into the world by the creation of animal life and to help develop faculties to resist the temptation and cunning insinuated by Venus. The astrologers of the north watched the complex patterns of Mercury and Venus around the rising and setting sun and understood that the destiny of humankind was tied up with the relationship between these two planets.

2. The stories of Odin and Asgard, like the stories of Zeus/Jupiter, record a time when great victories had been won over the forces of Saturn and Venus, the forces of materialism and delusion, but a time too when the war was by no means over on either front. The story-tellers knew that forces of materialism would rise again in the form of the sons of Saturn, the Titans and the giants. The forces of materialism were always threatening to encroach from the outside and Venus was the enemy within.

3. For a clear and concise account of morphic fields theory in relation to the latest developments in science, see Rupert Sheldrake's *The Science Delusion*, which I edited and published last year. It is published this year in America, on Deepak Chopra's list, as *Science Set Free*.

4. Mary Midgley, *Guardian*, 27th January 2012.

5. 'If all the world were paper/And all the sea were ink/And all the trees were bread and cheese/What would we have to drink?' This nursery rhyme points to an eternal mystery that still engages science today. The cosmos doesn't have to be the way it is, fine-tuned to be suitable for us and providing us with the conditions we need to live. It could be suitable, preferential in all sorts of ways but missing one small but element without which life as we know it would be impossible.

6. *The Corpus Hermeticum*: 'There is not one thing in the cosmos that is not alive.' (Book 12, *a discourse of Hermes to Tat*)

7. Traditional paintings of the Nativity are a wonderful symbolizing of this historical process.

8. Rudolf Steiner said that stones have a consciousness like deep trance consciousness in humans.

9. Pliny the Elder *The Natural History*, Book 2, chapter 102: 'The moon fills bodies by its approach and empties them when it withdraws. Blood increases and diminishes with it. It is the star of the animal spirit.' Eleazar, a Zealot from the first century, said the soul possesses great ability, even when imprisoned in the body, for it makes the body its organ of perception, but it is not until the soul is restored to its proper sphere that it is filled with untrammelled joy and power. The French mathematician and mystic Blaise Pascal famously said, 'The heart has its reasons of which reason knows nothing.' To the heart he might have added the lungs, the stomach, the genitals, the nervous system and indeed the brain.

10. Because the starting-point of idealism is the opposite of the starting-point of materialism, the ideas it generates may seem upside down and inside out to modern thinking. As we shall see, many great spiritual thinkers, from Jesus Christ to the Zen Masters, have played with this paradoxical quality. The Norse myths are more charged with this paradoxical quality – space and time mean little to them – than the more familiar Greek and Roman, which is perhaps why there are few popular retellings of them. Even the Victorians, usually so talented at this sort of thing, struggled with the Norse myths as did Roger Lancelyn Green in perhaps his least successful retelling.

CHAPTER 8

1. In the Koran, (Sura 27:16) Solomon says, 'We have been taught the language of the birds.' This means 'we know how to talk to higher intelligences' – birds here symbolizing angels. The same symbolism is used in the parable of the mustard seed, where the tree represents the world tree, the pole that passes through all levels of being and reality – and the birds of the air in its higher branches are the angels. Analysis after René Guénon. ('The Language of Birds', *Studies in Comparative Religion* vol 3, No.2 1969)

CHAPTER 9

1. Different religious traditions emphasize different eras. The entire corpus of Greek and Roman mythology is covered in a short passage in Genesis 6, alluding to angels taking human wives and the mighty men who were born from these unions.

2. Perseus is a sun hero, his deeds echoing the deeds of earlier sun heroes. He fights a Saturnine monster of materialism that wants to turn the whole world into dead matter. As we shall see, in idealism these repeating patterns in history carry with them no implication they are 'made up'. Patterns in history repeat as the wheeling stars and planets dictate.

CHAPTER 10

1. Lorna has written about a demon acting unwittingly. For a rare chance to see Lorna Byrne talking about 'the other side', see the filmed interview with Graham Hancock, available on his website.

2. The Enochian literature is liberally quoted and taken as an authority in the New Testament, and Jesus Christ alludes to it. *The Book of Enoch* was lost for over 1,500 years then rediscovered by the Scottish Freemason James Bruce in 1773, in territory that is today a part of Ethiopia.

3. Eleventh-century historian Said of Toledo records the tradition that Thoth or Hermes, called Enoch by the Jews and Idris by the Moslems, lived in Egypt, originated all antediluvian science, first spoke of the movements of the planets, built temples to God and warned of catastrophes, including the Flood. See also 'And I saw how the stars of heaven came forth, and I counted the portals out of which they proceeded, and wrote down all their outlets, of each individual star by itself, according to their number and their names, their courses and their positions, and their times and their months ...' (*The Book of Enoch* chapter 33); Robert Lomas and Christopher Knight suggested in *Uriel's Machine* that what was being described here was a megalithic monument and its function as predictor of the movements of heavenly bodies and so the seasons. Today many still hope to unearth Enoch's library in the deserts of north Africa, where traditions of the Hall of Records have survived. Some believe it is buried beneath the paws of the Sphinx. Lorna Byrne has given what I take to be a very vivid and

detailed description of this library existing in a spiritual dimension in her book *Stairways to Heaven*.

4. Malachi has a prophecy of 'the sun of righteousness', (Malachi 4:2–3) which St Paul and Christian tradition take as a prophecy of Jesus Christ. Jesus Christ has traditionally been portrayed using solar imagery and the association is often explicit in early Christian literature, such as the *Pistis Sophia*.

5. 'The vision caused me to fly and lifted me upward, and bore me into heaven... And I looked and saw therein a lofty throne: its appearance was as crystal, and the wheels thereof as the shining sun, and there was the vision of Cherubim.' (*The Book of Enoch* from chapter 14)

6. 'And the angels, the children of the heaven, saw and lusted after them ... and they began to go in unto them and to defile themselves with them, and they taught them charms and enchantments ... And they became pregnant, and they bare great giants, whose height was three thousand ells ... the giants turned against them and devoured mankind. And they began to sin against birds, and beasts, and reptiles, and fish, and to devour one another's flesh, and drink the blood.' (from chapters 6–7 *The Book of Enoch*) 'And it came to pass that the angels of God saw that they were beautiful to look upon ... and they took themselves wives of all whom they chose, and they bare unto them sons and they were giants ... And lawlessness increased on the earth and all flesh corrupted its way and every imagination of the thoughts of all men [was] thus evil continually ... And He said that He would destroy man and all flesh upon the face of the earth which He had created.' (*The Book of Jubilees* from chapter 5)

CHAPTER 11

1. Having said he will not prophesy, Elisha says, 'But now bring me a minstrel.' 'And it came to pass, when the minstrel played, that the hand of the Lord came upon him' (2 Kings 3.15).

2. There were men of deep wisdom in olden times who knew by intuition the feelings and ways of all living beings. They perfectly understood the languages of different kinds of animal. When they called, animals gathered together and listened to their teachings.

3. The ancient Greek Oreibasia was a midwinter rite dedicated to Dionysus. The women left the city at night and went to the mountains, where in imitation of Maenads they drank wine and danced themselves into ecstasy, thrashing their hair and dismembering and eating raw a young goat which represented the god. The Greek for goat is *tragos*, and this ceremony was the origin of tragic drama and prepared the way for all great art to deal with the important questions of life and death. The rite is a mixture of wild exaltation and repulsion, holy and barbaric at same the time. It is a paradoxical act. It is also an affirmation of the life force, because it confronts the worst that can happen and says that after all this the life force is still indestructible. It survives any individual death and is ultimately joyful. Life will go on.

James George Frazer's *The Golden Bough*, 1890 contains a missionary's account of a dance by cannibals in British Columbia which led to the tearing apart and eating of a human body. (Chapter 43)

As late as the early twentieth century the traveller Wilfred Thesiger witnessed the annual rite of a hill tribe in Tangier. The people were half-starved and in a drug-induced delirium. They danced to pipes and drums. Then a sheep was tossed into the village square and they fell on it, tearing it apart, eating it raw and quickly while the blood was still fresh. Thesiger is quoted by E. R. Dodds, *The Greeks and the Irrational*, 1951.

4. This information on bees comes from *The Parable of the Beast* by John Bleibtreu, 1970 an astonishing account of experimental biology, revealing intelligence at work in the natural world in many unexpected ways.

5. As Krishna, whose story we will tell in Chapter 15, said, 'That which is truly known knows that it is known.'

6. The greatest writers address the questions of life and death, the mysteries of the human condition, mysterious connections and mystical chains of events. To take a shining modern example, Jonathan Franzen, working in the grand high tradition of George Eliot, writes in *Freedom* of a character's 'really big life mistake'. Insecure because of a loveless childhood, Patty 'goes along with' her lover's version of her in spite of knowing that it isn't accurate. Her insecurity interlocks perfectly with his insecurity. The best and worst qualities of both of

them are engaged and this 'life mistake' becomes their great 'life test'. It is unlikely that this perfect interlocking would come about without the guiding hand of destiny. That things like this do happen in ways that sometimes only great writers can capture on the page is a profound mystery. What writers like George Eliot and Jonathan Franzen are saying is that we can try to put off consideration of these issues and immerse ourselves in other stuff, but we all in the end have to confront personal choices of extreme seriousness, and these great novelists show with psychological realism how this works out in the course of lives and generations. We will return to this topic in Chapter 42.

CHAPTER 12

1. In *Matsya Purana* (2.8–10) Vishnu tells Manu: 'Seven rainclouds will bring destruction. The turbulent oceans will merge together into a single sea. They will turn the world into one sheet of water. Then you must take the seeds of life from everywhere and load them into the boat of the Vedas.'

2. In *Meditations on the Tarot*, the Catholic scholar of mystical and esoteric wisdom Valentine Tomberg described the eye as a wound. I take him to mean that our physical eyes wound us because they blind us to the spiritual world. (Letter V)

3. 'And God arranged the Zodiac and commanded it to be productive of all the different types of animals that were to come' (*The Kore Kosmu*: 20). But the four Cherubim at the cardinal points of the zodiac – Taurus, Scorpio, Leo and Aquarius – together make a cross on the cosmos. ('These four constellations mark the extremities of a cross whose centre is the polar star, because of its immobility in the middle of the celestial rotation.' *Le Tarot des imagiers du moyen age,* Oswald Wirth) This is the cross on which the Sun god would later be crucified, so that matter could eventually be spiritualized according to cosmic plan.

4. The carving of the Sphinx on the Giza plateau in 11,451 BC represented a monument to a timelock. For the arguments on dating, see *The Fingerprints of the Gods* by Graham Hancock (William Heinemann,

1995), *Keeper of Genesis* by Robert Bauval and Graham Hancock (William Heinemann, 1996) and *The Egypt Code* by Robert Bauval (Century, 2006). One of the foundations of these theories is the redating work of Dr Robert Schoch. See 'Erosion Processes on the Great Sphinx and its dating' 1999.

CHAPTER 13

1. Some said this mystic mountain was made of crystal. Others said it was made of gold. Its caves were crammed with magical jewels guarded by serpents, and there were rumours, too, of underground cities and pathways spiralling down to the centre of the Earth.

In about 450 BC a mathematician and mystic called Pingala used the name Mount Meru for the Fibonacci sequence laid out as a pyramid. Mount Meru can be seen as a pyramid of holy thoughts emanating from the great Cosmic Mind and opening out to create the world below.

The third Panchen Lama, one of the traditional leaders of Tibet, said that going on a physical journey to find the sacred mountain would only take you so far. Intense and difficult spiritual and mystical exercises are needed too.

The pull of Mount Meru has been felt all over the world. Christian mystics such as St Augustine and Blessed Catherine Emmerich of the order of St Augustine have written about it. Thomas Vaughan, an Englishman inspired by Rosicrucian ideals, wrote under a pseudonym about a mountain 'situated in the midst of the earth or centre of the world which is both small and great. It is soft, also above all measure hard and strong. It is far off and near at hand, but by Providence of God's invisible. In it are hidden the most ample treasures, which the world is not able to value.' *Lumen de Lumine*, Part II by Eugenius Philalethes, 1651.

In the nineteenth century this sacred realm was widely known by the name Shambhalah. Tsar Nicholas II was convinced he was the reincarnation of a great mystic from the region and as a result built a Buddhist temple in St Petersburg in 1910. The Russian painter Nicholas Roerich carried holy earth, purportedly a gift from the

Mahatmas, supernatural spiritual teachers living on the mountain, to place in Lenin's grave. He was convinced that both Marx and Lenin had been secretly instructed by such masters.

Prophecies from the Kalachakra tradition of Buddhism from the second century BC predicted that Buddhism will be all but extinguished in Tibet, Mongolia and China between 1927 and 2027. They also predicted that between 2327 and 2424 a great war will take place. Armies will come down from Mount Meru, led by a king who will drive back the forces of materialism and bring a new golden age.

Rama is the ruler who archetypically absents himself from his subjects, like the caliph, Haroun al Raschid, in *Tales of the Arabian Nights* and the Duke in Shakespeare's *Measure for Measure*. Thomas Aquinas wrote that God and the angels sometimes absented themselves so that we might develop free will.

I was helping at the Dublin launch of Lorna Byrne's *Stairways to Heaven* when a man approached me and gave me an envelope containing material by an esoteric teacher whose work I was not familiar with. According to Brian Cleeve, each of us has a spirit that is part of a grouping of a thousand spirits. After death these spirits become integrated in a group mind, forming one being containing the experience of a thousand human lives within it. In this state we will retain our sense of individuality yet share the experiences of all the others in our group. I have lost this gentleman's details and been unable to thank him, but thank him now in case he is reading this. (Interesting to note the similarity with Isaac Luria's notion of 'families of souls' drawn to each other by a special kinship.) Lorna herself has sometimes said, based on her own experiences of heaven, that when we are there we lose all sense of life's unfairness in the face of something infinitely greater than all we experience on Earth as individuals. Some of Brian Cleeve's writings are online at *Seven Mansions: The Works of Brain Cleeve 1921-2003*.

CHAPTER 14

1. Zarathustra is one of the higher beings who watches over human history and intervenes at key turning points.

2. According to secular, academic scholarship, which assumes that angels and higher order spiritual beings aren't real, rumours of angels come about through cultural influence, and the angels of the Old and New Testament are modelled on Persian stories like the encounter of Zarathustra with the tall shining ones. See, for instance, *The Old Testament: A Historical and Literary Introduction to the Hebrew Scriptures* by Michael D. Coogan (Oxford University Press USA, 2005).

3. As a small boy Nietzsche was scared half to death when sitting in his father's huge armchair, alone in the library, he heard a man's voice suddenly call out to him from behind the chair. Petrified, he didn't dare turn around and look. Later in life the speaker would step out in front of him to greet him. It was Zarathustra, who had a terrifying aura of danger about him. We will return to Nietzsche and the history of his times later.

4. The divine is inside each of us, Plotinus says, 'like a face reflected in many mirrors'. The mystical doctrine of the Self and the self, perhaps more familiar to us in Hindu teaching, was taught in Christianity from the early days of the Church. St Augustine said, 'God is more me than I am myself.' What happens in the spiritual realm, in the world of the Self, will later happen to each and every one of us.

5. 'Christ' in Jesus Christ is not, of course, a surname. It's a title he acquired at his baptism, indicating that he was taking on the role of cosmic saviour.

6. After the battle Krishna raised Arjuna's grandson from the dead.

7. The Kali Yuga lasted from 3001 BC to AD 1899.

CHAPTER 15

1. The earliest writing that has come down to us is on cuneiform tablets from Uruk in modern-day Iraq.

2. Noah and Dionysus the Younger, figures associated with the transition to a post-Flood society, are both also associated with drunkenness. Alcohol helped human evolution because it was important for humankind to become intoxicated with the material world – and cut off from the spiritual dimension.

3. Enlil is Jupiter. The best translation of the epic of Gilgamesh, bringing out its underlying star lore, is *He Who Saw Everything* by Robert Temple (Rider, 1991).

CHAPTER 17

1. I follow David Rohl and the advocates of the 'new chronology' in identifying Dudimose, not Ramesses II, as the pharaoh of the Exodus. For a full account, see *A Test of Time* (Century, 1995) by David Rohl.
2. There were also instructions for the building of the Tabernacle, including two golden Cherubim stretched protectively over the ark. There were instructions on how to make the seven lamps and the priestly garments with a pocket to carry the Urim and Thummim – instruments of divination. Yahweh gave detailed instructions for sacrifice and ceremonial worship.
3. This story is from the Koran. (18:61–83)
4. For the identification of Bahrain as the site of the confluence of the two waters, see David Rohl's *Legend: The Genesis of Civilisation* (Century, 1998).
5. In Jewish mysticism there is a tradition that the first set of tablets that Moses brought down from the mountain contained a different and greater wisdom than that on the second set of tablets he brought down after the people had shown themselves unworthy by worshipping the Golden Calf. This greater wisdom was sometimes called the Kabbalah.
6. A. Lieber, 'Human aggression and the lunar synodic cycle', *Journal of Clinical Psychiatry* 39 (5), 1978: 296
7. In *The Advancement of Learning* Book II Francis Bacon said that the 'things invisible' were reflected by the moon.
8. The moon's light is constantly changing, often shadowy, and human thought likewise loses its clarity periodically and becomes fantastical. Moon demons are about the size of a six- or seven-year-old human. They howl at the full moon but fall silent at a new moon.
9. Joshua: chapters 5–6, The War Scroll found at Qumran and published in 1995 forbids the ritually impure to take part in battle, because holy angels will be fighting too. The angel who went before the Israelites

was St Michael. His mission at the time was to lead the Israelites to develop a rational, thinking consciousness. Michael, the messenger of Yahweh, is often depicted weighing the souls of the dead. By giving the Jews reason and the ability to choose rationally between right and wrong, he was also condemning them to be judged according to the path they took.

10. The 'new chronology' places the Exodus in at approximately 1447 BC. The latest excavations at Hisarlik in Turkey put the siege of Troy in the Late Bronze Age, approximately 200 years later. See David Rohl's *A Test of Time* (Century, 1995)

11. Pythagoras believed he recognized the shield he carried in a previous incarnation at the siege of Troy. Story preserved by Diogenes Laertins, available online at The Centre for Hellenic Studies, Harvard University.

12. For a perceptive critique of Jaynes, see *Voices of Reason, Voices of Insanity* by Ivan Leudar and Philip Thomas (Routledge, 2000). In my view this is a useful corrective to Jaynes, showing that he overstates his case. There are in Homer passages suggestive of the interior life, particularly and especially Odysseus, who says to himself, 'Why does my heart within me debate these things?' On the other hand, that it is Odysseus who says this is significant, because this cunning hero is the forger of the new form of consciousness. Like the Hebrew heroes, Odysseus succeeds by wits, not by his superior strength, like traditional Greek heroes represented at the siege by Achilles. It is instructive, too, to look at the work of earlier generations of scholars such as E. R. Dodds (*The Greeks and the Irrational*, University of California Press, 1951) and the 1948–50 Gifford Lectures of Wittgenstein's follower John Wisdom. They would have agreed with Jaynes in many respects, even if they might not have framed it so provocatively. It is also worth noting in this context that when Homer asks the Muses for help in writing, he is not asking for help with his writing style, he is asking for *factual information* about the course of the war and individual battles. He not only writes about people encountering spiritual beings coming to them from outside their own minds, he encounters such beings himself. This may remind us of Theosophists and Rudolf Steiner consulting the 'akashic chronicles', the cosmic memory bank. Similarly in *Paradise Lost*, Book 9, John Milton writes of his 'celestial patroness' whose 'nightly visitation is 'unimplor'd' and who 'dictates

to me slumbering or inspires easy my unpremeditated verse'.

13. This is a history of the world as it was understood and believed by people with a different form of consciousness to the one that dominates today. But the surprising thing is that many people today still have that form of consciousness, or something very like it – and if you have read this this book this far, that probably includes you!

CHAPTER 18

1. Wearing a chain and a ring, both of which had the name of God engraved on them, Solomon entered the throne room. The demon Asmodeus was sitting on the right of the throne, but when he saw Solomon, he raised his wings in fright and with a shriek flew away and vanished. (A Jewish legend preserved in Freemasonic lore. See *Masonic Legends and Traditions* by Dudley Wright, 1921, Chapter 3, available online in the excellent Ohio Grand Lodge Library of Masonic Books.)

2. This version of the ancient story of Hiram was reintroduced into the stream of Freemasonic tradition in the eighteenth century by the mysterious spiritual teacher and diplomat who called himself the Comte de St Germain. If angels influence our lives and if, as Christian tradition avers, some of those angels are the angels of the planets and constellations, then we have implicit in Christianity the outlines of a world-view that is at least very closely adjacent if not identical to the world-view of astrology. Currently the Church is in one of its astrology-denying phases, though for much of history astrological beliefs have been woven into everyday religious practice. Both the Old and New Testaments are bejewelled with stellar and planetary lore, and, like Solomon's Temple, Christian churches have traditionally been built and oriented according to astrological principles. One of the aims of this book is to look at what the great religions have in common, and there seems to be an astrological element in all of them. See also *The Secret History of the World* (Quercus, 2008).

CHAPTER 19

1. When he first appears he is called Elijah the Tishbite, but research has found no town, tribe or region associated with this name.

2. The attentions of the ravens indicate the presence of Zarathustra, a kindred spirit.

3. Of course it's hard not see an echo of this in the relatively recent Christian tradition of children leaving food and drink out for Father Christmas.

4. Elisha took on the mantle and had 'a double portion of spirit' (2 Kings 2.9). The Torah explains that he performed sixteen miracles whereas Elijah had performed eight. In esoteric literature this mantle is described as a mantle of fiery love. It refers to a stage in the transformation of the subtle body, a part of *merkabah* mysticism by means of which the subtle bodies are crafted into a chariot to carry the spirit up into the heavens.

5. Moses and Elijah continue to play great roles in the spiritual economy of the cosmos. Elijah intervenes in what the seventeenth-century mystic Jacob Boehme referred to as the Outworld and heralds the Second Coming, and Moses calls us to account after death. The sacred scriptures of the Jews show that the cosmos was made for us and moves both to help and to test us, both in this life and the next.

6. We may be reminded of the promise in the Psalms (91.11–13): 'He will give you his angels charge of you to guard you in all your ways. On their hands they will bear you up, lest you dash your foot against a stone. You will tread on the lion and the adder, the young lion and the serpent you will trample underfoot.'

CHAPTER 20

1. Immortality is a thread running through many incarnations. Highly advanced astrologers can trace it. It is said that Mother Meera can see it when you kneel in front of her and she looks down into your head. Great beings living and working in this world and in the spirit worlds are remembered in different cultures and in different times in different cultural clothing. The being who would be born to this queen

and would come to be known as the Buddha had lived earlier as Odin, according ot Rudolf Steiner. This great being has an essential role in the history of the cosmos: to lead us up and out of our animal bodies.

2. The tree the Buddha sits in front of is Odin's World Tree, the tree that connects us spiritually with everything in the cosmos. By also sitting against it, he is revivifying it and reconnecting humanity with everything.

3. For the Buddha's affinity with shepherds see also his appearance to the shepherds in the Gospel of St Luke. See *The Gospel of Luke*, lectures 2 and 3, Rudolf Steiner, 1909.

4. The Buddha's teachings about the principles underlying the cosmos have a wonderful clarity and they represent an epoch-making leap forward in conceptual thinking, as distinct from the traditional picture-consciousness of the ancient world.

5. The self is the individual's centre of consciousness. The Self is the Cosmic Mind. In idealism, the self is not the originator of its own consciousness, as it is in materialism, but 'borrows' consciousness from the Self. The Self is sometimes conceived of as undifferentiated, and sometimes its thoughts are experienced as gods or angels. Lorna Byrne has told me that she sometimes sees all angels connected to God by a cord.

6. The doctrine of the Eightfold Path of Virtue can seem highly abstract, but it is a way of working on the sixteen-petalled chakra, of moulding the petals in their ethereal plasticity in order to achieve spiritual gifts – but in a moral way. The Buddha taught holy living as the way to experience higher worlds.

CHAPTER 21

1. Given that Socrates is the father of Western philosophy, I have been surprised to find no account of his life with his daemon as its central theme, as I give it here. This is perhaps because his philosophy was seminal for rationalists and materialists. But, as this chapter shows, he did not believe what they believe.

2. In the play by Sophocles, Oedipus said that the daemon that had

urged him to his sorry self-blinding end had been Apollo, but he also insisted that the hand that had done the deed was his and his alone. (*Oedipus Rex* lines 1385–1390)

3. For an alternative view of the daemon of Socrates, Sir John Beaumont, the eighteenth-century squire whose early account of shamanism and poltergeists we will examine later, wrote that the daemon was clearly evil, because it led Socrates to an unnecessary death! (*An historical, physiological and theological treatise of spirits: apparitions, witchcrafts, and other magical practices. Containing an account of the genii . . . With a refutation of Dr. Bekker's World bewitch'd; and other authors . . .* , 1705)

    An interesting sidelight on the daemon of Socrates comes in the life of Plotinus, the Neoplatonist philosopher. He was persuaded by a friend to go to meet an Egyptian priest visiting Rome. This priest said he would show Plotinus his daemon, or familiar spirit, and invited him to come to the temple of Isis, where he would make the invocation, explaining this was the only place in Rome where the Egyptian language sounded pure and so reverberated effectively. But when the daemon was called to show itself, a god appeared. The Egyptian priest cried out, 'You are a happy man, Plotinus! You have a god for your daemon. Your guide is not of an inferior kind.' (Porphyry, *Life of Plotinus*, 10:1–2)

    Relating this story, Beaumont draws on comments from Hermes Trismegistus: 'Those who are committed to the more sublime angels are preferred before other men. For these angels that have care of them, raise them, and by a certain secret power subject others to them, which though neither perceive, yet he that is subjected finds a certain weight of presidency, from which he cannot easily disengage himself. Nay, he fears and reverences that force, which the superior angels influence the inferiors with, and bring the inferiors by a certain terror into the fear of presidency.'

4. The first philosopher to give a systematic account of atoms was a contemporary of Socrates called Democritus. An atom is literally that which is uncuttable. The atom was held to be the irreducible and therefore basic component of all reality – what was really real. Democritus's follower Epicurus and a hundred years later the Roman Lucretius developed atomism and with it a mechanical view of the

universe that was materialistic in the sense of proposing that matter was self-subsisting in a way that made spiritual explanation unnecessary. In *On the Nature of Things* Lucretius denied divine providence, celebrated pleasure as the highest good and said that world consisted of nothing but atoms and emptiness. Do the greatest periods of human creativity come from the drive to marry our everyday human experience of the divine with atomism – with science?

Epicurus founded one of the most popular schools in late antiquity. Similarly, atomism became very popular in the late nineteenth century, but was discredited by cutting-edge science in the 1950s.

CHAPTER 22

1. Other mystics who have had visions of the life of Jesus include Bridget of Sweden, Catherine of Siena, Anne Catherine Emmerich and Therese Neumann.

2. Quantum mechanics has revealed how human perceptions affect the behaviour of subatomic particles. This raises a weird possibility: perhaps the forming of the idea of atoms by Democritus and Epicurus brought them into existence? Perhaps matter was constituted differently before then?

3. 'In the deep dark night of the world Christ came.' Hildegard of Bingen. *Scivias* III, 7

4. In *Timaeus* Plato wrote: 'God laid the soul of the world in the shape of a cross through the cosmos and stretched out over the world body.' In *The Republic* he wrote that 'the Just Man will be crucified', which to many commentators seems to be an enactment on the human scale of the cosmic act described in *Timaeus*. These two passages are sometimes conflated to form a prophecy of the crucifixion, for instance by Rudolf Steiner.

5. Once human minds have been transformed by contact with Christ, divine consciousness will work outwards, refining and spiritualizing first animal consciousness, then vegetable life and finally matter. To begin this spiritual process you must first change your mindset and

then begin to change your physiology. As this mysterious spiritualizing process takes place, you will gain control of the animal, vegetable and, finally, when very advanced, the material dimensions of life. Some saints, for example, could control wild beasts, read other people's minds, heal and even fly. There is a complex and mysterious theology of matter here. Christianity does not argue for a turning away from the material dimension, a repression of the human body or of love and desire, but works towards a spiritualization of them.

6. Luke 10.38–42.

7. An oil used for anointing – *Christ* means 'the anointed one' – is an oil gently and slowly extracted from a tree or plant. It is its inner essence of living spirit. An anointment might give a spiritual glow.

8. Of all the non-canonical literature that narrowly missed out on inclusion in the canon, the Gospel of Thomas is the closest in form and content to the four canonical gospels, and is these days sometimes included in synoptic compilations and editions.

9. The earliest version we have on this text is damaged and the word 'mouth' is an assumption.

10. This story has been created by putting together some scraps of the Codex Borgianus, as interpreted by Lord Kingsborough and collected in *The World's Saviours* by Rev. C. H. Vail (N. L. Fowler & Co., 1913), and marrying them to ideas in Rudolf Steiner's lectures published as *Inner Impulses of Evolution: The Mexican Mysteries and the Knights Templar* (Anthroposophical Press, 1916). The Spider Woman is here the creator goddess/Isis of Chapters 4 and 5.

11. From the Gospel of Thomas, saying 82.

CHAPTER 23

1. There were various methods of inducing a visionary state in the ancient world. Chosen candidates were initiated in 'Mystery schools', secret enclosures attached to temples. Initiation meant dying to the world for three days and then being 'born again'. In Egypt in the Great Pyramid the candidate for initiation lay for three days in the granite coffin in the room we know as the King's Chamber. In initiation ceremonies in other parts of the world, the candidate was hung on a

tree. During the three-day period the candidate would undergo an experience like the one the human spirit experiences after death. When candidates awoke, they were convinced they had experienced higher realities. The most famous initiation centre in Greece, called Eleusis, lay just outside Athens. The Athenian intellectual and political élite initiated there included Sophocles, Plato, Pindar, Plutarch, Aristophanes and Cicero. (For a fuller account, see *The Secret History of the World* and *The Secret History of Dante*, Quercus, 2013)

2. Paul and other early Christians were well versed in mystical and esoteric lore. Iraneus, Clement, Tertullian and Jerome used the gematria, the mystical number symbolism more usually associated with the Kabbalah and the Old Testament, which we saw earlier in Greek myths.

    John Michell and David Fideler both made extraordinary breakthroughs in this field of studies in recent years, showing that the story of the miracle of the 153 fish in the unbroken net (John 21) and the story of the feeding of the five thousand contain a complex numerical symbolism. The fishing net of the gospels is the same net we saw on the omphalos stone in Greece: the process by which the thoughts of the Cosmic Mind are caught and pulled into the material world. They describe the process of precipitation of matter by mind with mathematical exactitude. See *City of Revelation* by John Michell (Ballantine, 1973) and *Jesus Christ, Sun of God* by David Fideler (Quest Books, 1996).

    Dionysius the Areopagite would be martyred on another hill just outside Paris, which we know as Montmartre as a result.

3. 1 Corinthians 15:55

4. Acts 2.24, 1 Peter 3.19, Gospel of Peter 10.38

5. For Nicodemus as an initiate, see Maurice Nicoll's *The Mark* (Vincent Stuart, 1954). When the gospel writer says that Nicodemus came to Jesus *by night,* he means that Nicodemus and Jesus were encountering each other out of the body, an ability that some initiations confer. The aim of initiation is to help prepare humanity for future evolution and therefore the nature of initiation evolves too. In the passage that follows Jesus explains to Nicodemus that the time has come for a new, more highly spiritual concept of rebirth. (John 3, 1–21)

6. Enoch and Elijah then describe how they are to return to battle with

the Antichrist at Jerusalem.

7. The three-day death and resurrection of Jesus had been in some way like the initiation ceremonies of the Mystery schools, except that it had been acted out in public. Moreover this was of course no symbolic death and rebirth. It was not simply a matter of altered states of consciousness. He really had died. In some ways, the initiations of the Mystery schools might be seen as prophecies of this historical event.

8. For an extraordinary modern rendering of this myth, told with a Miltonic grandeur, see the final chapter of Philip Pullman's *Subtle Knife* trilogy.

9. Blindness – to the material world – is sometimes symbolic of initiation, as in the case of Homer. See also Tomberg p.110

10. For a detailed account of the different degrees of certitude in Christian doctrine regarding angels, see the Fr Hardon Archives, www.therealpresence.org. See also *The Tibetan Book of the Dead*: 'The Good genius was born simultaneously with thee ... and the evil genius was born simultaneously with thee ...' (Book 2, part 2, the judgement)

CHAPTER 24

1. According to Sufis, saints are able to 'perform things that go against the customs'. For a modern account of regularities in nature accounted for as 'habits' rather than fixed, eternal immutable laws, see Chapter 3 of *The Science Delusion* by Rupert Sheldrake.

2. *The Book of Adam* is another text from this era with a vivid and immediate sense of the way that evil operates in history: 'This world is all night, full of twists and turns, tied up in knots and sealed with seals beyond measure.'

CHAPTER 25

1. Dirt is sometimes defined as: 'matter in the wrong place'. We might formulate a definition of evil along similar lines: 'wisdom in the wrong time'. After the falling apart of the civilizations of the ancient world and the closing down of the Mystery temples attached to the great

public temples, the priests, the *magi*, were forced to flee, and many arrived in Arabia. Outside the strictly guarded confines of the Mystery schools, their wisdom began to seep out, causing a widespread culture of occult experimentation. Part of Mohammed's mission was to stamp this out – reflected in the Islamic symbol in which Venus is enclosed by the moon. See also *The Secret History of the World*.

2. Origen made a clear distinction between asking angels for help and invoking them. See *The Westminster Handbook to Origen*, 2004.

3. Angels appear more than eighty times in the Koran and are a part of Islamic theology. 'Humanity's position at the centre of the cosmos is explained by reference to the angels, and over every soul, it says, there is a watcher.' Sachiko Murata in Seyyed Hossein Nasr, *Islamic Spirituality: Foundations* (Crossroad, 1987)

Significantly perhaps, Islamic intellectual leaders in America have been quick to take Lorna Byrne to their hearts: 'Lorna Byrne lifts the veil from our eyes by connecting the reader to an unseen angelic realm. At a time when the world is witnessing confusion, *A Message of Hope from the Angels* is a testament to the Divine love and assistance that constantly surrounds us—even if we don't always see or feel it.' Imam Feisal Abdul Rauf, author of Moving the Mountain and CEO of the Cordoba Initiative. 'Institutional religion and belief have been challenged and discredited by clergy scandals, "new atheists" and secularism, the growth of religious intolerance, and empty pews. Lorna Byrne's *A Message of Hope from the Angels* offers a message of hope that speaks to the crises and everyday problems that many struggle with in today's world.' John L. Esposito, University Professor at Georgetown University and author of *The Future of Islam* and *What Everyone Needs to Know about Islam*.

CHAPTER 26

1. Charlemagne gave the Sancta Camisia, the holy tunic of the Virgin Mary, to the church that would become Chartres cathedral. The cult of the Virgin Mary originated at Chartres, and spread out from there over the world.

2. Roger Bacon, the thirteenth-century scholar and founder of the

experimental method in European histories of science, quoted Sufi texts such as the *Hikmat el-Ishraq* and even dressed as an Arab in his perambulations around Oxford.

3. Ibrahim ibn Adham, who died c.790, was a Sufi saint.

4. Khdir was sent by God to the king of El Maucil to demand he convert to Islam. The king refused and ordered that Khdir be executed. The executioners did their job, but a few days later Khdir turned up at court again and renewed his demand. The king had him executed again, and again Khdir revived and reappeared, preaching. This time the king had him burned and his ashes scattered in the Tigris. The next time Khdir reappeared, the king and his city were destroyed by a terrible earthquake. (From *Curious Myths of the Middle Ages*, Sabine Baring Gould, 1866.)

5. Hildegard of Bingen: 'Listen to the sound in this music of fiery love coming forth in the words of this virginal youth who flowers like a green twig. Listen to the sound coming from the pouring out of the blood of those who are offering themselves faithfully and to the sound coming from the greenness of those flowering in virginity.' *Scivias*, The Third Part, Vision 13

CHAPTER 27

1. The father of the historical Perceval was one of Charlemagne's paladins called William of Orange.

2. John Donne's famous 1622 sermon 'Jesus Wept' is about how we may be deeply moved by the plight of another, how we may cry with love, and how this may become a sacred and miraculous process. When we cry holy tears, we are bathed in the tears of Jesus Christ, and this transforms both our innermost and outermost selves. According to the Catholic esoteric writer Valentin Tomberg, holy tears emanate from the heart, which is to say from the twelve-petalled lotus. *Meditations in the Tarot*, Letter XIV

3. The idea of a miraculous cup or bowl is universal. We find it in the Hindu *soma* and the Persian *homa*, the draught of immortality, and in the communion cup. In the Japanese tea ceremony there is a sense that the humble cup is the humble soul, poor in spirit and open to

being infused with the spirit of *wahi*, which is to say open to receive the inpouring of holy enlightenment. But the immediate antecedents of the Grail legend stories are obviously Celtic. One of the earliest surviving sources for stories of King Arthur, *The Spoils of Anwfn* (Welsh for 'Underworld'), features a cauldron of plenty.

The lance is like the legendary lance that is the only thing that can heal the wound it has caused, and in the story of the Grail its purpose is to heal human blood. Human blood carries animal consciousness – spirit – but, being animal, it is bestial. When it has been transformed, however, it can carry the spirit of Christ. For an account of the rediscovery of this lance during the siege of Antioch in 1268, see *The Secret History of Dante*, Appendix 1.

The Grail is like a flower that opens up when it receives the sun's beam – the holy lance of love. It therefore represents the vegetative dimension in the human being – the soul that connects us with the spiritual worlds. When our blood, our animal nature, has been fully purified by the spirit of Christ, our soul will blossom. There is an allusion here to the activation of the crown chakra, but also a looking forward to a time when humanity will be so far spiritualized and its animal nature so far transformed that it will return to the paradisal state described in Chapter 2. In this state it will no longer reproduce sexually but by the power of thought. 'At the resurrection people will neither marry nor be given in marriage: they will be like angels in heaven' (Matthew 22.30).

CHAPTER 28

1. 'Behold I have set thee today as a strong city, a pillar of iron and a wall of brass against the kings of Judah.' (Jeremiah 1.18) Henry Corbin, the great French scholar of Islamic esoteric philosophy, recorded a tale which is in a sense the mirror imager of this tale. In this story the hero's adventures take him to the fabulous world, the parallel dimension, where the mysterious Hidden Imam lives. He finds a part of it that looks remarkably familiar, and then realizes that he has arrived home. *Mundus Imaginalis*, Henry Corbin, 1964

2. 'There was one section of that tale which fascinated my gaze in a

degree that I never afterwards forgot. It was, in fact, one of those many important cases which elsewhere I have called involutes of human sensibility; combinations in which the materials of future thought or feeling are carried as imperceptibly into the mind as vegetable seeds are carried variously combined through the atmosphere, or by means of rivers, by birds, by winds, by waters, into remote countries.' Here again is de Quincey's sense of the interconnectedness of everything in the world. (Thomas de Quincey, *Autobiographical Sketches*, 1853)

CHAPTER 29

1. The skeletal remains of a wolf were said to have been discovered under the paving slabs of the church of St Francis in Gubbio in 1873.
2. The life of St Francis was one of constant inner struggle, and through this struggle the inner life of humanity became richer, more various, more subtly shaded, more deeply felt. This in turn had an effect on painting, leading to what Frank Auerbach described as 'a more direct and intense representation of human events', for example in the paintings of Giotto. (Quoted in *Dante the Maker*, William Anderson, 1980.)
3. Like Osiris and Jesus, St Francis lights up the Underworld. He is on a mission to all humanity, alive and dead. See also Chapter 45 re Padre Pio.

CHAPTER 30

1. A *hadith* is a saying or act attributed to the prophet Mohammed, sometimes conveying directly the word of God.
2. A similar chain of transmission may be traced among the great German mystics from Eckhart to Tauler to Valentine Andrae, the supposed author of the Rosicrucian Manifestos; see *The Secret History of the World*.
3. This is an existential desert, of course, a desert of non-being.
4. Ibn Arabi describes the experience of falling in love in beautiful, poetic

terms. Today this may seem like a universal experience, but it wasn't always so. Descriptions of falling in love enter European literature with the troubadours and Dante's falling in love with Beatrice on the streets of Florence in 1247. The notion of romantic love became more popular and more widespread because of the fashion for courtly love celebrated in, for example, *The Romance of the Rose* by Guillaume de Lorris and Jean de Meun, published in full in 1275. For a fuller account of Ibn Arabi, see *The Secret History of Dante.*

5. St Francis would always begin to preach using the phrase 'The peace of God be with you!' – of course, a distinctively Arabian greeting.

6. This Church practice invites comparison with the spells collected in, for example, Wallis Budge's *Egyptian Magic* (1899).

7. The place of sacred cows and bulls in Hinduism and ancient Egyptian religion is well known. Eusebe Salverte, sceptical author of *The Philosophy of Magic* (1829), preserved a record from Bury St Edmunds in England in 1487. It describes a ceremony in which a gentlewoman would choose a white bull that had never been tethered to a plough or baited. This bull would be led in procession to the shrine of St Edmund, with the monks singing, the crowd shouting and the woman walking by the bull stroking his milk-white sides and his 'pendant dewlaps' (the skin under his neck).

8. The distinction between soul and spirit was abolished by the Fourth Ecumenical Council of Constantinople in 869. We can see the resultant unease as much in the Cathars and Minnesangers as later in Luther and Calvin. Looked at this way, the Rosicrucians may also be seen as the extreme radical wing of the Reformation.

CHAPTER 31

1. When Dante wrote to a friend, the Lord of Verona, describing the effect he hoped his great poem would have on its readers, he was quoting Pindar on the benefits of initiation into the Mysteries: 'To take those living in a state of misery and bring them to an assurance of happiness.' Dante intended that reading his poem would be a form of initiation. (Epist.X.15) For a fuller treatment, including Dante's initiation into a tertiary order of the Templars, see *The Secret History*

of Dante by Jonathan Black (Quercus, 2013). The deeper I researched the Templars and their motives for wanting to control Jerusalem, to do with the prophecies of the Antichrist, the more it seemed to me that the least helpful system of thought when it comes to trying to understand them, is modern common sense.

CHAPTER 32

1. Hatha yoga is a type of practical mysticism involving breathing and other physical exercises so that physiological changes help bring about direct spiritual experience. Four texts in particular deal with the chakras; the *Shri Jabala Darshana Upanishad*, the *Chudamani Upanishad*, the *Yoga-Shikha Upanishad* and the *Shandilya Upanishad.* These texts describe the location of the chakras and provide symbolic descriptions for each of them. The alchemical teachings of Christian Rosencreutz involve similar work on the chakras – or 'the eyes of soul', as Teresa of Avila called them – but with a difference: in this 'Christian yoga' it is the heat of the Sun-god, Christ, which warms the lotus centres and causes them to open, blossom and mature in the light of the beautiful and the good.

    The twelve-petalled chakra of the heart is the centre of love. It is not fixed to the physical organism but can go out of the body, raying outwards to embrace others. This is one of the great esoteric secrets.

2. This story is very similar to – and originates in the same era as – the story of Venus and Tannhäuser. And of course, like *Sleeping Beauty*, it is a story that should be understood from the point of view of someone in the spirit worlds. When Matysendranath and Tannhäuser are captured in the enchanted world, they are in our material world, and they then escape back into the spirit worlds. Tannhäuser travelled to Rome to beg the pope to absolve him. The pope refused and said that Tannhäuser had as much chance of finding salvation as his staff had of flowering. After the troubadour had departed, the pope's staff did sprout flowers – but Tannhäuser had already returned to Venus and damnation.

3. The red on white cross is, of course, the cross of St George and, in others of its forms, the cross of the Knights Templar. In Rosicrucian lore and spiritual practice red roses symbolize the chakras.

4. With its horn in the position of the third eye, the unicorn is a symbol of intelligence raised to such a high level that it can see into the spiritual worlds.

5. Mercury plays a big part in alchemy, working on different levels. On one level, when the time comes for us to cease to reproduce sexually, Mercury will replace the moon as the nearest and most influential planet to Earth. The forces of Mercury, represented at different times by Odin and the Buddha, are the impulses working towards this transformation. Mercury is the messenger leading us to a transformed, spiritualized world.

6. The pearl is a symbol of the Higher Self. 'The Hymn of the Pearl' has come down to us appended to the Acts of Thomas. The story in the hymn is that a young prince is sent down to Egypt – which represents the material world – in order to retrieve a pearl. He takes off his robe of glory and descends. But while among the Egyptians he eats their food and falls into a deep sleep, forgetting he is the son of a king and what he is there for.

7. People sometimes read *The Yoga Sutras of Pantanjali* and react with incredulity to instructions on, for example, how to develop the strength of an elephant. In fact such gifts of the spirit can only be obtained, like the wonders alluded to in Christian Rosencreutz's dream, over several incarnations.

8. The vampire myth is an evil inversion of the story of Christian Rosencreutz.

CHAPTER 34

1. What was the nature of the being that William Noy encountered? It is important to distinguish between ghosts, whose after-death progress has been impeded in some unnatural way, and our loved ones in heaven, who may visit us fleetingly to prompt or guide us, perhaps even appear to us. David Bellamy gives us an example of the latter in his autobiography *Jolly Green Giant* (Century, 2002). While

finishing this book I was sent a book containing a most extraordinary and authentic first-hand account of the Power of Kundalini rising through the Chakras, written by a westerner. The chapter on enlightenment in *The Nine Freedoms*, by George King, 1963.

CHAPTER 35

1. Trithemius famously said: 'With the help of angels I can while sitting or walking communicate my thought to someone else over many miles without use of words, signs or signals.' Today we may have an anachronistic reflex of disapproval at the occult researches of magi like Trithemius and Cornelius Agrippa. There was a fine mix of attitudes at the time, but it is as well to remember that one of Paracelsus's contemporaries, Pope Sixtus IV, personally translated 72 Kabbalistic books into Latin.

2. In folklore goblins were sometimes said to be able to weave gossamer nightmares into the ears of sleeping humans.

3. In his memoirs, the Italian Renaissance sculptor Cellini famously remembers seeing a salamander in the Colosseum.

4. From the treatise *De Virtute Imaginativa*.

5. For Paracelsus, the soul of man is as intimately connected to the soul of the Earth as it is to the physical body. Invisible matter becomes organized and is made visible through the influence of the soul. If a living thing like a plant loses its material substance, the invisible form still remains 'in the light of Nature', and if we can reclothe that form with visible matter, we may make it visible again.

6. Practising a Paracelsus-influenced form of alchemy, the Jesuit priest Athanasius Kircher resurrected a rose from its ashes in front of Queen Christina of Sweden in 1687. Geoffrey Hodson, the remarkable Theosophist visionary from New Zealand, described spirits or fairies weaving into existence the ideal form of a flower – much as Plato might have conceived it – which, he said, was then filled by matter to create a physical flower. To view a magus miraculously reviving a flower, see Mooji, 'Flower of Life' on YouTube.

7. This is 'the Work' of the alchemists.

8. In the methodology of the experimental sciences – and we see the beginnings of it at this time – great emphasis is put on the collecting

of evidence to test theories. But of course the theory must have been arrived at by intuition.

If we look at the history of science in these terms, a paradox arises. The greater the leap forward that the discovery represents, the greater the role of intuition. The most brilliant ideas are usually the ones that come not after meticulous step-by-step calculation but 'out of nowhere', as you might say – if you are a materialist. Traditionally they were explained by angelic prompting. If you call the process 'intuition', you are not thereby offering an alternative explanation, only giving the same explanation a more scientific-sounding name.

CHAPTER 36

1. *Concerning the Three Principles of the Divine Essence* 1619. *Mysterium Magnum*, p.2, 1623

2. Second Epistle from *Sixty-Two Theosophic Epistles*, 1624

3. The Myers Briggs system of personality classification has become the standard method of assessment of employees by large organizations. It proposes four main types, three of which are primarily focused on sense data – sight, sound and touch. The fourth group – the 'digital' group – receives information not so much directly from the senses but after that information has been processed internally. This group, roughly a quarter of the population, is therefore more focused on the moving texture, the shifts and shades of the inner life. On the other hand, people who are autistic tend to be very focused on sense data and have less sense of an inner life in themselves or others. Science may therefore be said to represent a career opportunity for people with autistic tendencies. Moreover research also shows that people who are autistic seldom hold religious beliefs.

4. In 1894 a census of hallucinations was carried out by the English Society of Psychical Research and revealed that one in ten people experience an hallucination at some time in their life that is not the result of physical or mental illness. A similar survey in 1948 confirmed this.

5. Anglo-American analytical philosophy in the seventies. It may all have changed now.

CHAPTER 37

1. Steiner noted, in *The Karma of Untruthfulness* II: Lecture 20, '... the utterly British philosopher Francis Bacon of Verulam, the founder of modern materialistic thinking, [was] inspired from the same source as Shakespeare.' For Elijah working through both men, see *The Secret History of the World*.

2. Francis Bacon, *The Advancement of Learning*, Second Book, 1605

3. There is a fuller account of *The Taming of the Shrew* in *The Secret History of the World*, Chapter 20. There is an essay by Corbin on the *mundus imaginalis* freely available on the net.

4. The great prophet of this is of course Harold Bloom, Sterling Professor of Humanities at Yale University and author of *Shakespeare: The Invention of the Human* (Riverhead Trade, 1999).

5. The great book on the subject is Robert Burton's *Anatomy of Melancholy*, published in 1621. Burton gnomically comments that the real leader of the Society of the Rosie Cross was then still living.

6. 'Madness fascinates because it is knowledge,' said Michel Foucault in *Madness and Civilization*. But altered states of consciousness, mystical or otherwise, are only interesting if what they show is real; in Shakespeare, of course, the mad, the apparently mad and the crazy fool are often conduits for the higher wisdom. They see greater realities that the other characters cannot see.

CHAPTER 38

1. Robert Kirk, *The Secret Commonwealth of Elves, Fauns and Fairies*, finished in 1692. It was not published in Kirk's lifetime, only much later in 1815, by Sir Walter Scott.

2. Did this notion of fairy life give rise to Blake's idea of the ghost of a flea? Painting on permanent view in Tate Britain, London.

3. These accounts were taken from the testimonies of witnesses, but whatever their motives no one doubts they thought they saw what they said they saw. The Manningtree court records are available online.

4. In the twentieth century there was some emphasis on an additional criterion – that what a good scientific theory proposes should be not

only testable but also *falsifiable*. If no conceivable set of events would count against it, the argument runs, the theory is not really proposing anything. This was a stick used to beat religion.

5. During the course of scientism's emergence in the seventeenth century and the transition from an idealism world-view to a materialism world-view in the eighteenth and nineteenth centuries, the pioneers of science and maths held beliefs that would be anathema to today's radical materialists. Francis Bacon was a Neoplatonist who believed in angels and demons. Spinoza believed in angels. Descartes believed he might have been deceived by a *mauvais* genie. While still a young soldier he had a dream in which an angel appeared to him and revealed to him his mission in life – and how to achieve it. According to his own account of this dream, the angel said to him, 'The conquest of nature is to be achieved by measure and number.' Kepler and Galileo both believed in astrology. There was a strong spiritual dimension to all Kepler's work. He believed that astrology was 'a testimony of God's works' and a divine revelation, that at birth a celestial imprint of the positions of the stars and planets was made on the soul of an individual that would enable that person to hear celestial music and impel them to dance to the music of the spheres (see *Johannes Kepler and the Music of the Spheres* by David Plant). Even Locke advised that healing herbs should be picked at astrologically propitious times. Culpeper's *Herbal*, (1653) the first systematic herbal in English and the foundation stone of pharmaceuticals, was an extended commentary on the works of Paracelsus and Jacob Boehme.

6. A sense that our lives are meaningful is interwoven with our most heartfelt concerns by thousands of threads. To rip these out is a painful operation, but if you are an atheist and want to be intellectually consistent, this is what you must do, because the reality is that without a pre-existing Cosmic Mind to mean it, the cosmos and our part in it have no intrinsic meaning. This is a stark truth. I suspect that not many people who call themselves atheists face up to it and its implications for the way they understand their day-to-day experience. I suspect that they may compartmentalize their atheistic beliefs and carry on living their everyday lives as if they were full of meaning. Living life in a way that is rigorously consistent with atheism, constantly resisting the blandishments of meaningfulness and intuitions of something higher,

the temptation to believe that this or that was meant to be, may be hard work and even dangerous. Jean-Paul Sartre's *La Nausée* (Gallimard, 1938) is an autobiographical novel, an account of someone trying to live with complete intellectual honesty a life with no essential meaning. It is a painful account of a series of psychotic episodes. In the end the hero can bear it no longer and decides to give his life an arbitrary meaning – by becoming a writer. The biologist Lewis Wolpert, one of the leading proponents of atheism, has also written with great sincerity and sensitivity about his periods of debilitating depression. That atheism is depressing is, of course, not in itself a decisive reason to choose to believe in God, but it indicates that we may have a need for meaning hardwired into us.

CHAPTER 39

1. The philosopher Nicholas Berdayev wrote an essay on Boehme and his influences in *Studies Concerning Jacob Boehme* (1939): 'At the foundational basis of Hegel's philosophy lies an irrational principle. Hegel was as systematic in his rationalism as Aquinas or Descartes, but his whole system was based on an irrational vision – Boehme's. For Hegel, the Divinity is a primordially unconscious Deity, which comes to consciousness only through human philosophy. *The Roots of Romanticism* is a wonderful series of lectures given in 1965 by Isaiah Berlin introducing – to me anyway – many new writers and thinkers, part of a deep and intriguing vein of mysticism in German philosophy. I was intrigued to read of Herder's vision of God as a poet who speaks to us through history, of Fichte's idea that we do not act because we know, rather we know because we are called upon to act, and Schelling's idea of God as creative principle of consciousness. There is a direct line running from Boehme through these philosophers to Steiner.

2. Hegel, *On the Prospects for a Folk Religion*, 1793

3. Of course there are two main types of idealism – the mind-before-matter philosophy and the everyday sense of the mindset of someone prepared to sacrifice a great deal for the sake of a principle. But the two idealisms tend to go hand in hand, from the self-sacrifice of Socrates to the freedom-fighting of the Romantics. In fact the Romantics in

particular combined the two types, the Romantic tending to reject the everyday world, live in a garret and look to the stars.

CHAPTER 40

1. I learned from Patrick Harpur's excellent *Daimonic Reality* (Arkana, 1994) that when we talk about suffering a stroke, we are alluding to the 'fairy stroke', sometimes reported by people who had encountered 'the little people'. It rendered the recipient partially paralysed and unable to speak. The same effect has been reported by people who experience alien encounters and here by Bernadette of Lourdes.

2. This text has been taken largely from Bernadette's autobiography, supplemented with other contemporary accounts.

3. Swedenborg famously saw a fire in Stockholm and was able to describe it in great detail while it was happening – 300 miles away. He also quoted back to Sweden's negotiator word for word secret talks with Prussia and described the strangling of Peter III of Russia days before it took place. Like Joan of Arc and Lorna Byrne, Swedenborg saw angels with as much clarity as the rest of us see beings of flesh and blood.

CHAPTER 41

1. In 2006 I published a book called *Why Mrs Blake Cried* by an excellent scholar of the esoteric, Marsha Keith Schuchard. She was invited to a debate at United Grand Lodge in London, and when we had dinner afterwards, 'nabobs' was her humorous name for some of her hosts and opponents, who had dealt with her in a less than gentlemanly way in the course of the debate.

2. Whitley Strieber has written about feral children he saw in the same region, a prelude to encounters with otherworldly beings in *The Key*, 2000. I know of no writer who gives a better sense of what it is like to encounter a being from another dimension.

3. Henry Steel Olcott, *People from the Other World*, Cambridge University Press, New York, 1875

4. Ibid., Chapter 8

5. C. G. Harrison, *The Transcendental Universe*, George Redway, 1896

6. A certificate was issued to this effect by John Yarker, a senior British Freemason with strong American ties and member of at least one esoteric lodge. (See Mackey's *Revised Encyclopedia of Freemasonry*, 1929.)

7. Olcott quotes Lecky, author of *The History of the Rise and Influence of the Spirit of Rationalism in Europe* (1865), complaining of those who receive an account of a miracle taking place 'with an absolute and even derisive incredulity, which dispenses with all examination of the evidence'. I am reminded of Rupert Sheldrake's account of a recent conversation with his fellow biologist Richard Dawkins. 'I am not interested in the evidence!' said Dawkins, when pressed. As we shall see later, materialists have so framed the test that evidence is irrelevant.

8. *Hope Street* is an evocative memoir of a working-class life in Manchester by Pamela Young (Coronet, 2012). She was raised in the Spiritualist Church, then seen as a progressive, intellectually vibrant movement going hand in hand with socialism. Pam came from a long line of spiritually gifted women, none more so than her mother, a talented medium. The account of the materializations and other wonders that she and her brother witnessed in the 1950s are all the more powerful in the telling, because they were seen through the eyes of a child.

9. Bodily elongation is traditionally a phenomenon associated with saints and mystics, such as Veronica Lapelli in the seventeenth century or, in the eighteenth century, Blessed Stefana Quinzani. Over a hundred Catholic saints are said to have levitated.

10. For a well-researched article on the connection between Freemasonry and the Roscicrucians, see *An Esoteric View of the Rose-Croix Degree* by R.W.Bro Leon Zeldis, available online.

    Elias Ashmole published *The Theatrum Chemicum Britannicum* in 1651, a collection of alchemical poems. He had met a landowner called William Backhouse earlier in the year. Backhouse had adopted him as his 'Son' and he had accepted Backhouse as his spiritual master. Ashmole's spiritual education was long and drawn out, proceeding by fits and starts, until in May 1653 his notebook records: 'My father

Backhouse lying sick in Fleet Sreete over against St: Dunstans Church, and not knowing whether he should live or dye, about eleven o'clock, he told me in Silables the true Matter of the Philosophers Stone: which he bequeathed to me as a legacy.' Thereafter Ashmole's notes record no further alchemical experiments. He had attained. (By the word 'silables' he hints at the correct pronunciation of words according to a series of rhythmic vibrations, which in turn set up a succession of repercussions that may travel through the receding dimensions of a person's being. See *Maitri Upanishad*, VI)

CHAPTER 42

1. Published 1880. This is a shortened version of the Constance Garnett translation of 1912.
2. Vladimir Soloviev (1853–1900) founded the mystical philosophy called Sophiology. For an account of the prophecies of the Antichrist, see *The Secret History of the World*, revised edition (Quercus, 2010).
3. Like his friend Soloviev, Dostoyevsky predicts a hell on Earth precipitated by science, and both are inspired by Daniel's prophecies of the Antichrist. While a student, Soloviev had been hopping from one carriage to next of a moving train when in mid-flight he fainted. He was rescued from certain death by being dragged back on board by a young girl he had met earlier. He came to see that, really, she was a beautiful woman, whom he would call his Eternal Friend, a vision of wisdom, goodness and joy such as he had 'ceased to believe existed in this world'. His Eternal Friend would guide him through life. While he was on a study trip with Dostoyevsky to London, she summoned him to find her in the Egyptian desert. Dostoyevsky gives occasional hints as to his eschatological beliefs in his fiction: 'Your heavenly roses will bloom inside me forever,' he said. 'Men will transform the physical, and all thoughts and feelings will be transformed, all matter and the whole world.' (Dostoyevsky, *The Devils*, 1872)
4. A ratten – a short bamboo cane.

CHAPTER 43

1. William Blake: 'This world of Imagination is the world of eternity; it is the divine bosom into which we shall all go after the death of the Vegetated body.' *A Vision of the Last Judgement*, 1810.

2. There is a rare recording of Gershom Scholem lecturing on the *tzelem* in 1975 on the Book of Doctrines and Opinions, a site dedicated to Jewish theology and spirituality.

3. Biblical quotations distinguishing soul and spirit: I Thessalonians 5.25, I Corinthians 2.14, Luke 1.46–7. The distinction was 'abolished' by the Church in 669. Steiner and others have seen this as an attempt to prevent people attaining direct spiritual experience outside its aegis.

4. According to the *Maitri Upanishad*, 'He who sees with the eye, and he who moves in dreams, he who is in deep sleep, and he who is beyond the deep sleeper – these are a person's four distinct conditions.' The *Maitri Upanishad* is describing the whole human body as an instrument of perception and explaining that different elements of the body are vehicles for different forms of consciousness. (*Maitri Upanishad*, VII.II)

5. Athanasius, third-century bishop of Alexandria, said that in sleep the soul meets saints and angels as it is no longer confined within its earthly body. According to St Augustine, God works through dreams as through visions, and according to Tertullian, most people get their knowledge of God from dreams.

6. This is perhaps the commonly reported 'going into the light' experience. For a vivid account of this, see *Angels in My Hair* by Lorna Byrne. For a survey, giving an account of the remarkable consistency of such accounts across cultures, see *The After Death Experience: The Physics of the Non-physical*, which I commissioned from the historian Ian Wilson in 1987.

7. Interesting to compare with the medieval accounts of attacks by demons during the after-death experience by the Neoplatonist philosopher Proclus, who describes 'the rushing forms of troops of earthly demons'. See his *Commentary on the Statesman by Plato*.

8. In *On the Face on the Moon*, Plutarch wrote that after death the physical body is left behind as the soul and divine intellect – the *nous* – travel to the moon. After a while the divine intellect travels onwards

by itself. In accounts of death in the ancient world, such as the one given in what is today known as the Egyptian *Book of the Dead*, the self (the *nous*) has to go through seven gates and at each gate has to quote a magical formula, memorized during life on Earth. Here, in Steiner's account, it is moral and spiritual qualities that carry us through – a mark of humankind's spiritual evolution in the intervening period. Steiner also mentions in passing an intriguing idea: the spirits that live in the Mars sphere, for example, may sense us passing through. To them, we are like ghosts. See also *The Secret History of the World*, Chapter 10, for an account excavated in Iraq dating back to the third millennium BC.

9. E. R. Dodds, *The Greeks and the Irrational*, University of California Press, 1951, p.264

10. 'The world we live in,' wrote Steiner, 'is woven out of the material of which human thought exists.' (*Theosophy*, 1904, Chapter 3) We might picture this thought-material as being like water in a river, he suggested. Matter is like chunks of ice floating on the water – the same substance in a different state.

CHAPTER 44

1. For a list of books by Swedenborg borrowed by Jung, see the essay 'Jung on Swedenborg, Redivivus' by Eugene Taylor on the website of Philemon Foundation, www.philemonfoundation.org.

2. For a full account, see, *The Red Book*, W. W. Norton & Co., 2009, p.200.

3. Later he said the stories of Siegfried never appealed. German idealism can be a bit of a worry when it becomes *heroic*.

4. In *Alchemical Studies*, Routledge and Kegan Paul, 1967.

5. He kept the *Red Book* under lock and key during his lifetime – perhaps for fear people would think him mad. Philemon is an example of a Jungian 'archetype', the archetype of the wise old man, and, as the Swiss theologian Paul Tillich has pointed out, 'archetype' is here the Latin translation of Plato's 'idea'.

6. During the Crusades white-robed beings were seen to help the Christians in battle, which helped to give the Knights Templar a

supernatural aura. *The Knights Templar*, Stephen Howarth, Collins, 1982.

CHAPTER 45

1. In *The Church* (1967) Joseph Ratzinger's friend, the theologian Hans Küng, drew attention to similarities between the phenomena at Fátima and the prophecies of Joachim of Fiore – the predictions, the regularly recurring dates, the numerical symbolism. There are three children, three secrets and seven apparitions. The Lady appeared on the thirteenth of each month. Lucia would die on 13th May. The predicted assassination attempt on a Pope happened on 13th May 1981. It failed and the Bishop of Leiria-Fátima was given the bullet, which was later set in the crown on the statue of Our Lady of Fátima. For a fuller treatment of Joachim, see *The Secret History of the World* and *The Secret History of Dante*.

2. For further information on Catholic experiences of the supernatural in modern times, I recommend www.mysticsofthechurch.com. To give one further example, in 1968 two Muslim mechanics working in a garage in a suburb of Cairo saw a woman on the dome of St Mary's church. Assuming she was about to commit suicide, they called up to her not to jump. She did not reply, but when a woman pointed at her with a finger afflicted by gangrene, her finger was cured. Approximately a million people would see this luminous vision and photographs were taken too. For a good full account of this with photos, see *The Sceptical Occultist* by Terry White (Century, 1994).

CHAPTER 46

1. In 1946 Jung told a BBC radio audience that in 1918 he had begun to notice that a startling number of his German patients told him they were having dreams of an entity he identified as the Blond Beast. This entity was prophesied in the 1880s by Nietzsche when he wrote about what happens to noble men when they go amongst strangers, and the idea of it was adopted for their own ends by the Nazis. This is

another astonishing example of a powerful spirit or disembodied intelligence moving through many minds at once. (Friedrich Nietzche, *On the Geneology of Morals*, 1887)

2. There has been much speculation about Hitler's own occult interests, including *The Spear of Destiny*. Originally written by Trevor Ravenscroft as a novel. While working on this book I was sent an excellent book, *Whisperers* by J.H. Brennan, which produces a smoking gun in the form of a book called *Magische Geschichte / Theorie / Praxis*. Hitler owned a copy, which he annotated heavily – 66 times (chapter 18)

3. The only source for the story of Gitta and Hanna I know of is a little-known but wonderful book, *Talking with Angels* (Daimon Verlag, 1988).

CHAPTER 47

1. The ability to leave impressions in solid rock, though largely forgotten today, was also once a gift popularly attributed to high-level or spiritually evolved individuals in the West. An impression of the footprint of Hercules, easily two cubits long, was left in rock near Tyras in Scythia, according to Herodotus. Elijah's footprint was preserved on Mount Carmel. Moses left an impression of his back and arms in a cave where he had been hiding and there was an impression of Mohammed's head on the side of a cave near Medina. The stone on which St Catherine's body was laid out was said to have softened and retained an impression of it. For these and other examples, see *The Philosophy of Magic* by Eusebe Salverte (1829).

2. In the 1970s and 80s Father Thomas Keating, Fr William Meninger and Fr Basil Pennington developed a new form of contemplative prayer, based on the late medieval account *The Cloud of Unknowing*. The aim was to introduce the spiritual exercises and methods of meditation of a Trappist monastery to the outside world in order to create a Christian form of meditation to counterbalance the Eastern forms that were then becoming very popular among the young.

3. For an excellent account of scientists today clinging to a discredited mechanistic paradigm, see *The Science Delusion* by Rupert Sheldrake (Coronet, 2012).

4. The 'delayed choice' experiment was first carried out in 1984 at the University of Maryland by Alley, Jakubowicz and Wickes, and has been repeated many times since.

5. See Appendix II of *The Lost Key: The Supranatural Secrets of the Freemasons* by Robert Lomas (Coronet, 2011) for a clear account. In Chapter Eleven: 'Astronauts on Apollo 11 had reported seeing strange flashes, even with their eyes closed. NASA decided to investigate this effect, which only happened outside the Earth's natural electromagnetic shield. It was found that the flashes were caused by a single high-energy particle stimulating the astronauts' optic nerves or retinas.' Lomas goes on to quote from the official NASA report.

6. The plight of the Panchen Lama was brought to my attention by Sevak Gulbekian, publisher of Temple Lodge Publishing, the Rudolf Steiner Press and Clairview Books, and author of an excellent book, *In the Belly of the Beast: Holding your Own in Mass Culture* (Hampton Roads, 2004), which has a chapter on this subject.

7. *The Cycle of the Year as a Path of Initiation Leading to an Experience of the Christ Being* by Sergei O. Prokofieff (Temple Lodge Publishing, 1991), pp.337–8. Here Prokofieff, a leading Anthroposophical author, describes how materialistic influences on the living in the eighteenth, nineteenth and early twentieth centuries led to a drying up of their etheric bodies, impressed with dark imaginings, so that after death their etheric bodies were slow to dissolve and altogether formed a barrier, hindering encounters with Christ.

8. A full account can be found in the archives of the Religious Research Centre of the University of Wales.

9. David Hay, *Religious Experience Today*, Mowbray, 1990. See also David Hay and Gordon Heald, 'Religion is good for you', New Society, 17 April 1987.

10. ICM survey for the Bible Society reported in the *Daily Telegraph*, 17 December 2012.

11. Poll conducted by the Baylor University Institute for Studies of Religion and reported in *Time* magazine, 18 September 2008.

12. Survey by the Pew Forum on Religion and Public Life, available on: religions.pewforum.org/reports.

CHAPTER 48

1. Lorna's agent and manager, Jean Callanan, took us both to an exhibition of paintings by the Pre-Raphaelites at the Tate Britain earlier this year and Lorna picked out a painting of the Annunciation by Dante Gabriel Rossetti as capturing the perfectly the way that angels hover over the ground, down to the detail of the slight shadow. I hoped to show Lorna *The Dweller in the Innermost* by George Frederic Watts, which is perhaps a depiction of the Guardian of the Threshold, described by Edward Bulwer-Lytton, Rudolf Steiner and others. In the end we found a reproduction in the bookshop. For an interesting comparison, see this passage from *Experiences*, by Arnold Toynbee, Part II, Chapter 9: '. . . my concern with mankind is a concern for the spiritual facet of the psychosomatic presence that a human being displays to his fellow human beings and to himself. The truth (as I believe it to be) has been expressed visually by the Victorian English painter in a picture he has called '*The Dweller in the Innermost*.'

CONCLUSION

1. In the early chapters I tried to show that astrology only *seems* trivial – and that it is a component in a complex, sophisticated philosophical system that has served humanity well, and at least in the way it reconciles objecitve and subjective experience is the most comprehensive account of the world yet devised. Kant wrote that two things constantly filled him with awe – the pinpricks of the stars in the night sky and the pricking of the conscience within. In the philosophy outlined in this book the two are intimately connected.

2. Rupert Sheldrake was smiling mischieviously when he said to me in November 2012 that he thought that the Large Hadron Collider was a gigantic exercise in the quantum effect. All these scientists focusing on finding the Higgs Bosun particle will perhaps summon it into existence!

   In thousands of years, archaeologists may discover the remains of the Large Hadron Collider and consider them alongside the complex of pyramids on the Gizeh plateau, and, depending on their philosophical predisposition, they might see them either as gigantic follies or as massive machines designed to bring into focus a power from another dimension.

Is it clumsy to try to use the whole of history to trace back to its roots that most evanescent of experiences – the feeling that the thought you have just had isn't something you can really, safely, justifiably call your own?

Selected Bibliography

Avery Allyn, *A Ritual and Illustrations of Freemasonry*, 1831

William Anderson, *Dante the Maker*, Hutchinson, 1980

Bartholomaeus Anglicus, *Le Propriétaire des Choses*, 1490

Elias Ashmole, *Theatrum Chemicum Britannicum*, 1651

W. and G. Audsley, *Handbook of Christian Symbolism*, 1865

Francis Bacon, *The Advancement of Learning*, 1605

Philip Ball, *The Devil's Doctor*, William Heinemann, 2006

—, *Universe of Stone*, Bodley Head, 2008

Robert Bauval, *The Egypt Code*, Century, 2006

Robert Bauval and Graham Hancock, *Keeper of Genesis*, William
    Heinemann, 1996

Harold Bayley, *The Lost Language of Symbolism*, 1912

—, *Archaic England*, Chapman and Hall, 1919

John Beaumont, gent., *An historical, physiological and theological treatise of
    spirits: apparitions, witchcrafts, and other magical practices. Containing an
    account of the genii ... With a refutation of Dr. Bekker's World bewitch'd;
    and other authors ...* D. Browne, J. Taylor, R. Smith, F. Coggan and T.
    Browne, 1705

David Bellamy, *Jolly Green Giant*, Century, 2002

Nicholas Berdyaev, *The End of Our Time*, 1923

—, *Studies Concerning Jacob Boehme*, 1939

Isaiah Berlin, *The Roots of Romanticism*, Chatto & Windus, 1999

Jonathan Black, *The Secret History of the World*, Quercus, 2008

—, *The Secret History of Dante*, Quercus, 2013

H. P. Blavatsky, *Isis Unveiled*, vols I and II, 1877

John Bleibtreu, *The Parable of the Beast*, Paladin, 1970

Harold Bloom, *Shakespeare: The Invention of the Human*, Riverhead Trade,
    1999

Emil Bock, *Genesis*, Floris Books, 1983

Jacob Boehme, *The Signature of All Things, circa* 1612

—, *Mysterium Magnum*, 1623

Mark Booth, editor, with M. Basil Pennington and Alan Jones, *The Christian Testament Since the Bible*, Firethorn Press, 1985; published in the US as *The Living Testament*, Harper & Row

—, editor, *Christian Short Stories*, Crossroad, Continuum, 1985

Jorge Luis Borges, editor with Adolfo Bioy Casares, *Extraordinary Tales*, 1967

Patrick Bowen, 'The Ancient Wisdom in Africa' in *Studies in Comparative Religion*, volume 3, no.2, Spring 1969, pp.113–121

K. M. Briggs, *The Fairies in Tradition and Literature*, Routledge & Kegan Paul, 1967

Mick Brown, *The Dance of 17 Lives*, Bloomsbury, 2004

Richard Maurice Bucke, *Cosmic Consciousness*, E. P. Dutton, 1901

Robert Burton, *The Anatomy of Melancholy*, 1621

Lorna Byrne, *Angels in My Hair*, Century, 2008

—, *Stairways to Heaven*, Coronet, 2011

—, *A Message of Hope from the Angels*, Coronet, 2012

Joseph Campbell, *The Hero with a Thousand Faces*, Pantheon Books, 1949

Cicero, *On the Nature of the Gods*

Norman Cohn, *Europe's Inner Demons*, Sussex University Press, 1975

Michael D. Coogan, *The Old Testament: A Historical and Literary Introduction to the Hebrew Scriptures*, Oxford University Press USA, 2005

Henry Corbin, *History of Islamic Philosophy*, 1964

James Cowan, 'Wild Stones', *Studies in Comparative Religion*, vol. 17, nos 1 and 2

William Crookes, *Researches into the Phenomena of Spiritualism*, J. Burns, 1874

Nicholas Culpeper, *Complete Herbal*, 1653

Charles Dickens, *A Christmas Carol*, Chapman & Hall, 1843

Adolphe Napoléon Didron, *Iconographie chrétienne*, Imprimerie royale, 1843; *Christian Iconography*, 2 vols., Henry G. Bohn, 1851–1886

Dionysius the Aeropagite, *The Celestial Hierarchies*

E. R. Dodds, *The Greeks and the Irrational*, University of California Press, 1951

Fyodor Dostoevsky, *The Devils*, 1872

—, *The Brothers Karamazov*, 1880

Maureen Duffy, *The Erotic World of Fairy*, Hodder & Stoughton, 1974

Johann Peter Eckermann, *Conversations with Goethe, Conversations with Eckermann*, vols I and II, Gedichte, 1836; vol. III, 1848

Mircea Eliade, *Myth and Reality,* trans. Willard R. Trask, Harper & Row, 1963

George Eliot, *Scenes of Clerical Life*, Blackwood and Sons, 1858

Henry Nicholson Ellacombe, *The Plant-Lore and Garden-Craft of Shakespeare*, W. Satchell & Co., 1878

J. Fellows, *The Mysteries of Freemasonry*, 1860

David Fideler, *Jesus Christ, Sun of God*, Quest Books, 1996

David Foster Wallace, *Infinite Jest*, Little, Brown, 1996

—, *The Pale King*, Little, Brown, 2011

Michel Foucault, *Folie et déraison*, Librarie Plon, 1961; *Madness and Civilization*, abridged, Random House, Inc., 1965

Matthew Fox and Rupert Sheldrake, *The Physics of Angels*, HarperCollins, 1998

Jonathan Franzen, *Freedom*, Fourth Estate, 2011

James Frazer, *The Golden Bough*, 1890

Louis Ginzberg, *The Legends of the Jews*, The Echo Library, 1910

Joscelyn Godwin, *Robert Fludd, Hermetic Philosopher and Surveyor of Two Worlds*, Thames & Hudson, 1979

Rene Guénon, *Man and his Becoming according to the Vedanta*, 1925

—, *The Esoterism of Dante*, 1925

—, *The Lord of the World*, 1929

Sevak Gulbekian, *In the Belly of the Beast*, Hampton Roads, 2004

Graham Hancock, *The Fingerprints of the Gods*, William Heinemann, 1995

—, *Supernatural*, Century, 2005

Patrick Harpur, *Daimonic Reality*, Viking, 1994

—, *The Philosophers' Secret Fire*, Ivan R. Dee, 2002

C. G. Harrison, *The Transcendental Universe*, George Redway, 1896

Jane Harrison, *Themis: A Study in the Social Origins of Greek Religion*, Merlin Press, 1963

Hegel, *On the Prospects for Folk Religion*, 1793

—, *Lectures on the Philosophy of History*, trans. J. Sibree, 1837–1888

Geoffrey Hodson, *The Kingdom of Fairie*, 1927

—, *The Coming of Angels*, 1935

Stephen Howarth, *The Knights Templar*, Collins, 1982

Georges Huber, *My Angel Will Go before You*, Four Courts Press, 1983

Ted Hughes, *Shakespeare and the Goddess of Complete Being*, Faber and Faber, 1992

David Hume, *An Enquiry Concerning Human Understanding*, 1748

—, *An Enquiry Concerning the Principles of Morals*, 1751

Robert Irwin, *The Arabian Nights: A Companion*, Allen Lane, 1994

Toshihiko Izutsu, *Sufism and Taoism*, University of California Press, 1983

Julian Jaynes, *The Origins of Consciousness in the Breakdown of the Bi-Cameral Mind*, Houghton Mifflin, 1976

Leon Jenner, *Bricks*, Coronet, 2011

Carl Gustav Jung, *Psychology and Alchemy*, Routledge, 1944

—, *Memories, Dreams, Reflections*, Collins and Routledge, 1962

—, 'Paracelsus as a Spiritual Phenomenon', introduction (1942), *Alchemical Studies* (trans. R. Hull), Routledge and Kegan Paul, 1967

—, *The Red Book*, W. W. Norton & Co., 2009

Robert Kirk, *The Secret Commonwealth of Elves, Fauns and Fairies*, 1691, new edition with introduction by Marina Warner, New York Review of Books, 2007

Stanislas Klossowski de Rola, *The Golden Game*, Thames and Hudson, 1997

Brunetto Latini, *Li Livres dou Trésor*, Imprimerie Impériale, Paris, 1863

William Edward Hartpole Lecky, *The History of the Rise and Influence of the Spirit of Rationalism in Europe*, vol. I, 1865; vol. II, 1866

William Lethaby, *Architecture, Mysticism and Symbolism*, 1891

Ivan Leudar and Philip Thomas, *Voices of Reason, Voices of Insanity*, Routledge, 2000

Robert Lomas, *The Secret Science of Masonic Initiation*, with a foreword by Mark Booth, 2010

—, *The Lost Key*, Coronet, 2011

Robert Lomas and Christopher Knight, *Uriel's Machine*, Random House, 1999

Ignatius Loyola, *The Spiritual Exercises of Ignatius Loyola*, Antonio Bladio, 1548

Gitta Mallasz, *Talking with Angels*, trans. Robert Hinshaw, Daimon Verlag, 1988

Jean de Meun and Guillaume de Lorris, *The Romance of the Rose*, 1275

John Michell, *City of Revelation*, Ballantine, 1973

Seyyed Hossein Nasr, *Islamic Spirituality: Foundations*, Crossroad, 1987

Maurice Nicoll, *The Mark*, Vincent Stuart, 1954

Henry Steel Olcott, *People from the Other World*, Cambridge University Press, New York, 1895

Paracelsus, *De Virtutue Imaginativa*, c.1535

David Plant, *Johannes Kepler and the Music of the Spheres*, www.skyscript.co.uk/kepler.html

Alvin Plantinga, *Where the Conflict Really Lies*, Oxford University Press Inc., 2011

Plotinus, *Letter to Flaccus*

—, *The Enneads*

Plutarch, *Life of Marcellus*

—, *On the Face on the Moon*

Hope Price, *Angels: True Stories of How They Touch Our Lives*, Guidepost Books, 1993

Sergei O. Prokofieff, *The Cycle of the Year as a Path of Initiation Leading to an Experience of the Christ Being*, Verlag Freies Geistesleben, 1986; trans. Simon Blaxland de Lange, Temple Lodge Publishing, 1991

Philip Pullman, *His Dark Materials I: Northern Lights*, Scholastic, 1995

—, *His Dark Materials II: The Subtle Knife*, Scholastic, 1997

—, *His Dark Materials III: The Amber Spyglass*, Scholastic, 2000

David Punter, *Blake, Hegel and Dialectic*, Rodopi, 1982

Thomas de Quincey, *Autobiographical Sketches*, 1853

C. J. Richardson, *Studies from Old English Mansions*, 1851

John Robinson, *Honest to God*, John Knox Press, 1963

David Rohl, *A Test of Time*, Century, 1995

—, *Legend*, Century, 1998

Eusebe Salverte, *The Philosophy of Magic*, 1829

Jean-Paul Sartre, *La Nausée*, Éditions Gallimard, 1938

Marsha Keith Schuchard, *Why Mrs Blake Cried*, Century, 2006

Edouard Schure, *The Great Initiates*, 1889

Virginia Sease and Manfred Schmidt-Brabant, *Thinkers, Saints, Heretics*, Temple Lodge Publishing, 2007

Jean Seznec, *The Survival of the Pagan Gods*, Princeton University Press, 1940

Idries Shah, *The Sufis*, WH Allen, 1964

—, *The Way of the Sufis*, Jonathan Cape, 1968

Rupert Sheldrake, *The Science Delusion*, Coronet, 2012

Herbert Silberer, *Hidden Symbolism of Alchemy*, 1917

Ludwig Staudenmaier, *Magic as an Experimental Science*, 1912

Rudolf Steiner, *Philosophy of Freedom*, 1894

—, *Genesis*, 1910

—, *Inner Impulses of Evolution: The Mexican Mysteries and the Knights Templar*, Anthroposophical Press, 1916

—, *The Karma of Untruthfulness*, vols I and II, Steiner Books, 1916, 1917

—, *Knowledge of Higher Worlds and How to Attain It*, 1918

—, *The Temple Legend*, Rudolf Steiner Press, 1985

Whitley Strieber, *Christmas Spirits*, Coronet, 2012

Robert Temple, *He Who Saw Everything*, Rider, 1991

—, *The Crystal Sun*, Century 2000

—, *Netherworld*, Century, 2002

Keith Thomas, *Religion and the Decline of Magic*, Weidenfeld and Nicolson, 1971

Valentine Tomberg, *Méditations sur les 22 arcanes majeurs du Tarot*, published anonymously, Aubier, 1984; *Meditation on the Tarot*, trans. Robert Powell, Jeremy P. Tarcher, 1985

Arnold Toynbee, *Experiences*, 1969

Rev. C. H. Vail, *The World's Saviours*, N. L. Fowler & Co., 1913

Jacob de Voragine, *The Golden Legend*, 1275

HRH The Prince of Wales, Tony Juniper and Ian Skelly, *Harmony*, Blue Door, 2010

E. A. Wallis Budge, *Egyptian Magic*, Kegan Paul, Trench and Truber & Co., 1899

Marina Warner, *From the Beast to the Blonde*, Chatto & Windus, 1994

Terry White, *The Sceptical Occultist*, Century, 1994

W. L. Wilmshurst, *The Scientific Apprehension of the Superphysical World*, 1905

Ian Wilson, *The After Death Experience*, Sidgwick and Jackson, 1987

Oswald Wirth, *Le Tarot des imagiers du moyen age*, Claude Tchou, 1966

Francis A. Yates, *Giordano Bruno and the Hermetic Tradition*, Routledge, 1964

Pamela Young, *Hope Street*, Coronet, 2012

Carol Zaleski, *Otherworld Journeys*, Oxford University Press, 1987

R.W. Bro. Leon Zeldis, *An Esoteric View of the Rose-Croix Degree*, available online at Pietre-stones Review of Freemasonry, freemasons.freemasonry.com

Acknowledgments

Loving thanks to my daughter Tabitha for her beautiful illustrations, my son Barnaby for his help with corrections and my wife Fiona for being a book widow with such good grace. To Hannah Black, Kate Parkin, Sevak Gulbekian and Jean Callanan who cared enough to read the script and to make insightful and telling suggestions. I am more grateful than I can say. Heartfelt thanks to my starry agent Jonny Geller, who continues to support me and sell all around the world books which fit no category yet devised. Thanks, too, to everyone at Curtis Brown for being kind, supportive and thoughtful, but especially Kirsten Foster, Lisa Babalis, Melissa Pimentel, Kate Cooper and Eva Papastratis. At Quercus I'd like to thank roustabout Mark Smith, who has been a real pal, my mysterious and wise editor, Richard Milner, Iain Millar who has been ahead of the curve and key to the success of books there from the start, Josh Ireland who has been brilliant – tireless, deft and a joy to deal with throughout. Thank you to Roy Flooks for his excellent photographs of my rotting old books and Rich Carr for his brilliant design. Thank you, too, to my new American publishers, Judith Curr and Johanna Castillo at Atria for their publishing flair and innovative and far-thinking philosophy.

Index